Profiles in Diversity

Profiles in Diversity

Jews in a Changing Europe, 1750–1870

EDITED BY FRANCES MALINO AND
DAVID SORKIN

Wayne State University Press   Detroit

Originally published as *From East and West: Jews in a Changing Europe,
1750–1870,* by Basil Blackwell Ltd. Reprinted 1998 by Wayne State University
Press, Detroit, Michigan 48201. Copyright © 1990, 1998 by Wayne State
University Press. All rights are reserved.
No part of this book mat be reproduced without formal permission.

ISBN-13: 978-0-8143-2715-9   ISBN-10: 0-8143-2715-X

Library of Congress Cataloging-in-Publication Data

From East and West.
    Profiles in diversity : Jews in a changing Europe, 1750–1870 /
edited by Frances Malino and David Sorkin.
        p.   cm.
    Previously published: From East and West. Oxford, UK ; Cambridge,
Mass. : B. Blackwell, 1991.
    Includes bibliographical references and index.
    ISBN 0-8143-2715-X (pbk. : alk. paper)
    1. Jews—Cultural assimilation. 2. Jews—Emancipation—Europe.
3. Jews—Europe—Biography. I. Malino, Frances. II. Sorkin, David
Jan. III. Title
DS148.F76 1998
940'.04924'00922—dc21   97-37514

Contents

Preface to the
Wayne State University Press Edition

This volume has its origins in a conference held at Mount Holyoke College in April 1987, which was designed to introduce a general and university audience to the range of Jewish experience in the period 1750–1870. The enthusiastic response to the conference convinced us to think of a more enduring forum. We were also encouraged by many of our colleagues who joined us in lamenting the dearth of material available for teaching the period. Having the conference papers as the core of our volume, we invited additional contributions. Our goal was to present a selection of biographical and generational studies which in their diversity would be representative of the period. The result is a volume which will augment traditional textbooks and monographs.

We are delighted to have this volume back in print. Our experience in the classroom has convinced us of the pedagogical value of biographical and family studies: students find that the lives of individuals and families clarify historical developments that otherwise seem incomprehensibly abstract. For this reason we have also chosen to reissue this volume under a title that stresses its biographical contents. In addition, we have been motivated by the fact that while in recent years the number of monographic publications on European Jewry in the period 1750–1870 has multiplied, relatively little new teaching material has appeared.

We would like to thank Arthur Evans and the staff at Wayne State University Press for their enthusiasm for the volume and their efficiency in making possible its reissue.

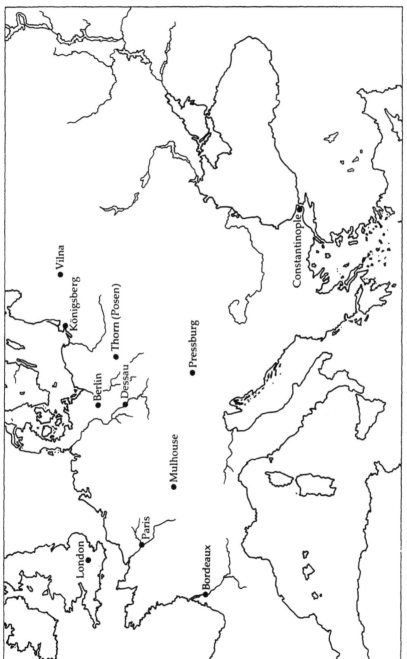

Map showing principal cities and towns connected with figures discussed in this volume.

Introduction

The years from 1750 to 1870 witnessed a momentous transformation in Europe, one which included an explosive growth in industry and trade, revolutions in politics and family life, and the unification of nation states. This transformation did not take the same form or proceed at the same pace in all the countries of Europe or even in different regions of the same country. It developed differently in the city from in the countryside, and varied according to social class and gender, occupation, residence and religion. Inevitably the Jews, too, experienced this transformation; the resulting diversity, however, has often been diminished, obscured or even obliterated.

Emancipation, the granting of equal civil and political rights, came both to epitomize this period and to define its history. For in Germany, where the process of removing traditional disabilities and restrictions and admitting Jews to the body politic was singularly intense and protracted, an ideological revolution accompanied the political one. New types of self-understanding developed, often helping to further emancipation; the very enterprise of writing Jewish history, as exemplified by the work of the nineteenth-century historian Heinrich Graetz, is a case in point. For Graetz, the past became in many ways the obverse of the present, ideology the subject of internal Jewish history and biography its method.[1] Subsequent historians, even if

---

[1] Heinrich Graetz, *Geschichte der Juden*, 11 vols (Berlin and Leipzig, 1853—76). English version: *History of the Jews*, 6 vols (Philadelphia, 1891). For Graetz's view of Jewish history see Ismar Schorsch (ed.), *The Structure of Jewish History and Other Essays* (New York, 1975). For Graetz's use of biography see Salo Baron, 'Heinrich Graetz, 1817—1891', in his *History and Jewish Historians* (Philadelphia, 1964) pp. 263—75. Graetz may have been influenced by the maskilic practice of didactic biography. For the justification

their own commitments lay elsewhere, continued to follow nineteenth-century German precedents, writing the history of Jewish communities through representative biographies of the 'modernizing elements'.[2] Such influential personalities as religious reformers and community leaders, pedagogues and philosophers became the 'vehicle for exhibiting the age'.[3]

This volume seeks to restore to the age some of its lost diversity. Drawing upon social history, it demonstrates that Jews experienced far more than increased rights and a changing ideology. Their transformation included changes in the full range of social experience — occupations, residence, family life, marriage, friendship and social integration. Through individual, and family studies, we link these less known changes to more familiar ideological ones.[4] Our portraits are not those traditionally used to represent the period: they are often of minor or less conventional figures. They are of merchants and bankers in Bordeaux, Istanbul and Alsace; intellectuals and pedagogues in Paris, Dessau and Lithuania; parvenus in London, Königsberg and Berlin; Orthodox rabbis in Moravia, Posen and London.

This then is a volume which relishes diversity, yet also reveals shared struggles, accomplishments and changes. Four themes highlight common threads of the period; the individual lives show variations in subtle and informative ways. The first theme concerns the ways in which Jews, both benefiting from and contributing to Europe's economic transformation, dramatically altered their lives and those of their co-religionists. 'Success in commerce',

---

of this practice see Isaac Euchel, 'Toldot Gedolei Yisrael', *Ha-Meassef*, 1 (1784), pp. 9–14, 25–30. For a recent discussion of the role of biography in early Jewish historiography see Michael A. Meyer, 'The Emergence of Jewish Historiography', *History and Theory*, supplement 27 (1990), pp. 160–75.

[2] Paula Hyman, 'The History of European Jewry: Recent Trends in the Literature', *Journal of Modern History*, 54 (1982), p. 303. See also the introductory paragraphs of Todd Endelman, 'The Checkered Career of "Jew" King: A Study in Anglo-Jewish Social History', *Association for Jewish Studies Review*, 7–8 (1982–3), pp. 69–71, which have not been reprinted in this volume.

[3] The phrase is from Barbara Tuchman, 'Biography as a Prism of History', in Marc Pachter (ed.), *Telling Lives* (Philadelphia, 1979), p. 133.

[4] On biography as a means of connecting cultural and social history see Robert Darnton, 'Intellectual and Cultural History', in Michael Kammen (ed.), *The Past before Us* (Ithaca, NY, 1980), pp. 341–2.

Richard Menkis demonstrates (ch. 1), was the salient motif in the lives of the Gradis family. They arrived in France in the seventeenth century as 'Portuguese merchants' or 'New Christians'. Inextricably linking marriage and business, they remained faithful to a crypto-Judaism until the 1730s, when the open profession of Judaism was finally permitted. As Bordeaux flourished in the eighteenth century, so too did the Gradis family. Their wealth enabled them to 'live nobly', their Judaism lost much of its traditional piety, but their attachment to the Sephardic Jewish nation remained firm. As leaders of their community, they filled the traditional role of intercessor; as benefactors of educational institutions, they simultaneously pioneered the new role of 'reforming philanthropist'.

Aron Rodrigue (ch. 2) highlights precisely this role for Abraham de Camondo, the 'Rothschild of the East' or 'Court Jew' of Istanbul. He too used his political connections to act on behalf of the Jewish community, and his extraordinary wealth to implement reform and change. But, in contrast to the Gradis family, Camondo lived in a country where merchants were protected by foreign connections and where Westernization became the key to commercial success. Struggling with its own need to modernize, the Ottoman State defended Camondo in his efforts to Westernize his recalcitrant co-religionists. The individual gestures of the Gradis family were institutionalized less than a century later when the Alliance Israélite Universelle ensured that Abraham Camondo's efforts would succeed.

As Camondo identified himself with the West, moving to Paris in his last years, so the Dreÿfuss family identified with the Calvinist enclave of French culture in the Alsatian textile city of Mülhausen. Michael Burns (ch. 3) takes us back to Jacob, the grandfather of Alfred, to explain the intricate tapestry of the Captain's life — the religious faith, personal honour, provincial loyalty and French patriotism behind the family's successful transition from rural pedding to selling textiles and then to manufacturing them. The family changed its name to Dreyfus, the city its to Mulhouse — signifying their identification with French as the language of progress and France as the true home of culture and civilization. The Franco-Prussian War, however, confronted the inhabitants of the city with a painful decision — to depart for France or to protect their business interests by remaining under German occupation. The Dreyfus family retained its Alsatian textile interests, but Alfred, the youngest son of Raphael, was sent to school in Paris. He brought with him financial security, impeccable French, and the unshakable faith of his family in the ideals of 1789.

Integral to Europe's transformation were competing versions of its past and opposing visions of its future. Here, too, individual Jews became both protagonists of one of the main ideological currents, the Enlightenment, and proponents of a Jewish version, known by its Hebrew name, the Haskalah. The Haskalah (our second theme) took a range of different forms — Western and Eastern European, moderate and radical — and changed over time, from the eighteenth to the nineteenth century. Born in a village near Lublin, employed briefly as a tutor in Berlin and best known for his active involvement in the French Revolution, Zalkind Hourwitz calls attention to the implications of the Haskalah when joined to political revolution. Frances Malino (ch. 4) traces his career as he petitioned government ministers, wrote a prize-winning essay, donated part of his salary to the revolutionary cause, enrolled in the National Guard and joined the ranks of political journalists. Rejecting the notion of any contract (be it religious reform or re-education) in exchange for civil rights, Hourwitz impatiently demanded full and unconditional equality for the Jews of France. And, like Jewish revolutionaries a century later, he believed that freedom for the Jews augured a future of universal peace and mutual toleration.

Joseph Wolf represents a more conservative side of the Haskalah. Wolf's intellectual development, as portrayed by David Sorkin (ch. 5), calls attention to the internal roots of the Haskalah in its revival of Hebrew, biblical study and more literal forms of interpretation. The personally timid Wolf helped found the new German-language media of the sermon and journal — both of which were essential in the struggle for emancipation. In those media, he subtly discarded the radical position of a Hourwitz, linking regeneration of the Jews to the granting of emancipation. Regeneration, however, denoted nothing more than fulfilment of the original programme of the Haskalah; and Wolf, a poor man with a rich intellectual life, dreamed of realizing that vision.

Through the figure of M. A. Günzburg, Israel Bartal conveys (ch. 6) just how perilous was the dream of the Haskalah when brought to East European soil. There it could only impose itself on a suspicious community leadership by forging an alliance with the government — a dangerous enterprise, since the government, albeit for different reasons, distrusted the maskilim no less than the Jewish community. How poignant appear Günzburg's sartorial changes as he travelled from Courland to Lithuania, and how threatening his commitment to popularize the scientific knowledge and business ethics that he believed essential for his co-religionists. And, finally, how delicate was the balance between commitment to a Germanocentric vision of Enlightenment and participation in a linguistically competitive milieu.

For Hourwitz, Wolf and Günzburg, the Haskalah offered the means of refashioning the Jews to ensure their survival in a freer and transformed Europe. But a new-found mobility unsettled the social order of the Jews no less than it did that of other peoples in Europe. Our third theme focuses on individuals and families for whom the Jewish community lost its significance and their identity as Jews much of its meaning. As Todd Endelman (ch. 7) illustrates through the example of 'Jew' King, there were many ways up, including the shabby and unsavoury. John King's exploitation of the addictions and fancies of Georgian gentlemen renewed the old stereotype of Jewish usury even as it gained him status and wealth. An ambitious young Jew with little education and capital but much familiarity with financial transactions, King wined and dined the elite of London. Characteristic of the Jewish parvenu in England, his status lasted only as long as his funds. But King was more than a calculating parvenu. He befriended Thomas Paine, involved himself in radical journalism and pamphleteering, and, with the freedom, even presumptiousness, of an outsider, attacked Christian sensibilities. Rebellious to the end, he nevertheless retained a commitment to Judaism which he proudly, if unsystematically, defended in books and pamphlets.

If 'Jew' King was an atypical scoundrel, the odyssey of the Itzig family which Steven Lowenstein evokes (ch. 8) was typical of the Berlin Jewish elite. Accumulating vast riches during the Seven Years War (1756–63), the family assumed a dominant role in communal affairs as well as an opulent lifestyle. While the first generation — which accumulated the wealth — continued to practise its faith in the traditional manner, the second served as patrons of the Haskalah, defenders of the maskilim and 'reforming philanthropists'. The third generation, in striking contrast to the Gradis family of Bordeaux, severed its ties to the Jewish community, intermarried and converted. Significantly, this generation suffered both moral and financial bankruptcy.

The portrait of the novelist Fanny Lewald suggests how similar events affected women differently from men. Deborah Hertz (ch. 9) weaves together the real and fictional lives of Lewald, and rightly so, since she explored alternatives and questioned objectives, not in the public, political and financial arena, but rather in the very private evocation of her character's dilemmas. Ironically, for the educated and ambitious Lewald, the emergence of a rich diversity of Jewish expression restricted her life every bit as much, if not more, than that of the previous generation. And so she imagined herself transported to the salon of Rahel Varnhagen, where wealthy nobles would aid her in her search for meaning and respectability. Lewald left behind her a faith she knew little about and an identity which meant even less; yet, however fragile and personal was her *modus vivendi*, and however ephemeral her fictional contributions, she exemplifies a loneliness and spiritual estrangement shared by many of her contemporaries.

Like political conservatism, religious orthodoxy becomes a doctrine only when challenged. Would there be a Burke, a de Maistre and a Genz without the French Revolution, or a Schleiermacher, a Chateaubriand or a Coleridge without the Enlightenment? And, without the challenges of religious reform, emancipation and social change, would Jewish Orthodoxy (our fourth theme) have emerged to create a new grammar for an extant but threatened language? Jacob Katz (ch. 10), Jody Myers (ch. 11) and Eugene Black (ch. 12) introduce us to very different expressions of orthodoxy in the figures of Moses Sofer of Pressburg, Zevi Hirsch Kalischer of Posen, and Nathan and Hermann Adler of London. All four rabbis, powerful personalities with extraordinary vision, exploited their political opportunities to reshape the institutions, even the objectives, of their faith.

Moses Sofer's reputation for Talmudic scholarship, moral rectitude and rigorous religious observance brought him from Dresnitz to Mattersdorf and finally to the city of Pressburg. There he witnessed the encroachments of modern life and, shrewdly averting his eyes from the minor accommodations of some of his congregants (for example, 'German' clothes and shaving), successfully confronted the challenges of religious reform. Elevating custom to a new level of sanctity, he defended Jewish law (halakhah) against innovation. Refusing to endanger the multifarious levels of meaning and mystery in the textual tradition, he opposed the efforts of the maskilim to produce a philosophy of Judaism or a Bible translation. Convinced that the alliance of the Haskalah with the government must be broken, he reshaped the rabbinate, endowing it with extraordinary authority. The rabbinate he created combined elements of the charismatic Hasidic *zaddik* with those of the modern German rabbi – not surprising, since Pressburg was geographically and culturally at the cross-roads between these two competing models.[5] Paradoxically, this

---

[5] On the *zaddik* see, for example, Samuel Dresner, *The Zaddik*, (London, 1960). On the modern German rabbi see Ismar Schorsch, 'Emancipation and the Crisis of Religious Authority – the Emergence of the Modern Rabbinate', in Werner E. Mosse et al. (eds), *Revolution and Evolution: 1848 in German – Jewish History* (Tübingen, 1981), pp. 205–47.

most influential exponent of an unchanging religious practice and belief made a family possession of the rabbinic leadership empowered to protect the traditions of Judaism.

The Hatam Sofer's defence of tradition was pragmatic: a charismatic rabbinate and a doctrine which precluded change. Zevi Hirsch Kalischer's effort was bolder and more visionary. Painfully aware of the spiritual deprivation attendant of life in exile, sensing a disturbing contradiction between the accepted theory of redemption — dependent on miraculous events — and his own commitment to rationalism, and perplexed by the signficance of such 'favourable' events as 'emancipation', Kalischer turned to 'active messianism'. The rebuilding of the altar and the offering of sacrifices in Palestine would re-establish an intimate connection with God and thus bring about the second and miraculous stage of Redemption. Kalischer formulated his theories in an isolated and insulated part of Posen. But the increased pace of social and religious change soon impinged there as well, and Kalischer, sensing his own life ending, turned to organization and propaganda to realize his vision. Less successful than the efforts of the Hatam Sofer to defend tradition, the messianism of Kalischer took on a new life in contemporary religious Zionism.

In many ways the legacy of Rabbis Nathan and Hermann Adler brings us full circle. For here one finds the reforming philanthropy of a Gradis and Camondo, a commitment to decorum, order and education worthy of the maskilim, a degree of social mobility and acceptance only dreamed of by the Itzigs and Fanny Lewald, and the state support that Moses Sofer coveted to preserve religious Orthodoxy. But this Orthodoxy resembled none other: its 'ministers' adopted a modified form of the language and garb of the Anglican clergy, and its houses of worship the architecture of the Church of England. The Adlers, both father and son, combined scholarship, community activism, the support of the lay elites and their own exemplary domestic lives to establish the enduring authority and influence of the Chief Rabbi. The Judaism that they fashioned, however, was one which their East European co-religionists found difficult to identify with their own.

By examining the complex relationships between experience and self-understanding, this volume hints at the extraordinary diversity and surprising continuities in the transition from early modern to modern Jewish history. While entire social strata remain unexplored and questions are raised which our twelve portraits cannot possibly satisfy, one undeniable conclusion can be drawn: the inviolability of individual experience foils the presumptions of grand teleology.

Part I

Getting on in the World

1

Patriarchs and Patricians: the Gradis Family of Eighteenth-Century Bordeaux

RICHARD MENKIS

Under the inevitable twentieth-century grime, present-day Bordeaux retains much of its *ancien régime* splendour. In the eighteenth century it became the leading colonial port of France. With the resulting wealth, royal intendants worked to transform Bordeaux from a medieval backwater into a respectable provincial capital, while prosperous colonial shippers built lavish homes. This frenzied activity resulted in a great eighteenth-century city, as can be appreciated by anyone who strolls through the public English garden, promenades on the boulevards, or simply admires the elegant *hôtels*.

From the façade of one of these buildings — now a café, formerly a comfortable home — several sculpted faces peer down on the activity below. This building was at one time the city residence of David Gradis (c.1665–1751), and his son Abraham (c.1695–1780), founders of the firm David Gradis et Fils, and, according to a family tradition, two of the stone faces represent father and son.[1] It is tempting to accept this tradition, and to imagine David and Abraham Gradis demanding a vantage point from which to observe what was happening in their city, for it was in this rapidly expanding port that they acquired their fortune and built a name for themselves and their firm.

Some of the salient features of the lives of the Gradis family have already been noted; in fact, the variety of perspectives on this family is astonishing. Members of the family have stressed its contribution to the protection of France during the various wars of the eighteenth century, as have patriots of Bordeaux. Jewish apologists of various stripes have attempted to use the example of the Gradis family to

[1] Jean Schwob d'Hericourt, *La Maison Gradis de Bordeaux et ses chefs* (Argenteuil, 1975), pp. 15 and 21.

demonstrate the dedication of the Jews to the lands in which they live. Québécois nationalists have on occasion argued a harsher position, taking the family to task for associating with the last intendant of New France, whom they considered corrupt and responsible for its downfall.[2] No one historian, however, has drawn together the various aspects of the lives of these successful shippers.

If there is any one characteristic that members of the family had in common, it was success in commerce: they were either striving for it or working to keep it. In this way, they were very much products of the occupational restrictions of the *ancien régime*. Nevertheless, their success led to some rather dramatic changes. They integrated into upper-class non-Jewish society and lived like their noble neighbours, although they could not be of the nobility. They assumed power within the emerging Jewish community, worked to strengthen and preserve it, but also to transform it in certain non-traditional ways. These various characteristics and transformations will be explored as we examine the history of the family, especially that branch of it which directed the firm David Gradis et Fils, over the course of the century that led to the French Revolution.

The first two generations: Diego and his children

Diego Rodrigues Gradis was the first member of the family to set foot on French soil, arriving in Bordeaux by the mid-1660s at the latest. His name reveals the origins of the family: the tiny Portuguese hamlet of Gradis, located in the region of Beira Alta.[3] This area was home to many *conversos*, those who were of Jewish lineage but lived,

[2] For a sampling of these perspectives see Schwob d'Hericourt, *La Maison Gradis*; Jean de Maupassant, *Un grand armateur de Bordeaux: Abraham Gradis (1699?—1780)* (Bordeaux, 1931); Heinrich Graetz, 'Die Familie Gradis', *Monatsschrift für die Geschichte und Wissenschaft des Judenthums*, 24 (1875), pp. 447—59, and 25 (1876), pp. 78—85; and Denis Vaugeois, *Les Juifs et la Nouvelle France* (Trois-Rivières, 1968). For a more detailed historiographical and bibliographical analysis see Richard Menkis, 'The Gradis Family of Eighteenth Century Bordeaux: A Social and Economic Study' (PhD thesis, Brandeis University, 1988), ch. 1.

[3] Genealogical information is derived from various registers in the Archives Municipales de Bordeaux (hereafter AMB) and the notarial documents in the Archives Départmentales de la Gironde (hereafter ADG). Owing to the exigencies of space, not all references can be provided in the notes. For information on the origins of the Gradis family, see the Archives Nationales

ostensibly as least, as Christians.[4] Exactly what drove Diego to France can, at present, only be the subject of speculation. Some *conversos* left the Iberian peninsula because of the threat of the Inquisition. If accused and convicted of Judaizing they could suffer both physical punishment and the loss of property. Others migrated from the Iberian peninsula in the hopes of expanding their business interests. By establishing family members along the Atlantic seaboard, *converso* merchants expected to capitalize on the profitable triangular trade which had Spain and Portugal, their overseas empires, and the Atlantic ports as its corners.[5]

If it is unclear under what circumstances Diego left the Iberian peninsula, two facts are certain: in Portugal he was living the life of a *converso*, and he chose to settle in a location in which he had to maintain the appearance of being a Christian. Diego could have lived openly as a Jew in Venice, Leghorn, Amsterdam or Hamburg. In Bordeaux, however, he and the other descendants of Iberian Jewry were not protected as Jews, but were, by legal definition during the sixteenth and seventeenth centuries, *nouveaux chrétiens* (New Christians) or *marchands portugais* (Portuguese merchants). They were offered physical security as well as protection for their property, which was theirs to dispose of at death instead of being subject to confiscation as property of the Crown. The operating fiction, however, was that these privileges were being extended to genuine

---

(hereafter AN), Conseil du Roi, E 3076[11], 'Rôle de rentiers de l'Etat', 23 Apr. 1709.

[4] Jews who had converted to Christianity, which in Portugal usually occurred under duress. See the masterly synthesis of the Portuguese Jewish experience in Yosef H. Yerushalmi, *From Spanish Court to Italian Ghetto. Isaac Cardoso: A Study in Seventeenth Century Marranism and Jewish Apologetics* (New York and London, 1971), pp. 1–50. I shall use the term *converso* to encompass both New Christians (those who converted to Christianity and were, in fact, believing Christians) and Marranos (those who converted but in fact identified as Jews, even if they did not follow all the traditional practices).

[5] The literature on the experience of the *conversos* in the Iberian peninsula and in the Marrano dispersion is vast. For an older, rather sensationalist, account see Cecil Roth, *A History of the Marranos*, 4th edn (New York, 1974); for a more sober evaluation see I.-S. Révah, 'Les Marranes', *Revue des études juives*, 118 (1959–60), pp. 129–77. Jonathan Israel's *European Jewry in the Age of Mercantilism, 1550–1750* (Oxford, 1985) provides a valuable synthesis of the activities of the Sephardic communities of Western Europe.

Christians.[6] As a result of this legislation, until the end of the seventeenth century these descendants of Iberian Jewry were baptizing their children, marrying in churches, burying family members in Christian cemeteries, and not openly organized as a community.[7] They were perforce integrated into the non-Jewish world.

Still, they probably retained some clandestine observances of Judaism, although a religious history of the descendants of Iberian Jewry remains a desideratum, especially for the period before the emergence of the professing Jewish community. In general, it is assumed that the descendants of Jews forcibly converted in Portugal at the end of the fifteenth century were likely to retain a higher level of observance than the descendants of those who had converted in Spain.[8] Whatever the case, Portuguese *conversos* in Bordeaux did maintain official connections with professing Sephardic communities where Iberian Jews were able to live openly as Jews. At the time of its establishment in 1615, a Bordeaux correspondent served Amsterdam's Santa Companhia de Dotar Orphãs e Donzellas, a charity for finding spouses for the poor, and the Portuguese of Bordeaux maintained contact with this organization throughout the seventeenth century. In addition to this explicit communal bond, these settlers aided their co-religionists elsewhere informally. In 1685 *conversos* from Bordeaux visiting Marseilles redeemed a Jewish woman from Kairouan held hostage, and returned with her to Bordeaux. The Jews of Bordeaux also assisted the survivors of the auto-da-fé in Toulouse in 1685, when *converso* merchants were accused of Judaizing, and deprived of the protections offered to *marchands portugais*.[9]

---

[6] For a summary of the legal history of the Jews in Bordeaux see Frances Malino, *The Sephardic Jews of Bordeaux: Assimilation and Emancipation in Revolutionary and Napoleonic France* (University, Ala, 1978) pp. 3–7. Some of the relevant letters patent are now available in Gérard Nahon (ed.), *Les 'Nations' juives portugaises du sud-ouest de la France (1681–1791). Documents* (Paris, 1981), pp. 21–35.

[7] Malino, *The Sephardic Jews of Bordeaux*, pp. 9–11.

[8] See the literature cited above, in notes 4 and 5.

[9] On Amsterdam see Gérard Nahon, 'Les Rapports des communautés judéo-portugaises de France avec celle d'Amsterdam du XVIIe au XVIIIe siècles', *Studia Rosenthaliana*, 10 (1976), p. 42. On the relation with Marseille see Meir Benayahu, *The Relations between Greek and Italian Jewry from the time of the Expulsion from Spain to the End of the Venetian Republic* (Tel Aviv, 1979–80), p. 76 and pp. 254–5 (in Hebrew). On the connection with Toulouse see below.

This is the background to Diego's early years in France; unfortunately, there is very little concrete information about Diego himself. He was married to Anne Henriques (d. by 1689), also known as Anne Bocarre, with whom he had at least four children: Antoine (*c*.1661–1726), Samuel (*c*.1661–1736), David (*c*.1665–1751) and Marie (?). According to a family tradition, Diego moved from Bordeaux to Toulouse, and both the close bonds forged between the Gradis family and the Mendes Moreno family in Toulouse and the tight relations between the two communities in general suggest that this tradition is accurate. Diego did not remain in Toulouse long, however, and returned to Bordeaux by the late 1680s. He most likely decided to leave Toulouse in the wake of a local persecution, avoiding confiscation of his merchandise by forwarding it to Bordeaux.[10] Diego may also, however, have perceived the economic potential of Bordeaux. As had already been observed by Dutch merchants, the native merchants were a rather unimaginative group who invested conservatively and worked only long enough to earn the necessary funds to buy an office for their children before abandoning commercial pursuits.[11]

In Bordeaux, Diego organized his business ventures along family lines, following the custom of his time and also initiating a tradition among the Gradis family. At first he worked in conjunction with his three sons Samuel, Antoine and David, but the business arrangements changed as members of the younger generation established new families. In 1690 Samuel married Françoise Mendes Moreno, the first of three daughters of Michel Rodrigues Moreno and Elizabeth Rodrigues Mendes of Toulouse to marry Diego's sons. After his wedding, Samuel started his own business, while Antoine and David continued working with their father for another five years.[12]

By February 1695, Diego's two remaining bachelor sons were prepared to marry. Diego arranged to provide for both himself and his sons by taking stock of his firm's total assets and dividing the value of

[10] For various family traditions see the memoir of David Gradis II, Private Archives of the Gradis family (hereafter AG), 10/108[4], 'Notice', fo. 1v. On the relations between Bordeaux and Toulouse after 1685 see AN, administrations financiers, G7 297, Bâville to the Contrôleur Général, 4 July 1687.

[11] Robert Boutrouche, (ed.), *Bordeaux de 1453 à 1715* (Bordeaux, 1966), pp. 496–500.

[12] For evidence of business activities see the discussion of the inventory of goods taken in 1695, below, and Pierre Goubert, *Familles marchandes sous l'Ancien Régime: les Danse et les Motte, de Beauvais* (Paris, 1959), p. 72, indicating that the Gradis family owed a total of 13,764 livres for textiles.

the merchandise into equal portions. The net financial worth of the business was, in fact, quite modest. The total value of the merchandise and grain, excluding amounts already credited to Samuel, was 9,638 livres, and father and sons should have received 2,400 livres each. Diego did not, however, grant his children exactly this amount, but withheld 900 livres from each of this three sons. He then awarded the resulting 2,700 livres to David, because he alone remained in business with his father. (Antoine had followed Samuel's example and decided to withdraw from his father's business after his wedding.) Diego also gave David access to all of his 2,400 livres, with the provision that David was responsible for maintaining his father in his home, and in fact Diego remained in David's house until his death in the first decade of the new century.[13]

The weddings of Antoine and David, to Agnes (Rachel) Mendes Moreno, and her sister Marie (Sara Esther), respectively, were celebrated in a double ceremony on 20 April 1695. Antoine was thirty-four years old, and David married − like his brother Samuel several years earlier − at the age of thirty. Like the other merchants in Bordeaux, these married only after establishing themselves as modest business successes, with the property and potential to attract suitable and profitable alliances.[14] And these alliances were indeed lucrative, particularly in comparison with the modest amounts that Diego gave his sons. The father of the brides was a wealthy merchant in Toulouse who provided each of the brothers with 7,250 livres in cash, together with furniture, household utensils and clothes valued at 600 livres.[15] Also significant in this marital arrangement were the close bonds formed. Every individual in the three couples was related to the other couples by both blood and marriage, and as a result the Gradis family

---

[13] David was to give his father an annual pension of 200 livres, which would be increased to 400 if they did not get along well and Diego went to live elsewhere. However, Diego reserved for himself the right to dispose at death of his 2,400 livres as he wished, and it was expected that David would then reimburse Samuel and Antoine the 900 livres withheld from their respective shares. (Belso-Dubos, Acte, 2 Mar. 1695; also in AG 2/5.) Antoine received his 900 livres, plus 100 livres resulting from the joint investment, in 1705. Samuel Navarre, husband of Marie, was also entitled to 100 livres. (ADG 3 E 15306, Belso-Dubos, quittance, 25 Nov. 1705.) Diego died sometime between late 1700 and 1704, probably close to the latter date (see ADG 3 E 15305, Belso-Dubos, reponce, 24 Aug. 1704).

[14] Paul Butel, 'Comportements familiaux dans le négoce bordelais au XVIIIe siècle', *Annales du Midi*, 88 (1976), pp. 139−41.

was well on the way to becoming a tightly knit clan. The various benefits of this closeness became increasingly apparent over the next twenty years.

While working towards the business success of his family in France, Diego set into motion the process of integration and acculturation. By the late seventeenth century, Diego was referred to as Jacques in various legal documents, and actually signed as such in 1700.[16] Around this time there was another important development, the transformation of the *marchands portugais* into a Jewish community, although the legal protections were not completely in place until 1723. Diego was apparently not far from the new developments, as his daughter Marie was married to Samuel Navarre, a leading figure in the fledgling Jewish community of Bordeaux.[17]

If details on Diego's life are spare, more information is available about members of the next generation. Their immediate context was the growing prosperity of Bordeaux. By the late seventeenth century the port was experiencing significant growth, which the War of the Spanish Succession (1701–14) only briefly disrupted.[18] Diego's sons prospered along with Bordeaux, all three eventually becoming colonial traders. In the early eighteenth century their trade was domestic, but Antoine, venturing on his own, also began sending small shipments to the colonies in the late 1710s and into the 1720s.[19] Samuel and David worked together as domestic traders and bankers well into the second decade of the century, for a time under the name Gradis Frères. The early trade of the Gradis brothers involved textiles. In

---

[15] ADG 3 E 15296, Belso-Dubos, mariage, 10 Mar. 1695. On Mendes Moreno, see also Elie Szapiro, 'Les marranes à Toulouse en 1685: groupe socio-économique, familiale, ou communautaire?', *Archives juives*, 14 (1978), pp. 68–9.

[16] ADG 3 E 15301, Belso-Dubos, protest, 10 Sep. 1700.

[17] Simon Schwarzfuchs (ed.), *Registre des délibérations de la nation juive portugaise de Bordeaux (1711–1787)* (Paris, 1981), pp. 73–4.

[18] Christian Huetz de Lemps, *Géographie du commerce de Bordeaux à la fin du règne de Louis XIV* (Paris, 1975), pp. 93–100.

[19] On Antoine see the will of his daughter Judith (ADG 3 E 15415, Dugarry, testament, 22 Feb. 1780), where he is called a retail merchant, but there is also evidence of some small-scale colonial trading in Zosa Szajkowski, *Franco-Judaica: An Analytical Bibliography of Books, Pamphlets, Decrees, Briefs and Other Printed Documents Pertaining to the Jews in France, 1500–1788* (New York, 1962), p. 97, no. 1123, ADG 3 E 15325, Belso-Dubos, procuration, 10 Nov. 1723; and in AG, journal entries, 20 Dec. 1724.

1705 they brought merchandise from Saint-Quentin in Picardy, an important weaving-centre. They also purchased cloth at the sales of the Compagnie des Indes in Nantes, which held the monopoly on various textiles from the East Indies. Around the turn of the century David and Samuel traded in merchandise of the Compagnie des Indes in partnership with two other Sephardic Jews, Antoine and Joseph Lameyre.[20] The Gradis brothers also acted as bankers in this crucial period of Bordeaux's growth. Familiar with the workings of the bill of exchange, they negotiated bills before their maturity date, and in return provided other bills, or cash, which was in particularly short supply in the early eighteenth century. Their financial circuits at this time encompassed Paris, Marseilles and Bayonne, and by 1715 extended to Amsterdam as well. These circuits reflected both the expanding trade of Bordeaux, and the Gradis brothers' participation in it.[21]

In the late 1710s David and Samuel decided to call a halt to their joint business activities, in part because the profits in exchanging currency (part of the earnings in redeeming and drawing bills of exchange) had declined. David joined the swelling ranks of those attracted to the colonial trade. In 1717 he sent to the Indies three newly acquired ships, the *David*, the *Ange Mikael* and the *Mignonne*. Several years later Samuel also began shipping overseas, and his branch of the family was subsequently engaged in colonial commerce through much of the eighteenth century, albeit on a far smaller scale than David's branch.[22]

---

[20] According to Henri Gradis, who had access in the nineteenth century to the early records of David Gradis, Gradis Frères operated from 1703 to 1707 (AG 2/8); the earliest example which I have noted of the signature Gradis Frères dates from 1704 (ADG 3 E 15302, Belso-Dubos, opposition, fo. 493). David and Samuel did, however, continue to work together into the 1710s. On the Picardy trade see ADG 3 E 15306, Belso-Dubos, attestation, 17 Aug. 1705. For information on the partnership with the Lameyre, see ADG 3 E 15306, Belso-Dubos, attestation, 12 Nov. 1705. By then they had been in partnership 'depuis plusieurs années'. The strong commercial links which existed between Nantes and Bordeaux in this period are discussed in Huetz de Lemps, *Géographie du commerce de Bordeaux*, p. 447.

[21] On the finances in this period see ibid., pp. 39–40. The discussion of the Gradis family is based on protests recorded in one notarial collection, that of Belso-Dubos, ADG 3 E 15301–25, 1700–24. For those locations specifically mentioned in the text see ADG 3 E 15301, 14 June 1700 and 13 Aug. 1700; 15307, 1 June 1706; and 15316, Apr. 1715, fo. 459.

[22] ADG 6 B 88, soumissions, 18 July 1717 and two undated (fo. 135, late 1717).

As in Diego's generation, marriages were arranged with careful attention to family business ventures. Samuel married David's daughter, Sara (Esther), after his first wife had died. The amounts of money promised between Samuel, the groom, and David, his brother and now father-in-law, totalled 39,000 livres.[23] Samuel and David, who were at his time business partners, protected their capital by passing dowries and bequests between them. This marriage between uncle and niece also eased the tension between business commitments and family responsibilities. David and Samuel had to travel widely on business, and each, when away, depended on the other to care for both families. Possibly this was the arrangement when David was away in Holland and England for a year, returning in April 1712;[24] it was definitely the case several years later. During Samuel's voyage in 1714 to Nantes, tragedy struck as his second wife died shortly after giving birth to her third child, Moïse.[25] Subsequently, David and his wife were expected to help take care of Samuel's children. Samuel could assume that this would be done with some care, as his late wife was also David's daughter, and their children David's grandchildren. In 1718, when David Gradis sent Samuel abroad, he reassured Samuel that his children were being taken care of 'as they are as dear to me and my wife as they are to you'.[26]

In addition to using marriage to exploit and reinforce existing bonds, fathers arranged marriages to extend business ties. David Gradis, striving to ride the rising tide of Bordeaux's colonial commerce, established useful connections in both the colonies and Northern Europe. In November 1718 he arranged the marriage of his daughter Rachel to Louis Lopes Depas. Louis's brother, Michel, was well-connected in Saint-Domingue, one of the destinations of the new colonial commerce. At the same time David arranged for another daughter to marry Jacob Peixotto, the son of Léon Peixotto, a banker of some note in Bordeaux. This marriage also brought an important foreign business contact into the family, Joseph Peixotto. This relative

---

[23] More specifically, Samuel promised promised 24,000 livres to his wife, and David 15,000 to his brother. See AG 2/6, notarial document dated 1 June 1710. Later, in his will, David gave 11,000 livres to the two surviving children of the marriage of Sara Esther with Samuel, so that the total amount given by David to that branch of the family was 26,000 livres.

[24] The travels of David are recorded in AG 2/8, substantiated by information in Huetz de Lemps, *Géographie du commerce de Bordeaux*, p. 500, n. 14.

[25] AMB GG 842, no. 96, circumcision of 'Moshe de Samuel Gradis' on 9 Oct. 1714; death of Sara recorded 15 Oct. 1714, AMB GG 366, no. 470.

[26] AG 2/8, excerpts from letter from David to Samuel Gradis, 5 May 1718.

of Léon lived in Amsterdam, and he had already proven his worth to the Gradis brothers by providing capital to the firm in 1715, a year when many firms in Bordeaux faced bankruptcy.[27]

Marriage also provided new sources of capital. In 1719 David arranged a marriage between his daughter Rachel and Samuel Alexandre. Samuel's father, Jacques, was a wealthy shipper and banker in Bayonne, whose brother-in-law and uncle, Alexandre *jeune*, had already served as a local correspondent of the Gradis family. This liaison was fruitful, as the Alexandres had a great deal of capital at their disposal, for which they found an outlet in the expanding colonial commerce of Bordeaux. Between 1719 and 1720 David Gradis formed a partnership with Samuel Alexandre, his son-in-law. They sent out at least one ship, the *Moyse*, under the business name Gradis et Alexandre Fils and extended bottomry loans to local shippers. The Gradis family exploited the valuable Alexandre connection throughout the eighteenth century.[28]

The business of David Gradis expanded, at least in part with the assistance of international connections and well-arranged marriages. David also attracted family members into other aspects of the business. Between 1717 and 1724 Abraham Mirande, whom David referred to as 'my clerk and relative' in his correspondence, worked in David's counting-room. In the 1730s Michel Depas, related to the Gradis family through the marriage of Louis Lopes Depas to Abraham's sister, Rica, served as clerk to David Gradis et Fils, to be replaced by Abraham Mirande's brother in the early 1740s. These relatives were expected to act in a trustworthy manner in attending to accounts, merchandise and correspondence.[29]

---

[27] On Louis Lopes Depas and Michel Depas see ADG 3 E 507, Banchereau, marriage, 9 Aug. 1733, and letters excerpted in AG 2/8. On Peixotto see AG 2/8, excerpt from letter to Joseph Peixotto, 30 July 1715.

[28] The Alexandre family was already involved in colonial commerce in the early eighteenth century. See the information in Raymonde Litalien (comp.), 'Minutes des notaires [concerant le Canada]' (This is an unpublished work which Ms Litalien of the National Archives of Canada kindly allowed me to consult while I was in Paris.) For other information on the Gradis — Alexandre connection see ADG 6 B 89, soumission, 21 Sep 1719, regarding the ship, and Litalien, 'Minutes des notaire', citing Archives Départementales des Pyrénées Atlantiques, 3 E 4630, Cassulet, 27 Feb. 1720, on the bottomry loan. For the later eighteenth-century ties to the Alexandre family see Menkis, 'The Gradis Family', pp. 163 and 169.

[29] On the various clerks serving in the firm see AG 2/8, excerpts from letters from David Gradis to Michel Depas in Saint-Domingue, 19 July 1724, and

But David Gradis drew, above all, his immediate family into his business ventures. By 1720 he had dissolved his partnership with his son-in-law, Samuel Alexandre,[30] looking rather to his sons, Samuel (d. 1732) and especially Abraham (*c.* 1695–1780), to perpetuate the firm. Certainly his children were already socialized into the world of commerce; years earlier, when David assured his absent brother Samuel that he was taking care of his children, he pointed out how he had taken them to see whether one of his ships had landed.[31] Most significant, however, was David's meticulous training of Abraham. In 1723 Abraham went on the European tour, a mandatory experience for the young merchant who had to know the intricacies of international trade. David left little to chance, writing in advance to his correspondents along his son's itinerary, asking them to treat Abraham well. David also provided his son with detailed instructions on matters ranging from business contacts to the art of buying and selling in busy Amsterdam. He encouraged his son to trust the banker (and relative by marriage) Joseph Peixotto, but warned Abraham to avoid his uncle Isaac (David's brother-in-law) at all costs, as he had proven himself unreliable in business. David instructed Abraham to buy textiles directly, not use brokers, and to monitor carefully – but unobtrusively – the dealings of one of his astute travelling-companions. For David, his son's training in Amsterdam represented a long-term investment against which he was willing to take short-term losses. Thus, although fully aware that certain merchandise in his warehouse could secure a better price in Nantes, David sent it to Abraham in Amsterdam so that his son could have the experience of arranging payments in the Dutch port.[32]

David continued this instruction when his son returned to Bordeaux, gradually increasing his responsibilities. In late 1723 he granted Abraham and Samuel a ship (the *Ange Mikael*) and cargo, estimated by David at a value of 25,000 livres, as well as some cash. David also wrote to Joseph Peixotto, who had just met Abraham, asking him to open a line of credit for his sons, promising to serve as the guarantor.

---

to 'M. Mirandelle' in Bayonne, 20 July 1724; excerpts from letters from Abraham Gradis to Michel Depas, 25 April 1741 and 2 June 1741, and to Abraham Mirande, 4 June 1741.

[30] AG 2/8, in numerous excerpts from letters dated late 1720.

[31] AG 2/8, excerpts from letter from David to Samuel Gradis, 5 May 1718.

[32] The information in this paragraph and the next is drawn from excerpts from David's correspondence transcribed in AG 2/8, and letters preserved in AG 2/11.

In 1726, when David went to La Rochelle and Nantes on business, David left matters in Bordeaux in the hands of Abraham, although he did direct his son's activities by correspondence. By mid-1728, however, David was able to send Abraham to Paris on a delicate legal matter, and not only offered suggestions on how Abraham should conduct himself, but also solicited his son's advice on various matters.

Abraham's apprenticeship was thus over. Father and son planned two related events: Abraham's marriage and the reorganization of the business. The details were recorded in the family's *livre de raison* — a genealogy, account book and book of guidance. Shortly after Abraham's return from Paris in late 1728, David Gradis established David Gradis et Fils, in partnership with his sons, Abraham and Samuel.[33] David and Abraham capitalized the firm with 162,284 and 26,000 livres respectively. Two years later, on 25 September 1730, or as stipulated in the *ketubah* (Jewish marriage contract), 14 Tishrei 5491, a double wedding was celebrated. David arranged with his brother Samuel that David's two children, Abraham and Esther, would marry Samuel's children Esther and Benjamin. Each daughter came with a dowry of 26,000 livres, but in fact no money changed hands, as the sums cancelled one another out. Both Samuel and David arranged for the marriages of their children without worrying about a loss of capital from the family businesses, while strengthening, once again, the bonds between the various branches of the family.[34]

---

[33] It is unclear what Samuel's involvement in the firm was; he died in 1732 in Martinique, and thus had little impact on the history of the firm.

[34] This sequence of business reorganization and marital arrangements is culled from several sources. Although the *livre de raison* has not survived, it is referred to in a later marriage contract (ADG 3 E 17550, Perrens, mariage, 5 Feb. 1748). On the *livre de raison* see Roland Mousnier, *The Institutions of France under the Absolute Monarchy: Society and the State,* tr. Brian Pearce, 2 vols (Chicago and London, 1979), vol. 1, pp. 50—1. The *ketubah* of Abraham Gradis has survived in AG 11/138, but is wrongly catalogued as that of Abraham, son of Benjamin. AG, journal entries, 15 Nov. 1751, provides the information on the firm's capitalization. It is likely that David and Abraham agreed to the marital and business reorganization in 1728, and that Abraham did not put the 26,000 livres into the firm directly, but that it was placed there by his father as compensation for the dowry which Abraham would not receive from his father-in-law. On business reorganization and marriage see Henri Lévy-Bruhl, *Histoire juridique des sociétés de commerce en France aux XVIIe et XVIIIe siècles* (Paris, 1938), pp. 75—6.

As was common in this period, marriage brought about a reorganization of the family business. David and Abraham agreed that Abraham would be an equal partner in the firm David Gradis et Fils, and that the bulk of David's wealth would ultimately devolve upon him. David continued to exercise his patriarchal authority and manage the family. It was David who arranged the marriage of his granddaughter to David Mendes in 1733, and thirteen years later — virtually blind, with Abraham signing his letter — it was once again the senior Gradis who responded to inquiries about potential marriages to members of the family.[35] But Abraham, as we shall see below, assumed increasing control of the firm's affairs over the last two decades of his father's life.

David had ensured that his children, especially Abraham, would continue the business that he had established. The two were moderately successful in their joint business ventures. A balance sheet drawn up after the death of David in 1751 shows that the profits of the firm were initially established at 318,193 livres, though they were reduced (because of various miscalculations and apparent overestimates of amounts owed) by over 56,000 livres to 262,284 livres.[36] With this modest success, David Gradis and his family lived comfortably. By 1720 David had acquired a home at the corner of the Fossés de l'Hôtel de Ville and Rue Cahernan, well situated in the middle of the Jewish community. In 1733 this building of seven rooms and storage areas housed David, his wife Esther, Abraham and his wife, and black servants.[37] Abraham requested permission from the municipality to add one or two rooms. The authorities granted this permission, under conditions which Abraham met.

Unfortunately, we are often in the dark about what went on within the walls of this house. It is difficult, for example, to re-create the religious life of David. There is no information at all on his behaviour in ritual matters; did he observe the dietary laws, or was he one of

[35] AG 2/8, excerpts from letters from David Gradis to David Mendes in Martinique, 28 Mar. 1733, and to Salomon Depas, 14 June 1746.

[36] Henri Gradis's calculations in AG 2/8 are borne out by the information in AG journal entries, 15 Nov. 1751 and 30 Oct. 1752.

[37] On the house see AG 2/3bis, and the architectural drawings in AG 2/24, probably dating from the 1740s. On their black servants see AG 2/8, excerpt from letter from David Gradis to Abraham Gradis and David Mendes, 31 Mar. 1735, and ADG 6 B 1228, 23 Aug. 1735, about the arrival of a slave named Henry at David Gradis et Fils.

the Jews of Bordeaux who was less than punctilious in these matters?[38] The evidence does suggest, however, that David's piety was spontaneous, sincere but not very sophisticated. David assumed that God's hand guided all affairs. 'God raises and lowers whomever He pleases. Blessed is His name...', he once stated to a correspondent, and in a will of 1746 David thanked God for 'the goods which it has pleased Him to give me'. Health and character were also God's handiwork; when David complained about the faults of a certain individual to his son Abraham, he interjected with the comment that 'God who gave me health and patience should make you a good man...' But David's God was not beyond the reach of mortal man, and David pleaded his case in several ways. His final wishes included the stipulation that money be provided to the Sephardic poor in Bordeaux and in Jerusalem, with the request that both 'pray for the repose of my soul'. The name on his tombstone indicates that David attempted to fight his fate and seek assistance from God, as there he is called Hizkiyahu ('God strengthens'), a name which he undoubtedly assumed — as did his brothers and others in the Sephardic community of Bordeaux and elsewhere — when he was ill, in an attempt to deceive the angel of death on its mission.[39]

[38] See the letters published by Gérard Nahon, 'From Bayonne to Bordeaux: Two Portuguese Letters of 1741', *Sephardic Scholar*, n.s. 3 (1977–8) pp. 48–62, and his analysis, for evidence that the Jews of Bordeaux were less punctilious in ritual matters than the Jews of Bayonne.

[39] For the sources cited in this paragraph see AG 2/8, excerpt from letter from David Gradis to Joseph Peixotto, 4 Jan. 1716; AG 3/31, will of David Gradis, dated 10 Mar. 1746, in which he also cited these first words of his will dated 29 Sep. 1733; AG 2/11, David to Abraham Gradis in Amsterdam, 27 July 1723. The oldest Jewish cemetery in Bordeaux has not been well preserved. I could not find David's tombstone, but part of the inscription was copied down and placed in the Gradis Archives (AG, chemise 275). On his brothers see the information in Georges Cirot, 'Recherches sur les Juifs espagnoles et portugaises à Bordeaux', *Bulletin hispanique*, 10 (1908), pp. 170 and 175: 'Hisquiyau Iahacob Gradis' (Samuel) and 'Hisquiyau Ishaq Gradis' (Antoine). For other examples of changing names in Bordeaux see ibid., pp. 161 and 167. A French translation of the prayer for changing a name in use among the Sephardim is included in *Prières journalières à l'usage des Juifs portugais et espagnols...par Mardoche Venture* (Nice and Paris, 1772), p. 534. See also Joshua Trachtenberg, *Jewish Magic and Superstition: A Study in Folk Religion* (New York, 1939), p. 305, n. 22, which cites the case of an Italian Jew who changed his name to Hizkiyahu while ill. On the phenomenon of changing names among both Sephardim

David was committed to his Iberian Jewish heritage. Both David and his wife resorted to Spanish phrases when providing counsel to their son, or when imploring God, as in the wish on Rosh ha-Shanah, the Jewish New Year, that his family be inscribed in the Book of Life.[40] Their tombstones followed the pattern of the community in that they were written in Spanish and Hebrew. In everyday use, however, Iberian languages did diminish in significance, as the process which had begun with Diego continued. David's earliest account books were kept in Spanish, but after 1711 French predominated in his letters and accounts. He did maintain strong, even exclusive, ethnic ties to the descendants of Iberian Jewry, and in his will the only non-family members granted charitable assistance were the Sephardic poor of Bordeaux and Jerusalem.[41]

David's commitment to the descendants of Iberian Jewry was firm in other ways as well. He encouraged *conversos* to return to Judaism, taking his cue from a Jewish community which was increasingly being tolerated legally as Jews rather than as Portuguese merchants. He served as the godfather of at least one *converso* who came to Bordeaux in 1718 to be circumcised at the age of thirty-seven, and thirty years later he was delighted to learn that a relative, Carlos Rodrigues Arpalhao, had left the Iberian peninsula and taken the step of being circumcised. David also displayed hostility to a member of his family who left Judaism; in 1715 his niece converted and took on the name Suzanne. When she announced that she wished to marry, Suzanne attempted to force her father, then, after his death, her uncle David, to provide a dowry, as had been done for Suzanne's sister Esther when she married Samuel Dacosta in 1720. When both father and uncle resisted, Suzanne appealed to the authorities, who subsequently seized the cargo of one of David's ships. After a decision of the Crown he agreed to pay 8,000 livres — the amount that he had paid for Esther's dowry — but immediately appealed against the decision. For David, Suzanne no longer was a member of the family,

---

and Askenazim see Leopold Löw, *Beiträge der jüdischen Altherthumskune*, vol. 2: *Die Lebensalter in der jüdischen Literatur* (Szegedin, 1875), pp. 108—9 and 390—1. The situation in Bayonne is surveyed by Gérard Nahon in 'Pour une approche des attitudes devant la mort au XVIIIe siècle: sermonnaires et testateurs juifs portugais à Bayonne', *Revue des études juives*, 136 (1977), pp. 3—123; for some parallels see esp. pp. 47—55.
[40] AG 2/11, letter from David to Abraham Gradis in Paris, 3 Sep. 1728: 'et que Dios nos escreva a todos en libro de vidas'.
[41] AG 3/31, will of David Gradis, 10 Mar. 1746.

and when he discussed family matters in his correspondence her name was' conspicuously absent.[42]

David, successful at business and deeply committed to other descendants of Iberian Jewry, assumed increasing power within the emerging professing Jewish community, or *nation*. The Jews were tolerated for their useful economic contribution to the state, and the community structure was controlled by a strong lay leadership, overshadowing clerical authority to a degree which probably surpassed even the strong lay influence in the Sephardic community of Amsterdam.[43] The process by which the Gradis family became one of the families exercising control over the community began with David. His name appeared among those of the forty contributors to the earliest known fund for supporting the Jewish poor of Bordeaux (1699). In 1718 he was co-opted into the power structure of the community as *gabbai* or syndic, the leading position of authority in the community. By virtue of this he automatically became one of the elders or *anciens*, the only members of the community with a vote in communal matters.[44] In short, David Gradis entered the upper echelons of power in the community and became a member of the Jewish patriciate of Bordeaux.

---

[42] On Arpalhao, see AMB, GG 842, no. 138; and AG 2/8, excerpt from letter to Salomon Depas, in London, 14 June 1746. The story of Suzanne is described, in part, in Théophile Malvezin, *Histoire des Juifs à Bordeaux* (Bordeaux, 1875; repr. Marseille, 1976), pp. 158–60, and in the documents published in Gérard Nahon, 'Dépêches des Secrétaires d'Etat des Affaires Etrangères et de la Religion Prétendue Réformée concernant les Juifs (1726–1765)', *Michael*, 4 (1976), pp. 194–7. See also ADG C 1086; and AG 2/23. David's continued silent anger is evident in AG 2/8, an excerpt from a letter he wrote to Salomon Depas, 14 June 1746. Other responses to conversions are described in Malino, *The Sephardic Jews of Bordeaux*, p. 10 and p. 120, n. 39.

[43] Although the Sephardic Jewish community of Amsterdam was, to a large extent, run by the wealthiest 20 per cent of the community (Israel, *European Jewry*, p. 198), Yosef Kaplan, in *From Christianity to Judaism: The Life and Work of Isaac Orobio de Castro* (Jerusalem, 1982), p. 169, n. 67 (in Hebrew), notes some limitations to the tight oligarchic control of the community in Amsterdam. No such limitation is evident in Bordeaux; see the pathetic letter of a rabbi in Bordeaux quoted in Malino, *The Sephardic Jews of Bordeaux*, p. 24.

[44] Malvezin, *Histoire des Juifs à Bordeaux*, p. 136; Schwarzfuchs, *Registre des délibérations*, p. 90, no. 15. On the role of the *anciens* see the communal decision of 21 Apr. 1716, ibid., p. 84, no. 11.

He subsequently assumed other communal responsibilities. Gradis was instrumental in acquiring land for the first cemetery in which the Jews of Bordeaux were buried according to Jewish rites. In 1724 he purchased the land for 6,300 livres, and in 1728 sold it formally to the Jewish community, although it had been ceded to the community less than one year after its purchase and was already being used for burials in March 1725.[45] David remained involved in communal affairs until the end of his life, by which time he had become one of the most respected and powerful, members of the community.[46]

The broad outlines of David's life and career are clear. After years of working with his brother, he was successful in drawing his son into the world of commerce, in which Abraham would ultimately excel. David was a member of the new aristocracy of wealth in the emerging official Jewish community, solid in his own observance and concerned that those leaving the Iberian peninsula should return to Judaism. He remained attached to his Iberian Jewish heritage, in language and in charitable activities, although the pervasive use of French for every-day matters does reflect the continuing process of acculturation among members of this branch of the Gradis family.

Abraham, Moïse and David Gradis et Fils

The firm David Gradis et Fils witnessed its greatest growth during the tenure of Abraham (c.1695–1780) and Moïse Gradis (1714–1788).[47] Abraham, about fifty-five years old when his father died in 1751, was already the driving force of the firm years before. Much of his day — certainly in the 1740s — was spent in the counting-room, digesting the mountains of paper accumulating there, as Abraham himself explained to one of his correspondents: 'Our books are up-

---

[45] On the actual purchase and sale see Cirot, *Bulletin hispanique*, 10, pp. 158–60, n. 3. In his accounts (AG, journal entries, 1 Apr. 1726) David refers to the 'chardin que javois achepte du Sr Perpignan lequel dit Chardin la Nation l'a pris'.

[46] For thirteen years (1733–46) one of the registers of the community containing important information on poor relief was entrusted to him. It remained in his possession until it was decided that each syndic should have it during his respective tenure of office. Schwarzfuchs, *Registre des délibérations*, p. 162, no. 105, and p. 192, no. 141.

[47] See Menkis, 'The Gradis Family', chs 4 and 5, for a description of the commercial activities of David Gradis et Fils in the eighteenth century.

dated daily and we do the same every Sunday to all our accounts. I am in charge of the waste-book and all the correspondence. I wake up very early in the morning and work until eleven o'clock, at which time I go to the exchange, and, after eating, I return to work [in the counting-room] until five or six o'clock'.[48]

Buried under the paper and books in this busy counting-room were several writing-stands,[49] since by the late 1740s Abraham was accompanied by Moïse, his nephew and brother-in-law. Moïse, about twenty years younger than Abraham, had virtually been a member of David's household, for, as we have already seen, Moïse's mother died just after his birth and his father Samuel travelled on business. Moïse left a profound mark on the firm while David was still alive, as Abraham gratefully acknowledged in granting Moïse one half of the assets not assigned to others in an early will of 1753.[50] The letters exchanged between Abraham and Moïse when they were separated reveal two like-minded men, passionately devoted both to each other and to the continued success of the firm.

Abraham and Moïse carefully divided their responsibilities. Abraham served as the firm's liaison with the Crown and its officials, an all-consuming task after 1744, when the firm conducted a significant portion of its business under contract with the Crown or in partnership with colonial officials. In addition to maintaining order while Abraham was away, Moïse was largely responsible for the accounts. Blessed with a phenomenal memory, he often neglected to record the relevant information, much to the chagrin of the book-keepers.[51] Moïse also served as a buffer between his brother-in-law and the everyday activities of the firm, especially during Abraham's later years.[52]

This division of labour functioned smoothly, and Moïse's absorp-

---

[48] AG 2/8, excerpt from letter to Michel Depas in Saint-Domingue, 2 June 1741.
[49] AG 3/41, 'Inventaire fait par Abraham Gradis au décès de son père David Gradis, 1751'.
[50] AG 4/45.
[51] AG 10/108[4], David Gradis II, 'Notice', fo. 17v. On Moïse's remarkable memory, see also 'Mémoire pour les sieurs David Gradis et fils, Négocians à Bordeaux, Defendeurs à la demande en homologation du rapport arbitral des divers articles dudit rapport d'une part. Contre sieur David Dasylva Demandeur en homolgation dudit rapport & Intimé, d'autre part', at the Centre de Documentation de la Chambre de Commerce et d'Industrie de Bordeaux (cat. no. 27802), p. 78.
[52] See David Gradis II, 'Notice'.

tion into David Gradis et Fils temporarily resolved Abraham's search for a successor, a concern because he and his wife Esther were childless. In his will of 1753, Abraham bequeathed Esther and Moïse half each of the assets not disposed of in minor bequests. Were Abraham to die before his wife, he could still rest assured that the firm's capital would be reunited, as Moïse was Esther's closest relative, and thus the logical heir of the childless couple. After Esther died, Abraham drew up a will which made Moïse the sole residuary heir, 'requesting that he [Moïse] accept this as the greatest proof... which I can give him of the justice which I owe him, and in so doing I am only according to him the fruit of his assiduous work, which has led to the success of our commerce and activities'.[53]

But Moïse was a bachelor, and thus the problem of succession after him remained. In response, Abraham attempted to draw his nephews, the sons of the marriage between Benjamin and Esther, into the firm in the 1760s. Two of Benjamin's children resisted Abraham's overtures, even though Benjamin's business had suffered during the Seven Years War[54] and David Gradis et Fils had prospered. Jacob (1731–91), was already arranging shipping-ventures on his own, while David preferred reading philosophy in his study to balancing the books in the firm's counting-room.

Abraham, relentless in his desire to pass on the firm to other members of the family, broke down the resistance of Benjamin's children. He drew David away from a life of intellectual pursuits, accusing his nephew of not recognizing commerce as the vocation of the Gradis family, and of pursuing glory outside the business activities which Abraham had so carefully cultivated. Abraham forcefully instructed David to abandon his studies to work permanently in David Gradis et Fils, and promised that one day David would direct it himself. David relented, and joined his brothers who were already working with Abraham and Moïse. By the late 1770s all the brothers – and, in Jacob's case, his wife and child as well – were living together in the house of Abraham Gradis and working with him.[55]

While Abraham was grooming Benjamin's sons for the ultimate succession, by granting the directorship of the firm to Moïse at his

[53] ADG 3 E 15416, Dugarry, testament, 9 May 1780, opened 25 July 1780.
[54] David Gradis II, 'Notice', fo. 9v. The last ship outfitted by Benjamin Gradis alone was the *Patriarche*, departing from Bordeaux on 16 May 1755 (ADG 6 B 101, soumission); in 1758 he outfitted the *Providence* with Raphael Mendes (ADG 6 B 102, soumission, 12 Feb. 1758).
[55] David Gradis II, 'Notice', fos 11v–12r.

own death he bequeathed it to the relative with the greatest experience in the firm and one for whom he had great affection. But he wished to keep the sons of Benjamin in the firm, and thus extended to them both carrot and stick. He made it clear that they would inherit the firm, and instructed Moïse to draw up his own will to that effect. Abraham, following the suggestion of Moïse, ensured that they would not start their own businesses by giving them virtually nothing in his own will, even though more distant relatives were promised money.[56]

Thus Abraham ensured the continuation of the firm despite the lack of a direct heir. Moïse faced a different problem: how was he to balance the needs of the firm with the existence of several heirs? In his will, Moïse exhorted his four nephews to continue their commerce together. But the director of the firm knew very well that he would have to be be more specific. How, for example, were final decisions to be made? Moïse was troubled by the problem, and apparently changed his mind on the issue at least once. Ever mindful of the possibility of family feuds, he diplomatically informed his nephews that, while all four were equally dear to him, and that all had been of assistance in the operation of the firm, David was the most experienced, and for this reason was to be the next director. Two conditions, however, were attached to his appointment. First, David had to keep his brothers fully informed of the firm's activities. Second, under certain conditions, all four brothers had the right to sign in the name David Gradis et Fils — that is, they had the right to commit the firm to various obligations. Hoping that all four nephews would work together in harmony, Moïse made them equal residuary heirs. But Moïse also made provisions lest his nephews should not fulfil his wishes and should thereby threaten the health of the firm. He warned that any nephew who separated himself from David's plan of action, wished to withdraw his share of the succession from the firm's pool, or did not participate fully in the activities of the firm would have his inheritance reduced to 400,000 livres. This represented a reduction of some 60 per cent, as the total value of the bequest to the four sons of Benjamin Gradis was over 4 million livres, or 1 million per nephew.[57]

[56] The only exception to this rule was Benjamin's son Moïse (1737–1825), who was granted jewellery in recognition of the care he took of Abraham while the latter was sick. See David Gradis II, 'Notice', fo. 19v; and ADG 3 E 15416, Dugarry, testament, 9 May 1780, opened 25 July 1780.

[57] In addition to Jacob, Moïse and David, already mentioned, there was Abraham (1740–90). The information on Moïse plans is drawn from ADG 3 E 26622, Baron, testament, 12 July 1788, opened 12 Feb. 1789.

Abraham and Moïse had thus passed David Gradis et Fils on to another generation of Gradises. The direction of the firm went to family members, as opposed to talented and well-connected employees of long-standing. In 1756 David Gradis et Fils had hired a Hyppolite Grignet, on the suggestion of both the former Minister of Marine, Maurepas, and a high-ranking official in the Ministry of Marine at the time, La Porte, who was also an influential contact for the firm. The treasurer of the General Farms of Paris suggested an individual by the name of Touya, and he too would work with the Gradis family during Abraham's tenure as director of the firm.[58] Both Grignet and Touya held responsible positions. Grignet was placed in charge of the operations of the counting-room, and maintained the firm's correspondence. Touya was responsible for the account books, and balanced the accounts, either alone or with Grignet. Abraham and Moïse trusted them, to the extent that David II felt that they were receiving preferential treatment. In 1777 Grignet parted on friendly terms to establish his own firm, and later served in the municipal administration. Touya left the firm at approximately the same time as Grignet, and became a treasurer of the city of Bordeaux. Both acquired their administrative positions with the assistance of the Gradis family.[59] The support accorded them was undoubtedly a token of gratitude for their contribution to David Gradis et Fils, and possibly a peace-offering for their exclusion from the firm once Benjamin's sons had proven their worth.

The maintenance of the character of the family firm was clearly a priority to Abraham and Moïse. This desire extended beyond purely commercial considerations: it was a matter of intense family pride. Abraham pointed out to his nephew David that, in inheriting David Gradis et Fils, he would also be inheriting the esteem accorded to the

---

[58] See David Gradis II, 'Notice', fos 12v—14v; and the correspondence between Abraham Gradis and La Porte, cited in Maupassant, *Un grand armateur*, p. 60, n. 25.

[59] Abraham granted a diamond to Moïse in his will (of 1780) with the request that Moïse give it to Grignet after his death. Moïse did in fact grant the diamond to Grignet in his will (ADG 3 E 26622, Baron, testament, 12 July 1788, opened 12 Feb. 1789). In 1781, a Gradis, probably Moïse, stood surety for Grignet when the latter acquired a position in the municipal administration of Bordeaux: AMB, Registres de la Jurade, BB 158, fo. 112r; 6 Mar. 1781. As for Touya see David Gradis II, 'Notice', fo. 17r: 'à la solicitation de mon oncle Moïse il eut été nommé Tresorier de la Commune de Bordeaux'.

firm.[60] Moïse also expressed this pride in his will, where he called on his four nephews to work with the same rectitude as he and Abraham had, and to sign the name of the firm David Gradis et Fils, as he and Abraham had also done while together, and as Möise had continued to do on his own.[61] As David II understood, these two men viewed the name of the family firm as the equivalent of a noble patrimony, and felt it their obligation to protect it, pass it on intact, and teach the next generation to serve the firm with the same loyalty and pride as they had felt.

This attitude emerged against the backdrop of the increased honour accorded commerce in the eighteenth century, as well as the specific role of commerce in the life of the Gradis family. Although involvement in commerce had once been sufficient to force a member of the nobility to surrender his rank (*derogeance*), in 1701 laws were relaxed so that a member of the nobility could engage in the wholesale trade without loss of status and the attendant privileges.[62] Against the detractors of this trend, others argued that nobles, especially those who were impoverished, should invest in commerce as an honourable way of serving the King. This thesis was advanced most forcefully by the Abbé Coyer in his work *La Noblesse commerçante* (1756). He sparked a heated debate by arguing that the nobility should engage in commerce 'for the good of commerce, which means for the good of France', and that 'Commerce has become the soul of political interest and of the balance of power.... The balance of trade and the balance of power are one and the same...'[63] The status of commerce was also enhanced by allowing merchants to purchase noble offices. Others proposed that commerce itself should be ennobled — that is, as a profession, and not just for the wealth which can purchase title.[64]

Although commerce was, in theory, accorded greater honour as a profession, many of the successful merchants in Bordeaux wished to concretize their success by formal affiliation with the nobility. Some purchased noble offices; many others married into noble families.[65]

---

[60] David Gradis II, 'Notice', fo. 11r, where he quotes Abraham referring to 'la haute consideration de notre maison de commerce'.

[61] ADG 3 E 26622, Baron, testament, 12 July 1788, opened 12 Feb. 1789.

[62] Guy Richard, *Noblesse d'affaires au XVIIIe siècle* (Paris, 1974), p. 38.

[63] Quoted in Mousnier, *The Institutions of France*, vol. 1, p. 192.

[64] Richard, *Noblesse d'affaires*, p. 66.

[65] William Doyle, *The Parlement of Bordeaux and the End of the Old Régime* (London and Tonbridge, 1974), pp. 16–17; and Paul Butel, *La Croissance commerciale bordelaise dans la seconde moitié du XVIIIe siècle*, 2 vols, (Lille, 1973), vol. 2, pp. 1059–73.

Not satisfied with acquiring a noble office, Jean Pellet of Bordeaux even fabricated a genealogy in order to argue that he was not just an ennobled merchant, but in fact a member of the old nobility.[66] Jews, too, aspired to the nobility, although they could not legally become members of it without conversion. This led in some cases to an unusual syncretism of religious background and eighteenth-century symbols. Charles-Paul-Joseph Peixotto, for example, created a genealogy in which he 'traced' his lineage back to one of the distinguished tribes of biblical times. In fact, during the Revolution Peixotto was accused of having striven for aristocratic status, and his fabricated genealogy and the crest which he had adopted were cited as evidence.[67]

The Gradis family followed another route. Drawing on the honour accorded commerce, they transformed the name of their firm into a surrogate noble title. The comment of David II cited above certainly suggests that Abraham and Moïse considered the name of their firm equivalent to such a title. Moreover, the exhortation in Moïse's will to preserve the family name of the business strongly resembles the pleas of members of the nobility to their sons to preserve the patrimony of the family out of pride, and not just out of material concerns.[68] For the Gradis family, pride in the name David Gradis et Fils was a theme from the time of Abraham onwards, and facilitated the passage of the family firm from one generation to the next.[69]

This heightened sense of pride in the firm was reinforced because Abraham and Moïse used their wealth to live nobly (*vivre noblement*). In the eighteenth century, 'nobility' not only described a legal status, but in a wider sense could include a manner of living open to all who could afford it. Abraham lived in an appropriately luxurious style in both town and countryside. In 1744 he was forced to move from his

[66] Jean Cavignac, *Jean Pellet, commerçant de gros, 1694–1772. Contribution à l'étude du négoce bordelais au XVIIIe siècle* (Paris, 1967), pp. 326–31; and Doyle, *The Parlement of Bordeaux*, p. 19.

[67] Malvezin, *Histoire des Juifs à Bordeaux*, pp. 269–71.

[68] Françoise Bluche, *La Vie quotidienne de la noblesse française au XVIIIe siècle* (Paris, 1973), pp. 34–5.

[69] See for example Schwob d'Hericourt, *La Maison Gradis* which is introduced (p. 7) with an excerpt from the will of Moïse, the son of Benjamin and brother of David II, who would ultimately be the head of the firm. For a similar phenomenon see David Landes, 'Bleichröders and Rothschilds: The problem of Continuity in the Family Firm', in Charles E. Rosenberg (ed.), *The Family in History*, (Philadelphia, 1975), pp. 95–114. Especially interesting is the demand that the Rothschilds made of a Montefiore who wished to enter the Rothschild firm: he could only do so if he would change his name to Rothschild (ibid., p. 108).

home by a decision of the municipality, and he subsequently built another nearby. His new home, occupied in October 1752, was splendid. He spent over 20,000 livres on it in 1751 and 1752, and at least 24,500 livres over the next fifteen years. By 1788 the value of the house was estimated at 120,000 livres.[70] Already in 1753 Abraham was inviting guests and promising them surroundings in the same general style as the great residences in Paris, albeit somewhat less grand. Visitors to his home, including the daughter of the Duc de Richelieu, were duly impressed.[71] Abraham also purchased magnificent estates in the country. In late 1748 he bought a *seigneurie*, an important step in maintaining the appearance of living nobly. He added to this holding in Talence in 1752, 1753 and 1759. By 1788 the family had acquired 103.5 *journaux*, the equivalent of 83 acres of land, worth an estimated 120,000 livres. Over the years Abraham busily improved these estates. He planted vineyards in Talence and, once the returns began in 1753, he constructed a new building on his domain.[72]

[70] In his will of 1780, Abraham specifically listed and granted annual pensions to three servants for their exceptional services, and leaves the impression that there were many others (ADG 3 E 15416, Dugarry, testament, 9 May 1780, opened 25 July 1780). On the value of the house, see AG, journal entries, 10 Aug, 1752, 2 Dec. 1752 and 28 Oct. 1788.

[71] Letters cited in Butel, *La Croissance commerciale bordelaise*, vol. 2, p. 108[4]; and Maupassant, *Un grand amateur*, p. 158.

[72] AG 3134, 'Achat de la terre noble de Monadey', copy of a notarial document from the *étude* of Perrens, dated 15 Dec. 1748. There has been unfortunate confusion on the purchase of *seigneuries*. It was not limited to the nobility, and it did not automatically ennoble. See Mousnier, *The Institutions of France*, vol. 1, pp. 482–3; and Pierre Goubert, *The Ancien Régime: French Society 1600–1750*, tr. Steve Cox (New York, 1974), p. 82. I suspect that those who have argued that Gradis was ennobled—Guy Richard, *Noblesse d'affaires*, p. 112; followed by for example, Robert Louis Stein in *The French Slave Trade in the Eighteenth Century: An Old Regime Business* (Madison, Wis., 1979), p. 159 – do so purely on the basis that he purchased a *seigneurie*. Jews were able to acquire noble land and seigneurial privileges, although these too were on occasion contested. (Thus the *cause célèbre* of Liefmann Calmer: see Szajkowski, *Franco-Judaica*, pp. 103–5, nos, 1199–244).

The acquisition of these properties shows a strong tendency among certain segments of the Jewish population to *live nobly*, which was an accepted method of climbing the hierarchy towards actual ennoblement (Goubert, *The Ancien Régime*, p. 155 and esp. pp. 185–6). For information on the holdings cited here see AG, journal entries, 10 Aug. 1753 and 28 Oct. 1788.

The profits of viticulture were, in fact, modest,[73] and even the convenience of having a relatively good wine for his own commerce was not crucial in Abraham's decision to acquire these estates. The residence in Talence was there for his recreation. Certainly in later life he spent much of his time at his estate; when the Palestinian rabbi Azulai passed through Bordeaux in November 1777, he went to visit Abraham in the countryside. His wife, too, went there with her friends.[74] It was on his estate that Abraham pursued his passion for horticulture, collecting seeds and specimens from both Europe and North America for his garden. On occasion he shared his interests with members of the nobility, exchanging expertise as well as samples for planting.[75] Abraham's garden — a tangible representation of the wealthy shipper's cosmopolitanism and refined taste — impressed its visitors. Azulai recorded with wonder that he was taken 'to [Abraham Gradis's] garden, where there was a large pool of water filled with fish, and delights of this world including flowers and trees from America and various plants and roses'.[76] Abraham and Moïse surrounded themselves with other 'delights of this world' as well. In 1788, the value of their silver was estimated at 21,000 livres, while their furniture and jewellery were valued at 5,359 and 8,036 livres, respectively.[77]

With their success in commerce, Abraham and Moïse were able to live nobly. The commercial activities of David Gradis et Fils also enhanced the standing of the family in both the non-Jewish and the Jewish worlds. By the mid-1740s the firm was a government contractor, which meant working closely with the Crown and its ministers, and had entered into a series of partnerships with members of the Ministry of Marine, many of whom belonged to the nobility.

Information on the actual size of the holdings has been kindly provided to me by Jean Cavignac, based on ADG Q, enregistrement, B 222, fo. 127v, 5 Mar. 1788.

[73] Robert Forster, 'The Noble Wine Producers of the Bordelais in the Eighteenth Century', *Economic History Review*, 2nd ser., 14 (1961–12), pp. 18–34: and Doyle, *The Parlement of Bordeaux*, pp. 86–101. Gradis's own profits followed the pattern and were uneven.

[74] Hayyim Yosef David Azulai, *Sefer ma'agal tov ha-Shalem*, ed. Aaron Freiman (Jerusalem, 1934), p. 116 (in Hebrew); and AG 6/65, letter from Abraham to Moïse Gradis, 4 June 1759.

[75] See for example AG4/49, letter from La Galissonière to Abraham Gradis, 8 Nov. 1752.

[76] Azulai, *Sefer ma'agal tov*, p. 116.

[77] AG, journal entries, 28 Oct. 1788.

Abraham Gradis also lent money to the members of the nobility —
particularly, once again, to officials in the Ministry of Marine.[78]
These economic activities, as well as the wealth of the Gradis
family, had repercussions on the social lives of family members. For
Abraham's father, social life revolved around his family and the
Jewish world. In his will, the only non-Jews provided for were his
servants; otherwise, his concern was totally for Jews, the poor of
Jerusalem and the poor of Bordeaux. Similarly, all indications from
Abraham's 'European tour' and from surviving correspondence up to
the early 1740s suggest that Abraham was surrounded by Jewish
friends, and that he shared family details with them alone. But this
changed dramatically in the late 1740s. When business was conducted
with the Crown, it was necessary to foster and maintain connections
with individuals in high places. When Abraham went to Paris in late
1749 he was in contact with the d'Harcourts, one of whom assisted
him in seeking reimbursement for his business with the Crown during
the war by presenting him to Rouillé, the Minister of Marine.[79] The
Baron de Rochechouart — an acquaintance of the d'Harcourts and a
debtor of the firm — also asked to be kept informed of Abraham's
meeting with the Minister. And the contacts with these people were
not just concerned with business. Abraham was invited to stay with
the d'Harcourts during that visit, and, although he initially declined,
he relented after their continued inviations and moved into their
residence in January. While there, Rochechouart kept Gradis informed of his hunting-successes, and promised to send him six par-
tridges from his latest kill.[80] The Duc de Choiseul, one of the most
powerful figures of the regime of Louis XV, addressed Abraham
Gradis with the familiar 'mon cher Abraham'.

Abraham maintained contact with the upper reaches of French
society closer to home as well. Already in the 1750s, his correspondents assumed that he had influential acquaintances in the *parlement*
of Bordeaux. He was the banker and friend of the *parlementaire*
Prunes, and paid close heed to much of his advice. He and his wife

---

[78] See Maupassant, *Un grand armateur* in pp. 150-8. This is also discussed
in Menkis, 'The Gradis Family', pp. 164–5 and ch. 5.
[79] On the d'Harcourt family see Maupassant, *Un grand armateur*, pp. 34–
5, and specifically AG 6/70, letter from Abraham to Moïse Gradis, 2 Jan.
1750.
[80] AG 6/70, letter from Abraham to Moïse Gradis, 27 Dec. 1749; and AG 3/
36, letters from the Baron de Rochechouart to Abraham Gradis, 11 Jan.
1750 and 28 Jan. 1750.

enjoyed visiting the spa at Bagnères, which was also a favourite place of relaxation for the *parlementaires*. And, as a major shareholder in the Grand-Théâtre of Bordeaux, he was also in the circle of the Governor of the Generality of Guyenne.[81]

Abraham's social life barely resembled that of his father, and this process was certainly facilitated by his selective attitude to ritual law. Abraham's letters reveal that he observed some of the holidays in one fashion or another. He would neither engage in correspondence nor go to the exchange on Passover. When he was in Paris in the late 1750s, he celebrated the holiday of Passover with his friend the representative of the Jewish community of Bordeaux in Paris, Jacob Rodrigues Péreire, at whose home he stayed. He assured Moïse in one letter that unleavened bread was being baked in Paris.[82] Abraham was not, however, punctilious in dietary matters, and ate at the homes of various members of the nobility in both Paris and Bordeaux. Azulai who complained that Abraham Gradis was 'one of the great heretics who eat forbidden foods in public',[83] was obviously irritated not merely by the fact that Abraham ate unkosher food — after all, Azulai refused to eat in the home of all but one member of the Sephardic community of Bordeaux[84] — but by the fact that he did so in public.

Clear and dramatic changes did take place in Abraham's religious attitudes. While David, spontaneously, even intimately, referred to God's involvement in all affairs, Abraham showed diminishing attachment to these forms of piety. In his first will (1753) he stipulated that the Jewish poor to whom he granted money should pray for him, but by the 1760s he no longer requested this. While most Jews of Bordeaux continued to engage in some form of religious discourse in their wills throughout the eighteenth century, in Abraham's last complete will (1780) there is no religious discourse at all, not even the

[81] AG 2/25, La Galissonière to Abraham Gradis, 10 Feb. 1754. On Prunes, see David Gradis II, 'Notice', fo. 11v, as well as numerous transactions recorded in the account books. Doyle, in *The Parlement of Bordeaux*, p. 129, elaborates on the significance of Bagnères for the *parlementaires*, while Maupassant, in *Un grand armateur*, pp. 54–5 and n. 23, draws attention to the social significance of the investment in the Grand–Théâtre.
[82] AG, Copieur d'Europe, letters from Abraham Gradis to Reynack, 13 Apr. 1756, fo. 85r, and to Mlle. d'Harcourt, 14 Apr. 1756, fo. 85v.; AG 5/63, letter from Abraham to Moïse Gradis, 30 Mar. 1759.
[83] Azulai, *Sefer ma'agal tov*, p. 115.
[84] Ibid., p. 36.

most casual reference to God, which could still be found in about two-thirds of wills of Jews of Bordeaux at this time.[85]

Succinctly but dramatically, Azulai recorded in his diary that Abraham was one of those heretics 'who do not believe in the Oral Law'.[86] Clearly, traditional religious beliefs had lost their hold over Abraham, as they had over other Jews, as well as many non-Jews, in the middle of the eighteenth century.[87] From Azulai's comment, as well as from the wills, we can infer that the Enlightenment must have had an impact on Abraham. Rabbinic tradition had come under severe criticism during the Enlightenment,[88] and even the towering

[85] On the first will see AG 4/45, testament, Sep. 1753. Abraham had no children, which could explain this request. In AG 4/45 there are also undated notes by Abraham on how to dispose of his wealth after his death. These notes clearly come from some time in the 1760s, certainly before 1771, as Benjamin Gradis (d.1771) was one of the inheritors specified in the will. The last will has been preserved in ADG 3 E 15416, Dugarry, testament, 9 May 1780, opened 25 July 1780.

On the wills of other Jews of Bordeaux, see Dominique Bourges, 'Les Attitudes des Juifs de Bordeaux devant la mort, 1745−1786, à travers les clauses de testaments', thèse de maîtrise, Université de Paris I, 1977−8), esp. pp. 110−11. A debate on the meaning of the decline of religious references in wills by Christians has taken place in French historiography. Unlike Michel Vovelle in *Piété baroque et déchristianisation en Provence au XVIIIe siècle. Les attitudes devant la mort d'après les clauses de testaments* (Paris, 1974), Philippe Ariès has argued, in *Essais sur l'histoire de la mort en Occident du moyen âge à nos jours* (Paris, 1974), that this does not indicate secularization, but shows rather that the will was increasingly seen as a business document.

It is clear from the last will of Abraham Gradis, however, that he viewed it as more than a document for the disposal of goods. Thus he specifically referred to the fond feelings for his late wife, a sentiment totally uncharacteristic of the wills of the time. On this, see Bourges, 'Les Attitudes des Juifs de Bordeaux devant la mort', p. 134. Clearly the lack of pious references in this will cannot be ascribed to Abraham's desire to use it merely as a vehicle for the disposal of goods.

[86] Azulai, *Sefer ma'agal tov*, p. 115.

[87] Bourges, 'Les Attitudes des Juifs de Bordeaux devant la mort', p. 113. For evidence on the decline in adherence to traditional religious values in Bordeaux, see Raymond Darricau and J.B. Marquette, 'Les Temps modernes', in Bernard Guillemain (ed.), *Le Diocèse de Bordeaux* (Paris, 1974), pp. 160−1: and Timothy Tackett, *Religion, Revolution and Regional Culture in Eighteenth Century France: The Ecclesiastical Oath of 1791* (Princeton, NJ, 1986), pp. 255−6, esp. p. 256, n. 18.

[88] Arnold Ages, *The French Enlightenment and Rabbinic Tradition* (Frankfurt am Main, 1970), ch. 2.

intellectual figure of Bordeaux, Montesquieu, who was generally tolerant on religious issues, privately held rabbinic tradition in contempt while valuing the divine inspiration of the Bible.[89] While it is still unclear whether Montesquieu had any direct contact with Abraham Gradis,[90] the latter would be well aware of these views of the Enlightenment.

Abraham not only adopted a non-traditional view of Judaism, but believed that it was worth propagating. Already in the 1760s he included in his will a donation of 500 livres per annum from a capital fund of 10,000 livres, so that a school could be set up for the Jewish poor to learn French and arithmetic. He clearly favoured a non-traditional type of education, aimed at making the poor 'useful' — an important theme in the development of the curriculum of the Talmud—Torah in Bordeaux.[91] In 1773 the community decided that there had to be changes in the curriculum, and a committee was set up to offer proposals. This group included, significantly, David Gradis II, and the proposals put foward were undoubtedly to some extent his, drawn up with the knowledge and encouragement of his uncle Abraham.[92] In fact, at the same time as the committee was set up, David Gradis et Fils, in co-operation with other firms, offered to provide interest of 6 per cent on capital funds deposited with the firm

---

[89] J. Well, 'Un texte de Montesquieu sur le Judaïsme', *Revue des études juives*, 49 (1904), pp. 150—3. See also Arthur Hertzberg, *The French Enlightenment and the Jews* (New York, 1968), p. 275.

[90] It has been suggested that a request for a bill of exchange by Montesquieu, addressed to 'mon cher Abraham', and dated 19 Mar. 1740, was directed to Abraham Gradis. See François Gebelin, (ed.), *Correspondance de Montesquieu*, 2 vols (Bordeaux, 1914), vol. 1, pp. 351—2 and Elie Szapiro, 'Trois épaves des Archives Gradis', *Archives juives*, 8 (1971—12), p. 22. Unfortunately, the family name of this Abraham is not indicated anywhere, but both of the above authors have tentatively argued that it was Gradis. I have not found a reference to this bill of exchange in the accounting records, but not all personal transactions were recorded there. There was at least one other Abraham who could have been the recipient of this request, Abraham Raphael. He was one of the Raphael brothers who served as bill-brokers in Bordeaux.

[91] Abraham promised the funding 'pour l'établissement d'une ecole pour que les pauvres de ma nation aprennent a lire, ecrire, le francois, les chiffres' (AG 4/45, undated will from the 1760s). On rendering the poor more 'useful' and discouraging them from 'vices', see Schwarzfuchs, *Registre des délibérations*, p. 299, no. 280, article 5, and pp. 446—7, no. 422, article 8.

[92] Ibid., and the educational proposals in AG 10/117. By this time, David II was living with his uncles Abraham and Moïse.

for the Talmud—Torah.[93] One year later, the Jewish community of Bordeaux approved the committee's proposal that French and arithmetic should be taught. Most significantly, the school rules clearly stated that Bible was to be studied only with the commentaries of the best grammarians, those who sought out the literal meaning of the text[94] — in short, no midrashic comments. This system of education effectively uprooted the Oral Law, much to the chagrin of traditionalists such as Azulai. Even Rashi's commentary, Azulai noted when visiting the school several years after these reforms were instituted, was not studied in the Talmud—Torah of Bordeaux, because it included too much rabbinic material.[95]

While possibly influenced by the *philosophes*, Abraham, like most other Bordeaux notables, does not seem to have experienced a serious intellectual conflict between religious tradition and the philosophy of the Enlightenment.[96] In fact, there is little evidence that he read much at all. When in Bagnères, he missed the gazettes with their news of events at Court and at sea.[97] While David II may have had his own reasons for minimizing Abraham's intellectual curiosity — his uncle was, after all, the one who who had drawn him away from his philosophical studies — David was undoubtedly correct in stating that Abraham was no 'litterateur'.[98]

Abraham's attachment to traditional forms of piety had clearly declined, but he continued to display the strong sense of identification with his ethnic group that had characterized previous generations. The Jewish community demanded his participation in communal matters, and he generally complied. He served as the syndic of the community between 1737 and 1738, and as an adjoint (adjunct) three times (1747—8, 1752—3 1753—4; he was nominated to serve again in 1774—5, but because of his advanced age he was exempted). As an elder — that is, a former syndic — he served on the powerful *bureau*

[93] Schwarzfuchs, *Registre des délibérations*, p. 427, no. 409.

[94] Ibid., p. 443, no. 422.

[95] Azulai, *Sefer ma'agal tov*, p. 114.

[96] The lack of a serious confrontation between Judaism and the Enlightenment, as happened in Germany, has been noted by Malino in *The Sephardic Jews of Bordeaux*, p. 26. See also Jean Cavignac, 'L'Apport des Israélites bordelais aux arts et lettres au cours du XIXe siècle', *Revue des études juives*, 144 (1985), pp. 343'—9; and Hertzberg, *The French Enlightenment and the Jews*, pp. 141—62. On Bordeaux as a whole, see Doyle, *The Parlement of Bordeaux*, pp. 130—6.

[97] AG 6/65, letter from Abraham to Moïse Gradis, 19 July 1759.

[98] David Gradis II, 'Notice', fo. 11v.

de treize,[99] and was even appointed to serve on that committee in August 1779, when he was about eighty-four years old.[100]

Even when Abraham had no official position in the Jewish community, he was called upon to plead its case before the various officials of the Crown. He became, at least on several occasions, the intercessor of the Jews, exploiting his connections in high places. In February 1759, Claude-Louis Aubert de Tourny, intendant of the Guyenne, attempted to make the Jewish community purchase the foundling-home in Bordeaux. The community leaders asked Abraham to work in conjunction with their agent in Paris, Péreire, to prevent this imposition, which they considered to be both a flagrant violation of their privileges and particularly humiliating.[101] The community considered Abraham suitable for this role because of the connections that he had in Paris through his government contracting, and they did not err in this. Over the next few days, Abraham met with Douin, the first secretary of Louis Phelypeaux, Comte de Saint-Florentin, the appropriate authority in this matter.[102] He may also have met with other highly place officials, as suggested by Douin. From Abraham's correspondence with Moïse it appears that the result was favourable, and Douin, convinced that the intendant had no right to force the Jews of Bordeaux to make this purchase, promised to look into the matter. Abraham's role was solely to intercede; once he had done that, he expected Péreire to keep the community leaders informed.[103]

---

[99] The committee would decide on appeals if an individual felt that the taxation imposed by the community was unfair.

[100] For a convenient list of the various communal officials and when they served, see Schwarzfuchs, *Registre des délibérations*, pp. 607–11.

[101] AG 6/66, letter from Daniel Mendes Furtado, syndic, and Raphael Mendes and D. Lameyre, *adjoints*, to Abraham Gradis, 9 Feb. 1759. This decree was considered humiliating not just because it was an imposition, but also because it was a working assumption in the eighteenth century that *enfants trouvés*, or foundlings, were illegitimate. See Olwen H. Hufton, *The Poor of Eighteenth Century France, 1750–1789* (Oxford, 1979), p. 319.

[102] Each region of France fell under the jurisdiction of one of the ministers of state. The region of Guyenne was initially the responsibility of the Secrétaire d'Etat des Affaires Etrangères, but from January 1747 it came under the Secrétaire d'Etat de la Religion Prétendue Réformée. There was a sizeable correspondence between the respective ministries and the various intendants over the course of the eighteenth century. See Nahon, *Michael*, 4, pp. 186–247.

[103] AG 5/63, letters from Abraham to Moïse Gradis, 20 Feb., 23 Feb. and 3 Mar. 1759, as well as several undated letters in that file.

The Jews of Bayonne, too, called upon Abraham to assist them. In 1761 the municipality of Bayonne granted the non-Jewish chocolate-makers the right to establish a guild, which would effectively exclude Jews from the very business which they had introduced to Bayonne. The Jewish community fought back, complaining to Saint-Florentin and making direct representations to the municipality. It was not enough, however, and in 1766 the community's representatives wrote to Abraham Gradis explaining what had happened and imploring him to do all that he could to correct a situation that threatened them with indigence. They approached him at the suggestion of his nephew, David Alexandre, in the knowledge that Abraham had powerful connections. While it is not clear exactly what Abraham did, if anything, in September 1767 the *parlement* suppressed the guild.[104]

The non-Jewish authorities, too, considered Abraham and Moïse their liaison with the Jewish community, regardless of whether these two had any official standing. In 1762 the intendant put Abraham in charge of collecting the various taxes on the Jewish community. In 1788, Moïse Gradis was asked by the local intendant, Dupré de Saint-Maur, to state his opinions on the Jewish community of Bordeaux and Judaism.[105] The intendant was, in fact, working with Malesherbes, who was looking into the desirability of granting Jews the same rights as he had granted to the Protestants the year before.

Abraham and Moïse expressed their identification with the Sephardic Jews of Bordeaux financially, as well as politically. Abraham contributed generously when money was needed to secure the registration of letters patent.[106] In 1762, in the midst of the Seven Years War and at a time when the financial situation of the Crown was particularly precarious, the Jewish *nation*, like other corporations, was expected to make a patriotic contribution, and in fact the sum of 24,000 livres was collected to purchase a ship. Once again, David Gradis et Fils headed the list of donors, offering 3,000 livres. In 1782, another subscription was arranged for a vessel for the King,

[104] Hertzberg, *The French Enlightenment and the Jews*, pp. 110–11, and the documents published by Nahon in *Les 'Nations' juives*, pp. 113 and 308–20, provide an outline of the affair until 1764. For the role of the Gradis family see AG 8/94, letter from the *nation* of Bayonne to Abraham Gradis, 21 Feb. 1766.

[105] Schwarzfuchs, *Registre des délibérations*, p. 319, no. 304; and Malvezin, *Histoire des Juifs à Bordeaux*, pp. 244–8.

[106] On Abraham's donation, see Schwarzfuchs, *Registre des délibérations*, pp. 228–9, no. 190.

and David Gradis et Fils was the most generous donor, this time offering 12,000 of the total of 160,000 livres required of the *nation*.[107]

Both Abraham and Moïse made special provision for the poor of their community. In his last will Abraham promised an annual distribution of 250 livres, setting aside 5,000 livres as capital. Similarly, Moïse provided a fund of 4,000 livres for an annual distribution of 200 livres, as well as 500 livres to be distributed on the day of his death.[108] The ethnic solidarity of Abraham and Moïse also extended beyond the local community, to other Sephardic Jews. Like David I, they both donated money in their wills to the poor of Jerusalem. Abraham granted the same amount to them as he did to the poor of Bordeaux, while Moïse gave 1,000 livres, to be paid in two annual instalments in the two years after his death. Although others in the Jewish community made such bequests,[109] they were few, and in some ways Abraham emerged as a defender of continuing support for the communities of Palestine. Though he was severely castigated by Azulai for his religious beliefs, he was Azulai's chief private donor in Bordeaux in 1777, giving him 240 livres.[110] During that same visit, moreover, Abraham, through his brother-in-law Moïse, told the community leaders that Azulai should be supported in his mission, although others clearly opposed it.[111]

---

[107] Ibid., pp. 318–19, no. 303, and pp. 532–4, no. 505; ADG C 4434. Although the community eventually decided that the money should be borrowed from some of its leading members, and that they would then receive some exemption from their annual taxes, the commitments were a gesture of patriotism on the part of the donors, as they did not receive interest on their loans.

[108] ADG 3 E 15416, Dugarry, testament, 9 May 1780, opened 25 July 1780, and 26622, Baron, testament, 12 July 1788, opened 12 Feb. 1789, respectively.

[109] Bourges counted seventeen wills which referred to donations to members of the Jewish community or the Jewish world, with five out of the seventeen (which includes David I and Abraham-she did not discover Moïse's will) donating money to the land of Israel. See Bourges, 'Les Attitudes des Juifs de Bordeaux devant la mort', pp. 102–3.

[110] See Meir Benayahu, *Rabbi Hayyim Yosef David Azulai* (Jerusalem, 1958–9), p. 456 (in Hebrew).

[111] On the dispute see Azulai, *Sefer ma'agal tov*, p. 116. There would later be some question as to whether these emissaries should be allowed to come to Bordeaux, or whether the money should be collected at one central location, for example Amsterdam, and subsequently have the money forwarded to the charity. Certainly this way travelling-costs would be saved.

But the generosity of Abraham and Moïse was not geared just towards the Sephardic Jewish communtiy, either in Bordeaux or in the Holy Land. In their wills they both made gifts to non-Jews as well.[112] Abraham gave 500 livres to the poor of the parish of Sainte-Eulalie, and 300 to the poor of Talence, while Moïse gave 500 livres to the impoverished Catholics of Sainte-Eulalie. In making bequests to non-Jews, the Gradis family stood almost alone in the Jewish community of Bordeaux in the eighteenth century.[113]

These bequests are rather startling. Several generations earlier the family had been in the land of the Portuguese Inquisition, and Abraham's grandfather may well have been a refugee from an outbreak of intolerance in Toulouse. But both the Gradis family and the world around them had changed since the mid-1680s. Less than one hundred years after Diego and his children had carefully divided their modest stock of textiles and grain, Abraham and Moïse were faced with the enviable problem of how to divide various holdings valued at over 4 million livres. Diego lived with David at the end of his life, reserving for himself a modest pension of 400 livres per annum, while Abraham and Moïse passed much of their later years in their country estate complete with a garden filled with tropical fruits, and spent their vacations with *parlementaires* at the local spa.

Abraham and Moïse correctly perceived that commerce was the basis of their success, and sought to instil a degree of nobility (in an *ancien régime* meaning) into their business house as well as their manner of living, which explains the great commitment to the family firm in each generation. Commitment to the firm was apparent in other ways as well. Marriages were arranged to foster new contacts,

---

There is, however, another reason why the community may not have wanted these *shelihim* (emissaries). Gérard Nahon has suggested that a community concerned about integration might feel it best to keep foreigners — especially those dressed in exotic garb — at a distance. See Gérard Nahan, 'Les Emissaires de la Terre Sainte dans les communautés judéo-portugaises du sud-ouest de la France au XVIIe et au XVIIIe siècles', *Studies in the History of the Jewish People and the Land of Israel*, 3 (1974), pp. 145–76 (in Hebrew), for a description of the various emissaries who arrived in southwestern France. For his comments on the decline of this phenomenon see ibid., p. 166.

[112] ADG 3 E 15416, Dugarry, testament, 9 May 1780, opened 25 July 1780, and 26622, Baron, testament, 12 July 1788, opened 12 Feb. 1789.

[113] See Bourges, 'Les Attitudes des Juifs de Bordeaux devant la mort', p. 137.

to develop a strong sense of family by multiple ties of marriage, and to prevent the loss of capital. Father and uncles worked assiduously to draw occasionally reluctant sons and rephews into the family firm, and family life was organized around the business. Abraham and Moïse could not purchase noble offices, but they certainly could, and did, live nobly, and were accepted as near-equals by the titled nobility. They reciprocated the openness extended to them, at least in part by extending their charitable activities to the non-Jewish world.

Certainly religious differences were no longer significant to the later generations. If Diego's private world still eludes us, David seems to have always been ready with a pious utterance. Abraham, on the other hand, abandoned features of traditional Judaism, and helped promote non-traditional attitudes in the educational system of Bordeaux. In other matters the Gradis family remained steadfast in changing conditions. Their attachment to the Sephardic community of Bordeaux specifically and the Sephardic Diaspora in general was strong in every generation. Diego lived at a time when there was no official Jewish community. Upon its emergence, his son and grandson ranked among its leaders, with the heads of other wealthy families. Moreover, Abraham became a *de facto* intercessor for the Jews at Versailles, thereby appropriating increased responsibility and power. When Moïse died in 1788, a remarkable era had come to an end for these acculturated members of the Sephardic elite of Bordeaux.

2

Abraham de Camondo of Istanbul: the Transformation of Jewish Philanthropy

ARON RODRIGUE

Near the bridge that crosses the now heavily polluted waters of the Golden Horn, and perilously close to the modern highway that links Istanbul to its international airport, stands a magnificent white marble mausoleum, very much in need of repair, dominating a huge cemetery full of broken stones and overgrown weeds. This is the oldest Jewish cemetery in Istanbul, that of Hasköy, and the mausoleum contains the remains of arguably the most famous Jew of nineteenth-century Istanbul, Abraham de Camondo. Both the ornate European baroque style of the mausoleum and the fact that it overlooks the main highway leading to the west, to Europe and the wider world beyond are fitting symbols for Camondo's life, pointing to the key process with which he was associated — that of Westernization.

Abraham de Camondo was born in Istanbul in 1780 to a comfortable but not particularly rich money-lending and banking family that had only recently established itself in the business. The family appears to have come to Istanbul in the late seventeenth century from Venice. Its first century in the Ottoman capital is shrouded in obscurity. Only in the second half of the eighteenth century, when we find members of the family trading with Venice, Trieste and Vienna,[1] did it begin its upward social mobility. As a result of their trade with the Hapsburg lands the Camondos obtained the 'protection' of the Austrian ambassador in Istanbul, and eventually acquired Austrian citizenship under Joseph II.[2]

---

[1] I am grateful to Lois Dubin for this information.

[2] The grandfather of Abraham de Camondo had to flee for his life from Turkey after falling out with the authorities. With the help of the Austrian ambassador in Istanbul, he made his way to Vienna, where he was given Austrian citizenship after being granted an audience with Joseph II. See

Under the Ottoman Capitulation treaties with the West, foreign protection and citizenship offered non-Muslim merchants and bankers in the Ottoman Empire a way of escaping Ottoman jurisdiction in matters concerning trade and taxation, and gave them access to European courts for commercial problems that involved litigation. The capitulations hence had created an enormous loophole in the *dhimma*, the covenant that regulated the protected but second-class status of Jews and Christians under Muslim rule. As a result, foreign protection became increasingly popular among non-Muslim merchants in the Levant, and acquisition of this status came to be a sign of upward social mobility.[3]

The involvement of the Camondos in trade and commerce with Italy and Austria led to their integration into the elite section of Jewish society in the Ottoman Empire. This elite was composed of Italian Jews, who were known as 'Francos'. Most had come from the Tuscan port of Livorno and had settled in Salonica, Istanbul, Izmir, Aleppo, Alexandria and Cairo in the course of the eighteenth century. They were all protected by foreign consuls and continued to maintain close ties with Italy.[4] Franco families such as the Allatini, the Fernandez, the Modiano, the Fua and the Morpurgo had become important members of the Levantine mercantile class, which was composed of many different ethnic and religious groups. The Camondos had forged business and family links with these families and had acquired a leading position by the middle of the nineteenth century.

There is no information about the education that Abraham de Camondo received in his youth. His predilection for the psalms, his building of small private synagogues in his numerous mansions, and his support of numerous yeshivot[5] suggest that it had a Jewish component. It is also clear that he was fluent in both Judaeo-Spanish, the mother tongue of the Sephardic Jews of Turkey, and Italian.

Ludwig August Frankl, *The Jews in the East*, tr. P. Beaton (London, 1859), vol. 1, p. 124.

[3] On the capitulations, see Nassim Soussa, *The Capitulatory Regime of Turkey* (London, 1933); and Necdet Kurdakul, *Osmanli Devletinde Ticaret Andlaşmalari ve Kapitülasyonlar* (Istanbul, 1981).

[4] On the Francos, see Abraham Galanté, *Histoire des Juifs d'Istanbul*, vol. 2 (Istanbul, 1942), pp. 213–24; Attilio Milano, *Storia degli Ebrei italiani nel Levante* (Florence, 1949); and Simon Schwarzfuchs, 'Sulam Saloniki', *Sefunot*, 15 (1971–81), pp. 79–102.

[5] See *Archives Israélites*, 34 (1873), pp. 227–36; and Edouard Roditi, 'Camondo's Way', *Grand Street*, 6, 2 (Winter 1987), p. 155.

The first forty-five years of Camondo's life were spent in the family business and not in the public arena. The Camondos were active as 'sarrafs' (money-lenders) in Istanbul until the business evolved into a merchant bank in the middle of the nineteenth century. Abraham was initiated into the financial world by his elder brother Isaac, who had put the Camondo bank on a firm footing in the Ottoman capital in the early decades of the nineteenth century.

The Jewish sarrafs of Istanbul were deeply involved in the financial affairs and the provisioning of the Janissary corps, that once glorious but now uncontrollable military group which had become a thorn in the side of all reform-minded sultans. Although Jews like everyone else suffered from the behaviour of this corps, which rioted all too frequently, the economic well-being of many Jewish merchants and bankers was dependent on the Janissaries, and Jews and Armenians were in fierce competition for the business. At the turn of the century, the Gabay, Aciman and Carmona families, the leaders of the Jewish community, were all active as sarrafs in the Court and had close financial dealings with the leaders of the Janissaries.[6] The Camondos appear to have been relatively minor figures at the time.

The year 1826, crucial in Turkish history, proved to be as significant for Abraham de Camondo as for the rest of the Jewish community. In that year the Sultan suppressed a Janissary revolt and abolished the corps altogether. At the same time he ordered the execution of the leader of the Jewish community, Behor Carmona, tax-farmer and money-lender to the Janissaries.[7] This action was designed to annul the debts owed to Carmona.

The Camondo brothers, under danger themselves from the Sultan, apparently for similar reasons, were saved by the protection and intervention of the Austrian ambassador, and the decree sentencing them to exile remained a dead letter.[8] The beheading of Carmona and other leaders of the Jewish community, and the Sultan's appropriation of their property, created a power vacuum in the community which was eventually filled by Abraham de Camondo, who had assumed the leadership of his family after the death of his brother.

---

[6] See Moïse Franco, *Essai sur l'histoire des israélites de l'Empire ottoman* (Paris, 1897), pp. 132–14; Abraham Galanté, *Histoire des Juifs d'Istanbul*, vol. 1 (Istanbul, 1941), pp. 24–9; Salomon A. Rozanes, *Korot ha–Yehudim be-Turkiyah u-ve-Arzot ha-Kedem* (Jerusalem, 1945), vol. 6, pp. 64–7.

[7] See Franco, *Essai*, p. 139. See also Ahmed Lütfi, *Tarih-i Lütfi* (Istanbul, 1290/1873), vol. 1, pp. 245–6.

[8] *Archives Israélites*, 34 (1873), pp. 229–30.

It is after 1826 that one begins to find Camondo active in both the non-Jewish and the Jewish public arenas. His bank grew steadily through the 1830s and 1840s and became heavily involved in financing of the Ottoman state's Westernizing and modernizing reforms of its army and institutions. The Camondo bank negotiated loans for the Ottoman state with Western banks. It also played the leading role in financing the Ottoman war effort during the Crimean War of 1854– 6.[9] Camondo became a close associate and personal friend of many Turkish political leaders, such as Reşit, Ali and Fuat Pashas.

It is quite clear that from the 1830s onward Camondo was a nineteenth-century Eastern version of the eighteenth-century Court Jew. Known as the 'Rothschild of the East',[10] with close business dealings with the leading Jewish banking families, such as the Rothschilds, the Bleichroeder and the Péreires in the West, and the Sassoons in the East, Abraham de Camondo was the most important and well-placed Jew in the Levant in the mid nineteenth century. It is not surprising that he was Sir Moses Montefiore's principal host in Istanbul in 1840, during Montefiore's visit to the region following the Damascus affair.[11]

His connections with Western bankers notwithstanding, Camondo did not appear very European to his important visitors. The Montefiores took note of the fact that his daughter, then seven years old, was already engaged to be married, following the custom of early marriages in the East.[12] Ludwig August Frankl, who spent the Passover of 1856 with the Camondos, described at length the family's rich 'Oriental' clothing:

Four generations were seated at the table; the patriarch of the house, clothed in silks of different colours, occupied a throne furnished with cushions of purple and gold....

In the corners of the large room, the floor of which was covered with the richest of carpets, was seated the mother of

---

[9] Abraham Galanté, *Histoire des Juifs de Turquie* (repr. Istanbul, 1985), vol. 2, p. 56.

[10] Frankl, *The Jews in the East*, vol. 1, p. 122.

[11] In 1840 the Jewish community of Damascus was charged with abducting a Catholic priest and seeking to use his body for purposes of ritual murder. Several Jews were tortured and two died before those remaining were freed L. Loewe (ed.), *The Diaries of Sir Moses and Lady Montefiore*, (Chicago, 1890), vol. 1, p. 266.

[12] Ibid., p. 267.

these children, grand-children and great-grandchildren, apart from the rest on a splendid divan. She wore wide trousers of red satin and a short white silk petticoat over them; on her feet were yellow slippers, round her waist was a shaded girdle; the upper part of her body was covered with a green satin tunic, with wide sleeves, and richly embroidered in gold. But her head-dress was the most valuable part of her costume; a white silk shawl was gracefully wound round a red fez, and adorned with pearls and precious stones of different colours. The old lady had been blind for some years, and was not seated at table, as she required special attention.[13]

Turkish Jewry, with whose fortunes Camondo was inextricably linked, was in a state of deep economic and social decline. The Jews had lost the distinction that they had enjoyed in the sixteenth century in both the commercial and intellectual spheres. The Greeks and Armenians had replaced them as middlemen in the lucrative trade with the West. The apostasy in the seventeenth century of the pseudo Messiah Sabbetai Zvi had left behind a deeply shaken community which frowned upon daring intellectual endeavours, a stance which narrowed horizons and discouraged learning.

The Jews were the smallest of the three main tolerated non-Muslim groups. It is estimated that there were 150,000 Jews in the Ottoman Empire as a whole in the middle of the nineteenth century.[14] Ludwig August Frankl, using figures supplied him by the Chief Rabbinate, states that there were 38,400 Jews in Istanbul in 1856.[15] Most of them were extremely poor and eked out a very meagre living.

Abraham de Camondo's connections at Court turned him into the principal *shtadlan* (intercessor) for the Jews in the Ottoman Empire. Any act against the Jews in the Ottoman realms — libels, riots, acts of petty oppression by local authorities, that seemed to call for intervention in Istanbul found him active on behalf of his less fortunate brethren. The same was to be true in the realm of philanthropy. As the richest Jew in the Ottoman Empire, he was the chief benefactor

---

[13] Frankl, *The Jews in the East*, pp. 122–3.
[14] A. Ubicini, *Letters on Turkey*, tr. Lady Easthope (1856; repr. New York, 1973), pp. 18–19, 22. This figure is based on the Ottoman census of 1844. See the discussion in Kemal H. Karpat, *Ottoman Population 1830–1914: Demographic and Social Characteristics* (Madison, Wis., 1985), p. 23.
[15] Frankl, *The Jews in the East*, p. 140.

of the principal Jewish institutions, such as the welfare bodies and educational and charitable foundations.[16]

So far we have a picture of the traditional Court Jew, who was also the *shtadlan* of his community and its principal benefactor — a recurring figure in Jewish history, found in different times and places. What makes Camondo particularly interesting, however, is the increasingly political character of his public activities from the mid-1850s onwards, his transition to an ideological commitment to reforming and Westernizing the Jewish communities of the East. Instead of giving simply as an act of charity, he began to set conditions aimed at altering the recipient institution in a particular direction.

This change in Camondo's activities is inextricably tied to the growing intervention by Western Jews in the affairs of Eastern Jews. Leading sectors of Western Jewry, deeply influenced by their experience of the emancipation process and the accompanying changes in Jewish society and culture, had become imbued with a missionary zeal to spread the new ideas to other Jewish communities. The growth of European trade and commerce with the Near East had by the middle of the nineteenth century brought many European Jews into contact with their brethren in the Levant, who became the subject of unflattering newspaper accounts published in the nascent European Jewish press. Eastern Jews were seen as fanatical, obscurantist and in great need of help to reform their society and culture in ways that would enable them to emulate their European co-religionists.[17]

Western Jews were actively assisted in their self-imposed reforming task by Abraham de Camondo. His association both with the Westernizers in the Ottoman government and with the Jewish banking *haute bourgeoisie* in Europe had convinced him of the need to institute change among Turkish Jewry. When Albert Cohn, the emissary of the French Rothschilds and the Parisian Central Consistory, arrived in Istanbul to open a school, Camondo played a leading role in securing the necessary financial backing for the new institution. This

[16] *Archives Israélites*, 34 (1873), p. 34.

[17] See Aron Rodrigue, 'French Jews, Turkish Jews: The Alliance Israélite Universelle in Turkey, 1860—1914' (PhD dissertation, Harvard University, 1985), pp. 18—43. See also Michel Abitbol, 'The Encounter between French Jewry and the Jews of North Africa: Analysis of a Discourse (1830—1914)', in Frances Malino and Bernard Wasserstein (eds), *The Jews in Modern France* (Hanover, NH, 1985), pp. 31—53.

first European-style school for Jewish boys in the Ottoman Empire was opened in 1854. The school taught French and other secular subjects as well as the traditional Jewish curriculum. Camondo headed the committee to oversee the institution's affairs. From 1858 onwards, he would be its sole financial supporter. The school continued to exist long after his death, supported by his descendants, and produced many of the leaders of Turkish Jewry.[18]

When, by its reform decree of 1856, the Ottoman state granted legal equality to all the non-Muslims of the Ottoman Empire, it also insisted that the communal administrations should be put in order and rationalized. This inaugurated close to a decade of conflict and crisis in the Istanbul Jewish community, with the traditionalists and the reformers pitted against one another. Camondo was the acknowledged leader of the reformers.

Trouble broke out in 1858 when, in response to attempts to enlarge the jurisdiction of the Committee of Instruction headed by Camondo, a rabbi excommunicated the school and all those who sent their children there, and condemned the teaching of French as contrary to the Jewish religion. The traditionalists also condemned the growing religious laxity among the Jews of Istanbul, especially among 'foreign Jews', a clear reference to the Francos. Camondo used his connections at the Ottoman Court to have the school reopened. Both sides compromised. It was agreed that religious subjects would be taught in the morning, secular subjects in the afternoon, and that the hours devoted to French would be somewhat reduced.[19]

A second conflict emerged in 1862. In 1860, Jacob Avigdor, a friend of the reformers, was elected Chief Rabbi. He created a council of notables to reorganize the administration of the community with Abraham de Camondo at its head. This council was composed of the leading figures of all Jewish sectors of the city. Its task was to reform the communal administration, to clamp down on bribery and corruption, and to enforce the collection of taxes. A Judaeo-Spanish newspaper, the *Jurnal Istraelit*, was created to conduct propaganda on its behalf.

A positive article on Freemasonry by the editor of this newspaper, who was also the secretary of the new council, caused a great commotion in Istanbul. The traditionalists denounced the newspaper and

[18] Aron Rodrigue, 'The Beginnings of Westernization and Communal Reform among Istanbul Jewry, 1854–1865', in Avigdor Levy (ed.), *Turkish Jewry* (forthcoming).
[19] Ibid.

those associated with it and asked the Chief Rabbi, whom they saw as in league with the reformers, to resign. Camondo himself was insulted and excommunicated when he invited one of the leaders of the traditionalists to his house to discuss the problems facing the community. In response, Camondo had this rabbi put in prison, an action which gave rise to mass demonstrations by the traditionalists in Istanbul, who petitioned the sultan for the rabbi's release. The petition was successful, and the rabbi was freed after a few days in jail.

Faced with a deeply divided Jewish community, the authorities intervened. Fuat Pasha, the Grand Vizir, appointed a new Chief Rabbi, Yakir Geron, a firm friend of the reformers. It is impossible not to see the hand of Camondo in this appointment, as he was a close associate of Fuat Pasha. Yakir Geron supervised the drafting in 1865, of a new communal constitution, which was heavily weighted in favour of the lay notables. Camondo, with his links to the Porte, had played a major role in the defeat of the traditionalists.[20]

It is important to note that this crisis erupted over the publication of an article defending Freemasonry. It has recently come to light that leading Francos belonged to the Freemasons' lodge, 'Union d'Orient', founded in Istanbul in 1863. Emmanuel Veneziani, who was one of the directors of the Camondo bank and ran it after the Camondos' departure from Istanbul, was the lodge secretary.[21] Many leading Francos associated with Camondo were also members, though there is no evidence that he himself belonged.

It is striking that the lodge was founded in the year when Adolphe Crémieux visited Istanbul. Crémieux, President of the Alliance Israélite Universelle, sometime Republican minister in the French government, and a leading member of the 'Grand Orient' lodge in Paris, had come to investigate the possibilities of opening new Alliance schools in the Ottoman Empire. There seems no doubt that he and Camondo established strong links during the course of this visit. On 21 November 1863, the regional committee of the Alliance for

---

[20] Ibid.

[21] Bibliothèque Nationale, Paris, Archives, Union d'Orient, Correspondance, letters received by the Grand Orient in Paris, 24 Apr. and 18 May 1863. See also Paul Dumont, 'La Turquie dans les archives du Grand Orient de France: les loges maçonniques d'obédience française à Istanbul du milieu du XIXe siècle à la veille de la première guerre mondiale', in Jean-Louis Bacqué-Grammont and Paul Dumont (eds), *Économie et sociétés dans l'Empire ottoman (Fin du XVIIIe—Début du XXe siècle)* (Paris, 1983), pp. 171–201.

the Ottoman Empire was founded in Istanbul in the presence of Crémieux, with Abraham de Camondo as its president and Emmanuel Venziani as its secretary.[22] From that time until his death, Camondo's public Jewish activities all took place within the framework of the Alliance's policies in the Near East.

The Alliance Israélite Universelle, founded in Paris in 1860 by French Jews, was the very incarnation of the reforming impulse of Western Jewry. It was active in defending the rights of the Jews throughout the world. But its real work was to be in the field of education. Starting in 1862 in Tetuan in Morocco, it opened elementary and eventually also secondary schools for Jewish boys and girls throughout North Africa and the Near and Middle East. By 1914, it had established a network of 183 schools with a total of 48,000 students in an area stretching from Morocco in the west to Iran in the east. Generations of Sephardim were educated in Alliance institutions, which provided essentially French instruction with the addition of Jewish subjects such as Jewish history, Jewish religion and Hebrew. The Alliance played a crucial role in the Westernization of Sephardic Jewry.[23]

Most Alliance schools were concentrated in the area controlled by the Ottomans. Camondo's contacts with the Sublime Porte proved invaluable in getting the Ottoman government to accept the organization. The regional committee that Camondo presided over from 1863 to 1869 laid the foundations of the Alliance's work in Turkey by energetically sponsoring the creation of local committees of reform-minded notables to help the work of the schools. It also kept the Alliance in Paris abreast of local developments, and collected and dispensed funds for the organization.

The views expressed by Camondo in his correspondence with the Alliance Central Committee in Paris echoed those of the Western Jewish reformers. He urged the President of the Alliance to do all that could be done to help 'the Jews of the East, who are so backward

---

[22] Archives of the Alliance Israélite Universelle, France III. A. 17, procès verbal, 21 Nov. 1863.

[23] On the Alliance, see among others André Chouraqui, *Cent ans d'histoire. L'Alliance Istaélite Universelle et la renaissance juive contemporaine (1860–1960)* (Paris, 1965); Michael M. Laskier, *The Alliance Istraélite Universelle and the Jewish Communities of Morocco, 1862–1962* (Albany, NY, 1983); and Aron Rodrigue, *De l'instruction à l'émancipation. Les enseignants de l'Alliance Israélite Universelle et les Juifs d'Orient 1860–1939* (Paris, 1989).

in civilization and for whom only *education* can open the path to progress'.[24] European-style schools were seen as the universal panacea by all the reformers, and Camondo was no exception. According to him, the rabbis did their best to keep the people in ignorance. This, and the opposition experienced by the school founded by Albert Cohn and supported by Camondo, made him pessimistic about the possibility of establishing Alliance Schools in Istanbul in the near future.[25] One had to wait for 'the spirits to turn by themselves towards civilization and look to education as the only means of leaving the state of profound ignorance in which they at present find themselves'.[26] Even though Camondo did not live to see the foundation of the first Alliance schools in Istanbul, in 1875, he created the infrastructure of support among the notables of the city which made it possible for these institutions to function properly. He was also active in helping and protecting the Alliance school founded in Edirne (Adrianople) in 1867.[27]

Camondo's evolution from local philanthropist to reformer to collaborator with the Alliance is a perfect illustration of an important development in the wider Jewish world: the transition from the old philanthropy of *tzedakah* (charity) to the new philanthropy of reform and then to the organizational philanthropy and politics which the Alliance exemplified. The actions of Montefiore and Camondo were rooted in the first stage of the transformation of Jewish charity. Both continued to make charitable donations to alleviate distress. But both eventually came to direct their prestige and financial power to reform and change the Jewish communities which they were helping.

By the 1860s, the heyday of the Jewish philanthropist who would act alone in trying to use his wealth to reform Jewish institutions and society seemed to be over. The new Camondos and Montefiores would continue to give to charity, but the bulk of their giving would now go to Jewish organizations with which they were associated, organizations which would try to implement a political and economic programme. Baron Maurice de Hirsch would support the Alliance, as well as the Jewish Colonization Association. The Rothschilds would initially strike an independent course, but would eventually relinquish the direction of the settlements that they had been fostering in Pales-

---

[24] Archives of the Alliance Israélite Universelle, France III A 17, letter from Camondo to Paris, 3 Mar. 1864.
[25] Ibid., letter from Camondo to Paris, 4 Apr. 1864.
[26] Ibid.
[27] *Le Judaïsme sephardi*, 5, no. 47 (1936), pp. 162–14.

tine to the Jewish Colonization Association. The Anglo-Jewish Association, the Hilfsverein der Deutschen Juden and eventually even the World Zionist organization would vie for the munificence of wealthy donors to implement particular programmes of action. Camondo's career, ending in his close association with the Alliance, is a perfect illustration of this trend towards the politicization and institutionalization of Jewish philanthropy in the nineteenth century.

Abraham de Camondo dropped his Austrian citizenship in 1866 when Venice became part of a united Italy. His munificent endowment of charitable institutions in Italy earned him and his descendants the title of Count from Victor Emmanuel.[28] By this time, the octogenarian patriarch of the family had handed over his business to his grandsons. When they decided to transfer the bank to Paris in 1869 and to settle permanently there, he followed in order to be with his family.[29]

Abraham de Camondo died in Paris in 1873 at the age of ninety-three. According to his wish, his remains were taken back to Istanbul and buried in the Hasköy cemetery. Perhaps his descendants should have returned with him, as they did not fare well in France. In 1917, during the First World War, Abraham's only great-great-grandson, Nissim de Camondo, became one of the first to be killed in the air battles involving the new French air force. The last direct descendants of Abraham were caught by the Germans in Paris during the Second World War, tortured at the transit camp of Drancy to extort money and information, and then deported to Auschwitz, where they all perished.[30] All that remains of the family today is monuments. In 1935 Nissim's father, Moïse de Camondo, bequeathed to the French state the lovely Camondo mansion at Parc Monceau in Paris, along with his priceless collection of Louis XV and Louis XVI antiques, the one great passion of his life. The mansion is now the largest museum in Paris dedicated to French art and furniture of the eighteenth century, and stands as a fitting tribute to the Gallomania of Levantine Sephardim in the late nineteenth and early twentieth century. And, of course, there remains the lonely, delapidated mausoleum of Abraham de Camondo on the road leading to the West from Istanbul.

[28] *Archives Israélites*, 34 (1873), p. 229.
[29] Ibid., p. 233.
[30] Roditi, 'Camondo's Way', p. 162.

3

Majority Faith: Dreyfus
before the Affair

MICHAEL BURNS

I

Maurice Barrès, so often wrong, was right about the minor role that
Captain Alfred Dreyfus played in his own Affair. 'Dreyfus was only a
pretext', said Barrès, and even the Captain agreed: 'I was only an
artillery officer, whom a tragic error prevented from pursuing his
normal career...', he wrote to a supporter; 'the symbol...is not I. It
is you who created that Dreyfus'.[1] The history of that Dreyfus, and
of his case, is a familiar one. Wrongly accused of transmitting military
secrets to the German attaché in Paris, the Captain, a French Jew of
Alsatian origin and a junior officer on the General Staff, was arrested
in October 1894. Court-martialled in December and officially 'de-
graded' in January in front of crowds shouting 'Death to the Jews!' he
was transported to Devil's Island off the coast of South America.
Surrounded by guards and a high wooden fence, occasionally shackled
to his bed and always forced to remain silent, he suffered four and a
half years of malaria and mental torture until he was called back to
France for retrial. New evidence confirmed his innocence and the
guilt of another officer, but old prejudices led to a shocking re-
conviction 'with extenuating circumstances'. Immediately pardoned
by a government which feared a worldwide boycott of the approaching Universal Exposition in Paris, Dreyfus returned to his family in
the early autumn of 1899 and began the long fight for his official
exoneration. Seven years later, a new government made up of many

---

[1] See the interview with Barrès in *Liberté*, 1 Dec. 1903; Dreyfus is quoted
in Stephen Wilson, *Ideology and Experience: Antisemitism in France at the
Time of the Dreyfus Affair* (Rutherford, NJ, 1982), p. 1.

former Dreyfusards proclaimed the Captain's innocence, reinstated him in the army, and awarded him the Legion of Honour.[2]

The struggle which pitted civil libertarians, anti-clericals and socialists against nationalist champions of militarism and anti-semitism was over; and, though the battle lines were never as clear as histories of the Affair suggest, and though vast numbers of French men and women outside Paris and provincial cities rallied to neither side, the legacy of the Affair, like that of the Revolution of 1789, helped shape the political landscape of modern France.

Dreyfus had been a hard man to convict and an even harder one to rally around — 'a poor focus', notes one historian, 'for commitment and loyalty'.[3] Enemies on the General Staff were obliged secretly to manufacture evidence to frame the junior officer, and supporters had to reconcile their crusade for the Captain's civil rights with their distaste for his exaggerated patriotism, rigid military bearing and almost mystical code of honour. While he refused to be anything other than a French officer under siege, the victim of a tragic judicial error, many of his allies wanted to see him as, to quote Charles Péguy, 'the symbol of the destiny of Israel offered as a sacrifice for the salvation of the other nations', or, in the words of Bernard Lazare, as a mirror image of 'Jews languishing in Russian prisons...Rumanian Jews who are refused the rights of man... Algerian Jews, beaten and pillaged...'.[4] Meanwhile, critics painted different portraits but with the same desire to fashion a symbol, and with a similiar focus on the Captain's Jewish origins. Edouard Drumont, the most powerful anti-semite of the *fin-de-siécle*, insisted that Dreyfus's Judaeo-Alsatian background was the key to his treason:

[2] The bibliography of the Affair now approaches 1000 titles: see Léon Lipschutz, *Une Bibliothèque Dreyfusienne: essai de bibiliographie thématique et analytique de l'affaire Dreyfus* (Paris, 1970). The most thorough study remains Joseph Reinach's *Histoire de l'Affaire Dreyfus* , 7 vols (Paris, 1901–11). The best overview, and the most recent, is Jean-Denis Bredin's *The Affair: The Case of Alfred Dreyfus,* trs. Jeffrey Mehlman (New York, 1986). For another assessment of the national impact of the Affair see Michael Burns, *Rural Society and French Politics: Boulangism and the Dreyfus Affair, 1886–1900* (Princeton, NJ, 1984).

[3] David Landes, 'Two Cheers for Emancipation', in Frances Malino and Bernard Wasserstein (eds), *The Jews in Modern France* (Hanover, NH, 1985), p. 299.

[4] Péguy is quoted in Wilson, *Ideology and Experience*, p. 4, and Lazare in Michael Marrus, *The Politics of Assimilation: A Study of the French Jewish Community at the Time of the Dreyfus Affair* (London, 1971), p. 188.

'As a Jew and a German [*sic*], he detests the French....A German by taste and upbringing, a Jew by race, he did the job of a Jew and a German—and nothing else.' Barrès put it more simply: 'That Dreyfus is capable of betrayal, I infer from his race.'[5]

Anti-semites warned that the Captain played on his cultivated French veneer to infiltrate the 'sacred ranks of the military', while behind that façade he was, like other 'refined' Jews, the 'brother of the dirty kikes'.[6] Drumont and his disciples would not be fooled by Dreyfus's impeccable French education and professions of patriotism; a Jew he was, and a (traitorous) Jew he would always be. For supporters, however, the Captain's high degree of assimilation and relative indifference to the anti-semitic dimensions of his case, signalled his rejection of Judaism, and, perhaps, his own anti-semitic sentiments.[7] He had been married by the Grand Rabbi of France, Zadoc Kahn, to a woman of strong Jewish faith, Lucie Hadamard, and he had confronted an anti-semitic superior at the Ecole de Guerre 'in the name of the Israelite officers'.[8] But his determination to separate his private beliefs from his public role as a French soldier — and, later, as a French prisoner — made it appear that he sought to distance himself from his co-religionists. Léon Blum, another French Jew of Alsatian origin, accused the Captain of 'servitude' to the military hierarchy, and doubted that Dreyfus himself would have been a Dreyfusard.[9] And histories of the Affair repeat the notion that Dreyfus had severed every tie to his Jewish heritage: His 'silence on his relationship to the Jewish tradition was absolute', notes Jean Denis Bredin in a masterful recent overview of the case. 'In his entire correspondence, there is not a single mention of the Jews, nor is the

---

[5] See Bredin, *The Affair*, p. 79: Landes, in Malino and Wasserstein, *The Jews in Modern France*, p. 296: and the coverage of Dreyfus's arrest and trial in Drumont's *La Libre Parole* after 1 Nov. 1894.

[6] Drumont first made the contrast in 1889 when he described the 'refined Parisian' Heinrich Heine (see Landes, in Malino and Wasserstein *The Jews in Modern France*, p. 298).

[7] The many reactions to Dreyfus are discussed in excellent essays by Pierre Vidal-Naquet and Jean-Louis Lévy (the Captain's grandson), in the recent edition of Alfred Dreyfus, *Cinq années de ma vie* (Paris, 1982). See also Marrus, *The Politics of Assimilation*, pp. 214–15 and *passim*.

[8] The incident is discussed in Archives Nationales (hereafter AN), BB 19/128, interrogation, 1894, pp. 434–5. See also Théodore Reinach, *Histoire sommaire de l'affaire Dreyfus* (Paris, 1924), p. 21; and Bredin, *The Affair*, p. 22.

[9] Léon Blum, *Souvenirs sur l'Affaire* (1935; Paris, 1981), p. 34.

drama in which he was caught up ever attributed to the fact that he was Jewish....He was French, Alsatian, the head of a family.'[10]

Rushing to create their own convenient and abstract symbol, to design their own profiles of the prisoner, Dreyfus's allies, enemies and historians rarely understood the mystery of the man. Fiercely proud of his Alsatian origins, he was a patriotic officer but not a 'military fanatic' (a 'fana mili' in the vocabulary of the Belle Epoque);[11] and he was intensely private about his faith. His prison letters and other papers do, in fact, contain more than a 'single mention of the Jews' and of anti-semitism, though such references are rare,[12] but those letters and notebooks kept on Devil's Island were public documents, scrutinized by legions of censors, and they provide only an incomplete portrait of a very private man.

A profile of Dreyfus must press beyond the hard, solid facts of his life and ask questions which elicit many answers, none of them certain. What were Dreyfus's unrecorded thoughts through those long years of solitary confinement on Devil's Island? Amidst that 'profound silence', as he described it, 'interrupted only by the sounds of ocean waves', to what source did he turn for strength? What were the 'heartbeats', as one poet put in another context, of his 'Nation in the night'? Letters to his wife Lucie start to point the way: 'devoted' to the nation to which he had 'consecrated' his life, he wrote shortly after his arrest, and committed to the reunification of his native province with his French fatherland, he would put his hope 'in God and in justice'.[13]

The powerful faith which sustained Dreyfus on Devil's Island had been shaped by the promise of justice embedded in the Declaration of the Rights of Man, by the curriculum of patriotism inculcated in schools of the fatherland, and, no less important, by the religious teachings of his family in Alsace — by Judaic traditions of justice,

---

[10] Bredin, *The Affair*, pp. 21–2, 86.

[11] The term is used in an article published in the *Journal d'Alsace* on 12 July 1975, the fortieth anniversary of Dreyfus's death.

[12] See, for example, AN, BB 19/128, interrogation, 1894, pp. 434–5; the prisoner's letter to the Grand Rabbi of France, dated 23 Dec. 1894, in the Dreyfus family private collection; and Dreyfus's letters to the Marquise Arconati-Visconti in the Bibliothèque Victor Cousin, Sorbonne (e. g. 22 Jan. [? 1903]). 'My only crime is to have been born a Jew!' Dreyfus shouted out in prison (see, Bredin, *The Affair*, p. 86n.).

[13] Bibliothèque Nationale (hereafter BN), NAF 16609, 5 Dec. 1894, and 24895, 18 Dec. 1894.

reason and deliverance which, for Dreyfus, were compatible with the legacies of the French Revolution and its 1791 edict of Jewish emancipation. 'It is to this good people, to these generous French', went one revolutionary manifesto which spoke for others, 'that we owe the first example of justice that the world has given to our ill-fated Nation. Yes, my children, behold your Fatherland, your Jerusalem, the land which God promised to our ancestors...'[14] Captain Dreyfus never felt comfortable as a uniquely Jewish symbol, as an embodiment of the persecution of the nation of Israel, because, for him and for so many others of his generation and background, religious faith, personal honour, provincial loyalty and French patriotism were four pillars of a single allegiance. But, like religious liturgy or the French language, that faith had to be learned, and long before he entered the most prestigious school of the fatherland, the Ecole Polytechnique, young Alfred Dreyfus had been tutored in the ways of allegiance by his family — and by the example of his family's history — close by the German border in southern Alsace.

II

In 1835, Jacob Dreÿfuss, Alfred's grandfather, took the savings he had accumulated after years of peddling and money-lending in the Alsatian countryside, and purchased a small flat in the centre of Mülhausen, a town only 5 kilometres west of his native village of Rixheim. Recent outbreaks of anti-Jewish violence in the hinterlands — upheavals sparked by hard weather, poor harvests and debts owed to local money-lenders — had pushed Jacob, his wife Rachel and their teenage son Raphael from the countryside; at the same time, economic opportunities in the rapidly expanding town of Mülhausen had pulled them to the promise of a better future. The old mill houses which had given the town its name centuries before were becoming quaint survivals of a slower artisanal age as mechanized cotton-spinning and weaving enterprises eclipsed the traditional small-scale production of leather and woollen goods and printed calico cloth. Cottage workers migrated to new steam-powered textile factories, Jewish pedlars moved into urban trades, and the road west from Rixheim became busy with industrial traffic. On their short

---

[14] Quoted in Béatrice Philippe. *Etre Juif dans la société française du moyen âge à nos jours* (Paris, 1979), p. 117.

journey into town, the Dreÿfuss family would make way for long convoys of up to fifty wagons with seven horse teams hauling massive balls of raw cotton and piles of charcoal to Mülhausen factories. Once an independent republic, but annexed by France in 1798, the town was fast becoming 'the Manchester of Alsace'.[15]

Jacob also remembered it as a place of refuge. During the Revolution and the Reign of Terror, when he was growing up in Rixheim, Jews under attack by peasant gangs had fled to Mülhausen on at least three occasions; and, in the decades which followed, periodic violence in rural areas pushed increasing numbers of Jews into the town. Local Protestants, like their Swiss neighbours in Basel, had opened the town gates, and, when they sheltered Jewish families from peasants 'in the mood for a new Saint Bartholomew's Day',[16] they repeated the gesture of their ancestors who had sent troops to aid victims of the sixteenth-century massacre. Unlike Lutherans in northern Alsatian towns, the Calvinists of Mülhausen recognized that Protestants and Jews, people of two diasporas, were linked by a 'similarity of suffering';[17] they also shared a sense of gratitude for the civil liberties granted by French edicts of emancipation.

A place of sanctuary remembered by the Dreÿfuss family, Mülhausen was also fast becoming an enclave of French culture in an overwhelmingly Germanic and Catholic Alsace. 'Spreading Calvin's language along with his heresy',[18] as their counterparts had done in other regions, Mülhausen's Protestant leaders established French schools and shielded their children from the coarse Germanic dialects of their mostly Catholic mill workers and servants. They made certain

[15] A. L. Walker, 'An Alsatian Manchester', essay in the Bibiliothèque de la Société Industrielle de Mulhouse. On the family's early history in Alsace, see my essay in Norman Kleeblatt (ed.), *The Dreyfus Affair: Art, Truth and Justice* (Berkeley, Calif., 1987), pp. 140–52.

[16] Altkirch sub-prefect quoted in Paul Leuilliot, *L'Alsace au début du XIXeme siècle: essais d'histoire politique, économique et religieuse*, vol. 3 (Paris, 1959), p. 244, n. 7. On Mülhausen as a refuge see Philippe, *Etre juif dans la société française*, pp. 107–8.

[17] The term was used by Protestants in southern France during the Dreyfus Affair (see, Burns, *Rural Society and French Politics*, p. 150). See also, Henri Sée, 'Dans quelle mesure Puritains et Juifs ont-ils contribué aux progrès du capitalisme moderne?'. *Revue historique*, 155 (1927) pp. 61–65.

[18] Eugen Weber discusses Protestantism as a 'powerful instrument of Frenchification' in *Peasants into Frenchmen: The Modernization of Rural France, 1870–1914* (Stanford, Calif., 1976), p. 84.

that French 'reigned exclusively in their homes'. To speak that language, and to speak it without a German accent, was one of the
'essential and distinctive signs of belonging to a good family'; and as
the town's 'manufacturing patriciate' — the Koechlins, Dollfuses,
Schlumbergers and others — developed French textile markets as the
source of their wealth, they cultivated the French language as the
source of their manners.[19]

Like most rural migrants, however, the Dreÿfuss family was not
immediately 'crushed into the mould'[20] of French culture upon entering Mülhausen, and the street on which they lived — the Rue de la
Justice — was French in name alone. With Protestant mill-owners
residing in the fashionable 'Nouveau Quartier' south of the old town,
Catholic workers and a growing number of Jewish merchants, artisans
and textile-brokers settled in neighbourhoods to the west, or in the
town centre. In their quarter, the Dreÿfuss family befriended Wolf
Salomon, a tailor; David Franck, a police agent assigned to the
synagogue; and Lazare Weill, a tradesman.[21] And they would share
with those neighbours visits to the Mülhausen synagogue, just across
the central Place de la Réunion, and a Judaeo-Alsatian dialect which
combined Hebrew—Aramaic, German and a smattering of French.
Setting them off from the city's Protestant elite and from Catholic
workers who used their own Germanic dialect, the family's Judaeo-
Alsatian was a 'decisive factor in their collective identity'; like the
religious customs they brought with them from Rixheim, it was the
language 'of a life apart'.[22]

The first member of his family to be born a French citizen,
Raphael Dreÿfuss was not the first for whom French was the mother

---

[19] Ernest Meininger, *Histoire de Mulhouse* (Mulhouse, 1923), p. 76; F.
Hoffet, *Psychanalyse de l'Alsace* (Paris, 1951), pp. 142–3; and Jean
Schlumberger (ed.), *La Bourgeoisie alsacienne: études d'histoire sociale*
(Strasbourg, 1954).
[20] Patrick Girard, *Les Juifs de France de 1789 à 1860: de l'émancipation à
l'égalité* (Paris, 1976), p. 251.
[21] Archives Départementales du Haut Rhin (hereafter ADHR), 5 E 337,
1838, 'Jacques Dreyfus' (Jacob Dreÿfuss). On Mülhausen society during
these years, see Raymond Oberlé, *Mulhouse, ou la genèse d'une ville*
(Mulhouse, 1985).
[22] Freddy Raphael and Robert Weyl, *Les Juifs en Alsace: culture, société,
histoire* (Toulouse, 1977), p. 406; and Daniel Stauben, *Scènes de la vie
juive (Paris, 1860), p. iii.* See also Honel Meiss, *A travers le dialecte Judéo-
Alsacien* (Nice, [? 1929]); and Paul Lévy, *Histoire linguistique d'Alsace et de
Lorraine*, vol. 1 (Paris, 1929).

tongue.[23] If he had any formal education in Rixheim, it included no more than occasional lessons in Hebrew in the village heder (elementary school), and his practical education — joining his father hawking goods as a country pedlar — was conducted in the Judaeo-Alsatian dialect of his rural community. A few years after settling in the new urban community of Mülhausen, however, Raphael learned German and rudimentary French, and was soon able to move beyond his first trade as a local merchant to become a commission agent, an intermediary between textile-manufacturers and buyers.

In 1841, Raphael married Jeannette Libmann, a seamstress from the Alsatian town of Ribeauvillé, the daughter of a kosher butcher. Three years later their first child was born. Following Jewish custom, the young couple named their son after Raphael's father, who had died in 1838; but with a simple difference which signalled a profound change. Jacob had kept the biblical form of his name in country and town, but his son and daughter-in-law blended Jewish tradition with Mülhausen's official language — a language they did not use and barely understood — and named their first boy Jacques. Four years later, on the fiftieth anniversary of the 'reunion' with France, the town council made a similar gesture and officially abandoned the Germanic name 'Mülhausen' for the French 'Mulhouse'.[24]

David Cohen's description of the Second Empire as a golden age for many French Jews, a time of unprecedented economic success in a climate of relative social and religious harmony, applies to the Dreÿfusses of Mulhouse.[25] Calling on his father's lessons of village trade, and on his own recent experience as a town merchant, Raphael started work as a commission agent dealing in printed and embroidered fabrics, a job as important to Mulhouse commerce as Jacob's peddling had been essential to the Rixheim market place. Well-situated to learn all aspects of the textile trade — fashion trends, labour costs, production techniques, distribution networks — Raphael kept clients informed of what products were in demand, and helped serve, with other agents, as a 'regulator of production'. He dealt in fabrics and in fortune, in a trade of chance. With his work highly sensitive to market fluctuations and to the ability of clients to pay commission fees, he would follow the lead of other agents and add loans to the services he offered. In a world where banking capitalism

---

[23] Later evidence confirms that French was not Raphael Dreyfus's mother tongue (see AN, BB 19/128, interrogation, p. 427).
[24] ADHR, 5 E 337, marriages, 1841, and births, 1844.
[25] David Cohen, *La Promotion de Juifs en France à l'époque du Second Empire*, 2 vols (Aix-en Provence, 1980).

and merchant capitalism were virtually synonymous, agents such as Raphael helped provide the funds needed to purchase land, building-materials and machinery for new cotton mills and chemical factories. With no salaries to pay and no shop to maintain, and with every reason to accommodate his clients, Raphael began to invest indirectly in the town's economy; and, as the manufacturers and buyers for whom he worked enjoyed their most prosperous and expansive years, his negotiations multiplied and his loans, at interest rates of 5 or 6 per cent, were made good.[26]

With assets from those transactions, Raphael began buying and selling small plots and buildings in the town's western and northern quarters. The pasturelands and fields that had once surrounded the town's medieval walls became prime properties for the development of new houses, mills and roadways, and Raphael sold his first two holdings to the municipality in 1855 and 1859 – one for the construc-tion of a road and small park, the other to create a second entrance to a primary school and 'assure the complete separation of the sexes'. Those negotiations brought the family nearly 1,000 francs – more than the annual salary of a Mulhouse mill worker – and helped pro-vide the capital for larger and more lucrative ventures.[27]

Fierce competition in the town led to failure as well as fortune during these years, and the pages of the local newspaper, the *In-dustriel alsacien*, often ran announcements of bankruptcies and fore-closures. On at least two occasions, Raphael made his way to the Mulhouse courthouse to bid for land at auction, and on both occasions he bought the land and sold it at a profit. For his largest purchase, however, an area north of the town which would soon be cut through by new streets, he needed help. On a trip to nearby Basel, or during his commission work in Mulhouse, he had met a Swiss banker, Jean Forcat, with a keen interest in the future of the southern Alsatian economy, and in November 1858 the two men raised more than 25,000 francs to purchase land north of the Rue Koechlin. A few years later they sold off a small section to the municipality – again, at a profit – and held the rest.[28]

---

[26] *Histoire documentaire de l'industrie de Mulhouse* (Mulhouse, 1902), pp. 951–2, 973; Henry Laufenburger, *Cours d'économie alsacienne*, (Paris, 1930–2), vol. 2, pp. 168ff; and Claude Fohlen, *L'Industrie textile au temps du Second Empire* (Paris, 1956), pp. 111–12, 310–11.

[27] Archives Municipales de Mulhouse (hereafter AMM), NIB 122, Raphael Dreyfus, 27 Feb. 1855, and N1B 103, 10 Oct. 1859. See also AMM, cadastres, 1856; and *Industriel alsacien*, 15 Mar. 1855 and 27 Oct. 1859.

[28] AMM, N1B, Raphael Dreyfus, 8 July. 1862.

If the 1850s were prosperous years for Raphael, the best was yet to come. In 1860 an Anglo-French free trade agreement, marking a turn toward lower tariffs, forced Alsatian mill-owners into new competition with their Lancashire counterparts, and after 1861 the closing of American ports during the Civil War spread a 'cotton famine' across Europe. For Raphael, these hard times were the best of times. As prices rose, so did the profits of bankers and commission agents, who, unlike factory-owners, had no raw materials to buy, equipment to maintain, mortgages to meet or workers to pay. 'This period so fatal for industry', went one report, 'has been a flourishing time for intermediaries... who, directly or indirectly, have got involved in businesses and have enjoyed extreme good fortune and considerable profits.'[29] So it went for Raphael. His business indeed flourished during these years, and his increased income enabled Jeannette to leave her job as a seamstress and care for her growing family in a new apartment on the Place des Victoires, close to the Town Hall. After Jacques, her first child, Jeannette had four daughters, two of whom died in infancy, and three sons. Her last childbirth, on 9 October 1859, when she was forty-two years old, was the most difficult, and she fell seriously ill in the days and months that followed. She turned to her midwife and to her eldest daughter, Henriette, for help with the new child, Alfred.[30]

Two years later, Raphael made a trip north from the Place des Victoires, across one of the town's canals and toward the vast symmetrical blocks of small houses which made up Mulhouse's *cités ouvrières*. Inspired by model dwellings displayed at the Crystal Palace exhibition in London, the town council fashioned its own plans to improve the conditions of mill workers by settling them in clean, efficient and orderly quarters close by their factories. By the early 1860s, hundreds of houses, back to back, with small garden plots and narrow pathways between, had been completed in the former fields and pasturelands north of the town centre. Beyond those houses, however, and reaching out to the forests and hills surrounding Mulhouse, more open land was available, and Raphael arranged for the purchase of one large triangular section at 20,500

[29] Fohlen, *L'Industrie textile*, pp. 310–11; Rémy Huber, *Les Progrès de la révolution industrielle en Alsace sous le Second Empire* (n.d.); Laufenburger, *Cours d'économie alsacienne*, vol. 2, p. 302, and Georges Weill, *L'Alsace française* (Paris, 1916), p. 109.

[30] ADHR, 5 E 337, births, 1848–59, and deaths, 1853–4; H. Villemar, *Dreyfus intime* (Paris. 1898), p. 7.

francs. This time he did not plan to sell, and for help with his scheme he again turned to the banker Forçat. Arranging a limited partnership, Raphael then approached André Koechlin — owner of a mammoth factory which would turn out 5,000 steam locomotives in the nineteenth century — about the possiblity of financing heavy machinery over eleven years at a fixed rate of 5 per cent. Koechlin agreed, and in 1862, at the height of the cotton crisis, with a flood of workers in search of employment, Raphael abandoned the profession of commercial intermediary to launch his own cotton mill on the Rue Lavoisier.[31]

The son of a village pedlar who had hawked second-hand goods along Rhine Valley roads so that his family could escape the violence of the countryside and settle in the town, Raphael matched Forçat's investment of 300,000 francs and began construction of a major Alsatian factory in the year when he turned forty-four. Gambling the profits of an intermediary on the promise of a secure niche in the town's economy, he joined the ranks of the few dozen Protestant and Jewish industrialists in Mulhouse, and gave his new enterprise the same French name as he had recently chosen for his family — Dreyfus.[32]

III

The town's powerful *grandes familles* did not rush to embrace this Jewish broker turned mill-owner — sober and private, they rushed at few things outside the competitive arena of business; but they had worked with Raphael in his role as a commission agent, accepted him as a client for their equipment, and now recognized the owner of Raphael Dreyfus et Compagnie as a fellow leader of Alsatian industry.

[31] AMM, J II E, cadastres, Rue Lavoisier; Fohlen, *L'Industrie textile*, pp. 110, 113, 310; and Michel Hau, 'L'Industrialisation de l'Alsace, 1803–1939' (thesis, Université de Paris X, 1985), vol. 2, pp. 588–9.

[32] In 1856, on the birth certificate of his daughter Rachel, Raphael signed his name 'Dreyfus', it seems for the first time (see ADHR, 5 E 337, births, 1856). Paul Lévy, who quotes A. Dauzat, believes that 'L'assimilation du nom...est un des aspects de l'assimilation des minorités ethniques: par la francisation de son patronyme, le naturalisé et ses enfants plus encore se sentiront mieux à l'aise dans leur nouvelle patrie; ce sera une garantie de loyalisme'—Paul Lévy, *Les Noms des Israelites en France* (Paris, 1960), p. 94. It would, of course, take more than a name.

'There exists among old and new enterprises within the same industrial centre', observed one leading manufacturer, 'a solidarity as undeniable as that which reigns among residents of the same commune.'[33] Like the Jews and Gentiles who traded together and worshipped apart in Raphael's Rixheim, the Jews of Mulhouse had been joining Protestants as commission agents and factory-owners for over four decades. The Katz and Lantz families opened agencies as early as 1818, and, shortly after Raphael launched his mill, another Jewish enterprise, Dreyfus-Lantz, with no relation to Raphael's family, began construction across the Rue Lavoisier. Lantz, Lang, Blum, Rosentiehl and other brokers and industrialists appeared on the membership lists of the Société Industrielle, the prestigious organization of Mulhouse manufacturers, and Lazare Lantz began a period of thirty-one years as a town councillor in 1860. Protestant notables subsidized the education of promising Jewish youngsters, and the city's prominent rabbi, Samuel Dreyfus, applauded the Protestant mayor as that 'honourable and much-loved' man who made a special effort to procure land for a new synagogue — a synagogue designed by a Protestant architect. The textile world which the town's leaders closed unofficially but effectively to Catholics (not one major Catholic enterprise would emerge in Mulhouse in the nineteenth century) they opened to Jews.[34]

Reared on the same biblical teachings — 'you shall open wide your hand to your brother, to the needy and to the poor, in the land' — Protestant and Jewish factory-owners had learned similar notions of justice and social responsibility. And if not all local entrepreneurs acted on those teachings, at least Raphael shared the sentiments of Engel-Dollfus, who insisted that 'manufacturers owe their workers something more than a wage'.[35] The city's working-class quarters — the dark back streets and tenements not yet levelled for new *cités ouvrières* — would have put Raphael in mind of the cramped streets of Rixheim where kosher butchers and leather tanners worked amidst the foul odours of slaughtered animals, and where his Jewish com-

---

[33] Engel-Dolfus, quoted in Laufenburger, *Cours d'économie alsacienne*, vol. 2, p. 355.

[34] Ibid., p. 127; Fohlen, *L'Industrie textile*, p. 112; Oberlé, *Mulhouse*, p. 227; François-Georges Dreyfus, *Histoire de l'Alsace* (Paris, 1979), p. 227; Georges Livet and Raymond Oberlé, *Histoire de Mulhouse des origines à nos jours* (Strasbourg, 1979), p. 213. For lists of Société Industrielle members see *Centennaire de la Société de Mulhouse* (Mulhouse, 1926); and for more on Lantz see *Histoire municipale de Mulhouse* (in AMM), p. 22

[35] Quoted in Laufenburger, *Cours d'économie alsacienne*, vol. 2, p. 354.

munity, his *kehillah*, looked after its poor. When he was growing up, local officials tried to outlaw Jewish 'beggars and vagabonds' only to be told by community leaders that the indigent would always be cared for 'because nature and religion demand it'.[36] In his village heder, Raphael would have learned that the Hebrew word *tzedakah* meant both charity and justice — 'the obligation imposed upon Jews to work for the reduction of inequality and the rectification of the iniquities which human will or blind fortune had visited upon mankind'[37] — and Raphael knew from his father that pedlars were given food and lodging in Jewish homes. The hungry and homeless took a prominent place at Rixheim's Sabbath meals and wedding-tables, and as a child Raphael would have heard of the 'chariot of cares' which travelled along Alsatian roads at night with rations for the needy. When he came to the city those memories remained vivid and those customs were respected by many members of his Mulhouse community. Charity was a *mitzvah*, a good deed commanded by the Bible as a form of justice and not as a casual gift, and Raphael set out to extend, within limits, those lessons to his new community of mill workers.[38] He may also have recalled the accusations of greed which his father had confronted as a money-lender in Rixheim — the myth of Jews out to profit from the misfortune of others — and perhaps he, Lantz, Lévy and other Jewish industrialists with ties to the country-side worked even harder than their Protestant counterparts to fufil their responsbilities to 'nature and religion' and to protect their families from old accusations rekindled. When Raphael joined the ranks of the town's industrialists, he followed their lead and im-plemented a progressive programme of accident insurance for his employees on the Rue Lavoisier. In a world where parents and children still worked upwards of fifteen hours a day with little sup-port in case of accident, or hope of relief in times of sickness, Raphael's programmes, however limited or paternalistic, were ap-preciated by mill hands, who later presented him with an ornate bronze medal as a gift of gratitude.[39] And those notions of social

[36] ADHR, V 604, 12 Feb. 1821.

[37] Marrus, *The Politics of Assimilation*, p. 77.

[38] On poverty, charity and justice among Alsatian Jews see for example Raphael and Weyl, *Les Juifs en Alsace*, pp. 302–3; and Stauben, *Scènes de la vie juive*, p. 9.

[39] The medal is in the private collection of Raphael Dreyfus's great-grandson, Jean-Louis Lévy. I thank him, and Mme France Reinach Beck, Raphael's great-grand daughter, for this information.

responsibility would set an example for the children who inherited his enterprise.

The family's observance of the High Holy Days and rites of passage at the Mulhouse synagogue, like the Hebrew inscriptions that they had chiselled on family grave-markers in the town cemetery, or the wig that Jeannette seems to have worn (in keeping with Jewish custom), had not hindered Raphael's entry into the textile trade. In fact, Rabbi Samuel Dreyfus, while working to maintain the integrity of his community of nearly 2,000 Jews, encouraged their integration into the larger society. In contrast to the Grand Rabbi of Colmar, his Orthodox superior to the north, Samuel Dreyfus was known for his liberal 'openness to reform', for the daily visits he made to public schools for the religious instruction of Jewish students, and for the close ties he maintained with the town's Protestant leadership. The first rabbi to earn the French *bachelier* degree, Dreyfus received his religious training at the yeshivah in Metz before coming to Mulhouse, a town he called 'one of the first in France where the spirit of equality and veneration for our religion has become deeply rooted'. He struggled with the Jewish Consistory to maintain the local rabbi's strong role, and his reformist tendencies did not lead him to abandon the traditional two sermons a year or other established customs; but his civic activism set an example, and the rabbi encouraged others to join what liberal contemporaries called 'la grande famille francaise'.[40]

One member of the Société Industrielle noted that increasing numbers of local Jews were receiving the 'proper instruction which introduces them to diverse professions and assures them a more comfortable, less precarious life while bringing them closer to the customs of the general population'.[41] Across four decades, in the pages of his publication *Lien d'Israel* and in his work to establish trades schools, philanthropic societies, hospitals and other municipal organizations, Samuel Dreyfus had been largely responsible for changes which secured a better life for Raphael's family and their co-religionists. Not all Jews in Mulhouse and its environs had been freed from the degrading poverty that their ancestors had known – town rag-pickers and village pedlars still tried to scrape a living from professions dead or dying – and not all had abandoned traditional

---

[40] On Rabbi Samuel Dreyfus see Livet and Oberlé, *Histoire de Mulhouse*, pp. 213–14; and, especially, Phyllis Cohen Albert, *The Modernization of French Jewry: Consistory and Community in the Nineteenth Century* (Hanover, NH, 1977), pp. 136, 260, 268, 291–2, 301.

[41] The comments appear in *Histoire municipale de Mulhouse*, pp. 96–7.

dialects and particularistic customs. But Rabbi Dreyfus made certain that the call of another Alsatian Jew, a manifesto sent out to Rixheim and other villages during the French Revolution, would finally and effectively be acted upon: 'French ought to be the Jews' mother tongue,' Berr Isaac Berr had proclaimed, 'since they are reared with and among Frenchmen...'[42]

Religious faith did not stand in the way of Raphael's economic success, as it did for Mulhouse Catholics, but, having been reared in a community where French was a foreign tongue, the question of language and culture threatened to slow his family's entry into the upper reaches of the town's manufacturing society. By the 1860s, the men who had directed the textile revolution in Mulhouse had conceived and financed an equally dramatic cultural and social revolution as well — a new French revolution. From libraries, schools and adult night courses in chemistry and literature, to museums of natural history, industrial design and fine arts, these men had worked to shape Mulhouse in their own image. Most were Protestants; some, such as Lazare Lantz, were Jews; but all were self-confident architects of the town's future who knew from experience that civilization was synonymous with France, and that French, not German or Alsatian jargon, was the language of progress. By the middle decades of the century, French had become the dominant language of the *haute bourgeoisie* throughout Alsace, the language that connected them to the markets and politics of the interior and set them off from their workers and rivals across the Rhine. In Mulhouse, where the Gallic roots went even deeper, French — along with an unwavering faith in science and reason and free enterprise — became a prerequisite for full membership of that town's industrial society.[43]

In the ornate leather-bound volumes published by the Société Industrielle, Raphael's name appears in the list of Mulhouse industries, but he is absent from the early photographic portraits of the Société's most illustrious members. This has less to do with the Jewish faith that he maintained than with his failure to master French and to assimilate French culture. Only the early signs of change were there: the children had been given French names, and by the late 1850s Raphael had abandoned the German spelling of his family name for

---

[42] Quoted in Paul Mendes-Flohr and Jehuda Reinharz (eds), *The Jew in the Modern World: A Documentary History* (New York, 1980), p. 109.

[43] Imbs and Dollinger, in Schlumberger, *La Bourgeoisie alsacienne*, pp. 311, 491; Weill, *L'Alsace française* p. 115; and *Centennaire de la Société Industrielle*, p. 14 and *passim*.

'Dreyfus'; also, along with other members of the Jewish community, he had rejected the constraints of Orthodoxy and adopted French customs of dress and more. His photograph, probably from the 1870s, shows him clean-shaven with short side-whiskers — a striking contrast to the long, full beards of his forefathers. His dark suit, silk tie and starched wing collar are those of a town businessman, far removed from the coarse black trousers, short blue frock coat and narrow-brimmed hat that Jacob Dreÿfuss, as a village pedlar, would have worn in Rixheim. Raphael and his family were among that 'large number of richly dressed persons' that one Mulhouse observer saw promenading in town on Saturday, though they would not have been 'quickly recognized as the children of Israel celebrating the Sabbath'.[44] Raphael's photograph, so similar to that of Auguste Dollfus and other prosperous, high-collared and confident Mulhouse manufacturers, would not have looked out of place in the publications of the Société Industrielle.

Raphael had entered the town's textile economy at the precise moment of extraordinary expansion, and as an intermediary at a time when manufacturers needed his services he made the contacts and amassed the capital necessary to start his own enterprise. But, as David Cohen reminds us, there is a profound difference between economic integration and assimilation.[45] Raphael's loan agreements, property contracts and requests for building and machine permits record both the rapidity of his economic success and the survival of his country ways; drafted by notaries in French, his contracts were then read aloud in German, the one official language that Raphael understood, and translated for his signature.[46] He could not have survived in the Mulhouse market place without some knowledge of French, and his Judaeo-Alsatian dialect contained some French words. In addition, he had to make his way through the pages of the city's most important paper, the *Industriel alsacien* (though raw cotton prices and bankruptcy statistics were part of a universal language), and he had to negotiate with French-speaking brokers and fellow industrialists at the Mulhouse stock exchange. But those conversations were punctuated with the German words and thick Alsatian accent of the hinterlands, an accent which often met with ridicule. A

[44] Quoted in the excellent article by Vicki Caron, 'The Failed Alliance: Jewish—Catholic Relations in Alsace—Lorraine, 1871—1914', *Leo Baeck Institute Yearbook*, 26 (1981), p. 7.
[45] Cohen, *La Promotion des juifs*, vol. 1, p. xiv.
[46] See the contracts in n. 27 above, and ADHR, 5 M 78, 1863.

few years earlier, the French Finance Minister, an Alsatian, had said of his economic programmes 'Mes projets sont détruits' ('My projects are ruined'), but critics of his policies — and of his accent — reported the statement as 'Mes brochets sont des truites' ('My sea-pike are trout').[47] The Finance Minister had his more modest counterparts in Mulhouse, and linguistic criticism was not always lighthearted. Raphael, now in his mid-forties, could not break all the habits of the countryside, or of his early years among migrants newly arrived in the city. He was still too close to Rixheim, and he was living proof of the observation made by Marc Bloch, another French Jew whose family was of Alsatian origin, that 'men fail to change their vocabulary every time they change their customs'.[48]

With Jeannette, however, and the rudimentary French she might have learned in her native Ribeauvillé — an Alsatian town with stronger French traditions than Rixheim — Raphael could follow the lead of Protestant colleagues who insisted that French should 'reign exclusively' in their homes. He and his wife could make certain that their children would master that language and perfect its pronunciation, the subtle sounds of belonging. They were not alone. It was in the 1860s that efforts to ensure the ascendancy of French over German in Mulhouse reached their peak, with the town's leaders mobilizing to sever ties to German and Germanic dialects among children of all classes, and radically to restructure a school system notorious for its indifference to anything unrelated to industry. A youngster in Mulhouse 'has no idea that speech is good for anything other than discussing budgets or explaining new ways of dying cloth', one journalist had noted, and contemporaries in Colmar had exaggerated only a little when they called their affluent neighbour to the south 'an ignorant and dull-witted town'. Unlike in the more refined administrative centre of Colmar, or the university city of Strasbourg, literature and the arts were in a 'savage' state in Mulhouse (like 'America before Columbus', said locals), and at school, home or workplace nearly all teaching was geared to the practical needs of a textile society. An inspector had called the Collège de Mulhouse nothing more than a huge industrial training-centre where 'the teaching of Greek and Latin is a joke' — and French had fared only slightly better. In most of France, educators worried about the poor scientific training of their students and feared that too great an emphasis on the

---

[47] Weill, *L'Alsace française*, p. 67.
[48] Marc Bloch, *The Historian's Craft*, tr. Peter Putnam (New York, 1953), p. 34.

classics would put them behind the more scientifically sophisticated Germans; but across the Vosges in Raphael's Mulhouse hard facts and the sums of industry, like Gradgrind's curriculum in Dickens's 'Coketown', had always been more important, because more relevant, than Plato, Virgil or the language of Montaigne.[49]

All that was changing, however, when the youngest Dreyfus children were growing up in the 1860s, and at every level of schooling. While technological innovations in the cotton industry led to new schools specializing in weaving, spinning, chemistry and commerce, other projects concentrated on the cultivation of French language and literature. Acknowledging that fully one-third of the children in Mulhouse were illiterate, officials confirmed that serious efforts were being taken to ensure that 'the generation now growing up will almost all speak French'. From industrial centres to isolated mountain villages, all youngsters 'will soon be able to express themselves in the language of their country'.[50] Inspired by Engel-Dollfus, and later by Jean Macé (an Alsatian schoolmaster whose Ligue de l'Enseignement was supported by the Société Industrielle and co-directed by the Jewish industrialist Lazare Lantz), plans were under way for the free and compulsory primary education of all Mulhouse youngsters; and, on the secondary level, the offspring of factory-owners, functionaries, leading merchants and highly skilled artisans would enter schools in which industrial arts, mathematics, statistics and geography were complemented by lessons in history, the classics and, above all, French language and literature. German, necessary for future Alsatian leaders, was still part of the curriculum, but French, the idiom of industry and emancipation, was given pride of place. It was a cultural campaign with many members, and its ranks included leaders of the Jewish community such as Rabbi Dreyfus, who believed that French was synonymous with progress and with the Rights of Man.[51]

---

[49] Livet and Oberlé, *Historie de Mulhouse*, pp. 210–12; and Weill, *L'Alsace française*, p. 124. Allan Mitchell discusses the German connection in *Victors and Vanquished: The German Influence on Army and Church in France after 1870* (Chapel Hill, NC, 1984), p. 143 and *passim*.

[50] Quoted in F. L'Huilier (ed.), *L'Alsace en 1870* (Strasbourg, 1971), pp. 52–3. See also R.D. Anderson, *Education in France, 1848–1870* (Oxford, 1975), p. 204.

[51] On Macé and his programmes see Katherine Auspitz, *The Radical Bourgeoisie: La Ligue de l'Enseignement and the Origins of the Third Republic* (Cambridge, 1982); and Livet and Oberlé, *Histoire de Mulhouse*, pp. 209ff.

By 1865, Raphael, Jeannette and their seven children – from twenty-one-year-old Jacques to six-year-old Alfred – made up a family universe of many accents and languages. With the parents' German and Judaeo-Alsatian and the youngsters' imperfect French, life in their apartment on the Place des Victoires must have sounded like a market day in Jacob's Rixheim. Working to soften the hard edges of their Alsatian accents, all the children would eventually perfect their French. But only the last two boys, Mathieu and Alfred, were young enough, and had time enough, to make it their mother tongue. Helped along by their eldest sister Henriette, acting as tutor, they began their studies at home while their parents prepared for the next step and considered schools not only in Mulhouse, but in Strasbourg, Basel and Paris. With Jacques and his closest brother, Léon, in line to manage the cotton mill, Raphael and Jeannette could afford, in every way, to provide their youngest boys with the French skills they would need to lead the family business into the twentieth century. And to do so as cultivated members of the Mulhouse patriciate.

IV

The Franco-Prussian War interrupted Mathieu and Alfred Dreyfus's schooling, but its consequences would provide another sort of education and bring them deeper into the French interior. Alfred's reaction to the sight of German troops marching under his Mulhouse window – 'my hatred, the hatred of my family for the foreigners'[52] – was as much an expression of fear and uncertainty, as it was the precocious patriotism of a ten-year-old boy. And, as the enemy advanced westward, it was felt by other French families. In late September 1870, after Strasbourg fell, one youngster much like Alfred was 'consumed with defiance' for the German invaders whom he watched enter his town with 'fite and drums'; a mil-owner, described in a novel about the war, 'had not ceased to rage since the Prussians had invaded the little town'; and the reaction of a character in a Maupassant story could have been drawn from young Alfred Dreyfus's life: 'I used to look at [the Prussians] out of the window' and 'it was more than I could stand. They made my blood boil and I

---

[52] Alfred Dreyfus later described his memories in a letter to the Minister of War (see BN, NAF 16464, 25 Dec. 1897).

cried with shame all day.'[53] Alfred called the Prussian violation of his homeland his 'first sorrow'.[54]

With the annexation of Alsace, confirmed by the Treaty of Frankfurt in May 1871, the French language became an idiom of *protestation*, and a habit which the German occupiers aimed to break. The authorities ordered that all official communication should be conducted in German and directed primary schools to teach that language alone. The Collège de Mulhouse, the secondary school that Mathieu Dreyfus had recently entered and Alfred would soon attend, continued the normal routine of French courses until the autumn, but it too planned to move German from its inferior place as a practical language and sharply reduce the emphasis on French.[55] The occupiers harboured a particular suspicion of Mulhouse as 'la ville la pius française de l'Alsace', ('the most French town of Alsace') and from the moment of annexation the linguistic battle set German authorities against local industrialists. Members of the Société Industrielle refused to translate the name of their organization and continued to publish bulletins in French. Some manufacturers organized a Ligue d'Alsace to combat the Germanization of their region and used Swiss newspapers as a forum for their campaign; smuggling French periodicals in from Basel, they helped make Mulhouse 'one of the most solid bastions of Alsatian protest against annexation'.[56] But resistance to German had little hope of success against a colonial administration armed with instructions from Bismarck and backed by his forces of order. A café-concert song, 'The Alsatian Schoolmaster', described the dilemma and enjoyed enormous popularity: 'La patrouille allemande passe./Baisser la voix, mes chers petits:/Parler français, n'est plus permis/Aux petits enfants

---

[53] Paul Appell, *Souvenirs d'un Alsacien, 1852–1922* (Paris, 1923), pp. 102–4; J.R. Bloch's novel *Et Cie*, quoted in Vicki Caron, 'Patriotism or Profit?: The Emigration of Alsace–Lorraine Jews to France, 1871–1872', *Leo Baeck Institute Yearbook*, 28, (1983), p. 160; and Guy de Maupassant, 'Boule de Suif', in *Selected Short Stories*, tr. Roger Colet (harmondsworth, Middx, 1982), p. 36.

[54] Dreyfus, *Cinq années*, p. 57.

[55] *Histoire municipale de Mulhouse*, p. 26; Weill, *L'Alsace française*, p. 250; and Dollinger, in Schlumberger, *La Bourgeoisie alsacienne*, p. 491.

[56] *Centennaire de la Société Industrielle*, p. 14; L'Huillier, *L'Alsace en 1870*, pp. 371ff.; and Dan P. Silverman, *Reluctant Union: Alsace–Lorraine and Imperial Germany, 1871–1918* (University Park, Pa, and London, 1972). pp. 23–4.

de l'Alsace', ('The German patrol passes by./Lower your voices, my dear little ones:/To speak French is no longer permitted/To the little children of Alsace').[57]

Raphael, whose first language, if not first allegiance, was German, faced different problems at his mill on the Rue Lavoisier. Cut off from markets and raw materials by train sabotage or by priorities of troop mobilization during the war, his industry was now officially detached from French markets and drawn into the Zollverein, the German customs union. The shift worried both German mill-owners and their Mulhouse counterparts. Technological improvements, sophisticated management skills and the expansion of French markets had helped Alsatian textile enterprises overwhelm most European competitors, and, with Mulhouse alone producing as much cotton as all the states in the Zollverein, the introduction of its goods into the German system on a equal footing could be catastrophic for enterprises across the Rhine. This, Mulhouse industrialists knew, would never be allowed. Moreover, the Dreyfus business and others in Alsace had been geared to an intricate network of branch factories across the Vosges which sent materials to Mulhouse for finishing-work, or took fabrics out for bleaching and dying. After May 1871, that network was dismembered. A compromise agreement struck in the wake of the Treaty of Frankfurt postponed economic chaos on both sides of the Rhine, but special tariff policies would last only a few months. As the deadline for 'option' approached — the Treaty provision which allowed Alsatians to 'opt' for French citizenship and to leave the region — Raphael searched for a way to save his mill, short of keeping his entire family under occupation and running the enterprise as a German subject.[58]

He had two choices: he could establish a new factory across the border in Belfort, a territory open to French markets and close enough to transfer equipment and draw on the local workforce; or he could divide the family, enabling some to become French citizens while others stayed behind in Mulhouse to manage the business. André Koechlin, the supplier of Raphael's machinery, joined members of the Dollfus family and others and moved branch enterprises to Belfort; but the Dreyfus company was still indebted to Koechlin, and

---

[57] The song appears in Frederick Seager, 'The Alsace–Lorraine Question in France, 1871–1914', in Charles K. Warner (ed.), *From the Ancien Régime to the Popular Front* (New York, 1969), pp. 114–15.

[58] Silverman, *Reluctant Union*, pp. 165–89; on the 'option' agreement see Caron, in *Leo Baeck Institute Yearbook*, 28.

Raphael, though one of the city's more successful factory-owners, did not share his colleague's abundant resources. The mill on the Rue Lavoisier was only in its seventh year, and the war had taken its toll.

Raphael's second choice became his only option when the German state announced its intention to draft Alsatian boys into the military. Among the few concessions offered the new subjects of the *Reichsland* was exemption for those who had already served with French forces. But that was as far as Bismarck would go: conscription would begin in the autumn of 1872, and in a few years the Dreyfus sons would be pressed into the German army and forced to wear the spiked helmets which had become, for local residents, the most dramatic symbol of the invader and a daily reminder of defeat.[59] In a city where German officers and their families faced hostility in shops and streets, and where the marriage of a French woman to a Prussian official caused such 'general indignation' that Alfred Dreyfus noted it among his most vivid memories of the annexation,[60] the prospect of serving in the enemy camp — a camp which continued systematically to discriminate against Jews in the military — only hastened the family's search for a way out.

Jacques Dreyfus had fought with the French Légion d'Alsace during the war and was exempted from German service;[61] and it was to Jacques that Raphael turned for help. As a temporary measure arrived at under the pressure of the citizenship deadline, he asked his eldest son to stay in Mulhouse to direct the factory and attempt to salvage the family fortune. A short time later, in May 1872, Raphael left Jeannette and the children in Jacques's care and travelled south from Mulhouse to the French town of Carpentras, where Henriette had recently settled with her husband, Joseph Valabrègue. Staying only long enough to appear before the town mayor and officially declare Carpentras as his French domicile — and the domicile of the six children who, as minors, were not permitted to 'opt' on their own[62] — he returned to Mulhouse to take advantage of a special pro-

---

[59] Caron, ibid., pp. 147–58; Silverman, *Reluctant Union*, pp. 66–70, 174; and Laufenburger, *Cours d'économie alsacienne*, vol. 1, pp. 130, 144.

[60] Letter to Joseph Reinach, BN, NAF 13567, n. d.

[61] On Jacques's service, see the document signed by the Minister of War on 30 Jan. 1921, and Jacques's statement notarized by the mayor of Carpentras (Vaucluse) and undated; both are in the private collection of the Dreyfus family. See also Capitaine Alfred Dreyfus, *Souvenirs et correspondance* (Paris, 1936), p. 41.

[62] The 23 May 1872 'Declaration d'option' is printed in Kleeblatt, *The Dreyfus Affair*, p. 143.

vision in the option agreement. With French citizenship confirmed, and with Jacques remaining in Mulhouse, Raphael prepared to move the family to Basel. From that temporary residence on the Rhine, at the junction of the French, German and Swiss borders, he could help direct the mill and hope for changes in the political climate of Alsace. And, if necessary, he could start the search for a permanent home for his family in the French interior.

'He who had sons departed,' went a popular Alsatian saying of the time;[63] but Raphael's option, made possible by Jacques's sacrifice, involved much more than saving sons from the German army. In October 1872, with Jeannette too weak to make the journey or unwilling to leave Jacques behind, Raphael took his three daughters and three younger sons along the same south-eastern road as Jacob Dreÿfuss had travelled as a country pedlar, a road which passed by Rixheim.[64]

Separated from his mother and from his native city for the first time, thirteen-year-old Alfred Dreyfus faced a particularly depressing autumn and winter in Basel. Immediately upon arrival his father followed the lead of other Mulhouse manufacturers and enrolled the boys in a *Realschule* (technical high school). Some courses were offered in French, but the primary language was German, and, though the Dreyfus sons knew enough to get by, it was a hard period of adjustment, especially for the youngest.[65] Nor were Swiss schools considered the ideal institutions in which to prepare the future leaders of French industry. That training, the Mulhouse *patronat* had always insisted, could only be achieved in Paris, at a college or *lycée* designed to ready students for the *baccalauréat* and for entrance into the Ecole Centrale des Arts et Manufactures, or the Ecole Polytechnique, the premier schools for young engineers, scientists, industrialists and military men.[66] Though too late for Jacques or eighteen-year-old Léon, Raphael knew that it was a dream within reach for Mathieu and Alfred. Early in 1873, with their parents, sisters and elder brothers remaining behind in Mulhouse, or in their nearby Swiss refuge, the two boys crossed the Vosges and set off for Paris.

[63] Quoted in Caron, *Leo Baeck Institute Yearbook*, 28, p. 148; see also p. 145, n. 30.
[64] Dreyfus, *Souvenirs et correspondance*, p. 41.
[65] Ibid, p. 42
[66] 'Beaucoup de patrons tenaient à voir leurs fils passer par l'Ecole Polytechnique avant de venir prendre place à la fabrique' (Weill, *L'Alsace française*, p. 112).

V

Raphael Dreyfus lived long enough to see his youngest son graduate from the Ecole Supérieure de Guerre, and then, as a captain full of promise, move on to become a junior officer on the French General Staff.[67] Honoured by his son's service to the fatherland, Raphael would be spared his degradation. Early in December 1893, upon returning to Paris from cavalry manoeuvres in the provinces, the Captain received word that his father had fallen seriously ill. With special permission from French and German authorities, he rushed to Mulhouse. Raphael died two days later, at the age of seventy-five.[68] On the next afternoon, family and old friends of the industrialist followed the funeral cortege north along the same route as Raphael had taken three decades before to survey the pasture and where his factory would be built. Turning west, the procession entered the Israelite section of the Mulhouse cemetery, a flat, open space with little vegetation and dense rows of small stone markers with Hebrew inscriptions and dates recorded according to the Jewish calendar. Jacob Dreÿfuss was the first member of the family to be buried in that plot, and Raphael, alongside Jeannette, who had died in 1886, and the two infant daughters they had lost many years before, was the last.

If Raphael's legacy to his seven children was far superior in worldly goods to the inheritance that he had received from his own father, many of the lessons he had given them were the same. Tutored by Jacob along the back roads and town markets of Alsace, he, in turn, taught his sons the intricacies of the textile trade, and, no less important to him, the duties which later came with membership in the Mulhouse patriciate and with French citizenship. While Jacob Dreÿfuss brought his family out of a hostile countryside and into 'la ville la plus française de l'Alsace', Raphael Dreyfus, in name and allegiance, led them deeper into the French interior. That he returned to live in his native province under German occupation was not a sign of divided loyalties, just as it was not for Jacques, Léon and Mathieu, who also stayed on − or returned − to live and work in Mulhouse: it was a practical strategy to save the family's resources, and the personal statement of a patriot who never accepted the

[67] For Alfred Dreyfus's service record, see AN, BB 19/101, feuillet du personnel.
[68] AN, BB 19/128, interrogation, p. 418; and AMM, état civil, 13 Dec. 1893.

inevitability of permanent occupation. As a devout Jew, a man of Scripture and of the belief, fashioned in his own lifetime, that France was itself a land of promise, he would have found in his later years as father and grandfather, new layers of meaning in Isaac's words of blessing to Jacob.

One year after Raphael died, his youngest son was confined to the Cherche-Midi prison in Paris awaiting deportation into the 'eternal exile' of Devil's Island. Prohibited from seeing his wife and two children, or any member of his family, he asked to be visited by the Grand Rabbi of France, Zadoc Kahn, a relative through marriage and a fellow Alsatian. The prisoner wanted to be 'comforted' by the rabbi's 'warm and eloquent words'. But the military judge advocate denied the request.[69] Lucie Dreyfus wrote to her husband on the night of the first anniversary of his father's death and told him that the entire family would go to synagogue. He wrote back that he, too, had been thinking of his father, and that the memories brought him both 'tears' and 'courage'.

Alfred Dreyfus was not an observant Jew — his request to see the Grand Rabbi was more an exceptional need for solace than a rule of faith; he had little interest in either the historical traditions of Judaism or the arguments of Jewish supporters who insisted that his 'unwavering hope...and almost fatalistic resignation' made him 'more Jewish' than he 'could ever imagine'.[70] Dreyfus was never resigned — his history attests to that — but he did possess an unshakable faith in what he described as the 'cult of humanity', and what the congregation of Rabbi Dreyfus of Mulhouse called 'la grande famille française'. The prisoner brought to Devil's Island, along with copies of Montaigne, Descartes and Montesquieu, four Bibles and three packets of sermons; and that says more about the man than any assessment of his allegiance, or lack of it, could ever do. Dreyfus had, in a sense, been 'baptized into a majority faith', but without being 'completely detached' from Jewish tradition.[71] For the Captain, as for his Alsatian family, the divine demand for justice had been answered by a new fatherland; and, if his belief was naïve, or romantic, or, in the end,

---

[69] See Dreyfus's letter of 23 Dec. 1894 asking Rabbi Kahn to 'venir me voir et me réconforter de votre parole chaude et éloquente' (Dreyfus family private collection); and the rabbi's letter of the same date to the Military Governor of Paris in AN, BB 19/75.

[70] Bernard Lazare, quoted by Vidal-Naquet in Dreyfus, *Cinq années*, p. 13.

[71] See Landes, in Malino and Wasserstein, *The Jews in France*, pp. 288−90.

wrong, it says more about those who broke the promise of the French Revolution than about those who struggled to honour it in their lifetime.

Part II

Redefining Community

4

The Right to be Equal: Zalkind Hourwitz and the Revolution of 1789

FRANCES MALINO

Travelling across France on the eve of the Revolution, one might meet in Bordeaux the urbane deist and philosopher Abraham Furtado, in Nancy the wealthy banker Berr Isaac Berr, in Strasbourg the factory-owner and Court purveyor Cerf Berr. Throughout eastern France one would encounter Jews whose lives remained within the confines of Ashkenazic tradition and whose language was Judaeo-French. And in Paris, near the Quartier Saint-Martin, where recent Jewish immigrants lived in poverty, peddled their wares and feared the surveillance of the police, could be found the Polish Jew Zalkind Hourwitz.

Hourwitz remains a shadowy figure, the source of a variety of observations which often say more about the authors' concerns than the subject's life. To his contemporary Michel Berr, for example, Hourwitz's peculiarity of dress and education loomed as large as his extraordinary intelligence. Robert Anchel, in 1937, to celebrate the presumed hundred-and-fiftieth anniversary of Hourwitz's arrival in Paris, applauded his zeal, bemoaned his indiscretion and defended the Jewish establishment past and present against such an iconoclastic antagonist. And Shmuel Trigano, French sociologist, accuses him of complicity in making French Jews hostages to a freedom which restricts them and a universalism which particularizes them.[1]

Zalkind Hourwitz lived during a pivotal period in history, both Jewish and non-Jewish. A compelling personality who fits none of the traditional portraits of eighteenth-century Jews, he challenges our

---

[1] Michel Berr, 'Zalkind Hourwitz', in *Biographie universelle ancienne et moderne* (Paris, 1828), pp. 54–5; Robert Anchel, 'Un Juif polonais en France: Zalkind Hourwitz', *L'Univers israélite*, 33 (23 Apr. 1937), pp. 505–6; Shmuel Trigano, *La République et les Juifs*, (Paris, 1982).

previous understanding of Jewish emancipation, provides an additional perspective with which to view revolutionary Paris and adds another dimension to the historiography of the French Revolution. Through his friends and enemies, the positions he sought and occupied, the fears, dreams and myths which sustained him, emerges a world of unexpected diversity. Hourwitz's importance, however, transcends the parameters of Jewish and French revolutionary history. His life provides a poignant example of one man's resolution of the charge of being an outsider — of being marginal to the society which moulded his self-perceptions. Lastly, Zalkind Hourwitz still speaks to the delicate and always precarious balance between the right to be equal and the freedom to be different.

Hourwitz was born in a small village near Lublin in the year 1751.[2] By the time he was twenty-two, he had abandoned the village and his family, their 'fear of devils, philosophers and philosophy' and his own abysmal ignorance, to which he would refer often in later years. How he managed to travel to Germany, when and with whom, unfortunately remain unknown. Quite probably, like his compatriot Solomon Maimon, he suffered physically and survived only because some kind-hearted souls — perhaps even from his own village — recognized in the unkempt youth great intelligence, a moral earnestness and a compelling integrity. Once in Germany, Hourwitz settled in Berlin, apparently earning his keep by tutoring children of the wealthy, whose mischieviousness (they tried to convince him that the strange language they spoke was Hebrew) subsequently inspired him to investigate the potentialities inherent in anagrams.

Neither introspection nor confession ranks high among Hourwitz's personality traits. For information on his early years, therefore, one must rely on his contemporaries and his own revelations, hidden as they often are behind some point of information or instructive example. Hourwitz may well have had France as his goal when he left his village, for in Metz there was a well-known yeshivah, a much revered Talmudic scholar and other students from Poland. And perhaps, as Hourwitz once declared, his father was himself a rabbi who intended that his son should further his education with the great rabbi Aryeh Loeb ben Asher (Sha'a gas Aryeh). But what Hourwitz brought with

---

[2] This is contrary to the date of 1740 quoted in all official biographical accounts. The census of 1809, however, which Hourwitz signed, lists his birth date as 1751, his place of birth Poland, his status that of a bachelor and his position that of 'maître de langues'. He had been in Paris for thirty-five years. (Jewish Theological Seminary, Mic. 8138.)

him to France in 1774 was less a commitment fo furthering his Talmudic education than a determination to acquire the very sciences and philosophies denied him in his youth.

Hourwitz never recovered from the feelings of embarrassment and linguistic estrangement to which he believed his birth, fortune and country had condemned him. I learned my ABC as an adult and only with the help of a Hebrew—German dictionary, he informed the French Minister Chrétien Guillaume de Lamoignon de Malesherbes, in a rare moment of personal reminiscence. Hourwitz also never abandoned his frustration with traditional Jewish life (undoubtedly nourished during his stay in Berlin), his disdain for what he believed to be the narrow vision of the rabbis, and his deeply held conviction that the selfishness of the lay leadership impeded the economic and intellectual well-being of his poor and oppressed co-religionists.

Metz may have boasted a fine yeshivah, but it also counted among its two to three thousand Jewish residents rebellious youth eager to frequent cafés, read forbidden literature and dress like their non-Jewish peers. The Jewish leadership, struggling to protect its moral and juridical authority at a time when internal tensions and government ministers competed to undermine them, quite probably suggested to the restless and outspoken Hourwitz that he leave the community.[3] By this time, however, he had found kindred spirits among his fellow Jews. He had also added to his already significant resentment of those who directed the affairs of the Jewish community.

Hardly 1,000 Jews lived in Paris when Hourwitz arrived in the capital. Yet in no other part of France could he find so many different Jews and Judaisms, such a wide variety of economic activities and lifestyles. Officially expelled from Paris since the fourteenth century, the Jews were subject to police surveillance (the Bastille or Bicêtre,

---

[3] In 1567, the French military governor of Metz gave permission to four Jewish families to reside in the recently occupied city. The four families increased to ninety-six in 1658 and ultimately to 480 families — the final number permitted by the royal letters patent. While the bankers and purveyors continued to satisfy the intentions and pocketbooks of the local offficials and the Crown, most of the Jews earned their living by lending money and trading in gold, silver and used clothing. From the beginning, the Jews were confined to the Saint-Ferroy quarter; they could neither own nor rent property in other parts of the city. The juridical autonomy of the Metz *nation* came accompanied with onerous taxes, the most notorious of which was the Brancas tax. In force until the Revolution, this tax required the community to become heavily indebted to Christian creditors and contributed to the increasing impoverishment of most of the city's Jews.

Chatelet or Fort l'Evêque awaited any 'recalcitrant' or 'rebellious' Jews) and had to reapply every six months for permission to reside in the city.[4] For Hourwitz, this discriminatory and often costly procedure was undoubtedly a small price to pay for a freedom from Jewish communal control. He was also free — as were most of the Ashkenazim — to live in poverty on the winding and tortuous streets in the Quartiers Saint-Martin and Saint-Denis, eating in tiny rooms where widowed Jewish women provided ritually prepared meals. On the left bank, by contrast, wealthy young Sephardic Jews carried swords and dressed and acted as gentlemen. Hourwitz's world, however, rarely impinged on their beautiful homes on the Rue Hautefeuille and the Rue Mazarine.

Hourwitz never escaped the poverty with which he first entered the capital. Whether hawking used clothing or eking out a living teaching foreign languages to the young, he barely avoided starvation and only then with the support of his friends.[5] He had no interest in the riches of the market place; his dreams were to acquire the treasures of the classical and contemporary world. And what better place than Paris to educate oneself! In his room on the Rue Saint-Denis à la Croix de Fer, he could be found each evening poring over torn copies of Ovid and Molière, Voltaire and Rousseau. Soon few languages or philosophical positions were unfamiliar to him.

The Hapsburg Emperor Joseph II had just promulgated a series of edicts which, while hardly motivated by concern for the Jews, nevertheless offered them along with other religious minorities increased

---

[4] The Sephardim of Bordeaux and Bayonne were probably the first to settle in the capital. Their success undoubtedly led Jews from north-eastern France and later Germany, Holland, England, Austria and Poland to follow. Some chose to settle permanently in the city; others came for a few months of business or 'study'. Many eked out a living as second-hand dealers, tailors and pedlars, while a few were wealthy merchants, bankers and manufacturers. Some got in trouble with the law, a few successfully defied the authorities, but most sought anonymity.

[5] For example, the diamond merchant Jacob Lazard. In his obituary, Lazard is criticized for having been stingy in his will. The reader is reminded, however, that he was always a friend of those Jews who embraced culture and literature. Lazard had arrived in Paris from Metz and like Hourwitz was impoverished. He went on to become one of the most important jewellers of Paris and after participating in the Napoleonic Assembly of Notables became a member of the Central Consistory. Hourwitz apparently spent some time in Lazard's home and received support from him. See the obituary of Lazard in *Archives israélites*, 1(1840), p. 469.

rights. Now King Louis XVI and his Council of State were examining plans and proposing reforms for the Jews of Alsace.[6] Attempts to ameliorate the condition of the Jews naturally brought forth dire warnings, hoary accusations of usury and ritual murder, and the offer of forgiveness through conversion. None of this escaped Hourwitz's watchful eye. Armed with an anti-clericalism no less vehement than Voltaire's and an intransigence toward any manifestation of prejudice, whether Jewish or Christian, he entered the political arena. The journals became his platform; satire, wit, sarcasm and outrage his weapons. His cause — freedom for his fellow Jews.

The Jews are the most sober, the most peaceful and the most docile of all people, Hourwitz argued in the 31 October 1783 issue of the *Courier de l'Europe*. Hourwitz was responding to a letter from Warsaw which this Anglo-French journal had published just two weeks earlier. Ostensibly attempting to explore what could be done in Poland for 'this unhappy people', the anonymous author (Hourwiz accused him of being a defrocked Austrian monk) had presented a scathing denunciation of the particularism, pretensions and financial activities of the Jews. The Jews never insult other nations, Hourwitz retorted, they do not seek to proselytize, and they never trouble the state. Do you find a usurer among them? Well then, punish him but do not accuse all Jews of the crime. Even the animals in the fables of La Fontaine are less unjust than this, for they would never hang all donkeys for the epicurism of one.

Explicitly defending the freedom to observe kashrut (dietary law) and prohibit intermarriage, Hourwitz paradoxically asserted that

[6] The Jewish population of Alsace increased dramatically throughout the eighteenth century, bringing the number of families to more than 4,000 in 1784 (approximately 24,000 people). Along with this sixfold increase came greater competition in the few occupations open to Jews and an explosive hostility between them and their peasant debtors. The false-receipts affair of 1777 — when peasants refused payment of their debts brandishing receipts duly signed in Hebrew — brought to the attention of all France the impecuniosity of the peasants of Alsace. The affair instigated an investigation by a royal commission, resulted in the abolition of the body toll for all Alsace and, most importantly, inspired the letters patent of 10 July 1784. These provided formal recognition of the authority of the syndics and rabbis, denied the right of local authorities to expel Jews legitimately dwelling in Alsace, and expanded the range of economic activities available to Jews. They also required an official list of those Jews permitted in the province (a census was conducted for this purpose) and denied Jews the right to marry without permission from the Crown.

belief in their chosenness distinguished the Jews not at all from the thousand and one Christian sects, each of which assured its adherents that outside of its temple there was no salvation. The final paragraphs of his impassioned response, however, were the most mischievous, the most misleading and also the most revealing. Refusing to accept that the onus was on the Jews to change and conform to the demands of the Christian world, he cleverly reversed the responsibility and initiative:

> There is a sweet, easy and infallible means of obliging us to embrace Christianity. End our captivity by giving us all the rights of citizens. You will then make the temporal Messiah we await useless and we shall be obliged to recognize Jesus Christ as spiritual Messiah, lest we refute the prophets. In the meantime, however, we shall remain faithful to our religion, loving God and our neighbour — that is, all men of goodwill of whatever nation.

Hourwitz would make this facetious offer on behalf of his fellow Jews more than once — surely aware that it would endear him not at all to traditional Jews or Christians or even to those who considered themselves enlightened. But Hourwitz concerned himself neither with celestial rewards nor with future redemption (his offer, never serious, only served to dismiss the issue altogether), but rather with the more concrete benefits of human justice and civic equality. That he could so easily dismiss the religious commitments and sensitivities of his contemporaries, however, facilitated and simultaneously complicated his struggle.

Hourwitz may have been isolated from many of his co-religionists, but he was not alone. Debates by and on behalf of Jews and Protestants, as well as publicized events illustrating the vulnerability of both, permeated the last years of the *ancien régime*. Millenarians, rationalists and humanitarians expressed a common theme. Their motivations might differ and their goals clash, but they all agreed that France must acknowledge its non-Catholics and grant them basic human rights. Both in his year-long correspondence with the French minister Malesherbes and in his essay submitted to the Metz Royal Society, Hourwitz sought to educate and influence those most likely to determine the future status of the Jews.

In November 1787 an edict 'concerning those who do not profess the Catholic religion' was promulgated. Primarily the work of Malesherbes, the edict granted limited religious tolerance to the non-

Catholics of the kingdom along with the freedom to exercise their commerce, crafts and professions. Nowhere were the Jews excluded. On the contrary, the edict explicitly stated that it included non-Christians and that it protected the 'concessions' of Lutherans and 'other subjects'.[7] Good reason, then, for the Jews to rejoice. For the first time, they believed themselves free to enter fully the economic life of the kingdom. Those living in Nîmes — many of whom had recently come to France from Avignon and the Comtat Venaissin — quickly registered Jewish births, marriages and deaths in the newly established registries. The Jews of Remoulins, Aix, Saint-Esprit and other small communities followed their example. Others — for example, Jews in Paris and Metz — sought admission to the guilds, and some purchased masterships.

The enthusiasm with which the Jews welcomed the edict, however, was matched with indecision and ignorance on the part of local authorities. And, while the *parlement* of Paris duly registered the edict, the *parlement* of Metz refused to do so, arguing that Metz would become a 'tribe of Jews'. The Crown finally assured Metz that no new rights had been granted to the Jews; Metz duly registered the edict, and the King, if Pierre-Louis Roederer is to be believed, advised Malesherbes, 'You have made yourself a Protestant, now I shall make you a Jew: occupy yourself with their future.'[8]

Malesherbes left few sources unexplored in this new task. He turned to friends such as Pierre-Louis de Lacretelle and Pierre-Louis Roederer, to the Jews of the south-west, the north-east and Paris, to the Police Inspector of Paris, and to ministers both in France and abroad. He gathered information concerning the laws and customs of the Jews as well as reports — solicited and unsolicited — from their friends and their enemies. He read their history and charted their settlements to provide him with the answer to one all-consuming question: could and would the Jews of France abandon their exclusiveness and particularity in return for the rights of Frenchmen? Were the Jews really comparable to the Protestants or were they a permanently separate and potentially dangerous people?

For well over a year, Hourwitz corresponded regularly with Malesherbes. He confided in the minister both his personal history as well as his biting criticisms of the establishment (Jewish and non-Jewish) and throughout offered compelling defences of his fellow Jews. 'You

---

[7] 'L' Edit concernant ceux qui ne font pas profession de la religion catholique'. See for example articles XXV and XXXVIII.

[8] *Journal de Paris*, 24 (An VII, 22 Frimaire).

will easily see', he informed Malesherbes at the beginning of their correspondence, 'that I know my nation well, that I am well instructed in the Talmud, without being its dupe, and that I speak less as a Jew than as a man...[9] And it was precisely this distinction which Hourwitz demanded for his 'unfortunate nation'.

Though his correspondence with Malesherbes (who left the Royal Council before any official edict on the Jews was promulgated) remained private and unknown even to historians, Hourwitz's participation in a contest organized by the Metz Royal Society received wide publicity. Every year the Society offered a prize for the best essay on a given topic; Robespierre had shared the prize with Lacretelle in 1784 for his essay concerning the origins of collective guilt.[10] On 25 August 1785, two months after the death of the celebrated and revered Rabbi Aryeh Loeb ben Asher of Metz, the Society decided to offer its coveted gold piece to the best essay concerning the means to make the Jews more useful and happy in France.

By 1787 nine papers had been submitted, but, according to Pierre-Louis Roederer, chairman of the judges and a member of one of Metz's leading parliamentary families, none of them adequately probed the depths of the problems raised. Returning the two best manuscripts to their authors (Grégoire, *curé* at Embermenil, and the Protestant lawyer Claude Thiery), Roederer asked them to explore the flexibility of the laws of the kingdom, the depth and power of popular prejudices and the means of ensuring the well-being of the national economy. He also asked them to consider the potential cost to the Jews were their particular institutions and 'virtues' to be destroyed.

Hourwitz too had sent the Society a manuscript, identified by a verse from Ovid's *Tristia*, 'Veniam pro Laude peto'.[11] The quotation, from a poem written when Ovid was in exile, is cleverly chosen, underlining Hourwitz's stylistic sensitivity and the importance that he assigned his work, as the passage from which the verse is taken

---

[9] Archives Nationales, 154 AP II 136. Hourwitz had probably consciously borrowed Christian Wilhelm Dohm's assertion 'The Jew is even more man than Jew.' His changes were both subtle and important. Christian Wilhelm Dohm, 'Concerning the Amelioration of the Civil Status of the Jews', in Ellis Rivkin (ed.), *Readings in Modern Jewish History* (Ohio, 1957), p. 14.

[10] *Mémoires de l'Académie de Metz* 1873−1874(Metz, 1875), pp 476−7.

[11] In order to ensure complete impartiality, the entries were to be identified by a quotation or some other distinguishing characteristic.

shows: 'And yet they [the verses] cannot be read in patience by anybody who does not know that they lack the final hand. That work was taken from me while it was on the anvil and my writing lacked the last touch of the file. *Indulgence, then, instead of praise I ask.*'[12] Roederer, however, had not returned Hourwitz's manuscript. Never willing to acquiesce when he felt a wrong had been committed, Hourwitz immediately requested that he too be given the opportunity to address the chairman's concerns and to resubmit his essay. Hourwitz's second version arrived in 1788. After receiving the three rewritten essays and deciding that further postponement would be unwise, the Society converted the award from a prize for the 'best essay' to three prizes. Hourwitz's *Apologie des Juifs* (with the purposeful reversal of the priority of goals announced by the Society) shared the honours with the essays of Grégoire and Thiery.[13]

Hourwitz's first and second entries, along with the published version, provide, as Hourwitz himself acknowledged, a rich and instructive canvas (similar perhaps to that of Hieronymous Bosch), as well as a test of any logician's patience. He attacks the establishment for not recognizing what is self-evident in their question, the rabbis for their stultifying restrictions, the lay leaders for their determination to oppress the poor and helpless Jews, the *philosophes* for their ignorance and nefarious influence, and the enemies of the Jews for their vicious accusations. He buttresses these charges with references to classical literature and contemporary fables. But, if he left few unscathed and many outraged, Hourwitz provided a powerful defence of the Jews and their 'extraordinary' qualities. And, if he argued for linguistic uniformity, advocated only voluntary religious associations and even repeated his conversion bait, he nevertheless refused to accept that Jews cease to be Jews as the price of their citizenship.

Hourwitz's *Apologie des Juifs* was quickly published (3 April 1789), providing its author with international publicity as well as some notoriety. But most important were the new friends that Hourwitz made and the access that he gained to government ministers and statesmen (to whom he could now personally plead the cause of the Jews). Their patronage, moreover, helped him to compete successfully

---

[12] Ovid, *Tristia*, I. vii. 31. The words cited by Hourwitz are emphasized in the translation.

[13] Zalkind Hourwitz, *Apologie des Juifs en réponse à la question: est-il des moyens de rendre les Juifs plus heureux et plus utiles en France?* (repr. Paris, 1968).

for the position of interpreter of oriental languages at the Bibliothéque
Royale. With a yearly salary of 800 livres, a position of respect and
even some influence, and the time and opportunity to immerse himself in his treasured books, Zalkind Hourwitz had arrived. But so,
too, had the Revolution: the date was May 1789.

In January, Louis had ordered the convocation of the Estates
General to address the pressing economic problems of his kingdom.
By May, deputies elected by all male French citizens over the age of
twenty-five arrived at Versailles armed with their constitutents'
grievances. Or, at least those of most of their constituents. The
Sephardim, protected by royal privileges as well as their own
economic utility, had participated fully in the electoral process. But
most of the Jews in France — those living in Alsace, Metz and
Lorraine — participated not at all. Officially excluded from the
general elections, they obtained belated permission to conduct their
own elections, prepare a list of their grievances and send six delegates
to Paris. The King would then decide how their demands would be
presented to the assembled deputies.

Hourwitz could barely contain himself with this news. Could the
fate of the more than 30,000 Ashkenazic Jews rest with the actions
and words of six of their leaders? He immediately set out to convince
the French ministers that he — and he alone — could honestly and
objectively convey the needs of his oppressed, impoverished and exploited co-religionists. For their oppression came, he wrote to the
Minister of State, not only from the intolerance of the French but
also from the superstitions of their own leaders; their poverty and
exploitation resulted from the exorbitant rents that wealthy Jews
charged them as well as from the economic restrictions and onerous
taxes of the kingdom. 'The syndics [the official lay leadership]
of Alsace, Metz and Lorraine will sacrifice the well-being of their
brothers to their superstitions and their private interests. It is absolutely necessary to join with our syndics some Jew instructed in the
laws of his nation and who is exempt from its prejudices.'[14]

Hourwitz's contempt for the Jewish leadership was well known
from his *Apologie* and because he often referred to the hostility with
which this award-winning work had been received by the Metz Jews.
What was also known, by both Parisians and the Ashkenazic leadership, was Hourwitz's uncompromising demand for full and equal

---

[14] Archives Nationales, AA42 dossier 1324, letter of 8 May 1789. See also
the letter of 15 May to Villedeuil in Archives Nationales, O¹ 609.

rights for the Jews of France. He feared — not all that unrealistically — that the Ashkenazic leaders and many of the French were inclined to compromise this equality.

By the time the Ashkenazic delegates finally arrived in Paris, on 6 August, the Estates General had become the National Assembly, the Bastille had been stormed, and the deputies had commissioned themselves to prepare a new constitution for France. The particular demands that the Ashkenazim brought with them to the capital would, along with the hundreds of other notebooks of grievances, soon be consigned to the archives.

Hourwitz followed the events of the summer of 1789 with great enthusiasm and no less commitment. He joined the National Guard and frequented the printing-press of the revolutionary Antoine Gorsas. He witnessed his friend and fellow prize-winner Grégoire call the National Assembly's attention to the volatile situation in Alsace, where debtor peasants chased Jews from their villages, pillaging their homes and destroying their gardens. He found himself singled out by the *Journal de Paris* as it turned for its defence of the Jews to his prize-winning *Apologie*.[15] And he observed with great consternation the divided and counterproductive responses of his fellow Jews to the Assembly's Declaration of the Rights of Man and the Citizen (26 August).

'All men are born, and remain, free and equal in rights', the Declaration asserted; 'no person shall be molested for his opinions, even such as are religious...' These were heady words whose implications would become clearer in the following months. The immediate concern, however, was to assure inclusion of the Jews. But how? The Sephardim, satisfied to have participated in the elections, suggested silence. The Ashkenazic deputies, now in Paris and anxiously awaiting the opportunity to address the National Assembly, edited their previous demands. They added civil rights to their request for freedom of residence and work, equality of taxation and — to Hourwitz's horror — retention of their synagogues, rabbis and syndics in the traditional manner and form. Only the Jews of Paris captured the revolutionary spirit in their response of 26 August. We are French, they asserted; we demand to be subject to French

---

[15] 'On s'occupe en ce moment à l'Assemblée Nationale du sort future de cette nation parmi nous', the *Journal* informed its readership. 'Ce qui la concerne est donc du plus pressant intérêt. Cette cause d'ailleurs est celle de l'humanité et c'est sous cet aspect que l'envoisage souvent M. Hourwitz' (*Journal de Paris*, 15 Sep. 1789).

jurisprudence, French police and French tribunals.[16] Occupying no official position within the community, Hourwitz was not among the eleven notables who signed this declaration. But Jacob Lazard, fellow rebel spirit from Metz, undoubtedly signed with his friend in mind.

Hourwitz's concern for his beleaguered co-religionists in eastern France was overshadowed by his fears that their leaders would barter equality for the Jews for promises of protection. These fears explain his behaviour in the autumn of 1789. The Ashkenazic delegates were finally to be called before the bar of the National Assembly. Once again Hourwitz attempted to add his words to theirs, to convince the revolutionaries that these leaders spoke less for the Jews than for their own interests. Just days before the scheduled appearance of Berr Isaac Berr and the other delegates, he wrote to the Committee of Reports of the Assembly,

> I have just learned with surprise that you have authorized my co-religionists of Metz to plead their cause...If everything I have told you and written to you is insufficient to convince you of the injustice of their pretensions, let me know. I flatter myself that I can satisfy you entirely and prove to you that the devout of my nation can practise their religion and pay their debts without tyrannizing the conscience of their fellow Jews with a rabbinical inquisition and without living in a cesspool...[17]

Understandably, Hourwitz would never be forgiven these biting words — not even two centuries later.

On 14 October the Ashkenazic deputies appeared before the National Assembly. They requested consideration for the 'timid demands that the Jews dare to make in the midst of their profound humiliation'.[18] With a defiance matched only by perspicacity and political acumen, Hourwitz publicly proclaimed a patriotic gift to the revolutionary cause — one quarter of his yearly salary in perpetuity.[19]

---

[16] *Adresse présenté à l'Assemblée Nationale le 26 Août 1789 par les Juifs* (repr. Paris, 1968).

[17] Archives Nationales, DXXIX 88

[18] *Discours des députés des Juifs des provinces...prononcé à la Barre de l'Assemblée* (repr. Paris, 1968).

[19] Records of Hourwitz's annual gift exist for 1789, 1790, 1791 and 1792. See Archives Nationales, AR 47 and 48. Hourwitz appears to have been the only employee of the Bibliothèque Royale to contribute in this manner. He

While the National Assembly promised the Ashkenazic deputies future discussion of the situation of the Jews, Hourwitz's act of revolutionary patriotism received instant publicity.

Hardly two months passed before the question of the Jews was publicly addressed. After several days of debate (21–4 December) followed closely in most of the city's journals, the National Assembly had welcomed Protestants and actors as active citizens but had deferred settling the status of the Jews. Neither the biting logic of Robespierre (the French had both created and exaggerated the vices of the Jews) nor the eloquence of Clermont-Tonnerre (leave man's conscience free and welcome the Jews not as a nation but as individuals) dispelled the fears of the majority of deputies. Instead, De la Farre, Bishop of Nancy, cleverly wove together the question of citizenship and that of French nationality, refusing the former on the basis of the Jews' presumed unwillingness and inability to assume the latter. France could not and should not admit to its family, De la Farre argued, 'a tribe whose religion, customs, physical and moral regulations differ profoundly from those of all other people: a tribe whose eyes turn incessantly toward a homeland which will one day reunite all its dispersed members and which perforce cannot commit itself to the land in which it dwells'.[20]

De la Farre grasped the central dilemma for both Jews and non-Jews. Were the Jews in France merely distinguished by different religious beliefs or were they a people whose 'native land' made them permanent foreigners in their present residence? Religious nonconformity could no longer be used to deny the Jews rights of citizenship — although Abbé Maury and others would continue to argue so — but estrangement from the nationhood of France certainly could. The *Chronique de Paris*, in a front-page article, turned for rebuttal to Hourwitz and urged its readers to purchase his *Apologie*, 'whose acquisition is indispensable to those who would wish to have clear ideas about this nation so disparaged and so poorly judged'.[21]

Hourwitz's retort to De la Farre, found in the *Apologie*, argued that the Jews were foreigners neither by nature nor by their religion but only as a result of the injustice of regarding them as such:

---

continued to earn the same salary of 800 livres a year throughout the early years of the Revolution; he obviously did not receive any additional income, since his taxes during this period were extremely low.

[20] *Opinion de M. l'eveque de Nancy, député de Lorraine sur l'admissibilité des Juifs à la plénitude de l'état civil, et des droits de Citoyens actifs* (repr. Paris, 1968).

[21] *Chronique de Paris*, 3 Jan. 1790.

Grant them the rights of citizenship and you will see that they are French just like all other subjects of the kingdom. It is true that they do not believe they will remain permanently in the country they inhabit and that they await the arrival of a Messiah who will re-establish them in Palestine, but they await death with even more certitude and this does not prevent them or for that matter anyone from sowing and planting wherever permitted.[22]

The debates in the National Assembly could not be left unanswered. On 28 January 1790 the Sephardim of Bordeaux and Bayonne, having called attention to past privileges, won their enfranchisement along with an explicit acknowledgement that citizenship for the Jews of the south-west could in no way predetermine the case of the Jews of eastern France. On the same day the Assembly received a 107-page 'Pétition des Juifs établis en France'. Signed by the Ashkenazic leadership of the east and Paris, the 'Pétition' bore the passion and eloquence of the young lawyer Jacques Godard. And on the very same day as well, the General Assembly of the Paris Commune admitted a deputation of the Jewish nation led by Godard. He had come to request from the revolutionaries a certificate attesting the worthy behaviour of the Jews of their city. You will not hesitate to grant them this certificate, Godard assured the deputies in a speech which would resound in all sixty districts and the numerous journals of the city,

> when you realize that but of 500 Jews in Paris, there are more than 100 who are enrolled in the National Guard and who sacrifice all their time, all their zeal, everything for the defence of the Constitution; when you know that in the midst of the deputies whom I have the honour to present to you is the famous Hourwitz, author of an excellent work crowned by the Society of Metz, interpreter of languages at the Bibliothèque du Roi, who, having as his whole fortune 900 livres [sic] and finding this too considerable, has just made a patriotic gift of one quarter of this sum...[23]

Moved by Godard's impassioned address, Abbé Mulot, President of the Commune, turned to the assembled Jews. 'The distance of your

---

[22] Hourwitz, *Apologie des Juifs*, p. 77.
[23] *Discours prononcé le 28 Janvier 1790 par M. Godard* (repr. Paris, 1968).

religious opinions from the truths that we profess as Christians can not prevent us, as men, from bringing ourselves nearer to you, and, if mutually we believe each other to be in error, . . . we are nevertheless able to love one another.'[24] Voltaire called himself tolerant, the *Courier de Provence* would subsequently remark, but he could have learned something from Abbé Mulot.[25]

During the next month, Godard took his delegation to each district in Paris as he and they tirelessly requested support for the Jews of France. Zalkind Hourwitz, Polish Jew and French revolutionary, was present, testimony to the integrity, honesty and patriotism of the Jews; present also were many of the arguments that he had publicized in his *Apologie*. Hourwitz and the revolutionaries of Paris had joined their causes.

The district of Carmelites — the home of Godard as well as the majority of the Jews of Paris — was the first to demand equality for the Jews. Soon the other districts followed suit, each emphasizing the patriotism of the Jews, their commitment to France and the justice of their struggle to obtain recognition by the Assembly.[26] But the deputies wavered as the enemies of Jewish emancipation issued dire warnings. And Hourwitz's patience was strained as Abbé Maury promised a memoir defending permanent exclusion of the Jews.

'In awaiting the publication of your memoir,' Hourwitz wrote to Abbé Maury in the pages of the *Chronique de Paris* and the *Courrier de Paris*,

> to which you defy us to respond, I defy you to reconcile the intolerant, impious Abbé with the Abbé Maury state pensioner and self-styled grand defender of the Catholic religion. I can only explain your conduct by assuming that you are ignorant of the principles of your religion. Learn them. They reduce themselves to the following: *love your neighbour as yourself, your country more than your gain and consider as brother* Zalkind Hourwitz, Jew.[27]

[24] *Réponse de M. d'Abbé Mulot*, ibid.

[25] *Courier de Provence*, 25 Feb. 1790. A deputation of the Commune had presented the distilled essence of the districts' reports to the National Assembly. As President of the Commune, Abbé Mulot had addressed the assembled deputies.

[26] The district of Mathurins, however, was a notable exception in refusing to support full rights for Jews.

[27] *Chronique de Paris*, 4 May 1790. In the *Courrier de Paris*, Hourwitz changed the final line to read '. . . and consider the Jews as your brother'.

Hourwitz's ire, however, hardly confined itself to the major foe of Jewish emancipation. Ostensibly criticizing gambling-houses, which he hated every bit as much as the practice of duelling, he could not resist castigating — in the graphic and sardonic style of the revolutionary journalists — the deputies of the National Assembly:

It is astonishing that the National Assembly has adjourned the business of Jews of all colours and men of colour of all religions, while it lets the directors and secretaries of gambling-casinos enjoy all the rights of citizenship. To be a citizen and even a legislator in this country of equality and liberty, it suffices to be the owner of a white foreskin and to have just enough honesty to avoid being hanged.[28]

The National Assembly slowly cut away at the disabilities of the Jews. Over and over again, the Paris Commune publicized its support for the Jews while Hourwitz satirized their enemies in his friends' journals. Sometimes he was joined by fellow Jews; they too used the journals to denounce those who stood in the way of full civil rights for them. And they contributed their pieces to the same journals — the *Journal de Paris*, the *Chronique de Paris* and the *Courrier de Paris*. But they rarely signed their names, often wrote only one article, and almost never departed from a straightforward approach. Like Hourwitz, they too resided in the capital — hardly surprising, since the Jews of Paris remained the most aware of contemporary events, the most radical in their political convictions and, except for the Sephardim of the south-west and the very rich syndics of eastern France, the only ones able to understand and write in French.

Finally, on the eve of the dissolution of the Assembly to make way for a newly elected legislative body, Adrien Du Port, deputy of the nobility of Paris, stood and demanded full rights for the Jews. He argued that freedom of religion permitted no distinction in the political rights of citizens because of their faith. A single voice resisted — the Alsatian Reubell — as the rest of the deputies tacitly agreed that to speak against Du Port's proposal was to fight the Constitution itself. Twenty-five months of agitation, discussions and debate ended in the full emancipation of the Jews (the decree of 27 September 1791 became law on 13 November). Throughout the next few months, Jews in the villages and cities would take the required civil oath, sometimes individually, often collectively. By the spring of 1792, the

[28] *Courrier des LXXXIII Départements*, 24 Jan. 1791.

Jews of France had officially renounced all previous 'privileges' and 'exceptions'.

Hourwitz now turned his attention to issues other than citizenship for the Jews. He wrote articles advocating protection of the rights of foreigners, support for the war against 'despots', and preservation of the Revolution from both Marat and Louis XVI. He once again publicly announced a patriotic contribution (this time omitting from his signature any reference to being either Jewish or a foreigner) and buttressed his defence of the war with Molière's sarcasm and an abridged version of the Ten Commandments.[29]

Soon, however, the journals to which Hourwitz contributed and the friends with whom he worked — Antoine Gorsas in particular — lost their voices and often their lives.[30] Hourwitz understandably resorted to silence as well as to a humiliating poverty, his position at the Bibliothèque Nationale (the former Bibliothèque Royale) having been abolished. Not until the Directory would he once again resume his role as journalist. Then he would address himself, in good *idéologue* fashion, to plans for improvement, appending his signature to proposals to prevent thefts, construct fire escapes, feed the poor (which quite often included himself) and educate the Parisians by renaming their streets and *quartiers*.[31] He would concern himself with things Jewish only when he saw a threat — either in law or in political philosophy — to equal rights for the Jews.[32]

Hourwitz would never regain the financial security he enjoyed during the early years of the Revolution. In a poignant letter in the autumn of 1799 to the Minister of the Interior, requesting consideration for the newly vacant chair in Hebrew and Syriac at the Collège de France, Hourwitz suggested that, if the position were already filled, he would be happy to return to his post at the Bibliothèque Nationale, where, he assured the Minister, he was often seen by men of letters. And, if this were also unavailable, he added, anticipating the Alliance Israélite Universelle of half a century later, perhaps he could be sent to Egypt to establish a French school 'among my co-religionists'.[33]

---

[29] *Patriote français*, 11 May 1792.

[30] Hourwitz's friends were generally associated with the Girondins and thus either fell to the guillotine or resorted to self-imposed exile from the city.

[31] The *idéologues* were those writers, scientists and philosophers of the late eighteenth century who, returning to the Enlightenment, sought both to vindicate and implement its main tenets.

[32] See for example *Journal de Paris*, 27 Oct. 1797; and *Ami des lois*, 11 June 1798.

[33] Archives Nationales, F 17 13556, dossier 36

In contrast to the revolutionary years, when barriers and privileges crumbled, Hourwitz now faced a restrictive world of a different sort. He never would have been able to obtain the position at the Collège de France, not only because it had in fact already been filled, and there was an insiders' network to which he had no access, but also because he was Jewish. Only in 1864 would the position be offered to a Jew, ironically also an employee of the Bibliothèque Nationale. But even the brilliant Solomon Munk would cause conflict and controversy among the members of the Collège. Some demanded to know how Professor Ernst Renan could be dismissed because he doubted the divinity of Jesus Christ and then be replaced by a man who denied it.[34]

Hourwitz remained frustrated in his appeal for useful employment; he never, however, abandoned the goals which had sustained him since the last years of the *ancien régime*. As in the past, however, he eschewed the position of the Jewish establishment. Even more, he defiantly stood apart.

In his eloquent and impassioned *Lettre d'un citoyen* (1791), Berr Isaac Berr sought to assure the religiously observant among his co-religionists that with the civil oath they renounced only their servitude. He explained; 'It is thus necessary my dear brothers to understand this truth, that, as long as we do not change our customs, our habits, in short our total education, we cannot hope to obtain the esteem of our fellow citizens.'[35] Berr Isaac Berr continued by outlining the educational, linguistic and professional changes necessary to make the Jews — or, more precisely, their children — respected and worthy Frenchmen. Many of the changes — for example, vocational diversification, education in the humanities and sciences, and linguistic assimilation — had been proposed decades earlier by Mendelssohn and the Berlin maskilim and had also found their way into Hourwitz's prize-winning essay.

But Hourwitz could never adopt the deferential style of Berr Isaac Berr. And when he was moved to righteous indignation on behalf of his people, he made sure that it was on non-Jews that he placed the onus. 'It is not up to us', he had written to the proselytizing Literary Society of Amsterdam, 'to justify our faithfulness to a religion whose antiquity and divinity you yourselves acknowledge; rather it is up to

[34] Ibid.

[35] *Lettre d'un citoyen membre de la ci-devant communauté des Juifs de Lorraine, à ses confrères, à l'occasion du droit de citoyen actif, rendu aux Juifs par le décret du 28 Septembre 1791* (repr. Paris, 1968).

you to justify to us your innovations and your desertion of our synagogue.'[36] Likewise, in the midst of the revolutionary debates, he had announced in the *Chronique de Paris*, 'Behold the men whom one seeks to deprive of the rights of man. And why? Because, having been burdened by taxes and deprived of the freedom to exercise most legitimate professions, they are found to include in their number some individuals who prefer to devote themselves to usury rather than to become highway thieves.'[37]

Hourwitz appeared at his most indignant, however, in June 1798. A Swiss orator had explained to his legislature that a man who would neither drink nor eat with him, who could not give his daughter in marriage to him, and who separated himself from all other men, could not be his fellow citizen. The *Patriote français* had agreed with this argument. Hourwitz responded in an article in the *Ami des lois*:

> One is reminded of the rantings of Abbé Maury against the Jews; they have just been repeated by M. Huber to the Swiss Assembly; he wishes to have the Jews contribute to all public charges but he contests granting them the rights of man and citizen on the pretext that their religion prevents them from eating with and marrying others. If the *Patriote français* were still edited by the *philosophe* Brissot, he would have found the motion by M. Huber very absurd, even in agreeing with its premises; for it would be necessary to deny citizenship not only to Jews, but also to Muslims, Quakers, Moravians and all other religious groups who do not marry outside of their faith and who abstain as well from certain foods. It would also be necessary to exclude former nobles who avoid commerce and marriage with former commoners. It would be necessary, finally, to exclude M. Huber himself, who would surely not give his daughter to the first in line or admit him to his table.[38]

Hourwitz's style, then, differed dramatically from that of the Jewish leaders. Much to their annoyance, moreover, he would use this same caustic tone when discussing them or describing the rabbis' recourse to excomunication.[39] But a more striking difference between

---

[36] Archives Nationales, 154 AP II 136.

[37] *Chronique de Paris*, 22 Feb. 1790.

[38] *Ami des lois*, 11 June 1798.

[39] In response to a request from the Minister of Cults in 1805 concerning the means of reconciling the interests of the religious leaders with those of

Hourwitz and the leadership lay in his determination to reject a paradigm of esteem and worthiness. Allergic to any assertion of the superiority of the non-Jewish world, or to Jewish deference to this notion, he found equally intolerable the re-establishment of communal control over the lives of individual Jews. Thus he sought to construct a new and improved world, one in which reason prevailed and mutual understanding led to mutual acceptance. In the final years of his life, Hourwitz devoted himself to this task — first by constructing a universal language (*Polygraphie*, 1801[40]), then by attempting to uncover the origin and nature of languages (*Origine des langues*, 1808), and finally by developing a system for writing as quickly as one spoke (*Lacographie*, 1811).

Throughout the century, philosophers, *philosophes* and the learned had attempted to probe the origins of language and thereby also the source of religious belief. Theories as diverse as those of Rousseau, de Brosses, La Metrie and Turgot all called attention to the dilemma of how man could become civilized without language, and, conversely, how language and speech could emerge from an uncivilized, even savage, human. Each had his answer or explanation; none gained more prominence than the prize-winning *Treatise on the Origin of Language* by Johann Gottfried Herder. Hourwitz's *Origine des langues* clearly belongs to this generation; he may well have been in Berlin when Herder submitted his essay, and certainly was familiar with the discussion in Moses Mendelssohn's *Jerusalem*.[41]

Hourwitz's determination to construct a universal language, while harking back to similar attempts in the seventeenth century, reflected too a renewed contemporary interest in the matter. His *pasigraphie* was one of many such proposals discussed by members of the Classe des Sciences Morales et Politiques of the Institut de France. Hourwitz

---

the faithful, Hourwitz once again castigated the rabbis (Archives Nationales, F19 11030). His attitudes undoubtedly kept him from participating in the Assembly of Notables or the Sanhedrin convened by Napoleon (1806–7), although his advice was sought by government ministers.

[40] Zalkind Hourwitz, *Polygraphie ou l'art de correspondre à l'aide d'un dictionnaire, dans toutes les langues, même dans celles dont on ne possède pas seulement les lettres alphabétiques* (Paris, An IX [1801]).

[41] In his *Jerusalem*, Mendelssohn describes the origin of language as a process in which man seeks to attach concepts to perceptible signs — tr. Allan Arkush (Hanover, NH, and London, 1983), p. 105. At the same time, however, Mendelssohn accepted the biblical view — which Hourwitz explicitly rejected — that God addressed man in Hebrew.

himself appeared before this prestigious body to discuss the implications of his completed *Polygraphie*, and in July 1801 the Accademia delle Scienze Dell' Istituto de Bologna devoted part of a session to it.[42]

Hourwitz's three monographs and an essay on the 'influence of habit on the faculty of thinking', attuned as they were to centuries of investigation and exploration, drew additional meaning and purpose from his personal experiences. An isolated Polish Jew speaks, seeking an escape from 'embarrassment', a refuge from linguistic estrangement, and dignity for himself, his co-religionists and mankind. Uncharacteristically, Hourwitz presents his vision of the future in symbolic fashion. The reader finds in the conclusion of the main part of *Polygraphie* a delicately drawn mantelpiece on which rests a globe, a book, a manuscript, a musical instrument and a caduceus. Hourwitz imagined a universe without divisions, ruled with justice, and surrounded by works of art, science and literature.

On Monday, 10 February 1812, at 10 o'clock in the morning, Michel Véron, justice of the peace, arrived at 25 Rue des Vieux Augustins. Hourwitz had suffered an attack of apoplexy two days earlier. His possessions remained under seal. Without heirs—Hourwitz had remained a bachelor — his property reverted to the state. Soon thereafter, a few torn items of clothing, a worn straw mattress with an equally worn wool coverlet, a library which included French, Hebrew, German, Portuguese, Italian and Latin grammar books, numerous dictionaries, the Hebrew Bible and the New Testament, and unsold copies of *Origine des langues*, *Polygraphie* and *Lacographie* were sold at auction.[43]

Hourwitz had explained that he entered the Metz contest because he believed that he could be useful, if not as advocate, then at least as witness. For us, too, Hourwitz is witness. Through him we hear the frustrations and impatience of an East European Jew. His criticisms of the rabbis and his disdain of the leadership travelled with him from his village in Poland, only to be given new import, if perhaps less validity, when expressed in his adopted home. Hourwitz, who had emancipated himself from ignorance and superstition, had neither respect nor understanding for the timidity and deference of his

---

[42] Minutes of the Institut de France, Classe des Sciences Morales et Politiques; Accademia delle Science dell'Istituto de Bologna, Registro degli Atti dal 1789 al 1804, TIT I.

[43] Archives de Paris, DQ[10] 1424, dossier 1660.

Westernized co-religionists. Yet he received from the Jews of Berlin a vision for his people which also gave meaning to his own life.

Unlike his compatriate Solomon Maimon, Hourwitz did not become an intellectual vagabond. Nor did he contemplate conversion. The Revolution of 1789 offered an alternative. Because he joined the legacy of Jewish life in Eastern Europe with the intellectual weapons of the West, he understood that choice. Even more, he embraced it as his own.

Hourwitz was a revolutionary, polemicist and utopian, not a reformer. He worried little about details of implementation, proudly rejected 'metaphysical' concerns, and placed his faith in reason, education and universal progress. Equal rights for the Jews became his personal commitment. But he never bartered the self-esteem of his people for their political rights as individuals. He was, however, all too willing to criticize publicly their leaders, their rabbis and their traditions. And, if he understood less well what to expect from the future than what to reject from the past, he also affirmed an abiding freedom to be different.

5

Preacher, Teacher, Publicist: Joseph Wolf and the Ideology of Emancipation

DAVID SORKIN

There are odd junctures in history when people of middling ability come to the fore. The revolutionary and Napoleonic era was such a juncture in Jewish history, especially in Germany. The intellectual leaders in the decades after Moses Mendelssohn's death (1786) were not his equals but epigones of mediocre talent and prosaic character.[1] Yet the tumult of the era goaded them into actions of which, a few years before, truly gifted men had only dared to dream. Joseph Wolf (1762–1826), for example, helped to formulate an ideology and found the media that were to serve the German-Jewish middle classes for the better part of the nineteenth century. But this achievement left him substantially unchanged: he remained meek, modest, impecunious, and at heart a conservative maskil.

Wolf was born in the village of Sandersleben in the duchy of Anhalt-Dessau in eastern Germany. This was one of the four duchies that comprised the ancient Upper Saxon principality of Anhalt, a region of some 250 square miles which, made fertile by the waters of a number of rivers (Elbe, Mulde, Wipper), was known in the eigh-

---

[1] Salo Baron made this point in his 'Moses Cohen Belinfante: A Leader of Dutch-Jewish Enlightenment'. *Historia Judaica*, 5, 1 (Apr. 1943), pp. 1–2. For France see Frances Malino, 'From Patriot to Israelite: Abraham Furtado in Revolutionary France'. in Jehuda Reinharz and Daniel Swetschinski (eds), *Mystics, Philosophers and Politicans: Essays in Jewish Intellectual History in Honor of Alexander Altmann* (Durham, NC, 1982), pp. 213–48. On the figures in Germany see Michael A. Meyer, *The Origins of the Modern Jew* (Detroit, 1967), pp. 115–43; and David Sorkin, *The Transformation of German Jewry, 1780–1840* (New York, 1987), pp. 124–34.

teenth century for its wool, fruit, grains, culinary herbs and tobacco.[2] Substantial Jewish settlement in Anhalt, as in so many of the German territories, was relatively recent. Although Jews had resided in the ancient principality as early as the fourteenth century, and traces of Jewish settlement can be found for the following three centuries, it was not until the late seventeenth century that a combination of geography and politics led to the establishment of a Jewish community.

After the Thirty Years War, the rulers of the myriad German territories adopted broadly mercantilist policies in an effort to rebuild their disrupted, and often shattered, economies. These policies included the admission of colonists who could promote trade, finance and industry. Since the available colonists were often either exiled Huguenots or Jews, mercantilism entailed a degree of religious toleration. In addition, the rulers often engaged the services of a wealthy Jew to improve the state's finances.[3]

Prince Johann Georg I of Anhalt-Dessau adopted both these policies. During the Thirty Years War, Jews had begun to settle in villages such as Sandersleben. This was probably because of the duchy's proximity to Leipzig (some 30 miles), a city that hosted a renowned fair Jews had long attended but which would not allow them permanent residence. In 1672 the Prince confirmed the settlements already in existence by issuing an edict permitting Jews to reside in Anhalt-Dessau. By 1685 some twenty-five Jewish families were living in Dessau, and more were in surrounding villages. In that year Moses Wulff (d. 1729), a descendant of the famous rabbi Moses Isserles, settled in Dessau and became the Court Jew. Wulff reorganized the currency, established postal and transportation services, funded the army and managed the Prince's estates and the collection of fees. The Jews were granted permission to build a synagogue in 1687 (26 November), and with that the modern settlement of Jews had begun.[4]

Little is known about Wolf's early years except that he was born into a humble family of teachers and thus experienced the mixture of bookishness and poverty typical of the maskilim and their successors.

---

[2] See the article 'Anhalt' in *Grosses vollständiges universal Lexicon* 64 vols (Halle and Leipzig, 1732–50), vol. 2, pp. 314–15.

[3] On mercantilism and the Jews see Jonathan Israel, *European Jewry in the Age of Mercantilism, 1550–1750* (Oxford, 1985).

[4] On Dessau and Moses Wulff see Max Freudenthal, *Aus der Heimat Moses Mendelssohns* (Berlin, 1900); and Ernst Walter, *Die Rechtstellung der israelitischen Kultusgemeinden in Anhalt* (Halle, 1934), pp. 3–10.

His father, Joseph Feibusch, a native of Dessau, struggled to support his young family from private tuition and died in the year Joseph was born. His mother, Malka (1741–1811), married another teacher, Mordechai Gumpel ben Abraham (d. 1799), with whom she moved to Dessau and had one more son. Wolf's early education was marked by his promise. At the age of four Wolf reportedly startled his teacher by asking a question about Hebrew spelling that resisted easy explanation.[5] After initial instruction in Dessau, he was given into the care of a paternal uncle who tutored gifted children. Having completed his preparatory Jewish education, celebrated by his Bar Mitzvah in 1775, Wolf began to attend the 'Yeshivah of Forty Students' in Berlin. In addition to his obvious promise, Wolf's education was also marked by his exposure to the influence of the Haskalah. A few words on the character and development of the Haskalah are therefore in order.

The Haskalah is generally dated from the 1770s and 1780s, when it emerged as a public movement. Yet it would be inaccurate to consider it merely a fledgling, or pale imitation in Hebrew, of the Berlin Enlightenment, which was then at its height. The Haskalah borrowed its forms and categories from the German Enlightenment, but its contents were largely derived from Jewish sources. This synthesis was possible because the Haskalah had had a long period of gestation in the revival of those traditions of Jewish scholarship which promoted a reasonable or rationalist understanding of Judaism. Central to such a view were Maimonidean philosophy and legal (halakhic) interpretation. But it also included an interest in those subjects that fostered the literal — as opposed to the mystical or casuistic — interpretation of Bible and Talmud: Hebrew language and grammar on the one side, astronomy, mathematics and geography on the other. The early Haskalah thus represented a renaissance of Judaism compatible with, and perfectly capable of assimilating, European science and philosophy. One might therefore designate the early stage (*c*.1700–60) an 'Orthodox Haskalah'.[6]

[5] On Wolf's early years see Phöbus Phillipson, *Biographische Skizzen* 2 vols (Leipzig, 1864), vol. 1, pp. 132–42; and Max Freudenthal, 'Ein Geschlecht von Erziehern', *Zeitschrift für die Geschichte der Juden in Deutschland*, 6 (1935), pp. 1. 156–7.

[6] Isaac Eisenstein-Barzilay, 'The Background of the Berlin Haskalah', in Joseph L. Blau (ed.), *Essays on Jewish Life and Thought Presented in Honor of Salo Baron* (New York, 1959), pp. 185–8; and Sorkin, *The Transformation of German Jewry*, pp. 41–62.

Dessau played a central role in the Orthodox Haskalah, and it was to be significant throughout Wolf's life, especially since he was to become a principal spokesman for the Dessau tradition in the early nineteenth century. Dessau's tradition was largely initiated by Moses Wulff. Like a number of other Court Jews, Moses Wulff had used his fortune to subsidize a traditional house of study (*Klaus*) but in addition took the unusual step of linking it to a Hebrew press (1695). The Wulffian press was active for over forty years publishing works on Hebrew grammar, science and geography, an effort that culminated in the republication of Maimonides' two major works: his code of law, the *Mishneh Torah* (1739), and his philosophical *magnum opus*, *The Guide for the Perplexed* (1742).[7] The *Klaus* attracted a succession of scholars and teachers who promoted study in the spirit of the Orthodox Haskalah. Rabbi David Fränkel, for example, who served Dessau from 1731 to 1743, published a famous commentary on the Palestinian Talmud that showed strong Maimonidean influence. He initiated and arranged funding for publication of Maimonides' *Mishneh Torah*, and gave tacit approval to the republication of the *Guide*. He was Moses Mendelssohn's teacher, and it was he whom the young Moses followed to Berlin.[8] A lesser figure in this Dessau tradition was R. Wolf Dessau (1751–84). One of Joseph Wolf's teachers, he had been educated in Polish and German yeshivot yet taught himself science and philosophy. His most important work was a commentary that aimed to elucidate the text of the book of Job.[9]

What Wolf imbibed from his teachers is impossible to determine. But his intellectual odyssey was thoroughly characteristic of the Haskalah in being virtually internal to the Jewish textual tradition, at least until its final stages. In keeping with the experience of earlier maskilim, Wolf acquired familiarity with Hebrew literature and developed an enduring attachment to the Hebrew language. His intellectual peregrination began when he started to study the Bible and

[7] Freudenthal, *Aus der Heimat Moses Merdelssohns*, pp. 219–22, 259; and Azriel Shochat, *Im Hilufei Tekufot* (Jerusalem, 1960), p. 207.

[8] Max Freudenthal, 'R. David Fränckel', in M. Brann and F. Rosenthal (eds), *Gedenkbuch zur Erinnerung an David Kaufmann* (Breslau, 1900), pp. 575–6 and 588–9.

[9] Max Freudenthal, 'R. Wolf Dessau', in *Festschrift zum siebzigsten Geburtstage Martin Philippsons* (Leipzig, 1916), pp. 184–212. The commentary on Job was *Pesher Davar* (Berlin, 1777).

the medieval exegetes in addition to the official curriculum of Talmud and commentaries. If the Bible awakened Wolf's aesthetic sensibilities, and became the focus for his love of Hebrew, the exegetes and the literature of the Middle Ages introduced him to a new period of Hebrew language and literature. In offering fragmentary glimpses of the medieval Jewish world, the exegetes excited his curiosity about the religious philosophy and poetry of that age. These, in turn, served as a gateway to the rationalist tradition in Judaism, in which systematic philosophy, whether Aristotelian or Neoplatonic, but always with Maimonides at the centre, was reconciled with religious belief. This reconciliation was to be crucial for Wolf's intellectual development, since he was to become a consistent advocate of the perfect compatibility of Judaism with science and philosophy. The medieval rationalists led him to contemporary exponents of that tradition, the maskilim and especially Naphtali Herz Wessely (1725–1805). And it was contemporary Hebrew literature, because of its reliance on German and French models, which served finally as the bridge to European culture.[10]

As far as can be ascertained, Wolf's odyssey was autodidactic. Despite the Dessau tradition and the Orthodox Haskalah, he had no formal instruction or teacher to guide him. He benefited from the experience of earlier maskilim and had a few friends at the yeshivah to aid him. A brief meeting with Wessely and the luminous example of Moses Mendelssohn inspired him. But by and large he was on his own. Although it had become increasingly common, since the beginning of the century, for students to make this intellectual trek, Wolf and his contemporaries, those born beetween 1760 and 1790, were to be virtually the last in Germany to do so.[11] The foundation of a new type of Jewish school, as well as the option of attending state schools, made the autodidactic journey of the eighteenth-century German yeshivah student the preserve of his nineteenth-century East European counterpart.

The material circumstances of a yeshivah student were hardly enviable. A student who attended the yeshivah in 1802, some twenty years after Wolf, described the dependence on a meagre stipend and occasional hand-outs:

[10] Phillipson, *Biographische Skizzen*, vol. 1, pp. 142–3,
[11] Ibid., pp. 144–5; Sorkin, *The Transformation of German Jewry*, pp. 124–39.

In Berlin at that time there was a Yeshivah of Forty Students. The students attended lectures in Talmud given by the three appointed [halakhic] judges ... The forty students received only two talers a month from the funds of the Talmud—Torah, but had some other income besides. In addition to the forty students there were another ten. When one of the forty left, one of the ten took his place. The ten could attend lectures, but they did not receive a stipend. But, since there were many pious people in Berlin at the time who set great store in the study of Talmud, the forty students as well as the supernumerary ten did not fare badly. Though they learned little, if they were able to fawn and appear sanctimonious they received support from the pious. There were also many private prayer chambers where morning and evening devotion was held. Since there had to be a quorum each time, students were retained by the owners of such prayer chambers and each time usually received twelve krone ...[12]

Wolf remained at the yeshivah in Berlin until he turned eighteen (1780), when he accepted a position as a tutor. In so doing he followed the traditions of both his family and the Haskalah, since the early maskllim were by and large employed as tutors or as clerks, or a combination of the two. His first situation, in the village of Feierswald in Brandenburg, left him little time for his own studies, though he did devote his spare moments to Mendelssohn's recently published Bible translation. In 1782 Wolf accepted what proved to be a more congenial post as tutor to a wealthy family in the neighbouring village of Wriezen on the Oder. The position offered both physical comfort and the leisure to pursue his own interests. He assiduously studied the work of his two idols: Mendelssohn's translation provided him with a model for German, and Wessely's epic poem, the *Mossaid*, one for Hebrew. From 1789 to 1796 he worked as a tutor in his home town of Sandersleben. Although he once again found himself in reduced circumstances, he did manage to read some contemporary German literature, including a mainstay of the Enlightenment, Lessing, and some writers representing the new sentimental and romantic sensibility, Klopstock and Goethe, as well as Mendelssohn's

[12] From the memoir of Jacob Adam (b. 1789) in Monika Richarz, *Jüdisches Leben in Deutschland: Selbstzeugnisse zur Sozialgeschichte* (Nördlingen, 1976), pp. 117—18.

political treatise *Jerusalem* (1783), and his last philosophical work, *Morning Hours* (1785).[13]

In 1796 Wolf married one Frädel Markus, the granddaughter of a shoemaker. This was a marriage of love. Wolf had to give up his position in Sandersleben and set up house, despite a lack of means. The couple decided to move to Dessau. Their first child, a son, was born there in 1797, and they were to remain in Dessau the rest of their lives. In Dessau, Wolf was to depart from the patterns set by earlier maskilim, however imperceptibly at first, and help articulate an ideology of emancipation. Yet he did so in keeping with the Dessau tradition which reconciled European culture with Judaism. Dessau was itself most conducive to this sort of reconciliation. The local authorities were on the whole benevolent. Typical of German governments at the time, Anhalt-Dessau pursued a policy of centralization in administration alongside mercantilism in economics that entailed an increasing encroachment on the autonomous powers of the Jewish community. Prince Leopold introduced new regulations for the Jews in 1764 and abrogated their juridical autonomy in 1774. Yet, in comparison to parts of Prussia, few harsh restrictions or burdensome taxation accompanied these changes.[14] At the same time, Dessau's location enabled its Jews to maintain their conciliatory tradition: Berlin was sufficiently distant (80 miles) and sufficiently different — as a large and growing garrison and Court boom town — to allow them to adopt only the positive elements of its Haskalah, while the Leipzig fair (30 miles) helped them to maintain their contacts with the Jews of Central and Eastern Europe. Finally, Dessau was the home of one of the German Enlightenment's showpieces, the Philanthropin School. Founded in 1774 by Johann Bernhard Basedow (1724–90), one of the Enlightenment's foremost pedagogues and educational philosophers, the school exemplified the goal of a 'natural' and 'reasonable' education. Basedow replaced rote learning with methods designed to develop all of a child's faculties: learning through play, and a practical orientation that emphasized the vernacular and technical subjects as well as providing for exercise. In addition, Basedow thought that education should be supervised solely by the state, and thus religious instruction in the school was non-denominational, being limited to those doctrines of 'natural religion' to which all faiths could allegedly subscribe. Although the Phil-

[13] Phillipson, *Biographische Skizzen*, vol. 1, pp. 142–7.
[14] Walter, *Die Rechtstellung*, pp. 10–12.

anthropin closed its doors after twenty years, it had an enduring impact. It persuaded the local authorities of education's significance, and Prince Leopold Franz soon thereafter sponsored a school for poor children.[15]

When Wolf arrived in Dessau, the community of approximately 1,000 Jews stood in obvious need of a school. This was evident from the fact that the local rabbi, Simha ben Zvi Hirsch of Halberstadt, had tried to initiate a reform of the three existing hederim (elementary schools) a decade before. His public call in 1785 led to the founding of a sort of Talmud–Torah, a heder somewhat more attentive to hygiene and pedagogy but which did not include secular subjects in its curriculum.[16] Wolf obviously had the requisite academic skills for founding a school. But he was a cautious and timid man who lacked initiative and the spirit of enterprise. He therefore persisted in familiar ways, setting himself up as a tutor of Hebrew, German and calligraphy, as well as writing letters on commission. When a new school did open in 1799, Wolf taught in it from the start.

The school was one of a number founded in the two decades surrounding the turn of the nineteenth century. The maskilim had asserted the importance of secular studies as complementary to and necessary for Jewish education, as well as for membership of 'mankind', the Enlightenment's ideal. Yet they did not succeed in founding schools before 1789, with the exception of the Berlin Free School, which a group of wealthy businessmen had established in 1778 for the poor children of the city. Only the radicalizing impact of the French Revolution, which resulted in the Jews' emancipation in France on the one side, and the German states' enlistment of education for political purposes on the other, led to the establishment of a series of schools: Breslau (1791), Hanover (1798), Dessau (1799), Sessen (1801), Frankfurt (1804), Wolfenbuttel (1807), Mainz (1814).[17]

The school in Dessau stood out among these in benefiting from a singular combination of community consensus and state support. The schools in Berlin and Breslau, for example, had been set up by militant maskilim who expected opposition and interference. The

---

[15] On the Philanthropin see *Studien über das Philanthropinum und die Dessauer Aufklärung*, Wissenschaftliche Beiträge der Martin-Luther-Universität (Halle-Wittenberg, 1970/3).

[16] Ludwig Horwitz, 'Geschichte der Herzoglichen Franzschule in Dessau, 1799–1849', *Mitteilungen des Vereins für anhaltsche Geschichte*, 6,4 (1893), pp. 504–5; and Mordekhai Eliav, *Ha-Hinukh ha-Yehudi bi-Germanya* (Jerusalem, 1961), pp. 87–9.

[17] Eliav, *Ha-Hinukh ha-Yehudi*, pp. 71–141.

founding of these schools presumed, and furthered, a rift between enlightened and traditional Jews. In Dessau, in contrast, the founders kept to the local tradition of moderation and sought support from all quarters. The 183 signatories to the 'Association for the Education of Youth' (Hinukh Neurim) desired a school which would balance religious and secular subjects while utilizing the sorts of pedagogical methods pioneered by the Philanthropin. The school opened in 1799; by 1801 the authorities had not only given it their support, regarding it as a welcome addition to their own efforts, but had also prevented competition by prohibiting the collective hiring (by two or more Jewish families) of private tutors.[18] The school's offering of religious subjects satisfied both maskilim and Orthodox parents (religion, ethics, Bible, Talmud, Hebrew); its secular subjects (German, arithmetic, French, geography, natural science) fulfilled the Haskalah's programme while also preparing students for the commercial occupations most of them would undertake. In 1804 an enterprising teacher opened a dormitory, and tuition-paying boarders from other parts of Germany (Hamburg, Posen, Dresden, Magdeburg) began to attend.[19] By 1809 the Dessau school had become the first of the new schools to serve as a general community institution. Rich and poor, pious, enlightened and indifferent all enrolled at the school, which was now heavily subsidized by community funds.

Wolf had a position at the school teaching German language, writing and reading.[20] Despite being the best-paid teacher at the school because of his age and experience, his financial worries and near-poverty were never alleviated. Wolf constantly sought other activities to supplement his income. In 1802 he became secretary to the organized Jewish community (*Gemeinde*), in which capacity he established a register of births and deaths (from 1811) and wrote memoranda on behalf of the community. A contemporary visitor described Wolf's domestic situation.

The entire family lived in one and the same room. His wife and children were there; he gave private lessons there, worked on his sermons and his writings, on petitions and other written

---

[18] Ludwig Horwitz, *Mitteilungen des Vereins für anhaltsche Geschichte*, 6, 4, p. 511, and 'Ein Bildungsverein am Ausgang des vorigen Jahrhunderts', *Allgemeine Zeitung des Judentums*, 61 (1897), p. 439.
[19] G. Salomon, *Lebensgeschichte des Hrn. Moses Philippsohn* (Dessau, 1814), p. 88.
[20] Horwitz, *Mitteilungen des Vereins für anhaltsche Geschichte*, 6, 4, p. 509.

documents for the Jewish community, all using a large rect-
angular table which simultaneously served as dinner, coffee and
work table. The furniture was most simple: the weak and always
sickly man had no sofa or easy chair on which he could relax.
Most of the linens were as a rule in the pawn shop.[21]

Mrs Wolf was rather inept as a housemistress, a tendency reportedly
aggravated by a weakness for coffee, which was then something of a
luxury. Wolf seemed to bear the situation with dignity and good
humour. A visitor reported, for example, that during a shockingly
spartan midday meal of buttered bread and ersatz coffee Wolf entertained himself with Kant's *Critique of Pure Reason*. In addition, Wolf
was known for his ready wit and ability to tell a story, skills he
was known to employ of an evening when working with his fellow
teachers.

Although teaching at the Franz School did not solve Wolf's financial
problems, it did significantly change his situation in other ways. The
existence of such schools marked a transition in the Haskalah from
theory to practice. The visionary programme for rehabilitating the
Jews was now being implemented in the key area of education. Such
a transition also entailed a change in status for the maskilim. The
school moved them from the precarious private position of tutor to
the ill-paid, but public, position of teacher. It likewise transferred
them from the periphery of the eighteenth-century autonomous
community to the centre of the emerging nineteenth-century voluntary
one. In addition, the school provided them with a locus for common
endeavour. The maskilim could co-operate in designing a curriculum, writing
textbooks, and related activities. [22]

In 1805, for example, Wolf collaborated with other teachers at the
Franz School in publishing a translation and commentary of the
Minor Prophets. This publication fell squarely in the Haskalah tradition. Since the Bible was the fount of Hebrew language, aesthetics
and morality, a proper understanding of it was central to the general
programme of a renaissance of Jewish culture. Mendelssohn's translation and commentary therefore appeared as one of the Haskalah's
towering achievements. Yet Mendelssohn had translated only the
Pentateuch; the other books remained.

Wolf followed Mendelssohn in rejecting the word-by-word Yiddish

[21] Philippson, *Biographische Skizzen*, vol. 1, p. 206; tr. in Meyer, *The
Origins of the Modern Jew*, p. 129
[22] Sorkin, *The Transformation of German Jewry*, pp. 131–4.

translations, which had been popular pedagogical devices from the late seventeenth century, and rendering the Bible into fluent idiomatic German printed in Hebrew letters.[23] He also aimed to make accessible the literal meaning of the text (*peshat*). His criterion in translation was 'that which is most reasonable' (*ha-yoter karov el ha-da'at*).[24] In a lengthy introduction he supplied the sorts of materials he thought would aid that literal understanding of the text: an account of the nature of prophecy in Israel, including the names and language of prophecy; a history of each prophetic book as well as a biography of the author; and a listing of relevant place names.

This introduction was typical of the biblical scholarship of religious enlighteners, both Jewish and non-Jewish, in that it was historical but not historicist: it recognized that the Bible had emerged in a distant and foreign setting that had to be elucidated, but did not attempt to restrict the Bible's validity. Wolf neither confined the Bible's message to a particular historical time nor dismantled the text into its historical components. Rather, he explicitly affirmed the authenticity of prophecy: 'for they are all the words of the living God, fruit of the spirit of prophecy, which flow through the soul of the prophets'.[25] Wolf's approach to the Bible, like so much of the Haskalah, drew heavily on the medieval rationalist tradition. He quoted Maimonides on the conditions of prophecy.[26] He used exegetes such as Rashi (eleventh-century), David Kimchi (thirteenth-century) and Ibn Ezra (twelfth-century), though he also felt free to diverge from them in establishing the text. In addition, on geographical and ethnographic issues he utilized non-Jewish sources or, as he called them, 'books of the sages of the nations' (*sifrei hakhmei ha-amim*). Yet Wolf's translation and commentary remained true to the Haskalah, and especially the conservative version of Wessely and Mendelssohn, in so far as it was intended to support traditional piety: 'and with all these we will desire to adhere to the tradition of our sages according to which we live and from which we will not depart'.[27]

---

[23] W. Staerk and A. Leitzmann, *Die jüdisch-deutschen Bibelübersetzungen* (Frankfurt am Main, 1923); and Werner Weinberg, 'Language Questions Relating to Moses Mendelssohn's Pentateuch Translation'. *Hebrew Union College Annual*, 55 (1984), pp. 197–242.

[24] *Sefer Minha Tehora, koleil Trei Asar* (Dessau, 1805), p. 4a. The volume was reprinted in Prague in 1835.

[25] Ibid., pp. 3a–b.

[26] Ibid., p. 4a.

[27] Ibid., p. 4b.

In the years immediately following the publication of the Minor prophets, Wolf also began to collaborate with his fellow teachers on projects of a different sort. The revolutionary era had encouraged the maskilim to found schools. The Napoleonic era brought the possibility of emancipation to Germany. In particular, after his victory at Austerlitz (December 1805), Napoleon eliminated the Holy Roman Empire and founded the Confederation of the Rhine (July 1806), in which French law prevailed. These events coincided with Napoleon's convocation in Paris of an assembly of Jewish notables and the subsequent Sanhedrin, which, in a grandiose manner, reaffirmed French Jewry's rights, though qualified by the so-called 'Infamous Decrees'. The Kingdom of Westphalia, founded in January 1808, introduced a communal structure on the French model, a 'Consistory', which immediately began to institute educational and religious reforms for its fully emancipated members.

By arousing an expectation of imminent emancipation, these events led Wolf to transform the Haskalah into an ideology of emancipation. What does this mean? From the inception of the serious discussion of emancipation in Germany in the concluding decades of the eighteenth century, emancipation had been conceived as a contract — namely, that the conferral of rights presupposed the Jews' regeneration. In Christian Wilhelm von Dohm's 1781 tract *On the Civic Amelioration of the Jews*, which largely determined the terms of the subsequent debate, 'amelioration' (*Verbesserung*) indicated both the granting of rights and the Jews' reciprocal regeneration. Napoleon's Assembly of Notables and Sanhedrin only reinforced such a notion by asking a series of questions designed to ascertain whether the Jews deserved rights. Yet the maskilim had adamantly resisted such a contract. Mendelssohn, representing the conservative maskilim, had argued in his political tract *Jerusalem* that emancipation must be given unconditionally. Like all people, the Jews merited emancipation on the basis of their natural rights. Even so radical a maskil as David Friedländer had asserted in 1793 that rights were the precondition for regeneration and not *vice versa*.[28] The Haskalah's Bible-based revival of the Hebrew language had manifestly developed as an expression of religious and cultural independence and not as part of an emancipation contract. Wolf took the bold step of accepting the prevalent notion of contract and merging it with the Haskalah tradition. That Wolf was able to do so without any apparent difficulty stemmed from the fact that he did not have to change his ideas. He retained his own

---

[28] Sorkin, *The Transformation of German Jewry*, pp. 23–8 and 63–77.

characteristic version of the Dessau tradition of the conservative Haskalah but gave it a radical turn by altering its context rather than its content.

The new context was the German-language media of the journal and the sermon. In 1805 Wolf began to give some of the first German-language sermons in the Dessau synagogue.[29] These were the exception in Central Europe. Unlike in Italy and England, where vernacular sermons were a longstanding practice among Sephardic Jews, in Central Europe the rule was the local rabbi's biannual Yiddish legal homily or the itinerant preacher's occasional hortatory one.[30] Wolf's sermons followed the best Enlightenment Protestant models of the time in their elevated diction, sombre tone and clearly demarcated three-or four-part structure. Here the religious Enlightenment, or at least its forms, seemed to have penetrated to the very heart of Judaism, the synagogue. Yet even in delivering vernacular sermons Wolf might well have thought himself faithful to Mendelssohn's example. Mendelssohn had written a handful of sermons in German, primarily for patriotic occasions, though someone else had delivered them, usually in Hebrew.[31]

In 1806 Wolf also helped to found the first German-language journal to be published by Jews in Germany, *Sulamith*. *Sulamith* was clearly heir to the Haskalah. It in large part imitated the Hebrew journal of the Haskalah, *Ha-Meassef* ('The Gatherer'; from 1784), adopting its format and range of topics: moral and religious subjects; translations of the Bible and other Jewish sources; reports on the customs and lives of various nations; and essays on technical subjects, especially commerce. Yet it differed fundamentally from *Ha-Meassef* in addressing a mixed Jewish and Gentile audience, rather than an exclusively Jewish one, and in attempting to promote the cause of Jewish emancipation.[32]

In the media of the sermon and the German-language journal, Wolf helped lay the foundations of a 'public sphere', the organs of

---

[29] *Allgemeine Zeitung des Judentums*, 51 (1887), p. 750.

[30] Alexander Altmann, 'The New Style of Preaching in Nineteenth-Century German Jewry,' in *Altmann (ed.), Studies in Nineteenth-Century Jewish Intellectual History* (Cambridge, Mass., 1964) pp. 65−116.

[31] Alexander Altmann, *Moses Mendelssohn: A Biographical Study* (University, Ala, 1973), p. 67−9.

[32] Siegfried Stein, "Die Zeitschrift 'Sulamith'", *Zeitschrift für die Geschichte der Juden in deutschland*, 7 (1937), pp. 193−226; and Sorkin, *The Transformation of German Jewry*, pp. 82−5, 90−1, 95, 98.

communication in which a collective identity and cultural–political consciousness could be created for the emerging German-Jewish middle classes. These organs of communication paralleled those of the German middle classes, and, alongside the dual-curriculum school, the temple or synagogue with a reformed service, and numerous associations, constituted the nascent voluntary German-Jewish community.[33]

In *Sulamith* and his sermons, Wolf marshalled his Haskalah ideals to support what became the central principle of emancipation: emancipation was a pedagogical process in which the Jews were to regenerate themselves in exchange for rights. As a pedagogue and the adherent of a fundamentally pedagogical movement, Wolf was no doubt at home with this idea. He managed, moreover, to espouse it without violating the Haskalah's independence. Wolf recapitulated the Haskalah's essential belief that a cultural revival was to develop from within Judaism itself, and especially from a recovery of its biblical heritage. Wolf wanted to keep that heritage pristine, vehemently protesting against the forced imposition of alien elements. The Jews should not abandon their own culture for European or German culture, but instead should take advantage of the possibilities offered by the new age of emancipation, in which 'Jew and man are no longer considered to be heterogeneous concepts',[34] to recover their true tradition of ethical and humane religiosity that had been distorted by centuries of persecution and obscurantism. What was required was that quintessentially maskilic idea that Wolf had first encountered in medieval Jewish philosophy, the synthesis of religion and reason.

Wolf argued for a 'reasonable and enlightened religiosity', asserting that the 'true value of mankind will first be recognized when reason and religion stand in heavenly alliance'.[35] German culture was not to replace Judaism, but to be enlisted as an agent of its renaissance. Wolf insisted that 'religion is the essential intellectual and moral necessity of the educated man'. Judaism is the source not only of ethics and morality, but of the Jews' very humanity: 'Fear God and observe his commandments; this is for all men.'[36] Wolf could there-

---

[33] Sorkin, *The Transformation of German Jewry*, pp. 79–138.

[34] 'Inhalt, Zweck und Titel dieser Zeitschrift', *Sulamith*, 1, 1 (1806), p. 6–7.

[35] 'Über die Vereinigung der Religion mit den Wissenschaften', *Sulamith*, 1, 2 (1806), p. 202.

[36] 'Über das Wesen, den Charakter und die Notwendigkeit der Religion', *Sulamith*, 1, 3 (1806), p. 317.

fore comfortably assign *Sulamith* a pedagogical function, declaring its *raison d'être* to be 'The development of the Jews' intensive educational ability'.[39] His pedagogical programme is a reiteration of the staples of the Haskalah. Secular knowledge, especially geography and history, are necessary to comprehend the Bible – the precise argument he had made in his introduction to the Minor Prophets – and geometry and astronomy to understand the Talmud. He even reached farther back in the Haskalah. He quoted a passage of midrash that had infuriated the rabbis when Wessely had used it in his tract *Divrei Shalom ve-Emet* ('Words of Peace and Truth'), the early manifesto of Haskalah: 'a pious scholar without knowledge is no better than an improperly slaughtered carcass'.[38] Yet Wolf enunciated this programme with an acute awareness of the emancipation contract. The Jews must 'dedicate their hearts' to the 'illustrious sovereigns' who 'restore to a humbled people their lost rights.'[39]

Wolf regarded his sermons as one means to effect the reforms he advocated in *Sulamith*. The sermon's purpose, he stated, was 'the ennoblement and completion of the human soul'. [40] The preacher was to train head and heart by revealing Judaism's ethical core. Thus, in a sermon delivered on Shavuot, the spring festival, Wolf asserted that, because the holiday had no outward ritual or symbol, it was eminently suited to a rediscovery of Judaism's true essence. 'To be sure, no religious image points to the origins of today's festival, no ceremony makes the memory of it tangible for us. Our divine service of today consists only in pure devotion, in the effusion of the heart and the elevation of the spirit', and, thus, 'it is perfectly suited to lead us to reflections which are commensurate with the dignity of man.'[41] In general Wolf adopted the Enlightenment's religio-pedagogical concept of 'edification' (*Erbauung*), transforming it into an instrument of emancipation.

Wolf gathered the best of his sermons into two volumes. When they appeared in 1812–13, they were the first volumes of published German sermons written and delivered by a Jew. Wolf's sermons inaugurated a veritable flood of sermonic literature, which continued unabated into the twentieth century. As early as the 1830s some observers were declaring the German-language sermon to be the most

---

[37] 'Inhalt, Zweck und Titel dieser Zeitschrift', *Sulamith*, 1, 1 (1806), p. 9.

[38] 'Über die Vereinigung der Religion mit den Wissenschaften', *Sulamith*, 1, 2 (1806), p. 256.

[39] 'Inhalt, Zweck und Titel dieser Zeitschrift', *Sulamith*, 1, 1 (1806), p. 11.

[40] *Sechs deutsche Reden*, 2 vols (Dessau, 1812–13), vol. 1 p. 30.

[41] Ibid., p. 2.

important of the abundant innovations aimed at rehabilitating Judaism and the Jews.[42] And by the 1840s the preacher had become a prominent figure in many urban and small-town communities.[43]

Despite his pioneering role in elaborating the ideology of emancipation and developing the rudiments of a public sphere, Wolf remained steadfast in his early allegiances and preoccupations. In 1808 he published a German translation in Hebrew letters of the book of Daniel.[44] At the same time as he was working on his sermons, he translated contemporary *belles-lettres* into Hebrew. This was a quintessentially maskilic enterprise, in that it aimed to prove the beauty of Hebrew by demonstrating its equality with European languages.[45] In successive issues of *Ha-Me'assef* in 1810, Wolf published his versions of two German poems. Both were typical Enlightenment products, the one concerned with an act of true philanthropy, while the other expressed the hope that the insatiable urge for wisdom would result in the ethical action that benefits mankind rather than in solipsistic pursuits such as sophistry and astrology.[46]

In the same year as Wolf translated the poems into Hebrew he did the same for his published sermons, asserting that the translations were for his 'compatriots' who did not yet know German.[47] Yet at first glance the crisp Hebrew versions seem startlingly different from the originals. A New Year's sermon concludes, 'mache unser Herz immer reiner und fester, unsern Geist immer aufgelärter und gebildeter, unsern Glauben immer sicherer und kindlicher' ('make our heart ever purer and firmer, our spirit ever more enlightened and developed, our belief ever surer and innocent'). The passage is rendered in Hebrew, *hazeik libeinu be-imrotekha, ve-haeir eineinu be-toratekha, ve-ameitz emunateinu be-kirbeinu* 'strengthen our hearts in your precepts, enlighten our eyes in your Torah, and strengthen our belief in our midst').[48] We should not suspect disingenuousness

---

[42] Ludwig Philippson, 'Volksbildung', *Israelitisches Predigt-und Schul-Magazin*, 1 (1834), p. 288.

[43] Sorkin, *The Transformation of German Jewry*, p. 131.

[44] *Sefer Daniel Meturgam be-Lashon Ashkenazi* (Dessau, 1808).

[45] Mendelssohn had translated contemporary English poetry i.e. Edward Young's *Night Thoughts*, in the *Kohelet Musar*, the Hebrew journal he published in 1758. See Altmann, *Moses Mendelssohn*, pp. 83–91.

[46] 'El ha-Hokhma', *Ha-Me'assef*, n. s., 2, 3 (1810), pp. 3–8; and 'Shir Sipuri', *Ha Me'assef*, n. s., 2, 4 (1810), pp. 45–51.

[47] *Sechs deutsche Reden*, vol. 1, p. ix.

[48] Ibid., p. 85, and Hebrew section, p. 47.

here. Though the German version does not mention the Torah, Wolf would not have thought that he had changed the sense of his words. The apparent discrepancy between the German original and the Hebrew translation points instead to the radicalizing context of the new German-language public sphere — the fact that thinking and writing in German could alter the implications of maskilic ideas.

Similarly indicative of the constancy of Wolf's outlook was his relationship to *Sulamith*. Although he had conceived the journal, written its statement of purpose and explained its title, he resigned after the first year. While the details of this resignation will probably never be known, it seems that he had both personal and policy conflicts with David Fränkel, the other founding co-editor, who was more enterprising, ambitious and politically radical. In 1810 Fränkel took the extreme step of changing the last words of the journal's subtitle, which had labelled it 'A Journal for the Promotion of Culture and Humanity within the Jewish Nation', to 'among the Israelites', an alteration which showed his willingness to implement the emancipation contract by adjusting Jewish self-definition.

Wolf's resignation from *Sulamith* did not mark a withdrawal from public activity. He continued to teach at the Franz School and to give sermons into the 1820s. In 1817 he co-authored a response to attacks on the Jews, Judaism and their already receding emancipation.[49] Together with Gotthold Salomon (b.1784), then a fellow teacher in Dessau and later a preacher in Hamburg, Wolf also compiled a series of texts drawn from the Bible, Talmud and rabbinic literature which were to show that Judaism was an ethical religion compatible with the Enlightenment and the demands of citizenship. Wolf and Salomon published the book themselves, and it sold well enough to go into a second printing.[50] This was one of the first instalments in the vast apologetic literature that German Jews would produce during the next century. In 1819 Wolf produced the first textbook of rabbinic Hebrew. Containing a grammar and a lexicon, this book contributed to the *Haskalah's* enterprise of restoring the Hebrew language in order to make available Judaism's textual heritage.[51]

Wolf had always been sickly, but in the early 1820s his health began to deteriorate. In 1824 he started to lose sight in one eye and travelled to Berlin to seek expert medical care. While the Berlin visit

---

[49] On Jewish emancipation and the Congress of Vienna see Salo Baron, *Die Judenfrage auf dem Wiener Kongress* (Vienna, 1920).
[50] *Der Charakter des Judenthums* (Leipzig, 1817).
[51] *Yesodei ha-Limud* (Dessau, 1819).

did not succeed in restoring his eyesight, it did enable him to visit Israel Jacobson (1768–1828), the former president of the Westphalian Consistory and advocate of reforms in Jewish ritual and education. Jacobson received Wolf warmly, praised his achievements over the years and gave him a generous sum of money which relieved some of his financial worries. In 1825 Frädel died, and in the following year Wolf succumbed to the cumulative effects of his ill health.[52]

To a latter-day observer the discrepancy between the modest circumstances of Wolf's life and his lasting accomplishmens are obvious. For, despite his life long poverty, Wolf left a rich legacy. By fashioning an ideology of emancipation and establishing the media of the journal and the sermon, he bequeathed a coherent set of ideas and the means to propagate them. The ideology became the idiom of self-understanding of the emerging German-Jewish middle classes, supporting varieties of identity ranging from secularism to neo-Orthodoxy while legitimizing the institutions of the nascent voluntary community.[53] Wolf's legacy was, moreover, personal. Among the preachers, teachers and publicists who disseminated the ideology in the post-Napoleonic era was Wolf's eldest son, Josef Wolfssohn (1797–1866). After education at the Franz School, an unsuccessful apprenticeship to a businessman and distinguished military service in the campaign against Napoleon, Wolfssohn taught alongside his father (from 1819) at the Franz School and preached in Dessau, Magdeburg and Leipzig.[54]

To Wolf's contemporaries his qualities overshadowed his accomplishments. The obituary that the elders of the Dessau community placed noted, 'What made him more estimable than all his knowledge, was his unassuming character, his willingness to help everyone, his philosophical composure in the face of physical suffering, and his friendliness in the company of his family and at school.' But, again to a latter-day observer, the inscription on Wolf's tombstone does cap-

---

[52] Phillipson, *Biographische Skizzen*, vol. 1 pp. 216–19.
[53] For the ideology and its impact see Sorkin, *The Transformation of German Jewry*.
[54] Wolfssohn subsequently taught in many places. He served as a tutor in Berlin, assumed his father's post at the Franz School in 1826, and then taught in schools in Seesen, Sondershausen, Breslau and Berlin. For Wolfssohn see Freudenthal, 'Ein Geschlecht von Erziehern' pp. 57–8. For Wolfssohn's sermons see *Predigten für warme Religions-freunde* (Dessau, 1826) and *Zwölf Reden. gehalten in der israelitischen Gemeinde zu Sondershausen* (Leipzig, 1838).

ture the fact that, among the men of middling ability whom the Napoleonic era propelled into radical action, Wolf stands out for having altered others more than himself. In the life of this impecunious teacher who forged an ideology for the affluent middle classes, the maskil devoted to Hebrew who devised German-language media, the elements of continuity far outweighed those of change. In a Hebrew preamble the tombstone inscription first described him as 'the wise scholar, perfect and complete' — in other words, as a traditional pious scholar (a *talmid hakham*). Then a poem in maskilic Hebrew sings his praises in two quatrains and a couplet:

> Sweet is the slumber of the just, loyal in spirit
> Resting in peace, joyfully reposing
> His heart is correct, trusting in God
> Morning — he will walk in the way of the righteous
>
> Alas! gloom will cover our faces
> Since, woe, the crown of our head is fallen
> Our memory of him standing before us is lovely
> Thus the flood of our tears is blue
>
> Righteousness shall go before him
> And his footsteps shall depart.

Finally, a German peroration: 'for the noble and unforgettable teacher and preacher, who combined so many gentle and charming virtues with a profound abundance of intellect and the inspired power of speech ...'.[55]

[55] Phillipson, *Biographische Skizzen*, vol. 1, p. 219.

6

Mordechai Aaron Günzburg: a Lithuanian Maskil Faces Modernity

ISRAEL BARTAL

TRANSLATED BY N. GREENWOOD AND L. SCHRAMM

I

Like a pilot who sails ahead in his tiny bark
To steer the giant craft that follows him
Between the treacherous reefs and hidden shoals,

So too you risked your life; your heart a beacon,
To ward off shipwreck from our generation,
You plied the sea of life with sense and wisdom.[1]

This sestet, from a sonnet signed with the initials Y. H. S. B. R. Y.
(= 'May God grant me favour'), expresses how one of Mordechai
Aaron Günzburg's devoted readers viewed that author when he read
his works. A pilot sailing a tiny boat before a ship threading its way
between the rocks — this was one reader's image of Günzburg, who
sought to guide the ship of his people through the shoals of the age.
The metaphor coincided with Günzburg's own image of the maskil
as pioneer and trail-blazer, marking out a safe path, based on knowledge and intelligence, for those advancing behind him:

Behold, the modern era has come upon you, and we authors are
the scouts sent before it to herald its advent and to command
you to seek out a resting-place and prepare what it lacks — for
its way is that of an advancing army, which sends out quarter-

---

[1] M. A. Günzburg, *Ha-Moriyah* (Warsaw, 1878), p. 8.

masters before it ... to procure food and lodgings, for if the citizens are notified and prepare what the army needs it will enter the town in good order and take the provisions laid out for it, rather than pillaging and destroying. But if the townspeople do not believe the quartermasters and fail to prepare — just as you do not believe us — the new age will come like an invincible army that enters the city that did not prepare for its coming, and will find their own billets and take whatever they find, looting and destroying ... Behold, I have warned you!

Therefore do what the time demands of you. Do not be apprehensive about changing some small point of the customs practised by your forebears, according to the needs of their time.[2]

The images of the new era as a storm-tossed sea in which the ship of the Jewish people is sailing or as an armed troop that conquers a city seem to be incompatible with the conventional idea of how the earliest East European maskilim related to the modern age.[3] The passage cited above seems to be rather an expression of a clearly Orthodox — defensive posture, which sees the shifts of the modern age as an unavoidable tribulation rather than as a positive advance. Could it be that Günzburg was not really a maskil — even though he considered himself to be one and was affiliated with a well-known circle of maskilim? Or is the historiographic image of the East European Haskalah not appropriate for this Lithuanian maskil, who feared modernity and wanted to steer his people past its obstacles?

II

Mordechai Aaron Günzburg was born in 1795 in Salant, Lithuania. As fate would have it, he was born just when Lithuania came under the rule of the Russian Empire: allegiance to it and its language were to be central to his life and work. During his early years, the Jews of Lithuania passed from Polish to Russian rule, experienced Napoleon's march on Moscow (the traces of the Grande Armée's passage through Lithuania were not forgotten for many decades after 1812), and

---

[2] 'Kikayon de-Yonah', ibid., pp. 47–8.

[3] On the optimism of early East European maskilim about the changes taking place in European society see I. Etkes, 'Li-She'lat Mevasrei ha-Haskalah be-Mizrah Europa', *Tarbiz*, 57 (1987), pp. 98–9.

were the arena in which two spiritual movements — Hasidism and Lithuanian scholarship — contended. Unfortunately, we have little solid information about this period in Günzburg's life. The biography written fifty-one years after his death[4] contains little more than a characterization of the future maskil's spiritual milieu. Its author, David Magid, relied on quasi-autobiographical material, most of it drawn from the collections of Günzburg's letters and from his autobiography, *Aviezer*. But these do not make it easy to distinguish the uniqueness of the man's life from the conventions of the *Bildungsroman* or Rousseau's *Confessions*.[5] Perhaps Günzburg, the adult maskil, was creating an exemplary 'making of a Lithuanian maskil'. Nevertheless, it is possible to point to several facts that shaped his life and influenced his activity, or which he considered to be noteworthy in the formation of his personality.

His father, Judah Asher Günzburg, was himself 'one of the noted maskilim of his time, who was also a fluent writer in the Holy Tongue'.[6] In Güenzburg's writings the father is identified with the educational and maskilic example. Thus, for example, his father taught him to distinguish 'on his own between absolute truth and apparent truth, and not to accept anything on hearsay without weighing it in the scales of his intellect'.[7] According to Magid, as early as the beginning of Günzburg's heder studies his father taught him to discriminate between beliefs based on legend and beliefs that can stand the test of criticism.[8]

Like other early maskilim in Eastern Europe, Günzburg took his first steps as a maskil under the influence of the traditional Jewish literary repertoire: *Yossipon, Tzemah David, She'erit Yisrael*.[9] These

---

[4] D. Maggid, *R. Mordechai Aaron Günzburg, 5556—5607 (1795—1846)* (St Petersburg, 1897), in Hebrew.

[5] On the nature of Haskalah autobiography see Sh. Vilna'i (Werses), 'Darkhei ha-Avtobiografia bi-Tekufat ha-Haskalah', *Gilyonot*, 17 (1945/6), pp. 175—83; A. Mintz, 'Guenzburg, Lilienblum and the Shape of Haskalah Autobiography', *AJS Review*, 4 (1979), pp. 71—111.

[6] Maggid, *Günzburg*, p. 3.

[7] Ibid., p. 4.

[8] Ibid.

[9] The *Book of Yossipon*, a Hebrew chronicle ascribed to Joseph ben Gurion and probably compiled in southern Italy in the tenth century, was a major source of information on the past for Jews in the Middle Ages. *Tzemah David* (Prague, 1592), compiled by David Gans, is a two-part chronological record of general and Jewish events. *She'erit Yisrael* (Amsterdam, 1741), by Menahem mann Amelander, is a Yiddish supplement to *Yossipon* updating it to the mid eighteenth century.

works, all of them Jewish chronicles widely disseminated in the Ashkenazic cultural milieu, were evidently among the early inspirations for his special affinity for historiography.[10]

Günzburg's father favoured Hebrew grammar and the Bible as the major subject of study, in contrast to the preference of the young man's teachers for Talmud. After he had been put off by Talmudic casuistry (*pilpul*), Günzburg himself accepted this order of priorities, which was a major attribute of the early Haskalah: 'For by nature he was not fit to follow tortuous paths to halakhah, when plain logic led him there by a short road.'[11]

Two books that Günzburg read at the age of seventeen, if we credit his later testimony in *Aviezer*, moulded his world view and influenced his writing as well as his works of translation: *Sefer ha-Brit* ('Book of the Covenant'), by Pinchas ben Elijah Horowitz (Brünn, 1797), and Moses Mendelssohn's *Phaidon*. The first, an encyclopaedic tome in which information about the natural sciences and geography is combined with traditional values, Kabbalah and ethics, includes several elements of a social and political critique of traditional life, but is far from being in the spirit of the Haskalah.[12] Mendelssohn's work, which deals with the immortality of the soul, led Günzburg to a position generally ascribed to non-maskilim; he cites his teacher's reaction when he asked him about Mendelssohn's philosophical inquiries:

It befits a man in whose heart there is perfect faith to inquire wisely into matters upon which the Torah has pronounced its verdict, for he thereby buttresses matters of faith by means of his intellect. But he must make faith paramount and intellect subordinate to it, and where the two are incompatible he must reject the subordinate in favour of the paramount.[13]

According to Günzburg, his study of Ecclesiastes with the commentary by Mendelssohn and the Berlin circle of maskilim consolidated his view about intellectual inquiry and criticism: 'let him hold fast to faith and not let it go, let him live by it and act by it,

---

[10] Maggid, *Günzburg*, p. 5.
[11] Ibid., p. 4.
[12] See also J. S. Raisin, *The Haskalah Movement in Russia* (Philadelphia, 1913), pp. 101–3; R. Mahler, *Divrei Yemei Yisrael, Dorot Ahronim*, vol. 1, book 4, (Merhavia, 1956), pp. 45–52.
[13] M. A. Günzburg, *Aviezer* (Vilna, 1863), p. 116.

while inquiry is his hobby, with which he hones his intellect and braces his feelings'.[14]

While the young Günzburg was crystallizing his areas of interest, he experienced an emotional crisis caused by his premature marriage. Because of a decline in his socio-economic status, his father, whom he admired so much, married him off to the daughter of a family that was inferior in its lineage and Torah learning. Günzburg came to connect the new groom's triumph over the impotence of the pubescent lad with his spiritual maturation: both were aided by the wisdom of a superb physician, a renaissance man of unknown origin (perhaps a member of the Frankist sect who had converted to Christianity). Whether this gentleman truly existed or was merely a literary fiction, Günzburg used him to develop the complex story of how he came to grips with the irrationality of traditional society and his own spiritual and theological problems.

The account of his premature marriage had affinities with similar descriptions in Haskalah literature, traceable to the memoirs of J. L. Peretz,[15] and reveals an unflattering aspect of the maskilic view of love and tender sentiments: Günzburg saw the proof of his virility, after he had overcome his impotence, as the full realization of his bond to his wife. In his eyes, the successful match was one based on rational considerations — that is, correspondence in socio-economic status. Günzburg's attitude towards married life was hardly different from that of traditional Jewish society in Eastern Europe. His criticism of early marriages and unsuccessful betrothals was not intended to undermine the basic principles of wedded life, but rather to base them on intellect and rational planning. Thus, for example, in the name of intellect and nature he criticized the deviation, in both Eastern Europe and Germany, from the rational age for marriage, contrasting the early marriages among Lithuanian Jewry with the late marriages common among the Central European bourgeoisie:

> For just as our brethren in Poland have tipped the scales too far out of balance, so too our brothers in Germany, who follow after the ways of the Gentiles — who are like beasts in the valley and scarcely wed until the brink of old age, after wasting their

[14] Ibid., p. 177.

[15] D. Biale, 'Eros and Enlightenment: Love against Marriage in the East European Jewish Enlightenment', *Polin*, 1 (1986), pp. 49—67. The definitive study of Ashkenazic family life is J. Katz, 'Nisuim ve-Hayei Ishut be-Motza'ei Yemei ha-Beyna'im', *Zion*, 10 (1944—5), pp. 21—54.

youthful vigour in the bosom of harlots and whores and squand-
ering their vitality on adulteresses — have caused the strength of
their youth to sin against nature by corrupting their way until
their vigour dries up like a shard.[16]

The medical concepts with which Günzburg explained the relationships between men and women were taken from medieval theories of
the humours as the source of the vitality of body and soul:

> For nature creates a balanced and tranquil regime: first it refines
> from the blood the moisture that the body needs for itself; after
> that it refines the most sublime humour to give life to others —
> and one who has lascivious thoughts forces nature to depart
> from its balance, because he compels it to quicken its race and
> change its course, to reduce other humours and multiply seed,
> giving life to others before he gives life to himself.[17]

One should remember, however, that such concepts were generally
accepted in European society at the beginning of the nineteenth
century.

From the perspective of a student of the early East European
Haskalah,[18] Günzburg's youth was typical of members of the Haskalah
during the first stage of their activity. As the son of a maskilic father,
he was exposed to the influence of rationalism from Jewish sources,
tended to prefer logical study to casuistry, and stressed the study of
Bible and the Hebrew language and its grammar — even while he was
adversely affected by the educational methods, marriage customs and
sexual mores of traditional society.

III

Had Günzburg never gone beyond these influences, we could hardly
say that he belonged to the Haskalah movement. True, many maskilim
began their careers under similar influences; but something more was
required to turn a son of traditional society into a maskil. What was
that extra something? Günzburg's autobiography, and perhaps even

---

[16] Günzburg, *Aviezer*, p. 75.

[17] Ibid., p. 126.

[18] Etkes, 'Li-She'lat Mevasrei ha-Haskalah', 57, pp. 97–8.

more his letters and essays, point to a number of changes affecting
the traditional milieu.

To begin with there was the European influence on language, dress
and thought. Even though Günzburg reiterated the continuity of
traditional values and the superiority of faith and religious observance
over intellectual criticism, the European model and the social and
economic values of the European Enlightenment clearly had a decisive
influence on him. In one place he writes, almost off-handedly that
the difference between his father's and his relationship to Hebrew is
'that I conceive German ideas and dress them in purely Hebrew
garments, whereas he begat his ideas on the knees of that language
[Hebrew]'.[19] That is to say, his father belonged to the traditional
society, which he experienced as a unity of thought and language,
whereas Günzburg himself thought in German and used Hebrew to
communicate his ideas to his more traditional co-religionists.

In a most instructive passage on the essence of faith, Günzburg
describes believers as follows:

> Those who have entered into a social compact, who have
> covenanted to be a single unit in which each man helps his
> fellows and works for the commonweal — every individual helps
> the society to his fullest strength, and the society the individual;
> the individual serves the collective, and the collective serves the
> individual.[20]

This demonstrates that Günzburg viewed traditional Jewish society
as a corporation, of which the individual, who lives his entire life
within it, is a part, bound by its laws (which he calls 'the register of
society', although he means the commandments of the Torah!). But,
continues Günzburg, in our day the traditional society has been
weakened and is unable to enforce observance of its rules or to
prevent the individual from living his life beyond them. Yet even
freethinkers ought not to give up the old rules — the religious observances — even though the coercive framework has been removed.
This idea, distinctly Mendelssohnian, reveals the Lithuanian
Günzburg as a man endowed with penetrating historical insight: he
understood long before his contemporaries in Eastern Europe
what the weakening of the Jewish corporation really meant. Even
though the implied support for the role of the community (the chief

---

[19] Guenzburg, *Aviezer*, p. 66.
[20] Ibid., pp. 46–7.

object of the maskilim's withering criticism) may seem somewhat strange coming from the pen of an East European maskil, his assertion that adherence to religion, even in the absence of communal powers of coercion, is a rational premise is far from a traditional position.

IV

Much can be learned about the new phenomenon represented by Günzburg from his topical writings and from his political and social activity. These stem from that period in his life when he clearly associated himself with maskilic circles and was so identified by his milieu. Evidently this identification coincided with the beginning of the confrontation between the maskilim and the traditionalists.[21] For much of his life Günzburg was among those maskilim who strove to conceal their beliefs, lest they should forfeit their source of livelihood or be condemned as deviants from traditional society. He came out into the open both because that society became more hostile to those suspected of maskilic tendencies and also because, in response to the change in the Jewish policy of the Tsarist government, the maskilim began publicly to promote initiatives in which they saw themselves as allies of the Russian authorities.

We do not know many details about the transition to open maskilic activity. Günzburg's autobiography goes no further than 1820; after that time we must draw whatever biographical information we can from his letters. So far as we know, at the age of twenty-one he was obliged to start travelling from town to town in order to support his family. The small legacy he received after his father's death some years later quickly evaporated. The Lithuanian maskil who, as his biographer puts it, 'was unsuccessful ... in every trade'[22] wandered among the towns of Lithuania and Courland (Latvia) and frequently changed jobs: he was a teacher, translated German documents for the lawcourts, was an innkeeper and tavern waiter — and even relied on the support of the generous patrons to whom he dedicated his books. For a time he lived in Vilna, later in Palengen and Mitau. In 1835 he returned to Vilna, remaining there until his death. At the start of this

---

[21] On the emerging clash between the maskilim and the traditionalists see I. Etkes, *R. Yisrael Salanter ve-Reshitah shel Tenuat ha-Musar* (Jerusalem, 1982), pp. 147–64; M. Stanislawski, *Tsar Nicholas I and the Jews* (New York, 1983), pp. 49–59.

[22] Maggid, *Günzburg*, p. 14.

second period in Vilna he worked as a clerk in the firm of the wealthy maskil Nisan Rosenthal and served as tutor to his son.

In his many journeys between Lithuania and Courland, Günzburg crossed the cultural divide between the Jews of Eastern Europe and those influenced by German culture. Thus the course of his life ran in one of the channels through which German culture and the Haskalah percolated into East European Jewish society. Because he lived so close to the cultural divide, he did not idealize the situation on the other side. He recognized its weaknesses as well as it strengths, and vigorously opposed uncritical use of the German model for the reform of East European Jewry. During his nomadic period, before he finally settled in Vilna — i.e. in the 1820s and early 1830s — he was already known as a maskil, but still endeavoured to disguise his opinions and soft-pedal his position on matters of dress and language. These were among the most important token's of identity, and came to occupy an increasingly central role in the confrontation between maskilim and traditionalists. The short German jacket, which the various reformers and maskilim favoured as a means of removing the barriers between Jews and non-Jews, became a symbol of all that the traditionalists in Eastern Europe rejected. The maskilim thought that it was essential for Jews to study the local language and acquire a knowledge of German, in order to show themselves loyal subjects of the Russian Empire and enhance their own value to the society in which they lived. The traditionalists sought to ban the study of languages other than Hebrew, and were deeply critical of the reading-matter favoured by the younger generation.

In one of his letters, Günzburg writes that he used to exchange his German clothes for Polish-Jewish garb every time he crossed into Lithuania, and do the reverse when he returned to Courland. Consequently he kept two complete sets of clothes in his trunk, 'in order to survive among the members of different sects.'[23] This story can help us understand Günzburg's character: in Courland he was a teacher, a Polish Jew trying to earn his bread, like thousands of other teachers, in a German-Jewish environment. In Vilna, German garb was considered to be the chief distinguishing-mark of those who challenged traditional values. After he began to work in tandem with the Vilna maskilim and to participate in the reform plans of the government of Nicholas I, Günzburg was among the representatives of the Vilna maskilim who petitioned the Russian authorities to compel the Jews to change their manner of dress. In his article

[23] Ibid., p. 17.

'About Dress',[24] written at the height of the intense campaign launched by Nicholas I in the early 1840s to bring about changes in Jewish life,[25] Günzburg wrote,

> Clothes alone constitute the wall that divides Jew and Christian and makes them think the other a different species of man ['eine andere Menschenrasse']. This is not the desire of the honourable kingdom, which loves all its children with a unifying love, because the Christians are ashamed to go in the company of Jews and the Jews fear to be seen in the company of Christians ... Even Jews who are upright in their hearts are afraid to walk with Christians in the streets, because other Jews, who recognize him by his garments, will think him an apostate — and, though there are some merchants compelled by necessity to associate with Christians for a brief moment, there is no true friendship between them. It is not on this basis that a human society will arise. But if the garments are alike, so, too, will the hearts be equal.[26]

Even at this time the maskilim, including Günzburg, feared the wrath of the traditionalists. The Vilna maskilim's petition on the matter of Jewish dress, submitted on 23 July 1843 to Uvarov, the Russian Minister of National Enlightenment, concluded as follows:

> Your excellency! We fervently hope that your highness's greatheartedness will not pass on to the rabbis the [names of the] Jews who wish to come closer to the other citizens, because the rabbis would take revenge for this deed.[27]

It is not by chance that, in a letter of the early 1820s expressing his fears of losing his post as a teacher, Günzburg associated maskilic dress with knowledge of languages:

---

[24] 'Al Devar ha-Begadim', in *Leket Amarim* (St Petersburg, 1889–90), pp. 90–1. On the Russian government's plans to make the Jews change their style of dress see Sh. Ginsburg, *Yiddishe Layden in Tsarishe Rusland* (New York, 1938), pp. 273–314.

[25] On this article see I. Klausner, 'Ha-Gezerah al Tilboshet ha-Yehudim, 1844–1850', *Gal-Ed*, 6 (1982), pp. 15, 20–2.

[26] Ibid., p. 20.

[27] Ibid., p. 25.

Who pays attention whether the garments of a day labourer are
wide like those of a Greek Orthodox priest or as short as a
man's palm [traditional Jewish dress versus the short German
costume]? Whether he speaks Ashkenazic, Ashdodic, Hittite, or
not [evidently an allusion to German, Russian and Polish]? ...
But for me, who am poor and destitute, that is not the case: my
clothes are open to all staring eyes, and they listen intently to
catch every word that falls from my lips. The jesters base their
ridicule and reproofs on every syllable that leaves my mouth,
and mourn bitterly about the great sin of the congregation that
employs such a teacher for its children.[28]

In this period, when he had to conceal his knowledge of German
from the traditionalists, Günzburg was already involved in translating
various works from German into Hebrew. He saw German as a
model for composition in Hebrew, as a tool for the acquisition of
knowledge and economic advancement, and as a factor of political
significance, in that it could hasten the integration of Jews into the
state. Twenty years later, in his article 'About Dress', he argued that

Similarity of dress, too, will increase ethical and moral behaviour; when the Jew wears Christian garb he will also learn
the manners and customs of the Christians and will learn at least
one or two languages well, so as to be able to speak the language
fluently and not be embarrassed in company.[29]

Günzburg saw the influence of German as a major factor in the
expansion of Hebrew. He explicitly spoke of liberating Hebrew from
the shackles of biblical syntax, ostensibly in order to create a simpler
and clearer style, but in fact also to secularize the language. Replying
to the criticism that he wrote in a simple, non-scriptural Hebrew
which had stylistic affinities with German, he stated that in his view
'the sin of Germanisms' was something that 'no Hebrew author can
escape unless he follows in the wake of the Holy Scriptures and
pastes together verses and fragments from the biblical books'.[30] His
view of language resembled that of the Berlin maskilim, who sought
to modify the bilingualism of German Jewry: the Holy Tongue
would be purified according to the model of the biblical language,
and its use extended to the sciences and *belles-lettres*, while Yiddish

---

[28] Maggid, *Günzburg*, pp. 16–17.
[29] Klausner, *Gal-Ed*, 6, p. 21.
[30] M. A. Günzburg *Kiryat Sefer* (Vilna, 1847), epistle 105, p. 117.

would be replaced by the German vernacular. The situation in Lithuania, as elsewhere in Eastern Europe, was more complicated than in Germany, since the Gentile vernacular was not German, even though German was the language preferred by educated Jews. In any case, Günzburg, as a member of the Haskalah, sought to enrich the Holy Tongue while making the broadest possible use of German texts. Even though one of his first translations from German was into Yiddish,[31] his attitude towards that language was strongly negative. He referred to it as 'A confused and strange Aramaic even for the celestial angels [who, according to tradition, do not understand Aramaic]; how much the more so for earthly men.'[32] Of the two elements of maskilic bilingualism, Günzburg preferred German and even asserted that he thought in German when writing Hebrew. There is no doubt that he was one of the first East European Jews thoroughly to internalize a European language and literature while continuing to use Hebrew and write in it. By his own testimony he preferred the 'living dog' (German) to the 'dead lion' (Hebrew).[33]

V

Dress and language were central to Günzburg's activities as a Vilna maskil. In Vilna he collaborated with those who shared his ideas in an attempt to reform the Jewish way of life. His co-operation with the Russian authorities was expressed in a number of ways, including petitions to impose European dress on the Jews. His literary and educational endeavours in Vilna revolved around his translations and adaptations from German and the establishment of a maskilic school, where he taught Hebrew.

His social and cultural circle, the Vilna maskilim, was a group of Hebrew writers and educators active in the capital of the Russian province of Lithuania during the reign of Nicholas I (1825−55). This group had been preceded by another in the 1780s and 1790s, the last years of the independent Polish kingdom.[34] Those earlier maskilim had not mounted a direct confrontation with traditional society, and,

---

[31] M. A. Günzburg, *Di Entdekung fun Amerike* (Vilna, 1823−4).

[32] Günzburg, *Kiryat Sefer*, epistle 101, p. 111.

[33] Maggid, *Günzburg*, p. 14.

[34] On late-eighteenth-century Vilna maskilim see I. Klausner, *Vilna bi-Tekufat ha-Gaon* (Jerusalem, 1941−2), pp. 46−9, and 'R. Yosef ben Eliyahu, Krovo ha-Naor shel ha-Gra mi-Vilna', *He-Avar*, 2 (1952), pp. 73−85; and Etkes, *Tarbiz*, 57, pp. 102−4, 110.

although they belonged to the Jewish social elite, their activities did not spawn a genuine movement. In contrast, their successors in the age of Nicholas I aroused hostile reactions among their neighbours, and their organization had the distinct air of a movement. Inspired by the ideas of the European Enlightenment, the group began to co-operate with the Russian authorities in order to modify Jewish life-styles and reform what they saw as the shortcomings of traditional Jewish society. On the one hand, this co-operation made them a force to be reckoned with, despite their pitifully small numbers and their lack of influence within the community. On the other hand, it branded them as turncoats collaborating with a hostile government.[35]

Günzburg, Samuel Joseph Fünn, I. M. Dik and the other members of the Vilna circle were enthusiastic about the new Russian Jewish policy and saw Nicholas I as an enlightened ruler on the model of his elder brother, Tsar Alexander I, the Austrian Emperor Joseph II, and Frederick the Great of Prussia. The Vilna maskilim identified with the Russian state and expected the Jews to conform to the demands of the regime by giving up the separatism of the Jewish corporation and becoming loyal Russian subjects. Already, in Posen and Galicia, the enlightened absolute monarchies of Prussia and Austria, forced to cope with a large Jewish population in these districts annexed from the dismembered Polish kingdom, had abrogated Jewish autonomy and in both states Jewish maskilim identified actively with the goals of the regime. For the Vilna maskilim, the tie to ruler and state now replaced the bond of the old corporation. They nevertheless did not see the abrogation of communal authority as a step towards the obliteration of Jewish existence. Rather, they looked forward to a reformed way of life, and saw themselves as the defenders of Judaism in an age when it could no longer be protected by the physical and spiritual walls of the Middle Ages. The following passage by Fünn on the need to shed the traditional garments typifies this view:

Both you and we know that, to the distress of everyone who loves his people, the bonds of religion have slowly weakened among our fellow Israelites and the vital spirit that has always quickened the Jewish heart has passed away because of the leaders ... and most of the people, who live only according to external laws without understanding or feeling the precious soul of the Torah ... To these men, who scent the incense of

---

[35] I. Etkes, 'Parashat ha-Haskalah mi-Ta'am ve-ha-Temurah be-Ma'amad Tenuat ha-Haskalah be-Russiyah', *Zion*, 43 (1978), pp. 274–80.

freedom almost as soon as they cast off their Jewish garb ... the residue of Judaism will be like a mountain hanging by a thread. This is truly awful, and everyone who loves his religion and people will mourn it ... The people of Jacob are ill, diseased in body and diseased in spirit, and to whom shall the experienced physician turn? What should he seek to heal in such a critically ill patient, if not the heart, the source of life, and the head, the source of intellect? Let him sacrifice a few external limbs [i.e. traditional dress] for the sake of the vital organs, so as to keep them alive and sustain them. To my sorrow I know that the period of change — the period of the changing of the garb — will have many victims. Every Jewish soul is as dear in my eyes as the entire world — but what can we change?[36]

Günzburg collaborated actively with the Russian authorities during the period of the 'official Enlightenment'. During the 1840s the Russian government undertook a series of steps intended to modify the Jews' status within the Empire. The maskilim were inclined to support the official policy even though they were aware that some of the new measures were directed towards goals other than the realization of the maskilic vision. But, alongside the understandable tension between them and the traditionalists, disagreement arose between the Vilna maskilim and the advocates of radical religious reform on the German model. Günzburg was one of the most prominent critics of Max Lilienthal, who was invited from Riga to St Petersburg in order to implement such a programme of reform. In *Kikayon de-Yonah* ('Jonah's Gourd'), published while the controversy was still raging (1843), Günzburg strongly attacked the idea of using the German model for East European Jewry and reiterated the two major principles of his moderate maskilic position.

First, the Jews of Eastern Europe have their own independent position and must not accept uncritically the opinions of the German Jews: 'Our land is not devoid of wise men, even though they are few compared to the masses and far from one another. The kingdom need not seek out wise men in a distant land, but only give a signal to the scholars of this land and assemble them together.'[37]

Second, while it is true that the German rabbis are versed in secular knowledge, they are not great scholars in Torah. If they want to come to Russia as teachers and preachers, they must first study the Torah:

[36] Klausner, *Gal-Ed*, 6, pp. 25–6.
[37] Günzburg, *Ha-Moriyah*, p. 43.

If there is no Torah there is nothing. Even if those who sleep in the earth should awaken and Aristotle himself rise from his grave, he would not have the merit to walk on the heads of the nation sanctified with the rabbinate. We would certainly honour him and utter in full the blessing on Him 'who has given of His wisdom to flesh and blood' [the blessing prescribed on seeing a learned non-Jew or any person of profound secular learning], but he would not be admitted among the assembly of the sages of Israel. He would be called a wise man, but he would not be called 'rabbi'.[38]

Günzburg did not spare the Lithuanian rabbis his critical shafts. He accused them of failing to play an active role in the relations between the Jews and the authorities, of lacking a secular education, and of doing nothing to improve education and the divine service in the synagogues. Rather than exchange them for German doctors, however, he wanted to train a new generation of East European rabbis who would combine traditional education and knowledge of Torah with European culture. He wanted these new rabbis to be involved in educational affairs and the life of the community. This preference for home-grown rabbis over imported German ones was not just the humiliated reaction of a 'native' culture to the penetration of foreign influence; it was also a strong manifestation of the internal-ization of the political changes wrought by the absolutist monarchy. The rabbis would be leaders and mediate between the Jews and the government, because the old apparatus of the East European *kehillah* would have vanished. Here, too, there is a striking parallel between Günzburg's attitude towards the rabbinate and that of Central European Orthodoxy. In the absence of official recognition of the old community organs, the role of the rabbi among Central European Jews had increased in importance, bringing him new responsibilities and authority. Like the other maskilim in Vilna, Günzburg believed that in a centralized state the rabbinate should be integrated into the government apparatus.

VI

Of all his maskilic activities, Günzburg's literary endeavours had the greatest influence. He specialized in a particular genre, which served

---

[38] Ibid., p. 44.

his goals faithfully: Hebrew translations and adaptations from German. Much of what he published, and nearly all his posthumously published work, was derived from German sources. Even *Aviezer*, his most original work, includes many passages based on German moral tracts. There is no doubt that his translations and adaptations were meant to realize a major goal of the Haskalah: the transmission of European knowledge and trends of thought to the Jewish reader. Naphtali Herz Wessely, in his important pamphlet *Divrei Shalom ve-Emet* ('Words of Peace and Truth'), argued that, in addition to theological subjects, Jews should study 'history, geography, the customs of the nations and the laws of the kings'.[39] Günzburg specialized in historical studies, but also showed a strong interest in geography. The maskilic message behind his publications in these areas was not only that Jews should have a wider knowledge of the world that they lived in and the species to which they belonged, but also that Hebrew, the Holy Tongue, was capable of serving as a modern scientific language.

Günzburg translated the chapters on the French Revolution and the Napoleonic era from *Die Weltgeschichte für gebildete Leser und Studierende* ('World History for Educated Readers and Students') by the German historian Karl Heinrich Pölitz (1772–1838), and incorporated them into a work called *Yemot ha-Dor* ('Annals of the Generation'), published posthumously in Vilna (1860). To promote knowledge of the country in which the Jews of the Russian Empire lived, he adapted material from Russian high-school textbooks for *Itotei Russiyah* ('Chronicles of Russia'; Vilna, 1839), which, as its sub-title announced, dealt with the period 'from the time this people became a nation until the present generation, with the annals of its kings and nobles, wars and activities, and all of its valour and its glory'. To promote knowledge of humanity in general, he published part of Pölitz's *Weltgeschichte*, which he had in fact translated in its entirety, as *Toldot Bnei ha-Adam* ('History of the Human Race'; Vilna, 1835).[40]

While struggling with these historical works, Günzburg encountered

---

[39] N. H. Wessely, *Divrei Shalom ve-Emet* (Berlin, 1782), ch. 1.

[40] On Günzburg's adaptations from the historical writings of Pölitz see Sh. Feiner, '"Mardut ha Tzorfatim" ve-"Herut ha-Yehudim"–ha-Mahapekhah ha-Tzorfatit bi-Temunat he-Avar shel ha-Haskalah ha-Yehudit be-Mizrah Eyropa', in *Ha-Mahapekhah ha-Tzorfatit*, Proceedings of the thirteenth annual conference of Merkaz Zalman Shazar and the Historical Society of Israel, Jerusalem, July 1989.

a problem that confronted all East European maskilim and which has been largely ignored by historians. Although the Russian authorities used the maskilim for their own ends, they distrusted them as a dangerous political element, suspecting the radical potential of the Haskalah. Even at the height of Nicholas I's reforms, traditional Jewish society appeared more loyal than the maskilim. Thus Günzburg was forced to make concessions in order to get his books published.[41] Their message, particularly where they were concerned with contemporary issues, was at odds with the regime's politics and only reinforced the censor's already exaggerated suspicions. Since Günzburg was utterly loyal to the Russian Empire and identified the good of his people with that of the state, it is not difficult to imagine the psychological dilemma that he faced.

Works on subjects that were not directly related to current events were less likely to provoke the censor and fared much better. The discovery of America and the wars of the Spaniards in the New World, for example, were topics that could expand the horizons of Jewish readers, historically and geographically, without raising politically contentious issues. The first book that Günzburg translated into Hebrew was of this sort: *Gelot Eretz Hadashah* ('The Discovery of a New Land'), translated from *Die Entdeckung von Amerika* by Heinrich Joachim Campe. This work was published in Vilna in 1823 by the mission press,[42] which may perhaps tell us something about the difficulty of getting it printed in the Jewish community (even though the volume had the imprimatur of the Rabbi of Vilna). Shortly thereafter, a Yiddish version of the book appeared — according to the introduction, 'in pure, easy Judaeo-German' — which also included 'a treatise on geography for learning to read maps, which I have added at the end'.[43] This appears to have been the first Yiddish work by a Lithuanian maskil intended to disseminate popular scientific knowledge.

Campe, an educator who wrote a number of the most important children's books of the German Enlightenment, had a profound influence on the Haskalah. Five of his books were translated into Hebrew, some more than once.[44] The choice of Campe enabled

[41] Ibid.

[42] Maggid, *Günzburg*, p. 25.

[43] Z. Rayzn, *Leksikon fun der Yiddisher Literatur*, vol. 1 (Vilna, 1926), pp. 573—6.

[44] Z. Shavit, 'From Friedlaender's *Lesebuch* to the Jewish Campe — the Beginnings of Hebrew Children's Literature in Germany', *Leo Baeck Institute Yearbook*, 33 (1988), pp. 406—7.

Günzburg to convey to his readers geographical and historical information in a moderate maskilic vein. The German author, moreover, was an intimate of Moses Mendelssohn, and in the maskilic consciousness was stamped as a proponent of the universal brotherhood of the enlightened intellectuals of all nations. In his labour of translation the young Günzburg was a link between the waning German Haskalah and an emerging Russian version which gave ideas originating in mid-eighteenth-century Central Europe new vitality in the Russia of the mid-nineteenth century.

Günzburg also published geographical and historical material in the anthology *Devir* (Vilna, 1844), which included, for example, the travel letters that Louis Löwe, later personal secretary to Moses Montefiore, had written on his trip to Palestine in 1838. These provide one of the first modern descriptions of Palestine written in Hebrew and intended for East European readers. The letters were initially published in the Jewish press in German, French and English; Günzburg added his readers to the emerging network of modern Jewish information.[45] *Devir* also includes a description of the Galilee earthquake of 1837 written by the British missionary Kalman,[46] and accounts of travels in Arabia and information on the Jews of North Africa and China from the pens of Christian travellers. From these texts the Jewish reader in Lithuania could acquire a totally non-traditional picture of the land of Israel and its Jewish residents and of remote and unfamiliar Jewish communities.

VII

One of the common literary devices of the Enlightenment and Haskalah was the letter. Günzburg used this form frequently, sometimes publishing actual correspondence — his own, or exemplary letters by others — and sometimes devising exchanges between fictional characters. Even though the letters he published include translations and adaptations of various sorts, they are perhaps the most original area of his writing. Collections of model letters, intended for actual use, were popular, and could be exploited to disseminate ideas. Because many of the letters composed by Günzburg

[45] I. Bartal, Preface to *Diary and Letters from Voyages, Palestine in the 1830s* (Jerusalem, 1974), pp. 1–10.
[46] Much information on the 1837 earthquake is to be found in A. R. Malachi, 'Ha-Ra'ash bi-Tzefat bi-Shenat 5597', in Malachi (ed.), *Prakim be-Toldot ha-Yishuv ha-Yashan* (Tel Aviv, 1971), pp. 22–64.

dealt with daily life, they can enhance our understanding of his world. Those concerning economic and commercial matters are the most valuable in this respect.

Günzburg's ideas on social and economic questions were no different from those of other maskilim of his generation. They all recognized the abnormality of the socio-economic structure of East European Jewry and proposed to amend it in accordance with the economic theories prevalent in Europe during the second half of the eighteenth century. Günzburg, like most of the maskilim, accepted the main points of physiocratic theory. He internalized the Protestant bourgeois ethic, saw virtue in making do with little, avoiding luxuries and rationally planning the use of time and money. *Aviezer* contains passages in which Günzburg complains that the pleasures and luxuries to which his upbringing habituated him weakened his ability to stand up to the severities of life:

> For had I not been enfeebled in childhood by eating delicacies by day and lying in silk all night, my strength would not have been overwhelmed in my youth by the toil of trade and fatigue of travel needed to bring my bread from afar; instead, now I can manage no wearying labour but must sit on a soft cushion and write.[47]

Günzburg combined views and theories taken from French and German sources with an awareness of concrete historical changes and contemporary economic events. This is evident in his 'Twenty-five Letters by Polish Merchants: In which a Manufacturer and a Merchant correspond about Wool and Cotton'.[48] These letters relate to a significant aspect of Lithuanian commerce in the 1820s — the blossoming of the textile industry and the important role played in this by the Jews.[49] This was not a modern factory industry of the type which sprang up some years later in Białystok and Lódz; rather, it belonged to a pre-capitalist economy, largely tied to the nobility's estates and feudal relations of production.

Günzburg presents the innovations of the English Industrial Revolution as a model for reforming Jewish commercial activity. The

---

[47] Günzburg, *Aviezer*, p. 6.

[48] Günzburg, *Kiryat Sefer*, pp. 27–54.

[49] R. Mahler, *Divrei Yemei Yisrael, Dorot Ahronim*, vol. 2, book 1 (Merhavia, 1970), pp. 39–41; P. Kon, 'Yidn in Industrie un Handl in Vilne Onheyb 19 Yorhundert', *Yivo-Bleter*, 8 (1935), pp. 78–85.

manufacturer is commended for buying his wool for spinning from estate-owners who practise scientific agriculture and improve their flocks by cross-breeding; his workshop contains sophisticated looms, in which 'all of the threads come from one loom and are so similar that they cannot be told apart (the spinning-jenny, a model for rational and uniform production under centralized control). By contrast, his old-fashioned competitor purchases his wool from farmers who make no attempt to improve their flocks; in his workshop 'many threads come from many different implements, each with its own qualities' and do not resemble one another.[50]

Günzburg not only advocates the economic innovations of the west; he also makes a plea for Western business ethics.[51] In his letters he recommends the trading-practices of the merchant as opposed to the pedlar, and, juxtaposing the thought patterns of the East European Jew, trained in Talmudic casuistry, and the thought patterns of a plain-dealing merchant, suggests that Talmudic reasoning is not the best way to conduct a business: 'Exegeses are appropriate for those who wear the rabbinical robe, not for merchants, and certainly not for me, a man who walks upright, whose heart is at one with his mouth, and who writes what his heart feels.'[52] Günzburg's 'Letters about the Commercial Estate'[53] presents a father's advice on business ethics to his son, Yedidah, whom he has apprenticed to a trading-house in Courland to learn modern German business practices. The father recommends 'the pleasant homily of the eloquent sage, our teacher Rabbi David Friedländer',[54] a Berlin maskil who was a prosperous merchant with connections throughout Eastern Europe and who held distinctly physiocratic views (though his views on matters of faith and religion were as far from Günzburg's as is East from West!). The recommended 'homily' was also structured as a collection of letters: *Briefe über die Moral des Handels* ('Letters on the Ethics of Trade'), written in 1785 and republished in 1817.[55]

There is no doubt that in the 1840s people in Vilna were already well aware who Friedländer was and what was going on in Germany, especially since the Lilienthal affair had aroused explicit opposition to the German model. We can assume that Günzburg made a sharp

---

[50] Günzburg, *Kiryat Sefer*, p. 46.
[51] Ibid., p. 46.
[52] Ibid., p. 43.
[53] Ibid., p. 130–142.
[54] Ibid., p. 137.
[55] *Jedidja*, 1, 2 (1817), pp. 178–213.

distinction between economic modernization, his views on which were strongly influenced by Friedländer, and religious modernization, which he distrusted in a similar way to the traditionalists. In the economic sphere, Günzburg like Friedländer, saw agriculture as the main pursuit, and trade as a necessary evil to preserve human society. He did not, however, suggest that Jews should devote themselves to agriculture — the radical vision of the productivization of the Jews — but favoured reforming and improving business methods. He thus was in agreement with the goal set by the absolutist regimes of Catherine the Great and Alexander I — the successful integration of the Jews into the Russian urban classes. Indeed, Günzburg's letters form a guide for the commercial entrepreneur who wants to succeed in trade or industry while remaining a loyal subject of the Empire and a religiously observant Jew.

VIII

Mordechai Aaron Günzburg endeavoured to reform his Russian-Jewish brethren and to imbue them with the spirit of the new age — a spirit that, while it heavily influenced him, also terrified him with the intensity of its innovations. His operating-methods were typical of the East European Haskalah: he criticized the rabbis, helped establish new educational institutions, and composed memoranda to the authorities about ways of reforming Jewish society. But his most important contributions to the spread of the Haskalah were his topical writings and, above all, his translations and adaptations from German. These works influenced readers in Eastern Europe decades after his untimely death at the age of fifty-one (1846).

The Orthodox in Vilna rejoiced at his death and took their revenge by refusing him a proper eulogy at his funeral. Their view of Günzburg as a dangerous innovator and a collaborator with the hated authorities is evident in the witty reaction of one anti-maskil. Asked why the preacher had not found it possible to say even one good word about the deceased, he replied,

> Our preacher, his honour remains with him, is a wonderful preacher. But he is accustomed to eulogizing rabbis who are great Torah scholars, pious and God-fearing. This is the first time he has had to eulogize a maskil. Is it any wonder that he did not find the strength to arouse dirges and laments? But wait a while: when God grants that another ten or twenty of your

maskilic brethren are carried to their graves — by then he will have learned to eulogize you appropriately as well.[56]

The witticism casts light on the climate of Vilna in the mid-1840s, when the differences between the maskilim and the Orthodox had sharpened, but condemnation of a maskil was considered to be somewhat dangerous. There is no doubt that Günzburg himself, like the other maskilim of Vilna, would not have been pleased by the image that the Orthodox had of him. He saw himself as a preserver of tradition who feared the radical influence of the Berlin Haskalah. In fact, to modern eyes, the Lithuanian author seems to be much closer to Orthodoxy than to the radical maskilim with whom he disagreed so sharply in his writings.

[56] A. Y. Papierna, 'Zikhronot u-Shmuot', *Reshumut*, 1 (1923—4), pp. 153—4. For a detailed study of this episode see Etkes, 'Parashat ha-Haskalah', *Zion*, 43, pp. 304—7.

Part III

Testing Assimilation

7

The Chequered Career of 'Jew' King: a Study in Anglo-Jewish Social History

TODD M. ENDELMAN

I

More than most European cities, Georgian London offered exceptional opportunities for advancement to ambitious Jews who had shed the constraints of traditional Judaism. There were few legal barriers to Jewish social and economic movement. The Jewish community exercised no police authority over individual Jews, since there was no organized community such as existed on the continent.[1] London itself was the largest city in Europe, with a population of over 900,000 in 1800 — almost twice that of Paris. Its complex and largely unregulated patterns of urban life allowed persons with ambition and drive much room for manoeuvre. Social relations between various groups were not rigidly fixed but, within certain bounds, remarkably fluid. There were fortunes to be made, social heights to be scaled, sexual favours to be won. English landowners, the governing class, flocked to London to enjoy its pleasures and entertainments. Their hedonistic ethic of consumption and expenditure, as well as their healthy regard for the pursuit of wealth in a variety of fields (rural and urban real estate; mining, fisheries, timber; stocks and bonds), made London a haven for adventurers and climbers who knew how to satisfy aristocratic needs and exploit aristocratic weaknesses.

John King — who was born Jacob Rey and known popularly as

Reprinted by kind permission of *AJS Review*.

[1] For the character of Anglo-Jewish communal life in the Georgian period and the legal status of English Jews see Todd M. Endelman, *The Jews of Georgian England, 1714–1830: Tradition and Change in a Liberal Society* (Philadelphia, 1979), pp. 10, 24–5, 45, 113, 122, 131–2, 142–8.

'Jew' King — was a notorious money-lender who flourished in the freewheeling atmosphere of late-Georgian London. He was not a leader of the Jewish community but was nevertheless one of the most well-known Jews in London between 1780 and 1820. His career exhibited many outrageous features and cannot easily be fitted into the usual categories for discussing the dissolution of traditional Jewish life and the integration of Jews into new spheres of activity. In one sense, however, his career is no less representative than that of Moses Mendelssohn, who was as unconventional in his own way as King was in his. Each moved in radically new directions — Mendelssohn in the realm of intellectual discourse, King in the sphere of concrete social relations. A comprehensive picture of the entry of the Jews into European society must include the lives of the 'Jew' Kings of history as much as the lives of the Moses Mendelssohns. The former are as instructive as the latter — if for no other reason than that there were many more Jewish parvenus and adventurers than philosophers.

II

Jacob Rey was born around 1753, presumably in London, although he may have been born abroad and have come to England as a young child.[2] His father, Moses Rey, was a humble street trader, un-

---

[2] The exact date of Jacob Rey's birth is unknown. According to Israel Solomons, in *Notes and Queries*, 10th ser., 9 (1908), p. 428, Rey was admitted to the charity school of the Spanish and Portuguese Jews in 1764 and was about eleven years old at the time. Solomons made this statement on the basis of a minute book of the charity school that was in his possession in 1908 and was sold subsequently to the library of the Jewish Theological Seminary of America. The library has been unable to locate the minute book for me, but a birth date of 1753 would fit well with other clues we have about King's age at different dates. Thus, around 1804, he wrote that he was 'in the evening of his life' — i.e. about fifty years old if we assume that he was born around 1753. [John King], *Oppression Deemed No Injustice towards Some Individuals, Illustrated in the Late Treatment of Mr. John King under a Commission of Bankruptcy* (London, [c.1804]), p. 27. As to the place of Jacob Rey's birth, there is a list of aliens in the Mansion House Sessions Book for 1796 (i.e. from the period of intense xenophobia and invasion hysteria associated with the revolutionary wars on the Continent) that includes the name John Rey. See Vivian D. Lipman, 'Sephardi and Other Jewish Immigrants in England in the Eighteenth Century', in *Migration*

doubtedly of North African or Gibraltarian origin, judging by the persona he affected to do business. According to one account, Moses Rey called himself 'Sultan' and dressed in 'Turkish' garb as he hawked cane strings, condoms, sealing-wax and bawdy books in the streets and coffee houses of London. Another source described Moses as a 'Turkish' Jew who had squandered his money in speculations and high living and consequently was forced to spend the last few years of his life travelling as a pedlar in the countryside from Monday to Friday.[3] Since Jewish hawkers of Gibraltarian and North African origin commonly wore Levantine costume while hawking their wares, it seems likely that Moses Rey was part of this stream of Jewish migration to England.[4]

Moses Rey differed from the mass of Jewish street traders in England in one important respect: he was sufficiently 'prosperous' to dispense with the potential earnings of his eleven-year-old son Jacob, who was thus allowed to continue his education into his adolescent years, an advantage which aided him in his later efforts to move in spheres of English society that were closed to most Jews. In 1764, Jacob Rey was admitted to the charity school of the Spanish and Portuguese Jews. Unlike the traditional Jewish schools of the Ashkenazim, this school offered instruction in both religious and secular subjects, with a marked emphasis on the latter. (For example, it was found in 1779 that most of the boys could not read even the daily service in Hebrew.[5]) When Jacob Rey left school in 1771, the wardens of the charity paid a premium of £5 to apprentice him as a clerk in a Jewish house in the City, again an advantage that few Jewish youth at the time enjoyed.[6]

---

and Settlement: Proceedings of the Anglo-American Jewish Historical Conference ... July 1970 (London, 1971), p. 61. No address, occupation, age, or place of birth is indicated. Nor is there any reason to believe that King would have given his name in such a peculiar fashion — half English and half Spanish. Nevertheless, there is a small possibility that this John Rey was the same person as John King.

[3] *Authentic Memoirs, Memorandums, and Confessions Taken from the Journal of His Predatorial Majesty, the King of the Swindlers* (London, n.d.), pp. 27–8; 'John King', *The Scourge*, 1 (1811), p. 1.

[4] For this aspect of Jewish immigration to England see Endelman, *The Jews of Georgian England*, p. 341, n. 5; and Lipman, in *Migration and Settlement*, pp. 42–3.

[5] James Picciotto, *Sketches of Anglo-Jewish History*, ed. Israel Finestein (London, 1956), p. 162.

[6] Solomons, *Notes and Queries*, 10th ser., 9, p. 428.

Unquestionably Rey was an ambitious young man. Within a few years of leaving school, he anglicized his name and was known thereafter as John King.[7] Since his Spanish name was hardly difficult to pronounce or spell, this decision probably represented a conscious effort to avoid the popular odium attached to Jews. The fact that it was common in mid-eighteenth-century England for stage Jews and other stereotyped Jewish characters to bear extravagant Spanish-like names provided an additional incentive for Rey to rid himself of his Iberian-Jewish pedigree. Such name changes, however, were not usual among the Jews of Georgian England. Even wealthy Sephardim who had severed their ties with the Jewish community, such as Samson Gideon, David Ricardo and Manasseh Masseh Lopes, did not trouble to anglicize their names. Thus, Jacob Rey's decision to become John King should be seen as a self-conscious move to de-emphasize his Jewish background.

After completing his clerkship, King became articled to an attorney for a short period — presumably to familiarize himself with the property and financial transactions that were the stuff of attorneys' business. At the time these low-rank legal functionaries were much-despised figures, although their services were essential for the trans-action of important legal matters. They routinely drew up wills and other property settlements, bills of exchange, and mortgages, for example. In addition, their knowledge of men and money allowed them to operate an informal credit system that brought together creditors and debtors who had not previously been acquainted. In the absence of well-developed credit and investment institutions, they assumed a financial role similar to that later performed by bankers, matching persons possessing idle savings with persons in need of ready cash.[8]

By the time that he was twenty-one, King was active as a money-lender. The newly married Mary Robinson, the future mistress of the Prince of Wales, recalled in her memoirs that her husband frequently borrowed money from King just after their marriage, which took place sometime in late 1773 or 1774. 'About this period I observed that Mr. Robinson had frequent visitors of the Jewish tribe; that he

---

[7] In 1775, in a Portuguese letter to the wardens of the Sephardic charity school, he signed his name 'Jacob Rey', but the English translation of the letter, which was inserted in the records at the time, was signed 'John King' (ibid.).

[8] *Authentic Memoirs*, p. 28; 'John King', *The Scourge*, 1, p. 2; *Gentleman's Magazine*, 94, pt 1 (1824), p. 1 184.

was often closeted with them and that some secret negotiation was going forward to which I was a total stranger. Among others, Mr. King was a constant visitor.' With much disdain she remarked that 'the parlour of our house was almost as much frequented by Jews as though it had been their synagogue'.[9]

King's choice of a trade appears as puzzling at first. One would not expect to find a Jew anxious for acceptance in social circles outside the Jewish community seeking his fortune in so opprobrious a calling. The association of Jews with money-lending was hoary, dating back to the High Middle Ages, when it was the single most important economic pursuit in the Jewish communities of England, northern France and Germany. Long after money-lending had ceased to play a critical role in the Ashkenazic economy, the myth of the Jew as grasping and usurious, hard-hearted and hard-dealing, remained alive. Even in so commercially sophisticated a society as Georgian England, critics of the Jews continued to view them *en bloc* as usurers, sometimes literally but more often in the sense that they transferred the standards of usury to other trades in which they had become active.[10] This association between Jewishness and a grasping, usurious sensibility was given expression in a quip attributed to Charles James Fox, a notoriously unsuccessful gambler who borrowed heavily from Jewish money-lenders. Thomas Townshend, so the story went, was talking with Fox and other parliamentary colleagues of the debates the preceding winter in the House of Commons and observed that Fox had never been oftener *on his legs* in any one session. "True," answered Charles, who loved to joke on his own misfortunes, "for the Jews left me not a chair to sit on."[11]

The attribution of a usurious outlook to Anglo-Jewry as a body reflected not only centuries of myth-making about the character of

[9] Mary Robinson, *Memoirs of Mary Robinson: 'Perdita'* (London, 1895), pp. 80–1.

[10] Captain Gronow, an observer of upper-class comings and goings in the Regency period, devoted a chapter in his memoirs to 'Jew Money Lenders', in which he made the link between Jewish usury and Jewish deviousness in other fields: 'if he [the Jew] can become the agent of any dirty work, [he] is only too happy to be so, in preference to a straightforward and honest transaction ... a class of traders who in all parts of the world are sure to embrace what may be termed illicit and illegitimate commerce' — Rees Howell Gronow, *Reminiscences of Captain Gronow*, 2nd rev. edn (London, 1862), p. 183.

[11] B. C. Walpole, *The Life of the Late Right Honorable Charles James Fox* (New York, 1811), p. 29.

the Jew, but also the persistence into the eighteenth and early nineteenth century of Jewish involvement in the personal money trade. These money-lenders acted not as suppliers of capital for industrial and commercial expansion, but rather as providers of loans for personal consumption to members of the upper class who lived beyond their means. The mania for gambling in the late eighteenth and early nineteenth century sent scores of well-connected young men in search of Jewish money-lenders. According to a censorious pamphlet of 1784, heavily capitalized, lavishly appointed gaming-clubs 'seduced' and 'ruined' the young inexperienced gentleman, who, as a consequence, was introduced by older associates 'to Jews, to annuity brokers, and to the long train of money lenders' who stood ready 'to answer his pecuniary calls'.[12] Charles James Fox, the Prince of Wales, the third Earl of Orford and the fourth Earl of Sandwich were among the better-known clients of Jewish money-lenders during the last decades of the century.[13] Thomas Rowlandson's 1784 engraving

[12] Andrew Steinmetz, *The Gaming Table: Its Votaries and Victims*, 2 vols (London, 1870), vol. 1, pp. 113–17. According to Steinmetz, there were only half a dozen gaming houses in London in the 1780s but nearly fifty by 1820 (ibid., p. 122). This passion for gambling, it should be noted, was fuelled by the agricultural prosperity of these years, which swelled the rent rolls of the gentry and aristocracy.

[13] Endelman, *The Jews of Georgian England*, pp. 212–13. Fox was £50,000 in debt before he came of age; in the winter of 1773–4, his debts amounted to £140,000; at his father's death later that year, they were over £154,000. He referred to the antechamber in his house in St James's Place as the Jerusalem Chamber because it was so frequently filled with Jewish money-lenders. See John W. Derry, *Charles James Fox* (London, 1972), p. 50; Steinmetz, *The Gaming Table*, vol. 1, pp. 309 and 316. A number of contemporary sources relate the following story regarding Fox's involvement with Jewish money-lenders. Charles's elder brother Stephen, heir to the title and property of their father, Lord Holland, was in poor health and himself without an heir, so it was believed that Charles would eventually succeed to the title. This probability gave hope to Fox's creditors that they would be paid some day. When a son was born to Stephen, Charles was called out of the Jerusalem Chamber, where a number of his Jewish creditors were gathered, to be told the news. When he returned, the Jews noticed a look of disappointment on his face and exclaimed, 'Vas is de matter? Vas is de matter, Master Fox?' 'Bad enough, indeed', replied Charles; 'here is a second Messiah come to plague you all' — Walpole, *Charles James Fox*, pp. 28–9. The story also appears in Edward Gibbon, *The Letters of Edward Gibbon*, ed. J. E. Norton, 3 vols (New York, 1956), vol. 1, p. 382; and Horace Walpole, *The Letters of Horace Walpole, Fourth Earl of Oxford*, ed. Mrs. Paget Toynbee, 16 vols (Oxford, 1904), vol. 8, pp. 367 and 370.

Money Lenders presents two heavy-jowled Jews with thick dark features carefully examining documents being offered to them by an elegant young buck seated at his breakfast table.[14] Much of the literature bewailing the passion for gambling fastened on the role of Jewish money-lenders in sustaining the mania. Captain Rees Howell Gronow, a Regency dandy and observer of London society, admitted that the 'Hebrew moneylenders could not thrive if there were no borrowers: the gambler brings about his own ruin', but also shrewdly noted that 'the mildness and civility with which the Christian in difficulties always addresses the moneyed Israelite contrast forcibly with the opprobrious epithets lavished on him when the day for settlement comes'. Thomas Erskine, the future Lord Chancellor, suggested that to extinguish the gambling-mania money-lending should be curbed: 'When the oil is spent, the lamp will go out of itself without an extinguisher; draw off the water from a man of war, and it is as great a victory as to blow her up or sink her. A gamester without his Jew is this very lamp without oil or this ship without water ...'[15]

With money-lending viewed as disreputable and as 'Jewish', why would John King, who presumably was eager to shed the taint of Jewishness, have made such a career choice? The answer may lie in the narrow range of opportunities open to a young Jew without capital and connections but with the ambition to rise above the place into which he had been born. Military, legal, clerical and parliamentary careers, which frequently offered mobility to clever young men without the advantage of good birth, were closed to unconverted Jews — if not legally in every case, at least in practice. A mercantile career could not have held out much chance of rapid advancement, since King was not connected to any of the great Anglo-Jewish families engaged in overseas commerce. Money-lending, on the other hand, could be very lucrative if the lender was both shrewd and lucky. Moreover, there was a well-established tradition in Anglo-Jewry of seeking one's livelihood in ways that respectable Englishmen considered marginal to the economic well-being of the country. As a minority group only recently arrived in Britain, Jews gravitated to the periphery of well-developed occupations and trades, establishing themselves in areas of the economy that were not dominated by

---

[14] This engraving is reproduced in Endelman, *The Jews of Georgian England*; and in Eduard Fuchs, *Die Juden in der Karikatur: Ein Beitrag zur Kulturgeschichte* (Munich, 1921), p. 46.

[15] Gronow, *Reminiscences*, p. 182; Thomas Erskine, *Reflections on Gaming, Annuities, and Usurious Contracts*, 3rd edn (London, 1777), p. 14.

native Englishmen, often on the fringes of social respectability or at least outside the mainstream of conventional routines and practices.[16] Of course, the precise calculations that led King to become a money-lender can never be known with certitude, since he left no account of his early years, but circumstantial evidence does permit speculation along these lines.

Whatever determined his choice, King rapidly left behind the world of hawkers and pedlars into which he had been born. In 1775, only a few years after setting out on his own, he sent £100 to the trustees of the Sephardic charity school in gratitude for the benefits he had received,[17] and in the spring of 1776 (19 Iyyar 5536) he married Sara, the daughter of Benjamin Nunes Lara and sister of Moses Nunes Lara, future benefactor of the Sephardic synagogue.[18] Both accomplishments clearly indicate that King had become a man of substance, if not standing, within a short time.

The lending-transactions in which King engaged differed markedly from those pursued by government loan contractors such as Samson Gideon, Joseph Salvador, the Goldsmid brothers and Nathan Rothschild. Lending money to dissolute womanizers and compulsive gamblers from the upper class was a high-risk, low-status business, plagued by uncertainties and irregularities. Georgian gentlemen were not known for their probity or fair play. The aristocratic ethos disdained money matters. Contracts were not to be taken seriously because money itself was a scornful subject. Cheating in sport, business, gambling and family matters was widespread and boasted of openly. As the biographer of William Crockford, the upstart gambling-house proprietor, remarked, 'Gentlemen of the Georgian era were not sportsmen; they lied and cheated outrageously, ... even an aristocrat would stoop to the lowest forms of trickery and down-right dishonesty such as were practiced by the rogues who infested Newmarket Heath.'[19] King complained bitterly about young men just

[16] For a fuller treatment of this theme see Todd M. Endelman, "L'Activité économique des Juifs anglais," *Dix-Huitième Siècle*, 13 (1981), pp. 113–26.

[17] Solomons, *Notes and Queries*, 10th ser., 9, p. 428.

[18] Lionel D. Barnett, (ed.), *Bevis Marks Records: Contributions to the History of the Spanish and Portuguese Congregation of London*, vol. 2: *Abstracts of the Ketubot or Marriage-Contracts of the Congregation from Earliest Times until 1836* (Oxford, 1949), p. 103.

[19] Henry Blyth, *Hell and Hazard, or, William Crockford versus the Gentlemen of England* (Chicago, 1970), p. iv. On this theme see also the examples cited in Gordon Rattray Taylor, *The Angel Makers: A Study in the Psy-*

out of Eton who rapidly learned 'all the mysteries of borrowing at high interest' and then just as quickly 'the mode of cancelling the obligation afterwards'. He thought that more money was made in one year by well-born 'sharpers' who failed to meet their obligations than by Jewish and Christian usurers in ten. Charles James Fox he singled out as particularly untrustworthy, addressing him directly in a pamphlet of 1783: 'There is not an usurer in London, Jew or Gentile, but shudders at your name; and the whole army of money-dealers fly at the first glance of your eye.'[20]

In an era in which cheating was the norm, a young man without connections, especially an outsider such as a Jew, had to have sharp wits and a dull conscience to prosper. Debts were contracted in an atmosphere that encouraged borrower and lender to seek to exploit each other's weaknesses. Honesty in such circumstances was a liability and an extravagance. In embracing fraudulence to secure his fortune, 'Jew' King was doing no more than giving expression to the spirit of the age, or, to be more precise, to the standards of those circles with whom he did business.

------

chological Origins of Historical Change, 1750–1850, 2nd edn (New York, 1974), pp. 99–100.

[20] John King, *Thoughts on the Difficulties and Distresses in which the Peace of 1783 Has Involved the People of England*, 5th edn (London, 1783), pp. 2–5. The most high-born defaulters in late Georgian England were the Prince of Wales and his brothers. In 1789 the Prince and the Dukes of York and Clarence asked Abraham Goldsmid to raise money for them in Europe through his correspondents there. Simeon and Abraham Boas of the Hague agreed to advance them 350,000 guilders for twelve years at 5 per cent interest, the loan to be repaid in four annual instalments beginning 1 December 1801. The Boas brothers received the joint bond of the three princes, payable to them and vesting in them power of attorney to divide the security into shares of 1,000 guilders each. The Boas brothers sold the whole bond. For two years, however, they received no money from the princes, so that they had to pay the interest themselves to the shareholders out of fear that the credit of their house would suffer. Eventually they were forced to stop payment and became bankrupts. When French troops overran Holland in the winter of 1794–5, they seized all of the Boases' property including the princes' bond. Soon after, both Simeon and Abraham took their own lives. When the Prince of Wales again approached Goldsmid some time later to negotiate a loan for him on the Continent, he wisely declined. See Robert Huish, *Memoirs of George the Fourth*, 2 vols (London, 1831), vol. 2, p. 137; *The Correspondence of George, Prince of Wales, 1770–1812*, ed. Arthur Aspinall, 8 vols (London, 1963–71), vol. 2, p. 49.

'Jew' King's conduct in money matters is known to us largely through the eyes of his enemies, and thus an accurate reconstruction of his manner of doing business is probably unattainable. Still, it is possible to describe some of the more characteristic lines along which he operated and to be reasonably sure that much of the notoriety and disrepute surrounding him was amply deserved, despite the tendency of the sources to exaggerate his wickedness. (Not all of his money-lending activity could have been conducted on a fraudulent basis; had it been so, he could not have remained active in the trade for four decades.)

Much of the time King functioned not as a money-lender, in the strict sense of the term, but as a money-broker — that is, as a middle-man who negotiated loans for others, taking a fee for himself, without risking his own funds. Money-dealers such as King existed because men of property wanted to enjoy a high rate of return on their money (a rate frequently well above the legal rate of interest of 5 per cent) but, at the same time, did not want their lending-transactions to be known. Usury, it should be recalled, was regarded as contemptible and odious, a disagreeable calling associated with Jews.[21]

One further advantage of employing a money-broker was that it saved the lender the bother of seeking out those in need of financial assistance. A money-broker's expertise consisted, in large part, of his knowledge of and access to those circles most frequently in need of ready cash. In pursuit of his trade, King actively cultivated the acquaintance of high-living men and women of fashion. According to the *Scourge*, a somewhat sensational journal devoted to exposing corruption, King first became familiar with London's *haut monde* at the time of his marriage, when he met 'many dissipated noblemen and ruined gamblers' among the visitors at his father-in-law's.[22] Later, having prospered, he entertained lavishly and frequently at a number of homes he rented in London at different times. The *Gentleman's Magazine* noted in his obituary that 'he lived in a very splendid style, keeping an open table everyday, to which such

---

[21] King, *Thoughts on the Difficulties and Distresses*, p. 4; Erskine, *Reflections on Gaming*, p. 31. Between 1714 and 1833, the rate of interest was fixed by law at 5 per cent, but, according to Jeremy Bentham, writing in 1787, nobody lent at that rate. The lowest usual rate, upon the very best security, was 8 per cent, with 9 and 10 per cent even more common. Interest frequently went as high as 13 and 14 per cent. See Jeremy Bentham, *A Defence of Usury*, 2nd edn (Philadelphia, 1842), pp. 52–4.

[22] 'John King', *The Scourge*, 1, p. 3.

company were invited as were likely to prove profitable, either by wanting, or by lending, money on annuities'. Indeed, so widespread was the belief that his hospitality was merely mercenary in motivation that the journalist John Taylor, a friend of King for over forty years, specifically denied the accusation in his memoirs: 'From all I could observe of Mr. King, I had never the least reason to believe that any of his invitations were for pecuniary purposes.'[23]

This defence of King's motives was beside the point: no money-broker eager to conduct business in the world of fashion could forgo personal links with its denizens or do without the financial information about the great families that such ties brought with them. Money-brokers had to know about the rent rolls, the mortgages, the debts and the wills of their clients' families. In this regard, King himself admitted that from 'the peculiar circumstances of my life, I had peculiar means of learning secret histories'. What Captain Gronow said of King's son Charles — a money-broker in his own right who was also known as 'Jew' King — might equally be applied to the father: he 'had made the peerage a complete study, knew the exact position of every one who was connected with a coronet, the value of their property, how deeply the estates were mortgaged, and what incumbrances weighted upon them'. ('Jew' King the younger, it should be added, was also known for the excellent dinners he gave, both at his London house in Clarges Street and at his Thames-side villa, Craven Cottage, at Fulham.[24])

King's money transactions were not limited, however, to the well-born and the well-connected. At various times he operated money-lending offices and advertised their services in the London press. Usually he did not conduct this kind of business under his own name but arranged for others to act as fronts for him. Early in his career, for example, he opened an office in Three Kings Court, Lombard Street, under the name Messrs John Dear and Company. As his name became known and his reputation spread, the need to hide his involvement in a venture behind a façade of Christian names and Christian clerks mounted. By the early 1780s, when his reputation had grown notorious, it was difficult for him to rent an office for his operations. On several occasions when it became known that he

---

[23] *Gentleman's Magazine*, 94, pt 1, p. 184; John Taylor, *Records of my Life*, 2 vols (London, 1832), vol. 2, p. 341.
[24] John King, *Fourth Letter from Mr. King to Mr. Thomas Paine at Paris* (London, [1795]), p. 6; Gronow, *Reminiscences*, pp. 183−8; Charles James Feret, *Fulham Old and New*, 3 vols (London, 1900), vol. 3, pp. 91−2.

was the proprietor of a money-lending office, the firm had to close down.[25]

Although King resolutely maintained throughout his life that his reputation had been unfairly blackened, there is considerable evidence to indicate that he took advantage of clients when the opportunity presented itself. One particularly well-publicized case involved Joanna Southcott, the millenarian prophetess. In 1806, three of Southcott's chief disciples — William Sharp, Major Robert Eyre and John Wilson — decided to borrow money to promote her mission and turned to 'Jew' King for help. They gave him bills of exchange, bearing their signatures, for over £2,000. King was to raise money for them on these bills by circulating them to third parties, but in the end he only provided a fraction of the sums they expected. King claimed that he had been instructed to raise the money at all risks and on any terms and that he had supplied them with money when they could not obtain it elsewhere. At the end of the year, when they refused to repay the full amount of the bills, King took them to court. They claimed in their defence that they had never received true value on the bills and that they had been arrested on bills for which they had never received a penny. Whatever King's conduct, the Southcottians also seem to have been contemplating a little fraud of their own: in the trial it became known that they were expecting the coming of the millennium before the repayment of the bills was due.[26]

King acquired a reputation for unsavoury financial dealings early in his career and never succeeded in losing it. He became entangled in numerous lawsuits stemming from his business ventures; his name appeared frequently in newspapers and journals, usually in an unflattering context. On two occasions, once in 1784 and again in 1802, he fled the country to avoid imprisonment. On Christmas Day 1790, *The Times* described King, with heavy-handed sarcasm, as

> without any matter of doubt one of the most respectable characters in this country; and until the later attack on him, the

[25] 'John King', *The Scourge*, 1, p. 14; 'Charles King', *The Scourge*, 1 (1811), pp. 412–13; *Authentic Memoirs*, pp. 35–6, 86–7.
[26] Joanna Southcott, *An Account of the Trials on Bills of Exchange wherein the Deceit of Mr. John King and His Confederates, under the Pretence of Lending Money, is Exposed, and their Arts Brought to Light* (London, 1807); J. F. C. Harrison, *The Second Coming: Popular Millenarianism, 1780-1850* (London, 1979), pp. 128–9.

breath of infamy never blew on his reputation. In all his dealings with mankind he has been the strict, upright, honest man. He never took advantage of the distresses of a fellow creature, in order to rob him of his property — he never exacted exorbitant interest for discounting a bill — he has justly paid every debt he contracted to the uttermost farthing, and in a domestic line of life has proved himself a fond — faithful — loving husband — a tender affectionate and praiseworthy parent, and a feeling steady and sincere friend. Chaste in all his actions — virtuous in every sentiment — and unsullied in his reputation as a Man, a Money Lender, a Jew, and a Christian.

Twenty years later *The Scourge* singled out 'Jew' King and his son Charles as the most unscrupulous money-lenders in London. It believed 'their influence to be more extensive and their plans more dangerous than those of all the other money-lenders collectively'. In 1824, Francis Place, the radical tailor, remembered 'Jew' King as 'an atrocious villain', claiming that if an account of his exploits were written no one would believe it: 'It could not be believed that any man would ever have attempt [*sic*] to do many things which he did, without incurring punishments which would put it out of his power to commit other offences.' A thinly veiled portrait of King in one of Pierce Egan's popular accounts of London high-and low-life, published in 1830, described him as 'an old scoundrel — a swindler — a rogue — a money lending vagabond'. Old Mordecai, as Egan called him, 'was so strongly aimed at all points respecting the quirks, quibbles, and the chicanery of the law, that any connexion with him in money matters was truly ruinous. His plans were well laid — he was cold, systematic, deliberate.' Indeed, his reputation was such that it was possible for a hack writer some years after his death to link King with the far more notorious fence Ikey Solomons, an Ashkenazic Jew thirty-five years younger than King, whom King probably never met, let alone had extensive business dealings with. Yet, according to this chronicler of Ikey Solomons' exploits, King and Solomons joined forces for a time to defraud young noblemen in need of ready money.[27] After all, was it not natural for one Jewish rogue to be in league with another?

[27] *The Times*, 25 Dec. 1790, p. 3; 'Charles King', *The Scourge*, 1, p. 457; Francis Place, *The Autobiography of Francis Place*, ed. Mary Thale (Cambridge, 1972), p. 238; Pierce Egan, *Finish to the Adventures of Tom, Jerry, and Logic in their Pursuits through Life in and out of London* (London,

Amazingly, despite the notoriety that clung to King throughout the years, he never suffered from a shortage of clients. There were always young gentlemen in need of ready money who were willing to take their chances with him. In their eyes, he probably appeared no more dangerous than London's other money-dealers, and, in the last resort, they were often fortunate to find anyone, honest or otherwise, to advance them money. In addition, gullibility, naïveté and common stupidity also played a part in keeping King in business. As Francis Place noted in his *Autobiography*, 'It would not be believed that people could be found who were so foolish as to be imposed upon and robbed to the extent they were robbed by King, much less would it be believed that such persons abounded to the extent his practice shewed they did.' (Place himself refused to borrow money from King even when he desperately needed it and could obtain it nowhere else — 'to have accepted any thing from him would have been downright baseness, so I remained in poverty, sometimes wanting food'.[28])

Equally notable is that King's Jewishness played almost no role in public attacks on his character. That he was a Jew was well known. But that his Jewishness or his Judaism was the source of his roguery was not a cardinal tenet of any of his detractors. His origins were not held responsible for his immorality. Similarly, attacks on King did not degenerate into condemnations of Anglo-Jewry as whole, nor did they call for the imposition of special laws to restrain Jews as a body, as had happened earlier in the century.[29] Of course, King's carryings-on reinforced the popular image of the Jew as untrustworthy in money matters, but they did not provoke generalized discussions of Jewish avarice or misanthropy. This may have been due, in part, to the relatively high degree of toleration already enjoyed by English Jews, at least in comparison to conditions on the Continent,[30] and, in part, to the absence of a rigorous code of commercial ethics at many levels of society. In short, King may have been thought of as one rogue among many, his Jewishness as incidental to his shortcomings, or, at least, as not responsible for them.

1830), p. 179; Moses Hebron (pseud.), *The Life and Exploits of Ikey Solomons* (London, [1829]), pp. 6–9. For a more sober account of Ikey Solomons see J. J. Tobias, *Prince of Fences: The Life and Crimes of Ikey Solomons* (London, 1974). A general introduction to Jewish crime in London during this period may be found in Endelman, *The Jews of Georgian England*, ch. 6.

[28] Place, *Autobiography*, pp. 174, 238.
[29] Endelman, *The Jews of Georgian England*, pp. 110–11.
[30] For a discussion of this point see ibid., ch. 1.

III

'Jew' King's notoriety did not derive solely from his conduct in money matters. Equally offensive to many of his contemporaries was his ambition. The barriers between Jewish and Christian society having been relaxed, although not erased, King was not content to remain within the social boundaries of Anglo-Jewry and seek companionship and recognition there. English in his dress, speech and tastes, he sought to make a place for himself in a non-Jewish world far removed from the society of street traders into which he had been born. In one sense, of course, all well-to-do Jews in this period were parvenus or the sons of parvenus. Some, like King, seemed inclined to break their ties to the Jewish community. Most were content to achieve a small measure of social integration into the non-Jewish world while maintaining their closest and most intimate ties with other Jews of similar wealth and acculturation.

The single most significant step taken by King in his striving for integration was the long-term liaison he established with Jane Isabella, Countess of Lanesborough, the only daughter of the first Earl of Belvedere, a Protestant landowner with considerable estates in Ireland. Born in 1737, and thus about fifteen years the senior of 'Jew' King, she was very beautiful as a young woman and had had many suitors, but, to please her father, had married in 1754 Brinsely Butler, a man of modest fortune who served as MP for Cavan from 1751 to 1768. For his loyal parliamentary service, the government rewarded Butler with a commissionership for revenues and, in 1756, with an earldom in the peerage of Ireland. He had few mental or physical qualities to recommend him to an attractive and spirited woman; they quarrelled frequently, and she left him in the late 1770s and moved to London, her husband dying soon after, in 1779. In the metropolis she entered into a dissipated and extravagant way of living. The settlement the Earl had made for her proved to be insufficient to cover her expenses and she was living far beyond her means. In financial distress, besieged by tradesmen and shopkeepers to whom she owed money, she applied to 'Jew' King for assistance in 1783.[31]

When King first met Lady Lanesborough, she still retained much of her earlier beauty. 'Though past forty, a considerable share of the extraordinary beauty of her youth has escaped the ravages of time and

---

[31] *Gentleman's Magazine*, 98, pt 2 (1828), p. 82; *Town and Country Magazine*, 19 (1787), pp. 297–8; *Authentic Memoirs*, pp. 233–4.

withstood the blights of a dissolute and profligate life.'[32] King's detractors claimed that he took advantage of her financial plight, extracting sexual favours in return for material aid. A gossipy portrait of the couple in the *Town and Country Magazine* in 1787 suggested that he supplied her pecuniary wants 'for a premium which at once indulged his sensuality and pride'.[33] If so, the Countess must have found it a satisfactory arrangement, for she remained with him, through thick and thin, for the next forty years. Thus a liaison that may have originated in squalid circumstances developed over time into a more substantial relationship. John Taylor, noting the vicissitudes of fortune experienced by King, recalled, 'I have sometimes seen him riding in his carriage with Lady Lanesborough and his family, and other times trudging through the streets arm in arm with her in very indifferent weather.'[34] When King had to flee England in 1784 to escape imprisonment, she went with him, and they lived together in Italy for five or six years on her jointure and, one imagines, his wits. When he had to find refuge on the Continent in 1802 to avoid debtors' prison, she again joined him, although this time they were abroad for only a year or two. In 1814 she inherited the income from the Belvedere family estates on the death of her brother, the second and last Earl of Belvedere, and some time after 1817 they retired to Italy, where they lived in comfort until his death in Florence in August 1823. (Four and a half years later she also died in Florence, in January 1828.[35])

'Jew' King's friendship with the Countess of Lanesborough began while he was still married to Sara Nunes Lara. Extra-marital relationships like this were not uncommon among acculturated English Jews of the late eighteenth century. Wealthy brokers and merchants openly kept mistresses and entertained ladies of easy virtue.[36] In the late 1770s, several years before meeting Lady Lanesborough, King had been publicly linked with the actress Mary Robinson, one of the great beauties of the day, mistress of the Prince of Wales in the early 1780s, and, not coincidentally, the wife of a well-born profligate to whom

---

[32] *Authentic Memoirs*, pp. 233–4.

[33] *Town and Country Magazine*, 19 (1787), p. 298.

[34] Taylor, *Records of my Life*, vol. 2, p. 344.

[35] *Gentleman's Magazine*, 98, pt 2, p. 82; George Edward Cokayne (ed.), *The Complete Peerage*, 13 vols. (London, 1910–59), vol. 7, ed. H.A. Doubleday and Howard de Walden (1929), p. 425.

[36] For more on the extramarital sexual activity of the Anglo-Jewish notability see Endelman, *The Jews of Georgian England*, pp. 130–1.

King had lent considerable sums of money. When the Prince of Wales abandoned Mrs Robinson for another woman and settled an annuity on her, King attempted, unsuccessfully, to blackmail her by threatening to publish her letters to him.[37] Some years before meeting the Countess of Lanesborough, King also appears to have had a longstanding relationship with a Scots woman, a Miss Mackay, by whom he had several illegitimate children.[38]

King abandoned his wife within a year or two of meeting Lady Lanesborough. When he fled abroad in 1784, he made no provisions for supporting his wife or their children. Sara King followed her husband to Livorno, however, and there, before a rabbinical court, obtained a divorce from him. Whether King married Lady Lanesborough, presumably in a Christian ceremony, before or after the divorce proceedings in Livorno, or whether they ever married, is unclear. Despite rumours to the contrary, King never converted to Christianity and, thus, could not have married Lady Lanesborough in the Church of England, at least according to the accepted practices of the Church. However, it was not unheard-of for an Anglican clergyman to perform the marriage ceremony for a Jew and a Christian without requiring the Jew to undergo baptism. What little evidence there is, however, points in the opposite direction. Writing in the early 1830s, John Taylor recalled that people had said that Lady Lanesborough had not really been married to King but only appeared as his wife. More significantly, when King himself referred to his companion in a pamphlet written around 1804, he never once spoke of her as 'my wife' but always as 'Lady Lanesborough'.[39]

Whatever the legal status of King's 'marriage' to Lady Lanesborough, it undoubtedly helped gain him entrée to social spheres that otherwise would have been closed to a Jew. Lady Lanesborough was not, of course, an intimate of the most elegant or most fashionable aristocratic society, but she undoubtedly made available to King a wider circle of acquaintances than he had had access to previously. In

[37] [John King], *Letters from Perdita to a Certain Israelite and his Answers to them* (London, 1781). The blackmail attempt is described in *Authentic Memoirs*, pp. 106–12, and in 'John King', *The Scourge*, 1, p. 13.

[38] *Authentic Memoirs*, pp. 59–60, 73–6, 80–3; 'Characteristic Portrait of a Modern Apostate', *The Scourge*, 10 (1815), p. 219.

[39] 'Characteristic Portrait of a Modern Apostate', *The Scourge*, 10, p. 219; Gainer *vs* Lady Lanesborough, I Peake, pp. 25–6; Taylor, *Records of my Life*, vol. 2, p. 342; [King], *Oppression Deemed No Injustice towards Some Individuals*.

the 1790s, among the frequent visitors to his home were the eighth Lord Falkland; his sister Lucia (the Hon. Mrs. John Grattan), a prominent figure in faro circles; his brother the Hon. Charles Cary (the ninth Lord Falkland), a captain in the Royal Navy; the fourth Earl of Sandwich, inveterate seducer, flagellist, and one-time member of Sir Francis Dashwood's Medmenham Monks; Delves Broughton, son of Sir Thomas Broughton, Bart.; and Henry Speed, banker and MP for Huntingdon, 1790−6.[40]

King not only sought out the well-born but also took pleasure in entertaining minor literary and political figures, especially political reformers. In the 1790s, he cultivated the friendship of leading members of the London Corresponding Society, such as John Ashley, Alexander Galloway, Richard Hodgson, Thomas Hardy, Thomas Holcroft and Francis Place, as well as the utopian anarchist William Godwin, the Jacobin poet and journalist Robert Merry, and the opposition journalist the Revd Charles Este. John Taylor recalled in his memoirs that he had 'enjoyed many pleasant hours' among 'accomplished and intelligent society' at King's house and that King was fond of having men of talent at his table.[41]

Like most parvenus, King worked assiduously to expand his circle of acquaintances. His relationship with William Godwin, a frequent guest at his table from early 1795 to late 1798, and possibly beyond, offers a fine illustration of the difficulties confronting a Jewish parvenu in search of social acceptance. (In King's case, needless to say, such difficulties were compounded by his reputation for sharp dealing.) When Godwin first began attending dinners at King's home, he found himself subjected to criticism from his friends. He defended himself by claiming, perhaps not altogether truthfully, that he had accepted 'Jew' King's hospitality for anthropological reasons: 'My motive was simple − the study to which I had devoted myself was to man, to analyse his nature as a moralist, and to delineate his passions as an historian, or a recorder of fictitious adventures; and I believed that I should learn from this man and his visitors some lessons which I was not likely to acquire in any other quarter.' In short, 'Jew' King was an exotic − his meals were to be enjoyed, his manners studied, his friends examined, all with the scientific detachment of the Enlightenment. Accepting his hospitality did not imply

[40] Taylor, *Records of my Life*, vol. 2, p. 341.
[41] Place, *Autobiography*, p. 236; Charles Kegan Paul, *William Godwin: His Friends and Contemporaries*, 2 vols. (London, 1876), vol. 1, pp. 146−7, 157.

becoming his boon companion or even a respectable acquaintance. In the winter of 1795–6, when King attempted to exploit the relationship by asking Godwin to appear as a character witness in a coming trial, Godwin angrily declined. He accused King of using his dinners as a kind of bribe and reminded him that the frequency of his visits was due to King's initiative, not his own. He told King point-blank that many of his friends objected to his visits to a man 'of whom, to say the least, the world entertained a very ill opinion'. Godwin informed King that he had replied that it was absurd to associate only with 'immaculate persons', adding, somewhat patronizingly, that the errors of the 'vicious' could not be corrected if honest men deserted them. These none-too-subtle slurs failed to cool King's ardour. He continued to seek Godwin's company, assuring him in one letter that Godwin would like him better if he got to know him more intimately.[42]

King's pursuit of Godwin symbolizes the plight of Jewish parvenus in England. Their only claim to respectable status was their wealth; their only weapons in the struggle for social integration were those that money made possible – generous hospitality, lavish entertaining, munificent and conspicuous charity-giving. Philosophical learning, literary sensibility and romantic yearnings – the accoutrements of status-seeking German Jews – counted for little in upper-class English circles, while wealth went further in establishing respectability than elsewhere in Europe. 'Jew' King's contemporaries, the government loan-contractors Abraham and Benjamin Goldsmid, set out to make a place for themselves in non-Jewish society through generous contributions to non-Jewish charities and lavish entertaining at their country homes.[43] 'Jew' King's fortune hardly matched that of the Goldsmid brothers or other Anglo-Jewish notables, but he used what he did have in precisely the same way – showering those whom he was wooing with invitations to dinner, treating those who accepted to a generous display of food, drink and furnishings. Francis Place once accepted 'with much reluctance' an invitation from King and recalled many years later, 'He gave us a sumptuous dinner of three courses and a dessert all served on plate, the table was attended by men in livery and one in plain cloaths. This disgusted me utterly ...'[44]

Place's disgust was a little priggish; many others whom King courted were not so fastidious. Nevertheless, King did not succeed in

---

[42] Kegan Paul, *William Godwin*, vol. 1, pp. 146–7, 154–7.

[43] Endelman, *The Jews of Georgian England*, pp. 251–4.

[44] Place, *Autobiography*, p. 237.

winning the social acceptance he wanted. Some well-bred Englishmen were willing to befriend him, but most had reservations about
nouveaux riches Jews, not to say notorious Jewish money-lenders.
There were definite limits to the willingness of established circles to
absorb social upstarts. The Jewishness of a parvenu was not easily
overcome, especially if that parvenu was a scoundrel. King himself
rationalized his failure by blaming the landed elite for closing its
ranks to new men whose fortunes were earned exclusively in commerce and finance. Men of rank, he observed, 'view with a jealous eye
opulence and splendour that is not derived from inheritance, as if
there was intrinsic and superior merit in adventitious birth'. They
believe it 'more creditable to be a member of a fashionable assembly
than director of a trading society; and more honourable to inherit a
fortune bequeathed from success at cards than from the honest
earnings of traffic'.[45] What King did not state, at least publicly, was
that his Jewish origins were also a barrier to social integration.

IV

As a young man, King was attracted to reform groups critical of the
existing political system, perhaps because, as a Jew who had grown
up in poverty, he was an outsider. This interest in political affairs,
which was unusual even for well-to-do, highly acculturated English
Jews, can be traced back to his school years. While still a student at
the Sephardic charity school, he became friendly with Thomas Paine,
who was living then in the same neighbourhood, and from whom
King received something of a political education. Many years later
Paine recalled that he had seen in King 'young as you was, a bluntness
of temper, a boldness of opinion, and an originality of thought that
portended some future good ... You used to complain of abuses ...
and wrote your opinions on them in free terms.'[46]

In 1783 King published an indictment of ministerial policy entitled
*Thoughts on the Difficulties and Distresses in which the Peace of 1783
Has Involved the People of England.* In this short pamphlet, King
contended that trade was languishing and population decreasing because the government was incompetent and corrupt and its policies

[45] John King, *Mr. King's Apology, or, A Reply to his Calumniators*, 5th edn
(London, 1798), pp. 43, 45–6.
[46] John King, *Mr. King's Speech at Egham, with Thomas Paine's Letter to
him on it, and Mr. King's Reply*, 10th edn (Egham, 1793), pp. 8–9.

detrimental to the well-being of the 'middling people'. During the war with the American colonies, ministers, generals, commissioners and 'a whole list of greedy vermin' had exploited the country's distress to increase their own fortunes. Government monopolies and restraints on trade retarded the economy. Mass emigration to India or America was no solution to Britain's economic distress, since India was governed by rapacious colonial administrators and had become a refuge for bankrupts and adventurers, while the American climate was unhealthy, its uncleared and uncultivated soil not suitable to 'the dainty sons of England'. What was to be done? Disinterested and sincere patriots had to drive out the designing sophists running the government. Tariffs and taxes had to be lowered, sinecures and pensions abolished, the monopoly of the East India Company broken.[47]

King's political thinking was unremarkable and in most ways typical of anti-ministerial circles prior to the French Revolution. Whatever Paine's influence, King's approach to politics in this pamphlet was reformist rather than revolutionary. What is remarkable about this foray into political pamphleteering, however, is that it marks one of the earliest occasions that a Jew anywhere in Europe sought to participate in national political life in pursuit of goals unrelated to Jewish communal needs. (The writings of Isaac de Pinto in the 1760s and 1770s, which appeared in French although he lived mostly in Holland, mark an even earlier – and perhaps the first – Jewish foray into general political life.) King's political involvement reveals the extent to which he wanted to identify with the English nation rather than with the Jewish community. Most well-to-do English Jews in the Georgian period probably thought of themselves primarily as Jews and only secondarily, if at all, as Englishmen; almost certainly most were apolitical. Public life in general mattered little to them unless it affected their status as Jews or their specific economic interests. Still others were reluctant to engage in political activity for fear of endangering the status of the community as a whole.[48] Since the legal basis for Jewish settlement in England rested on ill-defined grounds, they thought it best to avoid antagonizing any political faction, especially during the turbulent years of the American War of In-

[47] King, *Thoughts on the Difficulties and Distresses*, passim.
[48] John Goldworth Alger, *Napoleon's British Visitors and Captives, 1801–1815* (New York, 1904), p. 102; Lucyle Werkmeister, *A Newspaper History of England, 1792–1793* (Lincoln, Neb., 1967), pp. 32–3; King, *Mr. King's Apology*, pp. 36–7.

dependence, the French Revolution and the Napoleonic Wars. 'Jew' King was among a handful of Jews who broke with this apolitical outlook.

In the 1790s, King closely allied himself with groups calling for broader participation in the political process and an end to ministerial corruption. In the early years of the decade, he spoke frequently at a debating-club in Carlisle Street and espoused views more radical than those he had expressed in 1783. For two or three years (*c.*1790—2), he served as an editor of *The Argus*, a radical newspaper scathingly critical of William Pitt and his ministers and ardently supportive of Thomas Paine and the London Corresponding Society. King entertained leading members of the Society in his home near Manchester Square, and, when central figures in the Society were arrested and tried for high treason in May 1794, he contributed generously to the fund for their support.

Although King embraced the cause of radical reform for several years in the late 1780s and early 1790s, he did not remain a vociferous critic of the government for long. Late in 1792 he abandoned radicalism and at a public meeting at Egham in Surrey proclaimed his admiration for Pitt and his distaste for the French Revolution. This reversal of loyalties resulted not from any careful rethinking of principles but rather from government pressure. The story is involved, but worth recounting for what it reveals about the character of late-Georgian political life.

The chain of events that led to King's political turnabout can be traced to one of the shabbiest practices of the London newspaper world in the late eighteenth century — the extortion of 'hush-money' (as it was called) from prominent persons to prevent the publication of abusive material. *The Times*, for example, regularly composed unflattering letters about the morals of individuals, pretending that the letters had come to the paper with money for their insertion, and demanding payment for their suppression. In the late autumn and early winter of 1790, *The Argus* published a number of articles exposing the extortionate practices of *The Times*, and in December King sued the proprietor of *The Times*, John Walter, for libel, charging that *The Times* had accused him of swindling a Mr Rice, a goldsmith in Pall Mall, out of large sums of money. King maintained that Walter had told him that he had printed the allegation because it was accompanied by 3 guineas but had offered to retract it for 5 guineas. King's libel case against Walter was tried on 23 February 1791 and the proprietor convicted. However, the government interceded to save Walter, who at the time was already in Newgate Prison for having supported the Prince of Wales during the Regency battle, since *The Times* had previously been in the government camp. On the understanding that the paper would resume its firm support of the ministry, Walter was released from prison with a full pardon, the Treasury paying his fines. In addition, the government prevented King from pressing for judgement and may have given Walter some assurance that it would retaliate against King.

The next step in King's abandonment of radicalism began in a most unlikely fashion. In July 1792, two prostitutes appeared at the Bow Street magistrate's office to charge King with assault. They claimed that, while engaged in sexual activity of a sadistic character with King, they had been whipped with 'more than customary severity'. In all likelihood, Walter or other persons acting on behalf of the government had put the women up to this. Although they recanted every word of their story the following day and did not testify against King at his trial, he was convicted all the same and fined £3,000. When King thereupon appealed the case to the Court of King's Bench (with no success) and published a protest in *The Argus*, the fine was raised to £15,000, an enormous sum for the day, which King probably could not have paid. At the same time, the ministerial press launched a campaign to inflame the passions of others who had done business with King and had grievances of their own. Faced with a concerted effort on the part of the government and its friends to silence him, King reassessed his political loyalties and apparently came to some kind of understanding with the government. He dropped his association with *The Argus* and in December 1792 delivered his address at Egham.[49]

King's speech, which was published in the ministerial *Morning Herald* of 12 December 1792, and later republished as a pamphlet, was a defence of the English Constitution and an attack on the violent turn which the French Revolution had taken. Although King still did not altogether reject the need for reforms, he now argued that they had to come about in a constitutional manner through the correct parliamentary channels. It would be folly, he felt, for the English to seek political guidance across the Channel. The Revolution had come under the sway of men lacking either merit or genius; its furious and uncontrollable momentum was consuming those who had brought it into being. When Paine expressed his hurt surprise at King's about-face, King replied that his initial sympathy for the revolutionaries

[49] King, *Mr. King's Apology*, pp. 1–28; Werkmeister, *A Newspaper History of England*, pp. 24, 32–3, 113–15, 146.

had evaporated when they became dictatorial and oppressive, un-
leashing 'a second carnage on those who differ with them in opinion'.
He denied, however, that he had abandoned the cause of political
reform: 'When it is the proper season, I shall again exclaim against
the twenty millions of annual taxes, against pensions, sinecure places,
and unequal representation; but, instead of exclaiming against the
King as you [Paine] have done, I look to him to assist in the
reformation.' As for Paine's plans for the 'equalization' of society,
which King had never found attractive, they were illusory: under
every form of government, there always had to be labourers, just as
there always had to be governors to restrain the bad and guide the
ignorant. Paine's equality was a prescription for anarchy.[50]

King's defence of the English Constitution, including his warm
words for George III and property rights, marked a retreat from the
radical anti-ministerial stance of his years with *The Argus*, but it did
not represent a full swing from left to right. He remained committed
to the legislative reform of political abuses. In an open letter to Paine
published in the *Morning Herald* of 17 April 1793, he argued that,
although there were few radical evils in the English system, there
were many abuses. However, their reform had to wait for that time
when England's overseas enemies were no longer seeking to destroy
what Englishmen were striving only to amend.[51] In the middle of the
decade, he allied himself with the non-violent reformers of the London
Corresponding Society, contributing to the support of those arrested
for treason in 1794, defending the liberties of those whom the government sought to silence. By 1795 he was again moving into the anti-
ministerial camp. In another open letter to Paine, published in the
Morning Post of 13 March 1795, he again charged Paine's writings
with breeding confusion, disorder, and anarchy among the common
people, but he also strongly denounced the government's repressive
measures − the use of spies and informers, the suspension of Habeas
Corpus, heavy taxes and ruinous loans. Under the pretence of securing the Constitution, he argued, the ministers had violated many of
its fundamental laws. Moreover, by oppressing and exasperating the
people, the government's measures pushed them to seek redress,
paradoxically, in insurrection and violence.[52]

To some reformers, however, King's change of heart was suspect,

---

[50] King, *Mr. King's Speech.*
[51] John King, *Third Letter from Mr. King to Mr. Thomas Paine at Paris*
(Egham, [1793]).
[52] King, *Fourth Letter ... to Mr. Thomas Paine at Paris.*

perhaps because he was a Jew, perhaps because he was a usurer. Francis Place did not trust him and 'always suspected that he contemplated some iniquity' — i.e. that he was a government informer. But Place did admit that some reformers were willing to credit King for honest opinions and good intentions. King himself noted that his motives had been called into question when he had subscribed to the fund for those arrested for treason and that rumours circulated that he had provided secret intelligence to Pitt and the Duke of Portland, the Home Secretary. For King, such accusations were part and parcel of the blackening of his reputation by a sensationalist press.[53] As for their truth or falsity, there is no evidence one way or the other. In business matters King was certainly a scoundrel with few, if any, scruples. Yet his public denial of the charge of being a government spy and his longstanding concern with reform stretching back to the early 1780s suggest that his friendliness toward members of the London Corresponding Society was not mercenary.

V

King's absorption into spheres of activity outside the previous range of Jewish concerns diluted and diminished his Jewish identity. The more he moved in non-Jewish circles, embraced English habits of mind and identified himself as an Englishman, the more his Jewishness ceased to be central to his sense of self-definition. This does not mean that he replaced his old identity with a thoroughly new one and that all traces of his former 'Jewish' self disappeared. Human personality is not like a lump of clay, which can be moulded into new forms at will. Acculturation, integration and secularization reshaped and attenuated Jewish identity, but rarely did they extinguish it. External events and personal crises could at times reawaken loyalties long buried and neglected, as the history of Zionism in Western Europe and the United States clearly demonstrates. Even the apostate, seeking to wash away his Jewishness in the waters of the baptismal font, usually failed to loosen completely the hold of his Jewish past (although his children or grandchildren frequently were able to do so). At a minimum, the non-Jewish world rarely forgot the origins of even the most assimilated Jews. This was certainly the case with 'Jew' King, whose epithet bears testimony to the manner in which Gentiles continued to see him even after his change of name.

[53] Place, *Autobiography*, p. 236; King, *Mr. King's Apology*, pp. 36–7.

As a student at the Sephardic charity school, King had received a basic introduction to the fundamentals of Jewish tradition. He had learned to read the prayer book in Hebrew and possibly some biblical passages as well. He had also regularly attended services at the Sephardic synagogue in Bevis Marks, as did all charity students. After leaving school, he apparently ceased to observe even the most rudimentary of Jewish traditions. There is no indication that at this point he continued to attend services at Bevis Marks. In externals, he lived as a non-Jew, and, if we are to believe his testimony at a later date, he even had begun to think of himself as a Christian in a vague sort of way. As he told the Court of King's Bench in 1795, he had considered himself a member of the Church of England since he had been old enough to judge such matters for himself. However, when examined further on this point, he admitted that he had been married according to Jewish rites and had never been baptized or admitted to the Established Church; nor had he formally renounced Judaism.[54] King's testimony, which may not have been altogether truthful, nevertheless indicates his strong desire to be identified with the majority of Englishmen, as did his change of name two decades earlier.

King's testimony in 1795 raises the question of why he did not formally embrace Christianity, given his distance from Judaism and the Jewish community. When he went abroad for the first time with Lady Lanesborough in the 1780s, it was rumoured that he became an apostate in order to marry her. Although untrue, the rumour testifies to the widely held assumption that the obvious thing for someone in King's position to do would be to join the Church. At this time dozens of Jews whose links with Jewry were already weakened did precisely this in order to advance their careers or to merge more completely into society. King's unwillingness to take this step suggests that even at this early date radical assimilation did not necessarily lead to conversion. Unquestionably one major reason why he did not become a Christian was the areligious tone of the circles in which he moved. Conversion would not have enhanced King's standing in the

---

[54] Rex *vs* Gilham, I Espinasse, pp. 285–6. In Rex *vs* Gilham, King was called as a witness regarding the financial misdeeds of another party. He was sworn on the New Testament, and after he began giving testimony the defence attorney stopped him and began raising questions about whether King was a Jew, and, if so, whether his oath was binding since he was sworn on the New Testament. Lord Kenyon ruled that King's testimony was admissible since King now considered himself a member of the Church of England and bound by the precepts of that religion.

eyes of those groups whose approval he was courting. Similarly, conversion would not have brought him greater material success or have improved his civil status.

Equally decisive in King's case — and surely in many others — was a deeply rooted ambivalence about being Jewish. His testimony in 1795 was meant to give the impression that he had rejected his past altogether, but such a declaration can hardly be taken at face value. It is difficult, if not impossible, for a member of a self-conscious and persecuted minority to shed his or her past like an unfashionable suit of clothes. King had ceased to live as a Jew in a religious or cere-monial sense and was eager to break out of the confines of the Anglo-Jewish community, but it is unlikely that he had successfully suppressed all memories of and attachments to his origins. Perhaps he retained a muted pride in Judaism, for late in life, when he came under attack for personal and business misbehaviour, he proclaimed his Jewishness in proud, almost defiant terms. In defending his character in a pamphlet published in 1798, King noted that his faith was often called into question. It is unclear whether this meant that he had become the object of anti-Jewish animadversions or simply that his own attachment to any religion was being called into question. In any case, King answered his detractors by defending Judaism. In common with other European Jews who had been exposed to Enligh-tenment thinking, he first defined Judaism in highly rationalistic terms. The 'transcendent object' of his 'adoration' was 'not profaned by mythological fantasms, or incarnated like heathen Deities'. King believed that a superior intelligence or divine intellectual power had formed the world and that Judaism, divested of its ceremonies, was a religion of deism. However, not being a systematic thinker, King also defended Judaism on traditional grounds as well. He argued that Judaism's antiquity gave it an advantage over other religions. Furthermore, the very survival of the Jews over the centuries was evidence that Divine Providence was guiding their fate in history. Their conquerors had perished while they had remained, 'firm in their faith, steady in their religion, and numerous as ever'. Not only did King defend Judaism, but he went on to attack his critics as well. He accused Christians of failing to obey the morality of the gospels, citing the 'uncharitable temper' of Protestants and the 'intolerant spirit' of Catholics, as well as Christian attitudes regarding Jews. He reminded his adversaries that Jesus had been a Jew and that Christian persecution of Jews made it seem as if Christians regretted Jesus's origins.[55]

[55] King, *Mr. King's Apology*, pp. 38–41.

King's defence of Judaism was shallow, inconsistent and unlearned, more an emotional outburst than a reasoned polemic. His willingness to bruise Christian sensibilities, on the other hand, was remarkable. The community notables, who were extremely cautious about challenging Christian beliefs, consistently discouraged public defences of Judaism, believing (probably incorrectly) that any Jewish rebuttal of Christian polemics would endanger the community.[56] King obviously felt that he could write freely on this matter without risking serious consequences, either for himself or the community. His defence of Judaism was also notable in that it signalled a return to Jewishness on his part. This public avowal of the superiority of Judaism did not mean that King had become ritually observant, only that he had given up the attempt to bury his past and had become reconciled to his Jewishness. His former identity reasserted itself, although at an earlier period it certainly appeared to have been irretrievably lost. No doubt the mounting crescendo of press attacks in the 1790s, as well as his legal difficulties, served to provoke this awakening of older loyalties. Perhaps an awareness of the futility of radical assimilation, at least in his case, also played a part. Besieged, harassed and exhausted, he may have fallen back on an older identity as a means of reasserting his integrity.

From this point King became even more assertively Jewish. When he gave testimony in the matter of the Southcottian bills of exchange in June 1807, he took the oath on the Old Testament. Questioned about his religion, he acknowledged that earlier in his life he had taken the oath on the New Testament but asserted that now he was a Jew, not a deist, and 'performed this solemnity according to the Mosaic creed, although he did not observe all the ceremonies of the modern Israelite'.[57] It is likely that around this time King also began re-establishing more formal links with the Sephardic Jewish community. In 1812, in a number of letters to the Mahamad of the Sephardic congregation criticizing the state of the worship service, he mentioned that his infrequent attendance at the synagogue was due to the lack of devotion there, a criticism made by a number of writers at the time. He attributed the small number of worshippers to the absence of decorum in the service and, in particular, singled out for blame the unruly conduct of the charity-school boys. He even proposed a number of reforms to achieve greater decorum and offered

[56] Endelman, *The Jews of Georgian England*, pp. 282–4.
[57] Southcott, *Account of the Trials on Bills of Exchange*, p. 32.

his help in implementing them.[58] King's letters leave the clear impression that he had become a member of the Bevis Marks congregation and that he attended services there, if only infrequently. More significantly, his letters to the Mahamad demonstrate a concern with the character of Jewish worship and life in England, although the depth of this concern should not be exaggerated. Still, that he bothered at all to address the problem is significant. Jews who were thoroughly alienated from the community did not trouble themselves about abuses in Judaism. They did not become religious reformers; for them, Judaism had ceased to be a matter of concern altogether.

King's most forthright statement of his renewed adherence to Judaism and the Jewish community came in an introduction he wrote in 1817 to a new edition of David Levi's apologia for Judaism, *Dissertations on the Prophecies of the Old Testament*, which was first published in three volumes between 1793 and 1800. Levi, a learned hat-dresser, was one of the few Jews in late-Georgian England to answer Christian polemicists who sought to prove the errors of the Jews.[59] As the title indicates, his work attacked Christian interpretations of prophetic passages pertaining to the fate of the people of Israel. King republished Levi's polemic in 1817 in response to missionary work being conducted among the Jewish poor by the London Society for Promoting Christianity among the Jews. To this edition King added a sixty-page introduction, dedicated to the Haham, Raphael Meldola, in which he offered a surprisingly traditional defence of rabbinic Judaism. The integrity of Judaism, King asserted, rested on the fact that God delivered the Law, both written and oral, to Moses on Mount Sinai in the presence of 600,000 persons rather than in a private act of revelation. Those who were witnesses to the events on Sinai transmitted the text of the Mosaic Law to the next generation, and thus from generation to generation it was handed on, unaltered, unperverted, eternally binding. Everywhere in the world Jews observed their religion in precisely the same way as they had in the time of Moses, while Christianity, on the other hand, had undergone many mutations and schisms. Jesus himself, who was born and died a Jew, had never abolished any part of the Law or expressed any intention of founding a new religion, but continued to observe the commandments all his life. King pointed out that nowhere in Scripture was it asserted or even intimated that Jewish

[58] Albert M. Hyamson, *The Sephardim of England: A History of the Spanish and Portuguese Jewish Community, 1492–1951* (London, 1951), p. 270.
[59] 'Levi, David', *Dictionary of National Biography*.

law was the adumbration of another law. The Messiah of the Jews would be a supporter of the Mosaic code, not its destroyer. King also argued, as he had in 1798, that Jewish survival was itself both consequence and proof of chosenness: the Jews were God's peculiar people, their preservation an act of Divine Providence. He also mocked the pedigrees of the nations of Europe, pointing out that they were unable to trace their origins back into the distant past and that they were each a hybrid mixture of many peoples, while the Jews could deduce their genealogy from the beginning of the world.[60]

Alfred Rubens has described King's introduction to Levi's work as 'a competent and utterly hypocritical piece of writing'.[61] This judgement is wrong on two counts. To call it competent is too charitable. It is rambling, discursive and without a shred of originality. Yet to brand it hypocritical is to miss its importance completely. Whether King accepted the literal truth of the orthodox position he took is irrelevant. His boastful defence of Judaism should be seen rather as an autobiographical expression of his return to the identity, if not faith, of his fathers. His unambiguous defence of Judaism should be read as an affirmation of his Jewishness, not as a theological document. King had been the recipient of severe abuse for most of his adult life and in 1817 he was, by the standards of the time, an old man, being then in his sixties. This introduction was the defiant gesture of an old Jew seeking revenge on a world that he believed had treated him unfairly. By asserting the superiority of his ancestral faith over the Christianity of his detractors, King was both justifying his return to Judaism and settling a score with the non-Jewish world that he had once sought to conquer. When he died in 1824, he did so unequivocally as a Jew: in his will, he left £20 to the Sephardic congregation in London – half to discharge part of his debts to the synagogue and half to entitle him to be remembered in an annual memorial prayer.[62]

VI

The chequered career of 'Jew' King cannot easily be assimilated into the customary schemes for discussing modern Jewish history. He did

[60] David Levi, *Dissertations on the Prophecies of the Old Testament*, rev. edn with an introduction by John King, 2 vols (London, 1817).
[61] Alfred Rubens, 'Portrait of Anglo-Jewry, 1656–1836', *Transactions of the Jewish Historical Society of England*, 19 (1955–9), p. 39.
[62] Archives of the Spanish and Portuguese Synagogue, London, MS 111, entry for 1 June 1824.

not lead campaigns to make Jews more equal or productive members of society or to make Jewish worship more dignified. He did not sit on the board of any communal organization or associate with Jews who did. He did not contribute in any way to the debate within European Jewry over the shape of Judaism and the character of Jewish identity in the age of emancipation. He did not amass a fortune in government finance or international trade and buy his (or his children's) way into upper-class society. Indeed, during much of his adult life he had very little to do with Judaism in any sense of the term, although he never ceased to be identified as a Jew by the Gentile majority.

Yet the career of 'Jew' King is not merely a colourful footnote to the mainstream of modern Jewish history — unless the proper subject matter of modern Jewish history is to remain restricted to the activities of that handful of Jews who managed the affairs of the Jewish communities of Europe. If the adoption by Jews of non-Jewish values and modes of behaviour and their entry into new spheres of activity within state and society are major themes in modern Jewish history, then the experiences of a 'Jew' King are no less critical to understanding this period than those of a David Friedländer, an Abraham Furtado, a Benjamin Goldsmid. Regardless of their intellectual stature and material standing within the community, all Jews had to confront and adjust to a set of political and social conditions radically different from those that existed a half century or century before. They did so in a variety of ways. They did not enter the modern world like a well-disciplined army, tramping faithfully in the footsteps of Mendelssohn and the maskilim. The dual processes of acculturation and integration were acted out in countless thousands of private acts and encounters, mostly but not entirely unrecorded and unobserved, far from the limelight of public discussion. The life of 'Jew' King is part of this history. His career suggests that the scope of modern Jewish history has been defined far too narrowly and simply heretofore and that our understanding of the transition from early-modern to modern Jewish history requires the discovery and reconstruction of more Jewish lives outside the groups that have so far monopolized our historiographical attention.

8

Jewish Upper Crust and Berlin Jewish Enlightenment: the Family of Daniel Itzig

STEVEN M. LOWENSTEIN

Berlin was the first of the large Ashkenazic Jewish communities in Europe to be affected both by an intellectual movement favouring Enlightenment and by a social movement leading in various degrees to acculturation and assimilation. The relationship between the intellectual currents (which expressed themselves in Enlightenment philosophy, educational reform, and, later, religious reform)' and the social changes (expressed in language and costume change, the development of mixed social groups and, in many extreme cases, baptism) is very complex. This essay will restrict itself to a single case of that relationship by focusing on one of the leading Jewish banking families in late-eighteenth-century Berlin — the Itzigs.

The transformation of the Berlin community in the late eighteenth and early nineteenth century has been discussed at considerable length in most of the general histories of the Jews.[1] What happened

---

[1] Many general works on Jewish history contain extensive discussions of Berlin Jewry, including such topics as the influence of Mendelssohn and his Haskalah disciples, the epidemic of baptisms, and so on. The following examples have been chosen from among the more popular older histories: H. Graetz, *Volkstümliche Geschichte der Juden*, vol. 3 (Vienna and Berlin, 1888), pp. 469–86, 493–8, 506–15, 516–20; Simon Dubnov, *History of the Jews*, vol, 4 (South Brunswick NJ, New York and London, 1971), pp. 325–36, 343–7, 454–8, 588–602, 614–16, 635–55; Solomon Grayzel, *A History of the Jews: From the Babylonian Exile to the Establishment of Israel* (Philadelphia, 1962), pp. 542–5; Max L. Margolis and Alexander Marx, *History of the Jewish People* (Philadelphia, 1938), pp. 594–9, 619–624; Abraham Leon Sacher, *A History of the Jews* (New York, 1965), pp. 267–72.

In addition, the following are some of the more important monographs that discuss Berlin Jewry during the period covered here: Alexander

to Berlin Jewry was pioneering for its time, with few if any models to follow. Instead the Berlin Jewish community itself provided the models, both positive and negative, for later Jewish communities.[2] Jewish historians, too, saw Berlin Jewry as a paradigm for the modernization process, and this is one of the chief reasons why they devoted so much space to the community.

Although the Jewish Enlightenment and the *Taufepidemie* (epidemic of baptisms) were not the monopoly of any social class, there can be little doubt that they had a more rapid and more extreme influence on the Jewish upper classes of Berlin than on any other group. In the small circle of very wealthy families to which the Itzigs belonged, this influence is especially marked.

Daniel Itzig (1723—99) was one of three men who became millionaires during the Seven Years War (1756—63) by helping Frederick the Great manipulate the currency. The other two, Veitel Heine Ephraim (1703—75) and Moses Isaac-Fliess (1708—76) were related to Itzig by marriage, and their family history parallels that of the Itzigs.[3]

The Seven Years War was a landmark in the modernization of Berlin Jewry. Until that time, Berlin Jewry differed relatively little from other Ashkenazic Jewish communities. Tradition remained strong. Most Jews still spoke and wrote Yiddish, and observance of Jewish religious tradition seems to have been virtually universal. As

---

Altmann, *Moses Mendelssohn: A Biographical Study* (University, Ala, 1973); Deborah Hertz, *Jewish High Society in Old Regime Berlin* (New Haven, Conn., and London, 1988); Jacob Katz, *Out of the Ghetto: The Social Background of Jewish Emancipation, 1770—1870* (Cambridge, Mass., 1973). Michael A. Meyer, *The Origins of the Modern Jew: Jewish Identity and European Culture in Germany, 1749—1824* (Detroit, 1967).

[2] In part this is because of the intellectual influence of Berlin Jewish thinkers such as Moses Mendelssohn and Naphtali Herz Wessely, or of the religious Reform movement, one of whose first congregations was in Berlin. The remarkable social characteristics of the period, with its salon women, its epidemic of baptisms and its unparalleled mixing of Jews and noblemen, also played a part.

[3] Ephraim and Itzig were not themselves related. However, two of Veitel Ephraim's grandchildren — Henne Veitel Ephraim (d. 1776) and David Ephraim (1762—1835, later known as Johann Andreas Schmidt) — married Daniel Itzig's children Isaac Daniel Itzig and Rebecca Itzig. Moses Isaac-Fliess was married to Daniel Itzig's sister Bela (d. 1793). Fliess's son Joseph (1745-1822, later baptized as Dr Carl Ferdinand Fliess) married Daniel Itzig's daughter Hanne (1748—1801).

late as 1747 a Berlin Jew had been denounced to the government (by none other than Veitel Heine Ephraim) for shaving off his beard.[4] The community minute book in 1729 shows the observance of stringencies in kashrut (dietary law) not found in the countryside. The institutions of the community were traditional indeed.[5]

The main features which set Berlin Jewry apart from other Jewish communities were its unusual wealth, its relative newness (founded in 1671), and the boom-town nature of Berlin itself.[6] Not until the Seven Years War, however, did Berlin begin to diverge widely from other communities. The war marked the beginning of Enlightenment intellectual activity in Berlin (the first works of Mendelssohn appeared in the year preceding the war). Perhaps even more vital in changing the nature of the community was the fact that the newly enriched 'coinage' millionaires of the war period gained positions of influence.

That a new group of wealthy men achieved pre-eminence in the Jewish community was not in itself unusual. The ranks of the wealthy elite in Berlin were not very stable and there was a succession of individuals who first rose to positions of great wealth and then fell to relative financial insignificance. The domination of the community by the wealthy was not unusual either, but was in fact the pattern in most Jewish communities of the period. Nevertheless, the rise of the Itzigs and their partners did have a greater than usual effect.

First of all, their rise was rapid and overwhelming. In 1754 the richest 5 per cent of Berlin Jewish taxpayers paid 21 per cent of

---

[4] See L. Landshuth, *Veitel Heine Ephraim als Anwalt des Judenbarts* (1872; Berlin, 1909).

[5] See Joseph Meisl (ed.), *Pinkas Kehillat Berlin 1723–1854* (Jerusalem, 1962), p. 45, which describes the community's practice of not eating meat with questionable growths on the lung (*bosor shenisrecho*) – what is now known as 'glatt kosher'. Residents were forbidden to bring in such meat from communities that were not so particular. Those who violated the ban were subject to the large fine of 10 Reichstaler and their dishes were declared non-kosher. Such stringencies were extremely unusual for Ashkenazic communities of the period.

Among the traditionalist institutions found in Berlin were charity institutions for Israel (Gabbai Eretz Yisrael and Gabbai Hevron) and a Beth Midrash (traditional institute for Talmudic study). The latter institution was founded in 1743.

[6] The rapid growth of Berlin is demonstrated by statistics in Friedrich Nicolai, *Beschreibung der koniglichen Residenzstädte Berlin und Potsdam* (Berlin, 1786), pp. 240–41. In 1680 there were 9,800 inhabitants; in 1712 61,000; in 1740 98,000 and in 1780 140,625. Of these 140,000 inhabitants, almost 31,000 were members of the military garrison.

communal taxes; by 1764, after the war, the top 5 per cent were paying over twice as much (43 per cent). The Ephraim, Isaac-Fliess and Itzig families together paid no less than 26 per cent of all Jewish communal taxes in 1764. Daniel Itzig's weekly taxes rose from 2½ taler in 1754 to 47 taler in 1764.[7] His two partners' taxes increased as well, though less rapidly.[8]

Second, despite the unpopularity caused by the currency manipulations of the newly rich families, the Jews began to benefit from an improved legal status. In spite of Frederick the Great's personal antipathy to Jews and his Jewry law of 1750, frequently cited as an example of restrictive and oppressive legislation, the King rewarded those Jews who were useful to the Prussian economy with both economic and civic privileges. During the Seven Years War, he created a new legal category for Jews — the 'general privilege'. Possessors of a general privilege were exempted from most of the discriminatory laws against the Jews. The second and third persons to receive such privileges (in March 1761) were Ephraim and Itzig. A few dozen followed in the period before 1790.[9] In 1791 the Itzigs were granted the unique privilege of hereditary Prussian citizenship — the only Jewish family with such rights before promulgation of the Emancipation Edict of 1812.

Besides a change in legal status, the early 1760s were marked by a noticeable change in lifestyle among the newly wealthy families. The Itzigs, like virtually all Berlin Jews, lived in the Old Town (Alt-Berlin). They continued to live in this area, but began to purchase houses on some of its best streets. In 1765 Itzig moved from the family home on a back street, Geckhol,[10] to a mansion on the prestigious Burgstrasse overlooking the River Spree. This house had

---

[7] These taxes were actually paid forty-two times a year.

[8] Moses Isaac-Fliess paid 2 taler 3 groschen in 1748 (already a substantial sum), 4 taler in 1754, and 47 taler 3 groschen in 1764. Veitel Heine Ephraim was already very wealthy before the war. In 1745 he was already paying 4 taler 18 groschen 9 pfennigs in taxes, which rose to 7 taler 18 groschen in 1754 and 31 taler 12 groschen in 1764. All these figures come from *Pinkas Kehillat Berlin*.

[9] For a list of recipients of the general privilege see Heinrich Schnee, *Die Hoffinanz und der moderne Staat. Geschichte und System der Hoffaktoren an deutschen Furstenhofen im Zeitalter der Absolutismus* (Berlin, 1953), vol. 1 pp. 186–96.

[10] Later part of the Klosterstrasse.

Among the buildings previously purchased by Itzig were Neue Friedrichstrasse 36 (8,000 taler) and Neue Friedrichstrasse 42 (9,500 taler). The price of the house on Burgstrasse was 20,000 taler.

been built by a Pussian general in 1724 on the model of the aristocratic Hôtel de Soubise in Paris. Itzig expanded the house by purchasing five neighbouring buildings in order to make its wings symmetrical.

The interior of the building was decorated with wall paintings and contained an art collection, a private synagogue and a bath. Its garden had several fountains. The art collection contained works by Rubens and other masters as well as many items in the style of Watteau. Besides many landscapes, it showed such scenes from the Hebrew Bible as Moses striking the rock, and Eli and Elkanah with the prophet Samuel. Also present were some scenes from Greek mythology and at least two items with Christian themes (pictures of St Jerome in the desert and of Mary Magdalen). Similar art collections, also including Christian items, were to be found in the mansions of members of the Ephraim and Fliess families.[11]

Besides his magnificent main home, Daniel Itzig possessed several other properties in the city. In 1769 he purchased a house near the Royal Palace (outside the area where the Jews lived) built in 1749. This was later the home of his daughter, the *salonière* Sara Levy. A nineteenth-century description of this house, located at Hinter den Neuen Packhof 5, mentions its many portraits, its elegant eighteenth-century furniture, its large rooms and its large garden stretching down to the river bank.[12] There was also a large garden on Köpenickerstrasse, the Bartholdi Meierei (Bartholdi Dairy), 'which had formerly belonged to a government official and was bought by Itzig in 1771. This garden near the city gate was landscaped for the Itzigs by the royal gardener. It had hedges, shady walks, and thousands of fruit trees. Its outdoor garden theatre was adorned with statues.[13]

Itzig's partners also built magnificent buildings. The 'Ephraim Palais' at the Molkenmarkt remained a city landmark until demolished

---

[11] Nicolai, *Beschreibung der Königlichen Residenzstädte*, pp. 838–40. The collection belonging to Veitel Heine Ephraim's son Benjamin included a Caravaggio and two paintings by Poussin. Among them was *The Flight of Mary and Jesus to Egypt*. The collection of Dr Joseph Fliess included Rembrandt's painting of Ahasuerus, Haman and Esther, as well as a painting of Jesus appearing to Mary Magdalen.

[12] Felix Eberty, *Jugenderinnerungen eines alten Berliners* (Berlin, 1925), pp. 251–3.

[13] See Nicolai, *Beschreibung der Königlichen Residenzstädte*, pp. 934–5; and Hugo Rachel and Paul Wallich, *Berliner Grosskaufleute und Kapitalisten*, 2nd edn (Berlin, 1967), vol. 2, pp. 357–8.

in 1935. During the late eighteenth century, the Ephraim Palais and the Itzig home (later torn down when the Berlin Stock Exchange was built) flanked the Old Town at opposite ends, overlooking the River Spree. The Ephraim Palais, acquired by the family in 1762, was adorned with 10-foot-high statues and a fountain. The Fliess home also was decorated with statues, library and art collections. Ephraim's mansion served mainly as a place of business rather than a home. The Itzig mansion was so large that by 1812 it was inhabited by several wealthy Berlin Jewish families, among them Itzig's son-in-law David Friedländer, his grandson Moses Friedländer, and two leaders of the Reform Jewish community.[14]

Daniel Itzig's life changed in other ways as well. He dressed in contemporary style without a beard. Although he sometimes used the Hebrew alphabet, he endeavoured to write and speak High German rather than Yiddish.[15] His children acquired a knowledge of Western culture in addition to the Jewish religion.

On the whole, the wealthy were the protectors and patrons of the Enlightenment rather than its creative spirits. Certainly the new, more acculturated lifestyle with art collections and visits to the theatre encouraged an intellectual movement that favoured less separation from the non-Jewish world. It was not, however, in itself enlightened, for the Enlightenment was an ideology of rationalism and social reform, not merely an elegant and acculturated style of living. Nor did the wealthy begin the Enlightenment in Berlin. Many enlightened thinkers, notably Moses Mendelssohn, came from poor families outside Berlin. Others, such as Salomon Maimon, Isaac Satanov and Solomon Dubno, were East European Jews who had migrated to Berlin. The handful of very wealthy individuals who were also Enlightenment thinkers (notably David Friedländer and Saul Ascher) were the exception and not the rule.[16]

---

[14] The bankers Baruch Lindau (a contributor to the Enlightenment Hebrew journal *Ha-Me'assef*) and Ruben Samuel Gumpertz. Central Archives for the History of the Jewish People, Jerusalem, P-17/508.

[15] See for instance the entry in *Pinkas Kehillath Berlin*, pp. 398–9, in High German in Hebrew script.

[16] David Friedländer came from a wealthy Königsberg family. His taxes in Berlin ranged from 4 taler 6 groschen to 8 taler 16 groschen 6 pfennigs. Lazarus Bendavid's father paid from nothing to 2 taler 16 groschen 2 pfennigs; Saul Ascher paid 2 taler 16 groschen 2 pfennigs; his father had paid between 19 groschen 6 pfennigs and 2 taler 21 groschen. Markus Herz lived a very comfortable lifestyle as a respected physician with the title *Hofrat*, but he came from a very poor family. His father never paid more

Daniel Itzig and other wealthy men used their influence to support the Enlightenment. This was possible because of their power and status within the Jewish community. In 1762 Itzig became a Berlin communal elder, and from 1775 to his death he served as one of the two official leaders of Prussian Jewry (*Oberlandesältester*).[17] Daniel Itzig and seven of his children or sons-in-law, along with virtually all of the wealthiest Jews in Berlin, subscribed to Mendelssohn's Bible translation. Itzig and his family also subscribed to the Haskalah (Hebrew Enlightenment) journal *Ha-Me'assef* and other Haskalah works. When the Chief Rabbi of Berlin threatened to punish Naphtali Herz Wessely for writing his tract in favour of a radical change in Jewish education (*Divrei Shalom ve-Emet* ['Words of Peace and Truth'], 1782), Daniel Itzig's son and son-in-law convinced Itzig to take steps to protect the writer.[18]

Despite the support they received from the wealthy, and the fact that they sometimes socialized with them,[19] intellectuals such as Mendelssohn expressed reservations, both in private correspondence and in print, about their business ethics.[20] Another Enlightenment

---

than 9 groschen taxes. The approximate boundary between those classified as *benonim* (middle income) and those classified as *ashirim* (wealthy) in communal elections was approximately 1¾ taler. (A taler had 24 groschen.) The cut-off between *benonim* and *pahusim* (low income) was just under 1 taler.

[17] Veitel Heine Ephraim served as an elder of the Jewish community from an even earlier date, 1747, until his death in 1775. He was also an *Oberlandesältester*. The children of both Itzig and Ephraim also served in various communal offices. Interestingly, the same cannot be said of Fliess family members, who never seemed to display much interest in communal affairs.

[18] Altmann, *Moses Mendelssohn*, pp. 483–5.

[19] Mendelssohn both socialized and went on business trips with members of the Berlin elite (especially members of the Ephraim family). In his letters to his fiancee Frommet, Mendelssohn wrote in 1761 that Veitel Ephraim regarded himself as his protector and had given him a luxurious room in his house. See Dolf Michaelis, 'The Ephraim Family', *Leo Baeck Institute Yearbook*, 21 (1976), p. 209. In 1770 one of Frommet's friends who wrote to Mendelssohn on a round-robin letter was Veitel Ephraim's daughter Rösel. On a letter from Frommet in 1774, Zecharia Veitel Ephraim wrote a post script. In 1777 Benjamin Veitel Ephraim and Mendelssohn wrote a letter to their wives while on a business trip together. See Moses Mendelssohn, *Gesammelte Schriften, Jubiläumsausgabe*, vol. 19 (Stuttgart 1974), pp. 23–4, 148–9, 199, 219–20)

[20] Altmann, *Moses Mendelssohn*, pp. 97–8, quotes a letter from Mendelssohn to his fiancee in 1762 criticizing the wealthy Jews of Berlin and advising her

writer, Lazarus Bendavid, argued that the sudden wealth of the
Seven Years War was harmful to the Enlightenment. Before the war,
he said, the Enlightenment had been spread slowly through teaching.
This slow growth was later distorted:

> The Enlightenment of the Jew, which would have been ac-
> complished one step at a time in this manner, received a power-
> ful push all at once. Through this push, the Enlightenment lost
> in strength what it seemed to gain in time. The unfortunate
> Seven Years War broke out, in which a large portion of the Jews
> became rich. The Enlightenment of this people was started at
> the point where most peoples' end — with the improvement of
> the external at the expense of the internal.[21]

Even the Gesellschaft der Freunde (Society of Friends), the Enlightenment club founded in 1791 with many elite members, expressed
its fears of the power of the rich. For this reason, it excluded married
men from its membership during its early years.[22]

to avoid them. In the debate on Jewish emancipation in 1783 Mendelssohn
stated that 'Among the Jews ... I have found comparatively more virtue in
the quarters of the poor than in the houses of the wealthy — Paul Mendes-
Flohr and Jehuda Reinharz, *The Jew in the Modern World: A Documentary
History* (New York and Oxford, 1980), p. 43.

[21] Lazarus Bendavid, *Etwas zur Characteristik der Juden* (Leipzig, 1793),
pp. 34–5: 'Die Aufklärung der Juden, die solchergestalt stufenweise bewirkt
worden wäre, erhielt mit einenmale einen gewaltigen Schwung; durch ihn
verlohr die Aufklärung des Juden das an Kraft, was sie an Zeit zu gewinnen
schien. Der leidige siebenjährige Krieg brach aus. In demselben ward ein
grosser Theil der Juden reich, und man fieng bey diesem Volke mit der
Aufklärung da an, wo andere Völker gewohnlich enden — mit der Veredlung
des Aeussern auf Unkosten des Innern.

[22] See Ludwig Lesser, *Chronik der Gesellschaft der Freunde in Berlin*
(Berlin, 1842), p. 30. The exclusion of married men from admission was
finally repealed in 1807 (ibid., p. 46).

In Lesser's discussion of the reasons for the exclusion the fear of the rich
predominates: 'It was to be expected that only well-educated heads of household free of religious prejudices would ask for membership; but first of all
these were almost exclusively the wealthy, full of pride in their wealth and
reputations and therefore little suited to accept the rule of equality and
friendly association, which was the highest law of the new society. Secondly,
a large number of the young ... who were interested in the organization
were in a subordinate position to those men in their private life, for instance
as tutors, book-keepers, etc., and therefore had double the reason to fear
an aristocracy of money ...'

Whatever the reservations of the intellectuals, the fact remains that they were supported and protected by the rich. However radical the religious attitudes of some of the Haskalah leaders might be, they rarely turned to social radicalism. Since their chief supporters were the establishment of the Jewish community, it would have been folly to oppose this lay leadership directly. In addition, leading figures in the Enlightenment, including Mendelssohn's own son Joseph and Wessely, were in the employ of the leading families.[23]

Despite his worldly style of life and his support for Mendelssohn and his circle, Daniel Itzig, along with others of his generation, still retained certain elements of tradition. Like Mendelssohn, Wessely and others of his generation, born in the 1720s, he remained a traditional observant Jew. His home contained both a synagogue and a luxurious, painted room with a removable roof that could be used as a *sukkah* (booth).[24] At various points in his life he donated sacred items to the Berlin synagogue. Shortly before his death, he donated a large sum of money to the Jewish community to ensure that perpetual lights would be lit in the synagogue in memory of his beloved wife Miriam and himself.[25]

The men born in the 1720s seemed rather conservative to their successors. In the memoirs of some members of the later generation, the community leadership of the 1770s (presumably including such people as Daniel Itzig) appears as unenlightened and obscurantist. Henriette Herz, for instance, tells of the prohibition of a private theatre performance when she was about eight or nine (*c*.1773). She calls the community elders who forbade the performance 'the richest but also the most Orthodox community members'. (She does record however, that she was able to get them to relent.) Sara Meyer (born 1760), granddaughter of Veitel Heine Ephraim, blamed her mother

---

[23] In 1791 Joseph Mendelssohn was a book-keeper for Isaac Daniel Itzig, as was his co-founder of the Gesellschaft der Freunde, Aron Neo (Lesser, *Chronik der Gesellschaft der Freunde in Berlin*, p. 8). Wessely was an employee of the Ephraims' firm in Amsterdam (Michaelis, *Leo Baeck Institute Yearbook*, 21, p. 209).

[24] Nicolai, *Beschreibung der Königlichen Residenzstädte*, p. 852.

[25] *Pinkas Kehillat Berlin*, pp. 398–9. The traditionalism of Moses Isaac-Fliess is shown not only by the provision in his will disinheriting any child who converted to Christianity, but even more by a provision that the (non-kosher) wine in his wine cellar should not be sold to Jews.

Veitel Heine Ephraim's will seems to have threatened with disinheritance not only children who left Judaism but even those who abandoned practice of Jewish law. See Ludwig Geiger, 'Vor hundert Jahren', *Zeitschrift für die Geschichte der Juden in Deutschland*, 3 (1889), p. 210.

and Moses Mendelssohn for forcing her into an early and unhappy marriage. She also recalled that, when Mendelssohn caught her reading Goethe's *Die Leiden des Jungen Werthers* ('The Sorrows of Young Werther') a romantic novel in which the young protagonist commits suicide, he threw the offending book out the window.[26]

Daniel and Miriam Itzig had fifteen children who survived to adulthood. Fourteen of them married, all into the most prestigious Jewish families of Berlin, Vienna and Königsberg. The character of these marriages as family alliances is emphasized by the fact that several siblings married into the same families.[27] Marriage created a complicated set of interrelationships between the Itzigs, the Ephraims, the Fliesses, the Friedländers of Königsberg and the Arnsteins of Vienna.[28] Almost every Berlin Jew paying over 5 taler in periodic taxes in the 1770s was related to Daniel Itzig by blood or by marriage, even if sometimes rather distantly.[29]

The upbringing of the second generation still shows a mixture of the modern and the traditional, but the latter element virtually dis-

---

[26] J. Furst, *Henriette Herz, ihr Leben und ihre Erinnerungen* (Berlin, 1850), pp. 87–9; Dolf Michaelis, 'The Ephraim Family and their Descendants (II)', *Leo Baeck Institute Yearbook*, 24 (1979), p. 230.

[27] Isaac Daniel Itzig's first wife and Rebecca Itzig's husband were children of Ephraim Veitel Ephraim and his wife Jitel (*née* Marcus). Isaac Daniel Itzig's second wife, Benjamin Daniel Itzig's wife, the first husband of Zippora Itzig (later Cäcilie von Eskeles) and Jacob Daniel Itzig's wife were all children of Isaac Benjamin Wulff and his wife Händel (*née* Borchardt). I. B. Wulff was also the brother of Miriam Itzig, Daniel's wife. Moses Daniel Itzig and Henriette Itzig both married children of Rachel Joseph (later Rachel Oppenheim).

[28] Two of Daniel Itzig's children married grandchildren of Veitel Ephraim and one married the son of Moses Isaac-Fliess. A great-grandson of Ephraim, Johann Ebers, married the sister of Itzig's son-in-law and daughter-in-law. Two granddaughters of Ephraim married brothers of Daniel Itzig's son-in-law David Friedländer, while another Ephraim grandson married Friedländer's niece. Both Moses Isaac-Fliess and Daniel Itzig had children who married Eskeles and Arnstein siblings.

[29] Those paying over 5 taler in 1772 who were related in some way to Daniel Itzig were Ephraim Veitel Ephraim (father of his son-in-law and daughter-in-law), Isaac Dessau (brother-in-law and father of sons- and daughters-in-law), Aron Meyer (Ephraim V. Ephraim's brother-in-law), Rösel Bernhard (grandmother of daughter-in-law), Benjamin V. Veitel (brother of Ephraim V.Ephraim), David Friedländer (son-in-law), Edel Leffmann (mother of daughter-in-law), Zecharias V.Ephraim (brother of Ephraim V.Ephraim), Joseph V.Ephraim (also a brother of E. V. Ephraim), Joseph Fliess (son-in-law), Moses Isaac-Fliess (brother-in-law and father of son-in-law), Moses

appeared as the children grew to maturity. One very telling example of this is found in the names of the members of the second generation. All were given Jewish names by their parents, and the sons retained their distinctively Jewish given names for life. Many of the daughters, however, gave up their Yiddish names for more fashionable ones. So Vögelchen Itzig became Fanny (sometimes Franziska) von Arnstein, while her sister Zippora became Cäcilie. Jüttchen became first Jette and then Henriette. Zerelche (Zerline) kept a Jewish name but switched from the Yiddish version to the more biblical Sara. Bilka Itzig eventually became Bella (or Babette) Bartholdy. (Some of the daughters did, however, retain their original Jewish names.) The change in given names (and after 1812 of family names as well) is symbolic of the wholesale shift in identities taking place during the period.

The children of Daniel Itzig lived lives of refinement and culture as well as luxury. Their acculturated lifestyles are attested to in a number of ways. Their portraits show no remnants of traditional Jewish dress. The men are depicted with powdered wigs and are usually bare-headed; the married women are also bare-headed, in violation of tradition, and often wear the revealing fashions of the day. Two autograph albums of second-generation Itzigs also show the degree of acculturation. They contain miniature portraits and land-scapes and short epigrams in German, French and English (but never in Hebrew or Yiddish) written by friends and acquaintances. These acquaintances included members of the Berlin Jewish elite but also non-Jews, many of them foreigners.[30]

Three daughters of Daniel Itzig, Cäcilie von Eskeles and Fanny

---

Riess (brother-in-law of Ephraim V.Ephraim), Moses Bernhard (brother-in-law of Joseph Fliess, uncle of Itzig's daughter-in-law), Veitel Heine Ephraim (grandfather of son-in-law and daughter-in-law), Ephraim Marcus (uncle of son-in-law and daughter-in-law) and Hirsch Marcus (brother of above).

The only persons paying over 5 taler who seem to have been totally unrelated to Itzig by blood or marriage were Abraham Strelitz, Levin Marcus (father of Rahel Varnhagen) and Meir Eger.

[30] Both albums are in the archives of the Leo Baeck Institute, New York. One is in the Itzig Family Collection (AR 114, no. 3) and is labelled 'Souvenir de l'Amitié'. It belonged to an unnamed daughter of Daniel Itzig. (This is clear from the fact that Lea, Rachel and Cäcilie Itzig sign as sisters and Benjamin Isaac Wulff as a brother-in-law). Most entries date from 1784 to 1790. The other album belonged to Bunette Oppenheim (its archive number is AR 1952) and dates mainly to 1790. She was the sister of Daniel Itzig's son-in-law Mendel Oppenheim. Several of Daniel Itzig's children made entries in the album.

von Arnstein in Vienna and Sara Levy in Berlin, were hostesses of salons which were in the forefront of the social and intellectual life of the day. About Levy we know that she was a talented amateur pianist. In her old age she is said to have peppered her conversation with phrases like 'the last time I saw Lessing' and 'Haydn once told me'.[31]

While many of the women of the second generation were prominent in cultural and social life, some of the men continued Daniel Itzig's activity in Jewish communal affairs and later became involved in politics as well.

The most famous of Daniel Itzig's sons was Isaac Daniel Itzig (1750–1806). Isaac was active in a number of businesses including grain, wood and horse-dealing. He held the title of Chief Royal Banker (*Oberhofbankier*). In 1791 he received the unprecedented title of Royal Building Councillor (*Hofbaurat*) because of his work on government building-projects. In 1786 he bought an estate outside Berlin (Freigut Schöneberg) where he built a hunting-chalet (*Jagdschlösschen*) and houses for his labourers.[32]

Within the Jewish community Isaac D. Itzig was active as an assistant elder (one of the *ikkorim* – 1794–7), a treasurer (1780–6, 1789–2) and a tax-assessor (1785).[33] More influential were his activities in support of the Haskalah. In 1779, together with his brother-in-law David Friedländer, he founded the Jüdische Freischule (Jewish Free School), the first Jewish school with both secular and Jewish studies in its official curriculum. The first modern Jewish textbook was written for this school, with contributions by Mendelssohn and Friedländer. The school, which had eighty pupils in 1786, was housed in the old Itzig home, from which the family had moved in the 1760s. Isaac Itzig was titular head of the school till his death. In 1787 he was also the president of the Gesellschaft zur Beförderung des Guten und Edlen (Society for the Furtherance of the Good and Noble).[34]

Even better known was Daniel Itzig's son-in-law, David Friedländer (1750–1834). Born into a very wealthy Königsberg family,[35]

---

[31] Eberty, *Jugenderinnerungen*, pp. 254–5.

[32] Schnee, *Die Hoffinanz*, vol. 1, pp. 171–2; Rachel and Wallich, *Berliner Grosskaufleute*, vol. 2, 370–5.

[33] *Pinkas Kehillat Berlin*, pp. 325, 343, 361, 379, 395.

[34] Rachel and Wallich, *Berliner Grosskaufleute*, vol. 2, 370–2; Nicolai, *Beschreibung der Königlichen Residenzstädte*, pp. 699–700, 861.

[35] In the autobiography of Samuel Liepman Loewen (1750–1827) Joachim Moses Friedländer, the father of David, is described as one of only two Jews in Königsberg in the early 1770s who were not 'Pollacks in German clothing' (Archives of the Leo Baeck Institute, Valentin Family Collection).

Friedländer came to Berlin in his early twenties and became one of Moses Mendelssohn's favourite disciples. He was also the chief business adviser of his father-in-law, owned a silk factory and was a merchant. In 1808 he gave up his factory and other businesses to devote himself to public affairs.[36]

Friedländer's main activities were in intellectual and communal matters. An active Enlightenment writer, he translated the traditional prayer book into German. After Mendelssohn's death, he became progressively more radical. He ceased observance of Jewish ritual and became an active leader in the struggle for emancipation, writing most of the petitions on the subject submitted by the Berlin Jewish community. Friedländer wrote frequently and vehemently in criticism of those traditional Jewish religious practices and attitudes which he considered to be in need of radical change.

In 1799, just months before the death of Daniel Itzig, Friedländer wrote his most notorious work, the anonymous *Sendschreiben an seine Hochwürdigen, Herrn Oberconsistorialrat und Probst Teller zu Berlin, von einigen Hausvätern jüdischer Religion* ('Letter of Several Jewish Heads of Household to... Provost Teller'). In his desperation over the continued failure to procure political emancipation for the Jews, he proposed joining the Protestant Church, provided the petitioners did not have to declare belief in the divinity of Jesus.

Despite this provocative (and obviously unacceptable) proposal, Friedländer remained active in the Jewish community. He served as a community elder from 1806 to 1812, and was a leader in the struggle for reform of the traditional Jewish liturgy. He was also one of the fifteen members of the Berlin city council from 1809 to 1814. While Friedländer's writings often show a vehement opposition to tradition, even he shows occasional traces of the tradition in which he was raised. One example is the nostalgic stories he tells of the traditional days of his youth; another, the fact that, despite his acculturation, he conducted his Jewish communal business in Hebrew script as late as 1812 (though in High German). Despite his 1799 tract, he in various ways displayed opposition to conversion to Christianity.[37]

---

[36] Rachel and Wallich, *Berliner Grosskaufleute*, vol. 2, p. 378.

[37] See, for instance the story by David Friedländer about a 'Baal Teschuva' (penitent) retold by M. H. Bock in 'Gesammelte Blumen und Früchte zur neuen Sittengeschichte der Israeliten', *Sulamith*, 4, 1 (1812), pp. 148–9. His memo to the government of 1811 treats conversion to Christianity as a negative factor. His opposition to conversion (despite his 1799 tract) is also evidenced by the fact that his son Benoni waited till after David Friedländer's death to undergo baptism.

The other sons and sons-in-law of Daniel Itzig played a lesser role in public affairs. The third son of Daniel Itzig, Elias Daniel Hitzig, served as a town councillor in Potsdam, near Berlin, after 1808 and as an auditor of the Jewish community of Berlin (1789−92). Second-generation members of other prominent families such as the Fliesses and the Ephraims also participated to some extent in Jewish communal affairs, but even more in general public life.[38]

Until the last few years of Daniel Itzig's life, the influence of the family in the Jewish community and in the economy remained undiminished. In 1791, when they received citizenship, the members of the Itzig family paid over 10 per cent of the taxes of the entire Berlin Jewish community. Daniel Itzig's estate was valued between 700,000 and 1 million taler. Beginning in 1797, with the bankruptcy of the partnership of Isaac and Benjamin Itzig, the family's fortunes began to decline. Elias was left as the only solvent son. After Daniel's death in 1799, the situation deteriorated further. Daniel's son Jacob was arrested in 1805 and 1811 for various types of business manipulations. A son-in-law, David Ephraim, went bankrupt in 1805 and eventually fled to Vienna, where he was baptized and changed his name.[39]

During Daniel Itzig's lifetime no member of his immediate family converted to Christianity. All of his sons and daughters died at least as nominal Jews. Two of Itzig's sons-in-law[40] converted in the decade

---

[38] The political intrigues of Benjamin V. Ephraim in Poland, Belgium and France (in the early years of the Revolution) have been described by several historians (Schnee, *Die Hoffinanz*, pp. 162−6; Rachel and Wallich, *Berliner Grosskaufleute*, vol. 2, pp. 345−50). In 1806 he was arrested as a French spy, whereupon he wrote a memoir and justification entitled *Über meine Verhaftung und einige andere Vorfälle meines Lebens* (Berlin, 1807).

Dr Isaac Fliess was criticized for his lack of public-spiritedness in a collection of biographies of Berlin notables written in 1792. In the section on Lazarus Bendavid there is a passage which says, 'We wish that the very wealthy Dr Fliess had put him [Bendavid] in a situation where he did not have to worry about his support so that he could devote himself to study. He should have done this out of thankfulness for his [Bendavid's] supervision of him [Fliess] at the university ... [but] ... those who want to can't, and those who can − don't want to' quoted by Ludwig Geiger in 'Kleine Beiträge zur Geschichte der Juden in Berlin' (1700 bis 1817), *Zeitschrift für Geschichte der Juden in Deutschland*, 4 (1890), p. 54.

[39] Rachel and Wallich, *Berliner Grosskaufleute*, vol. 2, pp. 367−8 373−5, 377; Schnee, *Die Hoffinanz*, vol. 1, pp. 173−4.

[40] Joseph Fliess converted in 1804 after the death of his wife in 1801. When David Ephraim converted after his bankruptcy in 1805, he left town while his wife Rebecca remained in Berlin and lived as a Jew. Some sources believe

after Daniel's death. One of them did so after the death of his wife, while the conversion of the other precipitated a divorce. Two of the Itzig marriages ended in divorce. In a third case, the husband of one of Daniel Itzig's daughters had a series of illegitimate children by a Christian woman (whom he later married) while still living with his Jewish wife.

In later generations, the move away from tradition was even more marked. In virtually every branch of the family, Itzig grandchildren converted to Christianity. The first conversion of an Itzig grandchild was the case of Elias's oldest son, Isaac (later Julius Eduard Hitzig), who converted in Wittenberg less than three months after his grandfather's death.[41] This Hitzig was sent to Warsaw as a government official to keep him away from the family's influence. He later became a high judicial officer of the Prussian government (*Kammergerichts-director*) and a pious supporter of Christianity. His change of name became the subject of biting satire in a poem by Heinrich Heine:

So I straightway
Took a droshky and rushed to the
Court Investigator Hitzig,
Who was formerly called Itzig.

Back when he'd been still an Itzig,
He had dreamed a dream in which he
Saw his name inscribed on heaven
With the letter H in front.

What did this H mean? he wondered —
Did it mean perhaps Herr Itzig,
  Holy Itzig (for Saint Itzig)?
  Holy's a fine title — but not

Suited for Berlin...[42]

---

that Zippora (Cäcilie) Itzig's first husband, Benjamin Isaac Wulff, converted to Christianity after their divorce.

[41] Jacob Jacobson, 'Von Mendelssohn zu Mendelssohn-Bartholdy', *Leo Baeck Institute Yearbook*, 5 (1960), p. 254.

[42] Hal Draper (tr.), *The Complete Poems of Heinrich Heine. A Modern English Version* (Boston, Mass., 1982), p. 674. The quote is from 'Jehuda ben Halevy', IV. 38–42, part of book 3 ('Hebrew Melodies') of Heine's *Romancero*.

Julius Eduard Hitzig was soon followed into Christianity by a host of other Itzig grandchildren. Many of these baptisms took place in the 1820s and early 1830s (in some cases after the death of parents), though some seem to have occurred earlier in the nineteenth century. In at least two cases (Benoni Friedländer and Lea Mendelssohn-Bartholdy), Itzig grandchildren had all their children baptized years before they themselves converted. It is difficult to be sure how many Itzig grandchildren converted. The number is probably around twenty. In many branches of the family most of the grandchildren converted; in some branches, all did. Only a few can definitely be said to have died as Jews.[43] In many cases the grandchildren married Jewish spouses and converted together with them later in life. In other cases they were unmarried at the time of baptism. Some of these later married into the Prussian or foreign nobility. Others were granted noble titles after conversion.

By the early nineteenth century, the former influence of the Itzig family in the Jewish community was in eclipse. David Friedländer was the last member of the family to have influence in Berlin Jewry. Few members of the family played a role in the early Reform movement, in Jewish communal organizations, or even in the more general Berlin commercial community.[44] This was the result both of their

---

[43] Among those known to have converted to Christianity were: of the children of Isaac Daniel Itzig and his wife Edel (née Wulff), Marianne Cauer (baptized 1821), Jacob (1825), Benjamin Albert (1824), Johanna Nobiling (1830); of the legitimate children of Joseph Fliess and Hanne Itzig, at least Isaac Joseph (1824), as well as the illegitimate children of another son, Benjamin; of the children of David Friedländer and Blümchen Itzig, Benoni (1835); of the children of Levin Jacob Salomon and Bella Itzig (later Bartholdy), Jacob, Isaac and Lea Mendelssohn-Bartholdy (1822); Henriette von Pereira-Arnstein, daughter of Fanny Itzig and Nathan von Arnstein; eight of the children of Elias Daniel Hitzig (according to a list by David Friedländer dated 1811); of the children of Benjamin D. Itzig and Zippora Wulff, Lea Mendheim (1828) and Adelaide (1834); of the children of Henriette Itzig and Mendel Oppenheim, Marianne (1825; wife of Baron Schimmelpfenning von der Oye), Georg Moritz von Oppenfeld (1822), Louise Michalowitz and Carl Daniel von Oppenfeld (1827).

As against this long list, only the following seem to have remained Jewish: Moritz Jonathan Itzig (killed in battle 1813); Rebecca Seligmann, daughter of Bella Bartholdy; Moses Ilsing and Jacob Itzig (killed in battle 1809), sons of Benjamin Itzig; Caroline, daughter of Moses D. Itzig; Benjamin Jacob Barnhelm, (d. 1869, unmarried), son of Jacob D. Itzig and Sara Wulff.

[44] Besides David Friedländer and his son Moses, the following descendants of Daniel Itzig were to be found among the 265 families in the Reform

turning-away from the Jewish community and the decline in their economic power.

Much of the story of the Itzig family is repeated in other prominent Berlin Jewish families, such as those of Itzig's partners Isaac-Fliess and Ephraim. Although Isaac-Fliess was a traditionalist and was much older than Itzig, his family's abandonment of the Jewish community proceeded more rapidly than the Itzig's.

The conversion in 1780 of two daughters of Itzig-Fliess was among the earliest of all the conversions in the Berlin Jewish elite. The event was a *cause célèbre* not so much because Blümchen Isaac-Fliess had abandoned her husband Joseph Arnstein as because it led to a court case involving the family inheritance. Moses Isaac-Fliess had willed that any children who abandoned the ancestral faith should forfeit their inheritance. His sons tried to enforce the will, which the converted daughters contested. Daniel Itzig became involved in the case on the brothers' side, arguing not only against the converts but also warning of the spendthrift habits of family members. Eventually two other Fliess children converted. Not only did nearly all the children and grandchildren convert, but they produced many illegitimate children.[45]

---

congregation of Berlin around 1818: Mendel Oppenheim and Georg Moritz von Oppenfeld (son-in-law, and grandson), Recha Itzig and Sara Levy (daughters). In the lists of very wealthy Berliners subject to forced loans in 1812—15 the only firms listing a descendant of Daniel Itzig are Mendel Oppenheim und Wolff (son-in-law), listed at 15,000 taler (in about fifteeth place), and J. und A. Mendelssohn (husband of granddaughter) at about the same level. In the longer list of wealthy Berlin inhabitants in 1814 (including about seventy-five firms, perhaps half of them Jewish), only the following had connections with the Itzig family: J. and A. Mendelssohn (250,000 taler in capital), Bartholdy (100,000 taler), Mendel Oppenheim und Wolff (100,000 taler) and Moses Friedländer (50,000 taler). No one named Itzig is mentioned.

Among the members of the Berliner Kaufmannschaft (merchants' organization) in 1821 the only members of the family listed are Benjamin Jacob Barnheim, Moses Friedländer, Abraham Mendelssohn and Moritz Oppenheim.

Although these instances show that some Itzigs were still to be found in prominent places in the second and third decades of the nineteenth century, they generally played a quite secondary role.

[45] Between 1787 and 1798, Joseph Fliess, son of Moses Isaac-Fliess had five illegitimate children by Louisa Luza, whom he later married in a Christian ceremony. His brother Baer Fliess had two illegitimate children, besides his two legitimate ones. Joseph Fliess's legitimate son Benjamin seems to have

The Ephraim family followed a less extreme pattern, more like that of the Itzigs. The members of the first generation remained Jewish, and in some cases seem to have been more traditional than Itzig's children.[46] Many of Veitel Heine Ephraim's grandchildren converted, and, in a number of the cases in which they did not, their children did.[47] A few of the Ephraim descendants married into the nobility, and most of the male descendants eventually changed their surname to Ebers, Edeling or Eberty. The economic eclipse of the family was fairly slow. Several members of the third and fourth generation were still to be found on lists of wealthy Berliners in the early nineteenth century. A number of them were also active in the early Reform community before converting.[48]

---

had five illegitimate children by two different Christian women. Benjamin's brother Isaak Joseph Fliess also had an illegitimate son by a Christian woman. (Based on the 'Judenkartei' of baptisms of Jews in Berlin in the Evangelisches Zentralarchiv in Berlin.)

[46] Veitel Ephraim's older sons were roughly the same age as Daniel Itzig. Only the youngest son, Benjamin, was active in Enlightenment-type activities (even writing some amateur literary works). The third son, Zacharias Veitel Ephraim (1736–79), left money in his will for the creation of a traditional Talmudic house of study (Zacharias Veitel Ephraim'sche Talmudische Lehranstalt). The second son, Joseph (1730–86), was a head of the association for dowries for brides, and a member of the (traditionalist) burial society.

The descendants of Veitel Heine Ephraim's brother Marcus Heine Ephraim were even more traditional. Among the members of the very traditionalist, and frequently anti-Reform, burial society as late as 1813 were two grandsons, Ascher Marcus Ephraim and Heimann Ephraim Marcus. The latter was also a signatory of anti-Reform and pro-Orthodox petitions.

[47] Among the Ephraim grandchildren who converted were David Ephraim (1762–1835; changed name to Johann Andreas Schmidt), Albert Edeling (1764–1826), Jente Stieglitz (1764–1840, daughter of Benjamin V. Ephraim) and her sister Elka Emmerich (1774–1848), and the two daughters of Aron Meyer and Rösel Ephraim—Sara von Grotthuss (1760–1828) and Marianne von Eybenberg (d. 1814), both of them friends of Goethe. The great-grandchildren who are known to have been baptized although their parents remained Jewish are Victor Ebers (1776–1832), Joachim Ebers (1774–?), Ida and Gustav Eberty (b 1805 and 1806, baptized together with their mother Jeanette), Felix Eberty (1812–88) and Zacharias Friebe (1781–1842). Georg Moritz Ebers (1802–37) is a great-great-grandson of Veitel Heine Ephraim who was baptized. His father, Martin Ebers, seems to have died a Jew.

[48] In Berlin in the early nineteenth century, the Ephraim and Itzigs seem to

Many other Berlin elite families of the same period followed similar patterns of conversion and marriage into the nobility. In quite a few, the majority converted to Christianity by the third generation. There were some very wealthy families in which conversion and out-marriage were rare or delayed. One such family was that of Liepmann Meyer Wulff, the wealthiest man in Berlin around 1800 and grandfather of the composer Giacomo Meyerbeer. Another was the family of Joel Wolff Meyer.[49] However, the Itzig pattern was more common.

This pattern can be summed up rather simply. The first generation rapidly came into great wealth and influence. The second generation was raised in great luxury and cultural refinement. Many of its members were prominent in communal affairs and in the Enlightenment. The third generation was marked by the breakdown of communal ties and the loss of the family fortune. Conversion was only one manifestation of a more general turn away from traditional values, which was evident also in divorce, bankruptcy and dissipation. This

---

have participated in certain activities to about the same extent. For example, in 1818 the Reform congregation included four Itzig descendants and at least four Ephraims (Martin Ebers, Victor Ebers, Herrmann Eberty, Albert Edeling). Among those listed for forced loans in 1812–15 there were Zacharias Friebe (15,000 taler) and Veitel Heymann Ephraim (10,000). Both were in the list of the wealthy in 1814: Friebe with a capital of 250,000 taler, and Ephraim with 200,000. The Kaufmannschaft list of 1821 yields the names of Wilhelm Zacharias Friebe (officer), Victor Ebers, Martin Ebers and Herrmann Eberty.

[49] The rarity of elite families who produced few converts is shown by the fact that Stefi (Jersch-)Wenzel comments on the case of the Meyers as something quite unusual. See *Jüdische Bürger und kommunale Selbstverwaltung in Preussischen Städten, 1808–1848* (Berlin, 1967), p. 57.

Liepmann Meyer Wulff (1745–1812) was the richest man in Berlin at the time of his death. His son-in-law Jacob Herz Beer was the second-wealthiest Jew at the time. Wulff (known as Lippmann Tausk in Yiddish) endowed a private synagogue which lasted into the twentieth century. Beer was one of the founders of the Reform temple (sometimes known as the Beer–Jacobson temple). Although none of Wulff's four daughters converted, his son-in-law Victor Ebers did. Among the grandchildren, many remained Jewish, including the composer Giacomo Meyerbeer, who on hearing of his grandfather's death wrote to his mother promising always to remain a Jew. Even in this family, however, baptism was not uncommon. The children of two Wulff daughters converted. So did Meyerbeer's daughters and Wulff's great-grandson Felix Eberty. (It is noteworthy that almost all the family members who converted were also descendants of Veitel Heine Ephraim.)

is not to deny that, in some cases, conversion was the result of sincere conviction. In most cases, however, the desire for personal advancement, prestige or an advantageous marriage was a stronger motivation.

This pattern was so widespread in the Berlin Jewish elite of the period 1770–1835 that Jewish historians have tended to generalize it to the whole of German Jewry. Such a generalization is unwarranted for several reasons. First, the elite of Berlin Jewry was quite atypical of Berlin Jewry as a whole. The proportion of Jews resident in Berlin in 1812 who eventually converted is only about 7 to 8 per cent,[50] far below the proportion in the elite.

Secondly, the period 1770–1820 was also atypical, since it was marked, at least before 1806, by an extraordinary degree of social mixing — including marriage — between upper-class Jews and Prussian nobles and intellectuals. Such marriages were far more common in this period than they were to be later. Even more important was the pioneering situation of enlightened Jews at the time. There were no set models for Jews abandoning tradition, whether by neglecting kashrut and the Sabbath, mixing socially with Christians, moving from the Jewish district, or even playing the piano and collecting art. They did not have a sure idea of what could be reconciled with Judaism and what could not, since they lacked models of an acculturated type of Judaism such as religious Reform or of modernized Jewish cultural and social forms. Once these forms were established, later generations felt less tempted to abandon Judaism altogether as they abandoned tradition. For this reason and others, rates of conversion to Christianity as well as of intermarriage diminished in the generations after 1830 even among the elite.

The Itzig family's experience of fabulous riches in the first generation, leading to apostasy in the third, was typical of the Berlin Jewish elite in the late eighteenth and early nineteenth century. Despite what many of the standard texts of Jewish history assert, however, the experience of the Itzigs cannot be applied as a general pattern either to the majority of Berlin Jews or to the rest of German Jewry.

---

[50] Of the 3,493 Jewish residents listed in the Prussian-government list of Jews in Berlin in 1812 (Archives of the Leo Baeck Institute, Jacobson Collection, I, 82), 245 can be identified as having later accepted baptism. This would seem to be close to the real total.

9

Work, Love and Jewishness in the Life of Fanny Lewald

DEBORAH HERTZ

Although her name is all but unknown today, Fanny Lewald was well-known in mid-nineteenth-century Germany as both a writer and a public figure; it would mortify her to know that her novels have not 'stood the test of time'. She was productive: she published over twenty books, which sold well enough to support her, eventually in comfortable style. And she was courageous: when she refused to accept an arranged marriage at twenty-six, she risked condemning herself to an unsatisfying spinster daughter's life in her family home. She committed herself to Adolf Stahr and endured the long wait until he could obtain a divorce from his wife. Fanny Lewald's novels, laden with social critique, also reflect her bold, difficult life. She was a radical democrat in the 1848 Revolution, and a public advocate of women's rights before there was a feminist movement in Germany. She fought for and savoured the fame that she enjoyed in the last decades of her life. But, alas, posterity has judged her novels just not good enough.

Lewald came of age as a writer at a time when only a few German women were able to make careers as professional authors. The previous generation of female intellectuals, who came into adulthood around 1800 — the most famous were Rahel Varnhagen, Henriette Herz, Bettina von Arnim and Caroline Schlegel — published relatively little. In fact, even the most talented of them rarely made it into print. Rather, they made their literary contribution within the private world of love, salons, letters and diaries. By the time Lewald came of age, it had become easier for women to penetrate the public literary world. Young women had more opportunities to receive at least a primary education. Perhaps more importantly, it became more acceptable for a middle-class woman to use her education to earn a living. Writing was an especially quiet solution to the middle-class taboo on women's work, for it required no special training and could be done privately, at home. In addition, the increase in the number of newspapers, journals and books produced meant that there were more opportunities for women to publish. Earning a living from writing made a big difference in the private world as well, for only economic independence would allow women to exercise some control over their marriage choices.[1]

In spite of the relative advantages that Lewald's contemporaries enjoyed, writing for publication was still unusual for a woman, a project requiring ambitions and talents rarely encouraged even in daughters of the wealthier classes. Indeed, Lewald's fellow women authors were generally born into rather favourable circumstances. The noble authors in her generation included Therese von Bacheracht, Malwida von Meysenberg and Ida Countess von Hahn-Hahn, who were protected by their social position.[2] But, if one was born merely into the middle classes and, in addition, was politically radical, unlucky in love and a publishing author, then the result could easily be ostracism from polite society. Such was the fate of Luise Aston, Louise Otto, Kathinka Zitz-Halein and Luise Dittmar.[3] Lewald,

---

[1] For a good recent summary of female participation in the literary world of mid-nineteenth-century Germany see Patricia Herminghouse, 'Women and the Literary Enterprise in Nineteenth-Century Germany',in R. E. Joeres and M. J. Maynes (eds), *German Women in the Eighteenth and Nineteeth Centuries* (Bloomington, Ind., 1986), pp. 78—93. In the same volume, see also Regula Venske, 'Discipline and Daydreaming in the Works of a Nineteenth-Century Woman Author: Fanny Lewald' (pp. 175—92). In a parallel volume, John Fout (ed.), *German Women in the Nineteenth Century* (New York, 1984), see Renate Möhrmann, 'The Reading Habits of Women in the *Vormärz*', (pp. 104—17), and Lia Secci, 'German Women Writers and the Revolution of 1848 (pp. 151—71).

[2] On von Bacheracht see Gorzny (ed.), *Deutscher biographischer Index* (Munich, 1986), vol. 1, p. 83; on von Meysenberg see ibid., vol. 3, p. 1380; and on Hahn-Hahn see *Neue deutsche Biographie* (Berlin, 1959), vol. 7, pp. 498—500.

[3] On Aston see *Neue deutsche Biographie*, vol. 1, p. 423; on Otto (also known as Ott-Peters), see *Allgemeine deutsche Biographie* (Leipzig, 1893), vol. 52. pp. 737—42, and *Deutscher biographischer Index*, vol. 3, 1504; on Zitz-Halein see Stanley Zucker, 'Female Political Opposition in Pre-1848 Germany', in Fout, *German Women in the Nineteeth Century*, pp. 133—50; on Dittmar see Sophie Pataky (ed.), *Lexikon deutscher Frauen der Feder* (Berlin, 1898), vol. 1, p. 159. See also Hans Adler, 'On a Feminist Controversy: Louise Otto vs. Luise Aston', in Joeres and Maynes, *German Women in the Eighteenth and Nineteenth Centuries*, pp. 193—314.

however, was luckier. It took her a long time to find her voice, but, once she did, her output was steady and, at the time, rather well received. It also took her a long time to find and marry the right man, but again, once she did, their union was harmonious. Her devotion to hard work, her cautious liberalism and her novels' rather dutiful heroines smoothed the rough edges of her marginality and eased her way in society.

Lewald was the only Jewish woman among the better women writers of her era, making her life easier in some ways and harder in others. On the one hand, secular ideas, books and liberal politics were matters of passionate interest in her family. On the other hand, middle-class Jewish daughters were by no means encouraged to express themselves intellectually. There were no Jewish institutions, moreover, from which Leward could benefit. For although Jewish life was full of ferment at the time, none of the new movements enlisted Jewish women or addressed their problems.

In this essay, I tell the story of how Fanny Lewald found her way to a productive intellectual life. What she demanded of love and life 150 years ago were rarely available to women. And I explore her complicated identity as a converted Jew who nevertheless created fictional heroes who refused to convert. In telling Lewald's story, I demonstrate how inadequate existing models are for understanding the special plight of Jewish women. Although we know a great deal about how Jews 'in general' moved into the dominant culture, our knowledge is limited mainly to the lives of Jewish men. Once we enlarge the picture to include Jewish women's lives, we may find that none of the old paradigms quite fits any more, and that a new past awaits exploration.

Fanny Lewald's story began in Königsberg in 1811, as the first child of a reasonably well-to-do merchant family. Her early socialization was so lacking in Jewishness that she only discovered her Jewish origins from a neighbour. A young girl at the time, she only faintly understood what this meant. She later remembered the reaction at home:

> When I began to speak of these things at home, no one exactly denied it, but I was not allowed really to confirm it. And, when I became persistent, I received the answer that I could not yet understand such things; later I would learn all about it. To the very precise question 'Are we Jewish?' my father replied, 'You are our child, and don't go into it any further!'

She did indeed experience anti-semitism in the school she attended and on the streets of the city. But, by her own admission, she 'knew nothing of Judaism', and her mother, especially, preferred the family not to associate with other Jews. Her father changed the family name from Marcus to the less Jewish-sounding Lewald in 1812, when Fanny was just a year old. He arranged for two of Fanny's younger brothers to convert when they were thirteen and fifteen, although one of them did not want to abandon Judaism. Yet he actually forbade Fanny and her sisters to convert, arguing that they would never have an occupation that required it. Nor would they be the ones to initiate a relationship with a prospective Gentile suitor. Daughters could always convert if a Gentile groom appeared on the scene. As her father summed up his view, responding to Fanny's request to be converted alongside her brothers: she should wait to convert, 'because conversion binds you, whereas it makes your brothers free!' Fanny's father himself never converted, since it would have alienated his Jewish business associates in Poland.[4]

Fanny's early years were wonderfully happy, mainly because she loved school. But when she was fourteen her school closed, and she quickly grew bored with the regime of domestic tasks assigned to her as the eldest child in a large family. The only escape route was marriage. The first possibility was Leopold Bock, a local tutor and theology student whom Lewald met when she was in her 'teens. He was not only non-Jewish but also a devout Christian. Leopold came into her family's social circle through a mutual friend, a prominent minister in Königsberg. That Fanny should have met a Gentile theology student in this setting demonstrates the significant social integration of her family. Fanny later remembered how her mother

[4] The first quotation is from Lewald's autobiography, *Meine Lebensgeschichte* (Berlin, 1861–2), pt I, pp. 86–9. On her family's attitude to Yiddish and to discussions of Judaism, see ibid., p. 177. Her experience of anti-semitism at school and in the streets is discussed by Renate Möhrmann in her chapter on Lewald in *Die andere Frau* (Stuttgart, 1977), p. 121. Her brothers' conversions are discussed in *Meine Lebensgeschichte*, pt II, ch. 17. Her father's opposition to conversion by women is noted in Lina Morgenstern, *Die Frauen des 19. Jahrhunderts*, 3 vols (Berlin, 1888), vol. 2, p. 89; the quotation from him appears in *Meine Lebensgeschichte*, pt II, p. 113. His own decision not to convert is discussed in the abridged one-volume paper edition of *Meine Lebensgeshichte*, ed. Gisela Brinker-Gabler (Frankfurt am Main, 1980), p. 166.

'watched over our public conduct, over our speech and behaviour with such care and with such untiring patience'. To Fanny, her mother's goal was that she and her siblings should 'not marry Jews, and where possible [she tried] to keep us from any connection at all with Jews'.[5]

When she first met Leopold, Fanny's dreams were filled with images of fancy balls and friendships with famous people, certainly not the quiet life of a rural pastor's wife. Long conversations with him convinced her that a pastor's wife could play an important social role in a small town. Leopold asked Fanny's father for permission to marry her when she was seventeen, but her father insisted that he first complete his studies. No explicit objections were raised to her marrying a Gentile. But for some unknown reason Fanny's father forbade her to see Leopold ever again, even though he became very ill and pleaded, through mutual friends, for her to write and visit him. Fanny was despondent, but feared disobeying her father. Later a friend of the family explained to Fanny that her father had known that members of Leopold's family opposed the marriage because she was Jewish, and that this was Lewald's motive for breaking off the relationship. In the meantime, to prepare for her planned conversion, Fanny studied Christianity with a local preacher — also a friend of the family. And, even though she was no longer about to marry a non-Jew, her parents, especially her mother, pushed her to convert anyway, ostensibly to take her mind off Leopold. Her doubts about the Trinity notwithstanding, she went ahead with the ceremony. Leopold died not long after.[6]

Fanny's second great love was her cousin Heinrich Simon. She met him when she was twenty-two, when she spent the winter with his family in Breslau. Her Breslau winter was a restricted, female version of the classic German *Bildungsreise* (educational journey). Fanny's Aunt Minna was more sophisticated than Mrs Lewald, and their household was intellectually and politically lively. Heinrich and Fanny became close friends and corresponded regularly for many

[5] The quote is from the original *Meine Lebensgeschichte*, pt II, p. 166.
[6] For details of this episode see ibid., pp. 141−5. Ludwig Geiger argues that Lewald converted in order to 'assimilate', not for religious motives, that she was neither a believer nor a cowardly renegade. See his *Dichter und Frauen* (Berlin, 1896), pp. 330−1. Heinrich Spiero discusses Lewald's concerns at the time she converted in his *Geschichte der deutsche Frauendichtung seit 1800* (Leipzig, 1913), p. 25. A rather racist view is that of Hildegard Gulde, who wrote in her dissertation that it was not possible for Lewald to be a believing Christian, since she was born a Jew. See Gulde's 'Studien zum jungdeutschen Frauenroman' (University of Tübingen, 1931).

years.[7] But, once she returned to her Königsberg home, life continued in its quiet, mind-numbing way. When she was twenty-six, Fanny's father tried to persuade her to marry a rural tax-assessor in his thirties. She found his looks and personality repellent, and, hoping to marry Heinrich Simon, refused her father's entreaties. To oppose her beloved father pained Fanny greatly. When he complained of his difficulties in financing the marriages or even the upkeep of six daughters, she reiterated her willingness to earn her own income as a governess. He refused to allow it. Here was the dilemma that Lewald shared with many daughters of middle-class families in nineteenth-century Germany. Families such as the Lewalds were not rich enough to support a single daughter in cultivated idleness, yet too proud to allow them to work.[8]

And so, throughout her twenties, Lewald found herself living the quiet life of an eldest spinster daughter in the family home in Königsberg. She was to contribute her share to a large household. This entailed endless sewing and embroidery, as well as a hated daily stint practising the piano. Lewald was so intent on earning her keep that she kept a daily record of her household labour and its estimated financial worth. Her utter subordination to the will of her intellectually stimulating, but still rigidly authoritarian, father is best revealed in an incident that took place one night when she was at a party. He had a servant bring her home because she had left open a door somewhere in the house. He compounded her abject humiliation by forcing her to return to the party, thus revealing the embarrassing cause of her abrupt departure.[9]

[7] For a description of (August) Heinrich Simon see Morgenstern, *Die Frauen*, vol. 2, pp. 95–7. See also *Allgemeine deutsche Biographie*, vol. 34, pp. 371–6.

[8] For discussion of this classic nineteenth-century women's dilemma, see Herminghouse, in Joeres and Maynes, *German Women in the Eighteenth and Nineteenth Centuries*, pp. 78–93; Ute Gerhard, *Verhältnisse und Verhinderungen: Frauenarbeit, Familie und Rechte der Frauen in 19. Jahrhundert* (Frankfurt am Main, 1981); and C. M. Prelinger, *Charity, Challenge and Change: Religious Dimensions of the Mid-Nineteenth Century Women's Movement in Germany* (New York, 1987). On the particulars of the Lewald family finances and Fanny's attempts to support herself, see Brinker-Gabler (ed.), *Meine Lebensgeschichte*, pp. 1 165–73; and Möhrmann, *Die andere Frau*, p. 124.

[9] The story of her forced return from the party is discussed in Marta Weber, 'Fanny Lewald' (PhD dissertation, University of Zurich, 1921), p. 52.

Fanny was crushed to find out that her love for Heinrich Simon was unrequited. At this point she assumed that she would live out her life without useful work, without a husband and without a family of her own. But exactly what she would do with her days did not become clear until the following year, when she was twenty-nine. That was the year when Lewald found her way to a productive, and eventually a public, way of life. August Lewald, actor, playright and journal-editor in Breslau, and a cousin of her father, orchestrated Fanny's entry into the literary world by inviting her to write an article for his journal, *Europa*. Without her knowledge, he had already published excerpts from her letters in the journal.[10] He liked the article that she sent on the Prussian King's visit to Königsberg and encouraged her to write more. Lewald's first novel was *Clementine*, published anonymously in 1842. The absence of Fanny's name from the cover was a condition imposed by her father. She did not complain, but rather was grateful that he had granted her permission to publish at all. He also read through her manuscript and made suggestions. Fanny's father was clearly ambivalent about his daughter's publishing career. He could not provide her with an independent income, and by this time she no longer had any immediate marriage prospects. He did, moreover, sympathize with her misery darning socks at home. Yet he felt that his honour would be tarnished if it became known that his daughter earned money. The compromise was anonymity for her first two novels, along with a promise never to tell her sisters that she made money from publishing.

The contradictions in *Clementine* mirror Fanny's position in her own family, poised precariously between rebellion and conformity. The novel is the story of a woman unhappily married to an older man chosen by her parents. One day Clementine meets a previous suitor and falls in love with him. After a long struggle over whether or not to ask for a divorce, she decides to remain with her husband, whatever the cost to her happiness. The dilemma is portrayed sympathetically, but the resolution of the conflict is eminently traditional. To be sure, one might interpret Clementine's decision as emphasizing the cruelty of arranged marriages rather than as an argument that

---

[10] On August Lewald see Brinker-Gabler (ed.), *Meine Lebensgechichte*, pp. 184 and 192; the article on him in *Neue deutsche Biographie*, vol. 14 p. 408; and Ulrich Cruse, *August Lewald und seine zeitgeschichtliche Bedeutung* (Breslau, 1933).

women should stay trapped in them. The novel can in this way be read as Lewald's message to her father: she had been justified in rejecting the marriage that he had proposed several years earlier.[11]

In her second novel, *Jenny*, Lewald continued to focus on the difficulty of reconciling passionate love and social obligations.[12] This time, the particular problem for the hero and her brother is intermarriage. Jenny's life parallels Lewald's in an undisguised autobiographical fashion, at least in the character's first love. Jenny's family is Jewish but very assimilated. She converts in her late 'teens to marry a Christian theology student but later openly questions her acceptance of Christian doctrine. Her honesty costs her the man, for he refuses to marry a woman who is not a true believer, and lacks the will to resist his mother's opposition to the marriage. She remains proudly single for several years, until a nobleman falls in love with her. He is proud to marry a women of Jewish origins, and, when a fellow nobleman who is outraged by the marriage challenges him to a duel, he accepts. But he dies of his wounds, and Jenny proceeds to die of shock. The message: tragedy awaits those Jews who convert and the Christians who dare to marry them.

The world is also cruel to Jenny's brother Edward, but he is more consistently proud of being Jewish. Edward needs to convert to advance his medical career. He also loves a Gentile woman. Yet he refuses to convert, since he does not believe in Christianity and also is committed to the cause of Jewish political emancipation. He therefore requests permission from the state authorities for a civil marriage, a procedure that would not be legally available until 1847. His proposal is rejected, his woman friend marries his closest (Gentile) friend, and Edward goes on to dedicate his energies to the Jewish cause. The novel was based on contemporary events. Dr Falkson, a

---

[11] *Clementine* was published anonymously by Brockhaus in 1842. On *Clementine* see Möhrmann, *Die andere Frau*, p. 131; Margaret Ward, '*Ehe und Entsagung*: Fanny Lewald's Early Novels and Goethe's Literary Paternity', in M. Burkhard and E. Waldstein (eds), *Women in German Yearbook*, vol. 2 (Lanham, Md, 1986), pp. 57–77; and I. Stephan and S. Weigel, *Die verborgene Frau* (Berlin, 1983), p. 103.

[12] *Jenny* was published anonymously by Brockhaus in 1843. For a discussion, see Spiero, *Geschichte der deutsche Frauendichtung*, p. 26; and Sophony Herz, 'Treitschkes kritische Haltung gegenüber Berthold Auerbach, Rahel Varnhagen und Fanny Lewald', *Jahrbuch des Instituts für deutsche Geschichte*, 1 (1972), p. 142.

Königsberg physician, had recently brought a similar case before the Prussian courts.[13]

Jenny raises perplexing questions about Fanny Lewald's attitudes towards conversion. To imagine a protagonist who regretted converting and lost a potential Gentile husband because of her honest doubts was itself revealing. Fanny then imagined her fictional *alter ego* rewarded with the love of a nobleman who was willing to die to defend the honour of marriage to a converted Jew. The tragic end, however, shows that she saw this combination as doomed by the cruelty of an anti-semitic world. In the fictional character of Jenny, Fanny Lewald created a version of herself who was more loyal to Judaism. Jenny's brother was even more proudly Jewish. He could resist altogether the temptation to convert, lose his appeal to the state for permission to intermarry without converting, lose the woman, and emerge with dignity as a defender of Jewish rights. What was it in Fanny Lewald that had created this proudly Jewish Edward?

A year after *Jenny* was published, Fanny, at thirty-three, finally had the income and the self-confidence to leave her father's house. She found an apartment in Berlin and slowly began to build a new life for herself. Central to this life were new friends, many of whom had been prominent in the circle around Rahel Varnhagen. Rahel Varnhagen was a Jewish women of the previous generation whose writings remained mainly private, accessible primarily to her friends, but who created a public life for herself in her renowned salon. Varnhagen was at the centre of two literary salons, one in the 1790s and another in the 1820s and 1830s; she died in 1833, a decade before Fanny Lewald moved to Berlin. Among Fanny's new Berlin friends were Henriette Herz, another Jewish *salonière* famous in the previous generation, and Karl August Varnhagen von Ense, Rahel's husband. Fanny had an intense interest in Varnhagen's life story, and aspired to her *salonière* role.[14]

Her involvement with Rahel Varnhagen was so intense that in 1846 she cast her fifth book, *Prinz Louis Ferdinand*, as a historical novel

---

[13] For a discussion of Dr Falkson's case see Gulde, 'Studien zum jung deutschen Frauenroman', p. 149; also Ferdinand Falkson, *Die liberale Bewegung in Königsberg 1800–1848* (Breslau, n.d.).

[14] For background on the Jewish salons of the earlier period see my *Jewish High Society in Old Regime Berlin* (New Haven, Conn., and London, 1988). An accessible source on Karl August Varnhagen von Ense is Terry H. Pickett, *The Unseasonable Democrat: Karl August Varnhagen von Ense* (Bonn, 1985).

about Varnhagen. Once again she examined the complexities of Jewish identity. The Varnhagen of the novel is very glamorous, and popular among the Berlin nobility; her relationship with Prince Louis Ferdinand is the central theme. The Prince was a handsome hero, famous for his many love affairs, who died in battle against Napoleon in 1806. To be sure, in the novel Varnhagen's love for the Prince is ultimately unrequited, but she is portrayed as the Prince's trusted friend, the only woman to whom he can confide his political frustrations and his erotic entanglements. The matter of Varnhagen's Jewishness is explored in a few scenes near the beginning of the novel. Lewald recounts the very rapid improvement in the conditions of Jewish life under Frederick the Great, and how the salon women, as rebels, were forced to look outside their families for recognition and sociability. She suggests that the salon women's popularity was in part owing to their own families' wealth and their fathers' readiness to loan money to their spendthrift noble acquaintances. In one passage, she describes Yom Kippur Eve in the luxurious home where Rahel lives with her mother. Her mother takes Rahel to task for not having married a cousin proposed by the family, telling her that she should forget the 'princes and counts' who reject her in the end, as well as all of her 'reading and writing', and settle for marriage to a cousin. Rahel, resentful that 'God put my soul in the body of a Jew', passionately refuses to capitulate to any arranged marriage.[15]

Although in this exchange Lewald captures Rahel Varnhagen's real-life Jewish 'self-hate', elsewhere she portrays Varnhagen's Jewish pride. When asked by Prince Louis Ferdinand early in the novel how she bears injustice, Rahel replies, 'with pride, with anger, with great acts, and awaiting the revenge of Jehovah ... the Jews are the living symbol of oppression'. Later she commiserates with Dorothea Mendelssohn Veit Schlegel, who has just converted to Protestantism to marry Friedrich Schlegel. (In fact the conversion took place after Dorothea left Berlin.) Varnhagen pronounces that 'there is a curse on

[15] The full title of the novel is *Prinz Louis Ferdinand: Ein Zeitbild* (Berlin, 1859). The improvement in the situation of Berlin Jewry is described in pt I, ch. 8; the salon women's search for recognition outside their families is in pt I, ch, 9; loans to nobles are noted in pt I, p. 62; the Yom Kippur Eve scene is in pt I, ch. 14. Marieluise Steinhauer, in her *Fanny Lewald, die deutsche George Sand* (Berlin, 1937), p. 88, notes that Karl August Varnhagen did not approve of Lewald's portrayal of Levin's family as religious. For a critique of the novel on stylistic grounds see Robert Pruss, *Die deutsche Literatur der Gegenwart: 1848–58*, vol. 1 (Leipzig 1860).

the Jewish people, and I am dying from it'. Dorothea asks her why, then, she does not convert, since she has long held Christian beliefs. Rahel's reply is that Dorothea has no right to advise, since she has converted out of love for Friedrich Schlegel and not from true conviction. She continues lamenting the 'thousand barriers' she faces as a Jew, but intimates that she herself is somehow too principled to convert.[16]

Just as in *Jenny* Lewald created fictional characters more proudly Jewish than she, so too her fictionalized Rahel Varnhagen is less willing to abandon Judaism than was the real Rahel Varnhagen. Recent research, benefiting from previously unpublished letters, makes it absolutely clear that Varnhagen was not at all proud to be Jewish. True, she never pretended that she believed in Christian dogma. But there is no evidence that she had real doubts about converting in the late 1790s to marry her first noble suitor — who ultimately rejected her — or about converting to marry Karl August Varnhagen von Ense in 1814. Rahel Varnhagen's was on the whole a rather classic case of Jewish self-hate. Ponder this passage in a letter to her Jewish friend David Veit: 'I have a strange fancy: it is as if some supramundane being, just as I was thrust into this world, plunged these words with a dagger into my heart: "Yes, have sensibility, see the world as few see it, be great and noble ... But I add one thing more: be a Jewess!" And now my life is a slow bleeding to death.' Or consider this passage in one of the 'rediscovered' letters that Varnhagen wrote to another Jewish friend, Rebecca Friedländer: 'Should I always clean up the rubbish that others leave with me? It is so repulsive always having first to legitimize myself! That is why it is so disgusting to be a Jew!'[17]

Fanny Lewald clearly had a more measured, flexible sense of her Jewish identity than Varnhagen had. Still, her deep identification with Rahel Varnhagen made good historical and personal sense. With her many noble friends and her influential salon, Rahel Varnhagen

[16] See Sander Gilman, *Jewish Self-Hate* (Ithaca, NY, 1986), for a definition of the concept and numerous historical illustrations. Rahel's response to the Prince on how she bears injustice appears in pt I, p. 39, of *Prinz Louis Ferdinand*; her discussion with Dorothea Mendelssohn Veit Schlegel takes place in pt I, pp. 121–2.

[17] Rahel Varnhagen's comment to David Veit is cited in Hannah Arendt's *Rahel Varnhagen: The Life of a Jewess* (London, 1957), p. 7. The second quote appears as an undated letter, no. 128, in my *Briefe an eine Freundin: Rahel Varnhagen an Rebecca Friedländer* (Cologne, 1988).

was the first and the most illustrious Jewish woman in Central Europe to emancipate herself from traditional Jewish society and make her way in grand (if inwardly troubled) style in the noble world. At the time when she wrote *Prinz Louis Ferdinand*, Lewald's years of loneliness were still fresh in her mind, and she could empathize with Varnhagen's troubled love life. Having struggled for years to discover a vocation in writing, Lewald could also identify with Rahel Varnhagen's frustrated intellectual aspirations. And, having moved to Berlin in search of a glamorous social life, she emulated Varnhagen's popular salon.

Yet in other respects her choice of Varnhagen as a role model strikes the modern reader as paradoxical. Varnhagen had lived constantly in the shadow of anti-semitism, whereas Lewald's transition from the Jewish to the Gentile world was relatively smooth. Surely Lewald would have seen herself as living under more favourable circumstances than had Varnhagen. Consider how far Prussian Jewry had come in the years between 1800 and 1846, the year when Lewald began work on the novel. Was not her own life the best demonstration that it was better to be a thirty-five-year-old female intellectual of Jewish origin in 1846 than it had been in 1807? The Prussian Edict of Emancipation of 1812 had granted the Jews a good measure of civic equality and considerable, if not complete, access to educational and occupational opportunities. Many Prussian Jews moved to larger cities and improved their social position in the decades that followed the Edict.[18] Family businesses expanded, and Jewish bankers, merchants and entrepreneurs became richer and more powerful. Sons of cobblers, pedlars, rabbis, Hebrew-teachers, and Torah scribes could now learn German, attend gymnasium, enroll at university and become physicians, lawyers and journalists. Nor was opportunity limited to the public world of residence and employment. The private worlds of religious affiliation and marriage reflected similar changes, as measured in conversion and intermarriage statistics for the period. Beginning in about 1790, the number of conversions in Berlin increased steadily until about 1840. Before 1790 the yearly average was

---

[18] For a general overview of the improvements in this era see Ismar Elbogen and Eleonore Sterling, *Die Geschichte der Juden in Deutschland* (Wiesbaden, 1982), ch. 8; and Thomas Nipperdey, *Deutsche Geschichte 1800–1866* (Munich, 1984), p. 252. On the withdrawal of some of the rights granted in the 1812 Edict see Julius Carlebach, *Karl Marx and the Radical Critique of Judaism* (London, 1978), p. 59.

usually under ten converts; subsequently, it was usually about forty converts a year. Intermarriage rates show a similar increase.[19]

For decades after the 1812 Edict, conversion to Protestantism was required for marriage to a non-Jew as well as for appointment to civil-service positions in the universities and government bureaucracy. For the ambitious, to give up hope of these glittering prizes could be a large sacrifice in the context of the mid-nineteenth-century German-Jewish world, precisely because Jewish life was changing so quickly. It was new for converted Jews to hold high civil-service positions and be thought desirable marriage partners for Gentiles. Was the price of conversion too high, or was it, as many argued, a sign of progress?

This is a large question. Let us keep it in mind as we return to the contrast between the views of Varnhagen's and Lewald's generations on the question of conversion. For Rahel Varnhagen's generation, the absence of a viable movement for the religious reform of Judaism was a notable factor, and may help explain why she and many of her friends decided to convert. The extreme crisis of Judaism at the end of the eighteenth century is illustrated by the activities of David Friedländer, a colleague of Moses Mendelssohn, a banker, entrepreneur and community elder. In 1799 Friedländer proposed that the Jewish community should undergo a 'mass dry baptism' into a rational sect poised between Christianity and Judaism. Friedländer's proposal was ultimately rejected. But that he even conceived of such a solution to the contemporary Jewish dilemma, and proposed it semi-publicly to a prominent Protestant minister, is one of many examples in the previous generation of the widespread optimism that the two religions would merge sometime in the future. The deistic and later the pantheistic religious tendencies in the wider intellectual world made conversion seem more rational, since both ways of thinking minimized the institutionalized differences between Judaism and Christianity. In contrast, the new movements within Judaism that had developed by Lewald's time made the choice of whether or not to convert more complex than it had been for the previous generation. It was harder to justify converting when efforts were under way to reform the Jewish religion and to gain more civil rights for Jews.[20]

---

[19] See my 'Seductive Conversion in Berlin, 1770–1809', in Todd Endelman (ed.), *Jewish Apostasy in the Modern World* (New York, 1987). For extensive discussion of nineteenth-century patterns, see Peter Honigmann, *Die Austritte aus der Jüdischen Gemeinde Berlin 1873–1941* (Frankfurt am Main, 1988).

The larger story of Prussian Jewry's achievements in the decades after 1812 is relevant to Fanny Lewald's biography. Many members of her own extended family and friends of her family converted, attained professional positions, and married Gentiles. Although he never converted, her own father was one of the first Jews to become a city councillor in Königsberg. Fanny's father's cousin August Lewald, who did convert, was a prominent editor and playwright. Her beloved cousin Heinrich Simon was a noted liberal politician active in the 1848 Revolution. Her brother Otto became an officer of the judiciary and eventually a judge in Berlin.[21] As we have seen, Lewald's male relatives' successes in secular society opened the way for her to succeed as a writer.

Despite this, however, the patriarchal style of her father — and the wider social values that his style reflected — obviously presented her with obstacles to overcome. To condone assimilation did not necessarily imply encouraging an intellectual daughter. In the years after her school closed up to the time when she began to write, in her late twenties, Fanny was in fact passionately envious of her brothers' lives. She later remembered how 'just as father kept us daughters under strict discipline, he guaranteed great freedom for the sons as soon as they came of age. He generously took care of their financial needs, [and] supervised them little ... '[22] Her experience suggests

---

[20] On Friedländer's proposal see my 'Seductive Conversion', in Endelman, *Jewish Apostasy*, pp. 71–2. For background on Reform Judaism, see Jacob Marcus, *Israel Jacobson: The Founder of the Reform Movement in Judaism* (Cincinnati, 1972). See also David Philipson, *The Reform Movement in Judaism* (New York, 1967), pp. 183–4 and 398ff. (on women), as well as Caesar Seligmann, *Geschichte der jüdischen Reformbewegurg* (Frankfurt am Main, 1922). For background on the movement for Jewish civil rights see an article on a key leader by Moshe Rinott, 'Gabriel Riesser', *Leo Baeck Institute Yearbook*, (1962), 11–38.

[21] On the entire Lewald family see Heinrich Spiero, 'Die Familie Lewald', *Altpreussische Monatsschrift*, 47 (1911), pp. 318–24. On Fanny's father's election to the Königsberg city council see the article on Fanny Lewald in the *Neue deutsche Biographie*, vol. 14, 409–10. On August Lewald see the sources cited in note 10 above.

[22] The quotation is from the original *Meine Lebensgeschichte*, pt II, p. 235. On Lewald's jealousy of her brothers' lives see Möhrmann, *Die andere Frau*, p. 119. On this question, the notion of Ludwig Geiger that Lewald was 'masculine' in her character is of interest: see Geiger's article on Lewald in his *Dichter und Frauen*, pp. 326–40.

that Jewish women experienced only a pale reflection of the new way of life pioneered by so many Jewish men. Her sufferings as a Jewish daughter who was only allowed to participate in high culture within the walls of her home helps explain her complex nostalgia for Rahel Varnhagen's life. For, in the previous generation, Varnhagen and some of her women friends, rather than their brothers, had been the pioneers in the assimilation project.

Lewald's liberalism also contributed to her yearning for Varnhagen's popularity with the nobility. For, like so many liberals of her generation, Lewald craved noble connections in her private life even as she condemned the nobility politically in her publications. Her desire for noble friends may seem anachronistic, but it was bound up with the very different opportunities that the two classes − the nobility and the bourgeoisie − offered 'their' women. When Lewald was growing up, in provincial Königsberg, the class to which her family naturally sought admission was the merchant bourgeoisie. Forty years earlier, in Berlin, Rahel Varnhagen and her Jewish friends' parents were wealthy enough, and the nobility in enough of a financial crisis, for that to be the class into which the Jewish elite tried to assimilate. The two generations of fathers sought to join different classes, and this made all the difference in the world for their daughters when it came to intellectual ambition, love and marriage. Though the Prussian nobility of the late eighteenth century was scarcely decadent, women of that class enjoyed more freedom than women from equally wealthy middle-class families.[23]

Thus Lewald's sufferings as a daughter in her particular family, generation and city made her yearn to belong both to a different religion and to a different class. Her family's bourgeois values deprived her of the possibility of living the life of a cultivated, idle single woman. Yet the wider changes taking place at the time only increased her desire to emulate Varnhagen. Whereas in the previous generation private homes had been a central location for socializing, by Lewald's time more and more public dialogue took place in coffee houses, male clubs and the universities. This meant that it was more difficult for Lewald − while single and living at home − to put her secular education to work in a salon of her own. That would have to wait decades, until she was installed in Berlin and properly married

---

[23] I discuss many aspects of the comparative freedom of noble women in eighteenth-century Prussia in ch. 6 of my *Jewish High Society in Old Regime Berlin*.

to Adolf Stahr.[24] Her education had given her a better preparation for salon life than Rahel Varnhagen had had, but, while still a prisoner in her parents' home, she had no easy opportunity to use it.

Lewald's complete inability to build an intellectual or a social life as a spinster daughter in her parents' home naturally increased the pressure to marry. Unlike among Varnhagen's friends, a free and lively crowd who fell in love and actually seem to have made love frequently, without necessarily following the road to marriage, romance was a deadly serious business in Lewald's world.[25] Marriage was her only exit from a life spent darning her sisters' stockings in front of the window, whereas Rahel Varnhagen had been able to live an interesting, albeit painful and workless, life as an unmarried woman. That Varnhagen had such glamorous noble friends must have blinded Lewald to the fact that these so-called friends caused Varnhagen endless humiliation with their snubs. Perhaps, for Lewald, the wounds inflicted by such eminent people were themselves a badge of honour. In any case, she had plenty of reasons to be nostalgic for Varnhagen's social life as a single woman.

Lewald's initially perplexing envy of Varnhagen suggests that an increase in opportunites for Jews in general did not necessarily extend to Jewish women. But was this true with regard to conversion? Leaving the Jewish community was certainly easier for Lewald than for Varnhagen. Rahel Varnhagen's Jewish identity had been quite brittle. The rapidity of her entrance into the secular world and the elevated social circles in which she moved drove her to self-hate and a near-complete repudiation of Jews and Judaism. Lewald, in contrast, had a less polarized Jewish identity. In Rahel Varnhagen's time, there was little overlap between the small Jewish world and the large Gentile one. Entering the larger world usually involved a stormy exit, both subjectively and objectively, from the small one. By the time Lewald came of age, many more Jews had converted and there

---

[24] Lewald's long wait for a salon is noted by Möhrmann in *Die andere Frau*, p. 122. Her Monday-night salons after her marriage to Stahr are described in Weber, 'Fanny Lewald', p. 41. It should be noted, however, that not all observers found the Lewald—Stahr salon stimulating. Georg Brandes noted that the younger generation 'saw her salon as a place where boring cleverness and clever boredom showered down from the roof' — Georg Brandes, *Gesammelte Schriften*, vol. 1: *Persönlichkeiten* (Munich, 1902), p. 347.

[25] Lewald herself notes the differences in sensual and marital standards in the two eras on the very last page of her novel *Prinz Louis Ferdinard*.

were also more versions of Judaism itself. Thus more complex and subtle shades of Jewish identity existed. In *Jenny* and *Prinz Louis Ferdinand*, for example, Lewald created fictional characters who refused to convert, though she herself had been willing to convert at the age of seventeen, when her parents proposed it to her.

Was the contrast between her own life, in which she readily converted, and her novels, whose heroes agitate about whether or not to convert, a contradiction? The answer here can only be suggestive, but it would seem to be 'no'. For a convert to imagine created selves who rejected conversion mirrored the ambiguities of the age. The third and fourth decades of the nineteenth century in Germany were years of extraordinary ferment for Jews. Choices were often tormented, and changes of mind were sometimes swift and surprising. Ponder the case of Eduard Gans, the founder of the academic study of Judaism, who suddenly converted in 1825 to obtain a professorship and never spoke out on Jewish issues again. Or consider the case of Heinrich Heine, who had converted earlier that same year but did not get the coveted professorship. Ambivalence about Jewishness certainly fuelled Heine's creativity, and determining the balance between his love and his hate for Judaism is a rather intricate business.[26]

In comparison to those of Gans and Heine, Lewald's choices were' less contradictory, her contradictions less problematic. As a teenager she was in love with a theology student and enthusiastic for Christianity. She converted with the full approval of her parents and even of her extended family. As she came into her own intellectually, she distanced herself inwardly from Christian doctrine in favour of a Spinozistic pantheism, and became more concerned about Jewish civil rights. The mildness of Lewald's ethnic and religious conflicts reflected the fact that she was not, after all, a terribly emotional soul. She was able to live quite easily with having converted without fully believing in Christianity, and still commit herself, at least in a novel, to the cause of Jewish civil rights. Her feminism and her liberalism revealed similar contradictions.[27]

---

[26] The literature on Heine, especially, is rich and thorough. Gans's conversion and Heine's poem about if are discussed in, S. S. Prawer, *Heine's Jewish Comedy* (Oxford, 1983), pp. 10–18. There is a sensitive discussion of Heine's Jewishness in Arthur Elösser's essay 'Literatur' in Siegmund Kaznelson (ed.), *Juden im deutschen Kulturbererch* (Berlin, 1962). See also Ruth Jacobi, *Heinrich Heines jüdisches Erbe* (Bonn, 1978).

[27] For critiques of the contradictions in Lewald's feminism see Margaret

The considerable psychological flexibility that Lewald had as a converted Jew she somehow could not achieve in her role as the intellectual daughter of a Jewish family. Her family encouraged her to leave Judaism but did not allow a parallel freedom when it came to paid work and social independence. Contrast her constricted life with that of the Jewish men of her time. They faced difficult decisions, to be sure, but at least they had some control over their education, their career, their choice of marriage partner, and their religious and political affiliations. Depending on the relative strength of the temptations of the outside world and their inner convictions, they could decide whether or not to convert. For Jewish women, the single act of marriage freed them from patriarchal fathers, determined their standard of living, inserted them into a new extended family and friendship group, and allowed them to have children. Yet they often had no say at all in choosing the man whose circumstances would have such a huge impact on their lives. For a Jewish woman who dreamed of participating in high culture and meeting glamorous people, the pressure to convert and marry out of the faith must have been intense indeed. Although Lewald eventually found a public voice and a public role through her work, she was the rare exception. Jewish women in mid-nineteenth-century Germany found no place in either the movement for religious reform or in the movement for civil rights. Neither movement paid much attention to Jewish women's special problems, a failure which was no doubt inevitable. The religious reformers, for example, clearly lacked sympathy for Jewish women's complete dependence on marriage. David Fränkel, in an 1807 article in *Sulamith*, a leading journal in the early years of the Prussian Haskalah, exorted Jewish men to focus on 'sciences and arts' rather than on earning money. He continued,

> also as a result you will not find it necessary to amass and save
> considerable capital sums so that this can be given to your son-

---

Ward, 'Fanny Lewald and George Sand: *Eine Lebensfrage* and *Indiana*', (unpublished paper, German Department, Wellesley College), p. 12; and Geiger, *Dichter and Frauen*, p. 330. Some critics, it should be noted, voiced nothing but praise for Lewald's feminism: see Fedor Mamroth, *Die Frau auf dem Gebiete des modernen deutschen Romans* (Breslau, 1871), p. 28; and Karl Frenzel, *Gesammelte Werke*, vol. 1: *Erinnerungen und Störungen* (Leipzig, 1890), pp. 154 and 157. On Lewald's contradictions regarding the nobility see Weber, 'Fanny Lewald', pp. 40 and 58; and Geiger, *Dichter und Frauen*, p. 331.

in-law as a means of support when he marries your daughter; rather artisans, labourers, soldiers and civil servants will often appear and will find acceptable as a bride a virtuous home-loving girl, even if she has no dowry.[28]

Fränkel's advice to Jewish fathers may have made sense in the context of his critique of contemporary Jewish values. But it could never make nineteenth-century German-Jewish daughters happy. Inside the painfully limited universe within which they could make choices, a good dowry represented potential independence and at least a wide choice of husbands.[29] It would take many decades indeed before Jewish reformers would address Jewish women's particular issues and Jewish women in Germany would found their own political movement.[30] From the long period before that time, Fanny Lewald's voice has survived to give us a glimpse of how very difficult it was for Jewish women to become intellectually productive, find happiness in love, and all the while stay loyal to Judaism.

[28] The Fränkel quote comes from *Sulamith*, 2 (1807), pp. 377–9, as cited in David Sorkin, 'Ideology and Identity: Political Emancipation and the Emergence of a Jewish Subculture in Germany, 1800–1848' (PhD dissertation, University of California at Berkeley, 1983), p. 91.

[29] See the essays in Marion Kaplan, (ed.), *The Marriage Bargain: Women and Dowries in European History* (New York, 1985), especially Kaplan's own essay on the marriage strategies of Jews in imperial Germany.

[30] Here again, Kaplan is indispensable: see her study *The Jewish Feminist Movement in Germany* (Westport, Conn., 1979).

Part IV

Inventing Orthodoxy

10

Towards a Biography of the Hatam Sofer

JACOB KATZ

TRANSLATED BY DAVID ELLENSON

I

Modern Jewish historiography has established Rabbi Moses Sofer, the Hatam Sofer (1763–1839), as the leader of pre-modern Orthodox Jewry in its battle against the initial manifestations of the Reform movement. The special position of the Hatam Sofer is apparent when his responsum to the Hamburg Bet Din (rabbinical court) of 1819 is juxtaposed to the others received. In that year the Bet Din had enlisted the support of German, Austrian, Hungarian and Italian rabbis in a stand against the reformers, on two grounds: first, opposition to the building of the Reform temple in Hamburg; and, second, general disapproval of any innovations in liturgy and ritual.

Most of those whose opinions were solicited by the Bet Din (and whose responsa were later collected in the book *Eleh Divrei ha-Brit*: 'These are the Words of the Covenant') held positions of stature in the rabbinical world, and several of them were leading halakhic authorities: among them, Rabbi Akiva Eger (1761–1837) of Posen, Rabbi Mordecai Benet (1753–1829) of Nikolsburg, Chief Rabbi of Moravia, and Rabbi Jacob of Lissa.[1] Even among these champions of the Law, however, the Hatam Sofer was distinguished by his articulate reply, which both grasped the full significance of the problem and took a principled, aggressive stand.

It is doubtful that, before the Hatam Sofer wrote this responsum,

---

[1] H. Graetz, *Geschichte der Juden*, 11 vols (Leipzig, 1853–76), vol. 11, p. 380, lists these persons as the major responders. Sh. Bernfeld, *Toldot ha-Reformazion ha-Datit be-Yisrael* (Cracow, 1900), pp. 83–4, adds four more names.

his authority was perceived as greater than the others rabbis'. Though he had already attained fame as a scholar by disseminating Torah among the masses and issuing responsa for some twenty years, the other rabbis who replied to the court were equally well-known. Rabbi Jacob[2] and Rabbi Mordecai Benet[3] had already published books, and all the rabbis in question occupied prestigious posts. Though the rabbinical office of Pressburg was an honoured one, it could not be compared to the offices of Nikolsburg, Lissa and Posen. Moreover, Rabbi Moses Sofer never published a book during his life. His fame and authority emanated from his words and the distinguished personality reflected in them.

One outstanding indication of the man's historical significance is that his contemporaries thought it important to tell his life story. The first biography of the Hatam Sofer was written six months after his death in 1839 by his second son, Simon,[4] and the second was composed by his faithful pupil Rabbi Hezekiah Feivel Plaut, more than a full generation later.[5] This student had seen his master's manuscripts, had heard the Hatam Sofer himself tell stories of his early life, and had known him well. The Hatam Sofer was a conversationalist and loved to tell his students and family about the days of his youth, which had been far from uneventful. Many of these stories are included in Lev Landsberg's *Eleh Toldot* ('These are the Generations'), which has been almost completely forgotten,[6] and the biography written by the Hatam Sofer's grandson, Rabbi Solomon Sofer. This book, entitled *Sefer Hut ha-Meshulash* ('The Triple Cord'),[7] is the most substantial and well-known of these biographical works, and

[2] The editor of *Eleh Diveri ha-Brit* (Altona, 1819) describes Rabbi Jacob as the author of six books (p. 10).

[3] Three books of his were published during the years 1805—6.

[4] This biography was included in Sh. Weiss, *Avnei Beit ha-Yozer* (Paks, 1900), pp. 48—55. At the beginning of the narrative Weiss complemented (p. 48n.) the son's account, using the source referred to in the next footnote, but did not alter the text itself.

[5] H. F. Plaut, *Likutei Hever Ben Haim*, (Munkács, 1879), introduction to pt 2. Rabbi Plaut's own autobiography is in the introduction to the first part of the book.

[6] L. Landsberg, *Eleh Toldot* (Pressburg, 1878). This author received information from his father, a disciple of the Hatam Sofer, and from members of the Sofer family.

[7] Sh. Sofer, *Sefer Hut ha-Meshulash* (Paks, 1887). There are several later editions of this book, which the author enlarged. Here the Tel Aviv edition of 1963 will be used.

also inculdes biographical portraits of Rabbi Akiva Eger, the Hatam Sofer's father-in-law by his second marriage, and of Rabbi Samuel Benjamin Sofer, the Ktav Sofer, son of Moses Sofer and father of the book's author. The book is hagiographic in tone and nothing more than a fountain of uncritical praise for the Sofer family. Though Rabbi Solomon Sofer inserted important documents into his book, he not only failed to extract their factual content, but also, and more importantly, failed to interpret them historically. Even today, however, his book remains the principal source of biographical information on the Hatam Sofer.

In these books, the pupil's adoration for his master and the grandson's praise for his forebear are joined by the desire to see the Hatam Sofer as a model fighter in the conservatives' war against the innovators—a war in which the biographies themselves play a part by completely identifying with the man and his approach. By contrast, historians writing in the same period directly opposed the Hatam Sofer's position. From a negative appraisal of his theory, they arrived at a criticism of its proponent as well. Jost,[8] Graetz,[9] and especially Isaac Hirsch Weiss[10] perceived the stature of the Hatam Sofer, but they judged him negatively because he seamed to them to have fled the struggle with contemporary problems.

When the question of national existence came to overshadow the controversy over the religious dimension of his theory, it became possible to see a positive side to the Hatam Sofer's work without necessarily subscribing to his views.[11] Historians and writers in the national period discovered that the Hatam Sofer had built a fortress against national self-denial by assimilation. It was now possible to interpret even his reservations about emancipation not as an obstinate stand against the flow of history, but rather as a vision of the results of that flow. The Hatam Sofer's stand against emancipation, his interest in Jewish settlement in the land of Israel, and his defence of

---

[8] I. M. Jost, *Neuere Geschichte der Israeliten* (Berlin, 1846), vol. 3, pp. 70–1.

[9] Graetz, *Geschichte*, p. 380.

[10] I. H. Weiss, 'Le-Toldot ha-Ga'on Rabbi Moshe Sofer', *Mi-Mizrah umi-Ma'arav*, 2, 3 (1895), pp. 17–29. His judgement is given in apt metaphorical language: 'One very energetic and accomplished man stood up to delay and reverse the whirlwind. Nor did he fear that his hand would be crushed in his effort to do so' (p. 17). Weiss frequently mentions the Hatam Sofer in his memoirs: *Zikhronotai* (Warsaw, 1894).

[11] Bernfeld, *Toldot ha-Reformazion*, p. 85.

Hebrew in opposing the translation of sources were all evaluated positively by nationalist writers.[12]

Of course, this positive evaluation by later generations of historians is no less biased than was the negative assessment offered by their nineteenth-century predecessors. Thus, it is necessary to reinterpret the Hatam Sofer's life so that he, like any other historical personality, may be viewed in light of the totality of his actions and accomplishments.

II

It was a crucial moment in Rabbi Moses Sofer's life when, at the age of nineteen, he left his home town of Frankfurt am Main for the unfamiliar environment of the cities of Moravia and western Hungary.[13] Throughout his life he consciously maintained his attachment to the famed Frankfurt congregation and always signed his letters 'Moses the Humble, a Sofer from Frankfurt am Main'.[14] He even observed — though not without halakhic reservations — the special day of remembrance in Frankfurt, Purim Vincets (20 Adar), commemorating the community's restoration in 1614.[15] His recollections of the things he saw and heard in his youth appear throughout his writings, often in the context of legal rulings, customs, and decisions on questions of religion and law. Most of the allusions, however, are not to the particular customs of the Frankfurt community, but rather to things he saw and traditions he received from his masters. He counted several sages among his teachers in Frankfurt and Mainz, where he studied during the years 1776–7.[16] These men he referred to as 'my teacher' or 'guide of my youth', for they had

---

[12] Sh. Weingarten, *Ha-Hatam Sofer ve-Talmidav — Yahasam le-Eretz Yisrael* (Jerusalem, 1945); A. Katz, *Ha-Hatam Sofer, Rabbi Moshe Sofer, Hayav ve-Yezirotav* (Jerusalem, 1947); Z. Zehavi, *Me-ha-Hatam Sofer ad Herzl* (Jerusalem, 1966). Sh. Weingarten justly criticizes Zehavi's book in *Sinai*, 1967, pp. 77–85.

[13] He was born on 7 Tishrei 1762.

[14] He discussed this usage in *Teshuvot*, 6 vols (Pressburg and Munkács, 1841–1912), 6.59.

[15] *Teshuvot*, OH 191: 'In order to avoid any doubt whether the meal on that day should be regarded as a "meal of commandment", he would complete a Talmudic tractate on that same day.'

[16] Sh. Sofer, *Hut ha-Meshulash*, p. 25; *Derashot*, ed. Yosef Naftali Stern, 2 vols (Cluj, 1929), 1.77b.

educated him in his early years.[17] The two outstanding rabbis from whom he received his major doctrines, were Rabbi Pinchas Horowitz (1730–1805) and Rabbi Nathan Adler (1741–1800).[18] The esteem in which the Hatam Sofer held these two sages is wellknown, but significance of his relationship to them has not been fully assessed.

Rabbi Pinchas Horowitz was born in Poland and became Rabbi of Frankfurt in 1771.[19] Hasidic tradition holds that he was the 'long-standing disciple' of one of the movement's early leaders, Rabbi Dov Baer (the 'Maggid'; d. 1772) of Meseritz.[20] There is tangible proof, however, of only one visit by Rabbi Pinchas to the Maggid. He was accompanied on this visit by his brother, Rabbi Shmelke (1726–78), and it occurred on the eve of their departure to the West—Shmelke to Nikolsburg and Pinchas to Frankfurt.[21] We are uncertain as to the impression this visit made. The Hatam Sofer testifies that privately, but not in public, Rabbi Pinchas prayed from the prayer book of Isaac Luria (1534–72), which was used by the Hasidic community.[22] However, we cannot conclude from this that Rabbi Pinchas was a disciple and follower of this great teacher of Hasidism. Indeed, neither the names of Hasidic teachers nor traces of their doctrine appear in his writings. His style of homiletical interpretation is similar to the pre-Hasidic pattern. The central value in his system of thought is the study of Torah according to its plain meaning, and it is through this intellectual engagement with 'the words of the Living God' that the quality of *devekut*, i.e. the clinging to God, can and should be attained by every individual.[23] If he retained a secret attachment to Hasidism, it completely escaped the notice of his outstanding pupil,

---

[17] Rabbi Stern, in his introduction to *Derashot*, lists the teachers of the Hatam Sofer. In his preface to *Hatam Sofer al ha-Torah* (Jerusalem, 1958) he added one name.

[18] The title 'Mori ve-Rabi' was sometimes bestowed on Rabbi Tevele Scheuer, who studied in Mainz before him. See *Derashot*, 1.77b, editor's note; and *Teshuvot*, 7.17 (10a).

[19] M. Horowitz, *Frankfurter Rabbinen* (repr. Jerusalem, 1969), p. 208.

[20] A. Valden, *Shem ha-Gedolim he-Hadash* (Warsaw, 1879/1880), 1.115

[21] Information in the introduction to *Shulhan Arukh shel Ba'al ha-Taniah*, by his sons. I owe this reference to Dr Abraham Rubinstein. See M. Teitelbaum, *Ha-Rav mi-Ladi u-Mifleget Habad* (Warsaw, 1910), appendix II, p. 252.

[22] *Teshuvot*, OH 16.

[23] In the introductions to his halakhic books, *Sefer ha-Hafla'ah* and *Sefer ha-Miknah*, Rabbi Pinchas Horowitz presented his views as part of a homiletical interpretation.

the Hatam Sofer. Indeed, the Hatam Sofer knew nothing substantive regarding Hasidism until a later phase of his life, when, as rabbi in Pressburg, he came into contact with several of the greatest Hasidic masters of Hungary and Galicia. Even then, however, his relationship to Hasidism was cool, if not actually hostile, and during his time in Mattersdorf he used an expression of revulsion with regard to the Hasidim.[24] In the eulogy he delivered on behalf of Rabbi Nathan Adler, he described Adler by saying that he had 'attained the essence of Hasidism, namely piety and abstinence', and added, 'but not like the Hasidim of this age, Heaven forbid.'[25]

The Hatam Sofer's admiration for Rabbi Pinchas Horowitz was nurtured by his recognition of the man's Talmudic genius and halakhic authority. He called him 'the Master of all the sons of the Diaspora',[26] an apt title for the man who was rabbi of the venerable Frankfurt congregation and issued responsa to those who asked him about halakhic issues. In contrast to Rabbi Pinchas, Rabbi Nathan Adler served as a teacher and guide to only a few followers and left nothing in writing.[27] In describing both his character and actions, we therefore must depend upon the testimony of witnesses — both hostile and enthusiastic. Foremost among the enthusiastic was his pupil the Hatam Sofer. The derogatory testimony, on the other hand, is included in an anonymous pamphlet, *Ma'aseh Ta'atuim* ('The Deceitful Act'), written in 1790 by a Frankfurt Jew, Judah Wetzlar, who was inclined toward the Haskalah.[28] If we examine the testimony

[24] *Teshuvot,* OH, 15, 16, 197.
[25] *Derashot,* 2.372a.
[26] *Teshuvot,* OH 15: 'Thus I received from my masters, may the memory of the righteous be for a blessing. They are my teacher, His Excellency, the Pious One who serves in office, our teacher and Rabbi Nathan Adler, may the memory of the righteous be for a blessing; and His Excellency, Rabbi Pinchas Horowitz, rabbi of all the sons of the difficult Exile, may his memory be for a blessing, from whose waters I drank Torah for its own sake and from whose sources I hewed...' The combination proves that the choice of titles was not accidental.
[27] See Z. B. Auerbach, introduction to *Mishnat Rabbi Natan* (Frankfurt am Main, 1862). A. Y. Schwartz, in *Derekh ha-Nesher ve-Torat Emet* (Galanta, 1928), collected quotations ascribed or referring to Rabbi Nathan Adler, without distinguishing between truth and fiction. Y.N. Stern, in his commentary to *Derashot he-Hatam Sofer* 2.375a–372a, indicates the references to Adler in the writings of the Hatam Sofer.
[28] See A. Geiger, 'Natan Adler und sein Dajjan Leser', *Ha-Mazkir,* 1862, pp. 77–9.

of both sides, however, we find that they agree on the essential facts
of Adler's life.

Wetzlar contends that Rabbi Nathan Adler's followers were bent
'upon destroying the foundations of our customs ... by constructing
new practices ... Furthermore, out of their stupidity, they would
produce a new religion just as if the Torah had been given them as an
exclusive possession.'[29] Among the examples given of their deviations
from the norm are changes in the liturgy; differences from the rest of
the community on the times when Sabbath and holy days were
reckoned to begin; stringent rulings on dietary matters, the impurity
of women in childbirth and the observance of purity by priests; and
the unusual requirement that women should wear fringes (*tzitzit*) on
the corners of their garments.[30] Wetzlar emphasized the social implications of these changes. The different liturgical customs,[31] the
method used to fix times for reception of Sabbath and holy days,[32]
and the stringent dietary rules[33] all separated Adler and his followers
from other members of the community — a major infraction in
rabbinic Judaism. The result, Wetzlar concludes, is a mockery 'of our
holy fathers and our sages who established these good customs',[34] a
rebellion 'against the rabbis who served us as eyes'.[35]

We have evidence from independent sources for many of these
deviations. The Hatam Sofer testifies that Rabbi Nathan, when
leading the community in prayer, did so from the prayerbook of Isaac
Luria;[36] and from two of his contemporaries, Aaron Horin and
Abraham Löwenstamm, we know that he deliberately used the
Sephardic system of Hebrew pronunciation — another practice characterstic of Hasidism.[37] Also, the Hatam Sofer's custom of reciting
the prayer 'Grant us peace' in the evening service was obviously
received from his master.[38] As for Rabbi Nathan's stringent decrees
on matters of purity and impurity, we possess a tradition that Rabbi

---

[29] [J. Wetzlar], *Ma'aseh Ta'atuim* (Frankfurt am Main, 1790), p. 3.
[30] Ibid., pp. 5—9.
[31] Ibid., p. 7.
[32] Ibid., p. 8.
[33] Ibid., p. 9.
[34] Ibid., p. 4.
[35] Ibid., p. 6.
[36] *Teshuvot*, OH 15.
[37] A. Chorin in *Nogah ha-Zedek* (Dessau, 1818), p. 24; A. Löwenstamm,
Zeror ha-Hayyim (Amsterdam, 1820), 58b—59a.
[38] Plaut, *Likutei*, 3.3b.

Abraham Trier, an opponent of Nathan, nevertheless saw them as revealing a deep concern for holiness.[39] An indication of the special importance ascribed to fixing the right time for the commencement of holy days is contained in the Hatam Sofer's own testimony that, on taking leave of his master in Fürth in 1784, he received from Rabbi Nathan precise instructions on a number of matters of religious practice, including how to calculate the exact time for the beginning of the festivals.[40] Finally, though Wetzlar does not mention it, it was apparently Rabbi Nathan's custom to recite the Priestly Benediction daily.[41]

All this makes it clear that Rabbi Nathan established a pattern of religious life which was distinct in several ways from that which was generally accepted in his city. Indeed, the Hatam Sofer later claimed in his arguments with the Hasidim that his teachers, and among them Rabbi Nathan, 'did not gather a community'.[42] At the same time Adler's brand of Hasidism was not, as the Hatam Sofer maintained later on when he developed his own theory, one of individual piety. A group of followers accepted his customs — with the possible exception of his use of the Lurianic liturgy[43] — and the Hatam Sofer himself, in a letter dated 1803, speaks of a student who

> did not neglect even a single teaching, either great or small, of our teacher and rabbi, may the memory of the righteous be for a blessing, on how one should conduct one's self ... Moreover, the way in which he educates his young son and studies with him is most wonderful. Indeed, the son prays with amazing exactness and does not alter the correct version one iota, as he taught him in an admirable way.[44]

Whether intentionally or not, Rabbi Nathan did in fact gather around himself a group which was considered deviant in matters of religion and law. Even a less conservative community than Frankfurt would

---

[39] Auerbach, *Mishnat Rabbi Natan*, p. vi.

[40] Solomon Sofer had access to a notebook in which the Hatam Sofer took notes from his teacher (*Hut ha-Meshulash*, p. 32).

[41] Horowitz, *Frankfurter Rabbinen*, p. 218, souce unnamed.

[42] *Teshuvot*, OH 197.

[43] The Hatam Sofer stresses, regarding both his teachers, 'For they prayed only in accordance with the liturgical rite of the Ari [Isaac Luria]' (*Teshuvot*, OH 15).

[44] *Igrot Sofrim* ed. Sh. Sofer (Vienna, 1929), 2.1–2.

have been likely to protest against them. Indeed, the deviant practices of the Hasidim in Eastern Europe, which aroused public wrath, were no more serious than the deviations of Adler and his followers, although their social significance was similar.[45] In 1779 events in Frankfurt finally came to a head.[46] Rabbi Nathan was forbidden to continue his *minyan* (prayer circle), stripped of rabbinical functions, and deprived of his authority to render legal decisions. Ten years later the ban was renewed.

It is more important to understand the motives of Adler and his followers than of those who pronounced the ban. Unfortunately, we do not know his precise religious teachings. There is no doubt that he engaged in Kabbalah, he and his students living in a constant state of mystical splendour and visions, for one of the charges levelled against the group in the second stage of this struggle was that the visions they recounted terrified people. Indeed, it is evident that in this respect several members of the group went to extremes.

Rabbi Nathan himself must be regarded as the primary source of this agitation. At the same time, it is essential to view him as an original and sensitive personality for whom customary religious activity seemed insufficient. Through his considerable learning, he sought to determine the norms of religious belief and practice, and to apply them assiduously, without compromise and without regard for prevailing custom. It is likely that he taught a special Kabbalistic doctrine, but its nature remains unknown to us.[47] In any event, a charismatic personality clearly stands behind this entire phenomenon. This is expressed in his denial of the value of custom and, even more, in the loyalty that he inspired in his students and followers.

This last phenomenon is exemplified in the relationship between Adler and his greatest student, the Hatam Sofer. According to each and every biography, there was a conflict between Rabbi Moses Sofer and his father, who himself was learned and high-born and who took an active part in the education of his son.[48] The story goes that the

---

[45] Horowitz, *Frankfurter Rabbinen*, pp. 220–1, has noted a resemblance between the proclamation against Rabbi Nathan and anti-Hasidic expressions in Poland. He also suggests that the events in Poland influenced the Frankfurt community leaders. In fact, Rabbi Nathan's deeds provoked no less astonishment than those of the Hasidim in Poland.

[46] This is described in Horowitz (ibid.).

[47] Geiger (*Ha-Mazkir*, 1862) aptly characterizes Rabbi Nathan's personality and circle.

[48] Weiss, *Avnei Beit ha-Yozer*, 48b–49a.

son, while lecturing on a problem raised in a book (*Kos Yeshu 'ot,* 'The Cup of Salvation') written by his great-grandfather, completely contradicted the solution offered there. According to one text he said, 'My forebear erred.' The Hatam Sofer's father rebuked him publicly for this — one text says that the father slapped him in the face.[49] In this dispute Rabbi Nathan sided with the son,[50] and, consequently, the bonds between student and rabbi were strengthened while those between son and father were weakened.

This deep attachment between rabbi and student was demonstrated later, when Rabbi Nathan, after the first ban on his activities had been issued, became Rabbi of Boskowitz in Moravia.[51] According to the tradition received by early biographers, the pupil intended to accompany his master a short way, but at the moment of separation was so overwhelmed by sorrow that he could not bear to part from him. The rabbi, instead of dulling the student's enthusiasm, encouraged it. Thus Moses Sofer departed the city of his birth without saying farewell to his mother and without visiting the grave of his father, who had died three years previously.[52] This scene of the faithful pupil clinging to his master was enlarged upon and embellished by those who retold it.[53] Indeed, in the eulogy which the Hatam Sofer offered for his master, eighteen years after the event, he himself alluded to it: 'As is well known to all, I ran after him a hundred parsangs and thus left my mother's house, the place of my birth.'[54] He clearly recognized, then, that this youthful act had established a place for him in the public consciousness.

III

Rabbi Nathan Adler remained in Boskowitz three years, from 1782 to 1785. During that time the Hatam Sofer lived in his master's home

---

[49] Ibid., 49a; Landsberg, *Eleh Toldot,* p. 9; Plaut, *Likutei,* 1b; Sh. Sofer, *Hut ha-Meshulash,* pp. 20–2.

[50] Ibid.

[51] Horowitz, *Frankfurter Rabbinen,* p. 220.

[52] The epitaph is recorded in M. Halevi Horowitz, *Avnei Zikaron* (Frankfurt am Main, 1901), item 3638. The Hatam Sofer's father died on 16 Sivan 5539, (1779).

[53] According to Sh. Sofer, *Hut ha-Meshulash,* 49b–50a, Sofer expressed the wish to be able to serve Rabbi Nathan in Boskowitz, and the rabbi told him that his wish was to be regarded as an oath. Plaut merely relates that the Rabbi took his disciple with him.

[54] *Derashot,* 2.372a–b.

and accompanied him everywhere. His relationship with the famous rabbi also brought him into contact with great scholars of Torah and persons of high social rank. While still on their way to Boskowitz, they went through Prague, and were welcomed into the home of the city's rabbi, Ezekiel Landau (1713–93). After their first meeting Adler and Landau continued to exchange views on matters of Torah, employing the young Sofer as their intermediary.[55] Upon his departure from Boskowitz, Rabbi Nathan travelled via Vienna, and again his student met some of the greatest sages of the generation.[56] The Hatam Sofer also saw the luxury enjoyed by the Viennese elite, and witnessed the first signs of the Arnstein family's lapsing observance.[57]

Nathan Adler did not succeed as a community rabbi. It seems that he attempted to impose on the whole community the stringent standards of kosher slaughter that previously only his coterie of followers had adopted.[58] As a result, he was embroiled in controversy with the town's inhabitants and abandoned his rabbinical position; he and his pupil arrived in Vienna in spring 1785, with nowhere to turn.[59] Finally he returned to Frankfurt. The Hatam Sofer, however, settled in Prossnitz, Moravia, and married a local woman, Sarah Yerwitz. Two qualities which remained characterstic of him throughout his life were revealed by this incident. The first was entirely personal: the Hatam Sofer made decisions on ethical grounds without regard to utilitarian considerations. For example, we have no idea why he wanted to marry Sarah Yerwitz in the first place. According to the notions of the time, she was not a good match: the Yerwitz family was not wealthy, and the bride was an older widow.[60] Once Moses

---

[55] *Teshuvot,* YD 338.

[56] *Teshuvot,* YD 294: 'and prominent scholars of Torah were among that party'. See also Sh. Sofer, *Hut ha-Meshulash,* p. 31. According to the second source quoted, they spent Passover there.

[57] Plaut, *Likutei,* 1b.

[58] Auerbach, *Mishnat Rabbi Natan:* 'Scoundrels arose against him as he had been stringent about Kosher slaughtering, and they complained about him to the overseer of the city.' See also Sh. Sofer, *Hut ha-Meshulash,* pp. 31–2.

[59] See above, note 56. There is also testimony on Rabbi Nathan's 'several months' in Vienna in Horin's account; see above, note 37.

[60] The Prossnitz community minutes record what Hirsch Jerwitz said of his future brother-in-law: 'And many turned eagerly to him for marriage. But he was unconcerned with money and he despised the "high and mighty". Rather, he chose the good and this humble man married the woman Sarah mentioned above. His entire orientation was to do the right thing and marry the daughter of a scholar' (*Ozar ha-Sifrut,* p. 21). It is also mentioned that the

Sofer had consented to the marriage, however, he did not waver, despite major obstacles among others, the opposition of his two mentors and his family.

The second quality was typical of someone rooted in Torah culture. According to this system of values, the prime duty of man is the study of Torah — either alone or in a group. Indeed, this, and related activities, should occupy the major portion of a Jewish scholar's time and energy. All other activities — except for fulfilling the commandments, the time for which is fixed and measured — should be purely incidental and kept to an absolute minimum. In diligence and perseverance Talmudic scholars attain at times a measure of virtuosity, and during a time of personal sadness these qualities become a source of strength. Sanctified intellectual engagement seizes a man's entire being, allowing him to sublimate other needs and worries. Thus, even when his life was burdened with trouble, most of the young Moses Sofer's energy was devoted to learning. Not only did he study Torah privately, but he also studied with anyone who contacted him, either in person or in writing. Of a despairing letter that he sent at the time to Rabbi Abraham Bing in Frankfurt, nearly half was devoted to a halakhic matter. Even at a time of distress, it would not have been seemly for a Jewish scholar to send a letter without bearing witness to the essence of his activity; all the more so in a time of tranquillity. Thus, after his wedding, when the Hatam Sofer wrote to Rabbi Nathan Adler, it was not primarily a personal communication. After the summary statement 'And thus the wisdom of the Lord, may His name be blessed forever, was decreed' came a report on his Talmudic studies. Then Sofer submitted a query concerning the problem to hand and even proposed a weekly exchange of letters with his master on the subject (a programme that certainly was never carried out). It was as if Sofer had said, 'We are not permitted to ponder the decree of the Creator, nor have we the leisure to so ponder. Come, let us turn to our work, the task of study and the business of halakhah.'[61]

---

bride's father, 'after his death, left a prize...the woman Sarah, may her days be long. And when he still lived, this great man exerted much effort to betroth her to a distinguished man,...but he found [no one].' She was thus a middle-aged widow, as oral traditions have recorded as well (Landsberg, *Eleh Toldot*, p. 15). L. Goldschmied, 'Geschichte der Juden in Prossnitz', in H. Gold (ed.), *Die Juden und Judengemeinden Mährens in Vergangenheit und Gegenwart* (Brünn, 1929) p. 103, speculates about the mediator between Moshe Sofer and the Jerwitz family, but the speculation is unfounded and certainly does not explain the motives for the match.

[61] In his old age he produced a similar self-characterization in a letter

The Hatam Sofer's first halakhic novellae were composed when he lived in Boskowitz in the shadow of his teacher, and, when he first came to Prossnitz, he continued to work along the same lines.[62] His surviving papers from this period include notes for his novellae, and exchanges of view with other Jewish scholars in the nearby area — Semnitz, Boskowitz and elsewhere — on particular problems. He took advantage of these years to consolidate his exceptional mastery of rabbinic texts, and he did this by clarifying items and searching for an answer to every problem which he encountered in the course of his study. Yet, his mastery of the material was still not complete. Once he said that he was not an expert in the *Hoshen ha-Mishpat* (the part of the sixteenth-century law code, *Shulhan Arukh,* dealing with civil and criminal law),[63] and on another occasion he said that he wished his correspondent would forget something he had said since it was mistaken.[64] His confidence in his ability to get to the heart of a matter, however, was absolute. Once, when someone who opposed him took exception to his explanation of a contradiction in the Rambam, he answered,

> You are right since I have dared to stand in the place of greats ... But I say, God's Torah is not in heaven and anyone who wishes to come and interpret it is permitted to do so. And, even if this was not the opinion of the Rambam, if my words are true we need to reach this decision because of the reasons I have cited, though it is our custom in this generation to be dependent on the great authorities.[65]

Rabbi Moses Sofer occupied himself as a teacher in the months prior to his wedding. It seems probable that he did this for economic reasons: before the marriage he was in dire financial straits. Thus, having started to teach, he continued in his post until the end of the school year, i.e. Rosh ha-Shanah 1788. For the next four years he was assured support at his brother-in-law's table, as stipulated by the wedding-contract. There is no indication, however, that his brother-

---

to Rabbi Zakharia Yeshayahu Hacohen Yaltes. He describes himself as a teacher first and foremost, 'and the other things I do out of necessity, as one walks on top of coals' (quoted in Weingarten, *He-Hatam Sofer ve-Talmidav,* p. 45).

[62] *Teshuvot,* pt 7, is from this period.

[63] Ibid., 17 (9a).

[64] Ibid., 20.

[65] Ibid., 21.

in-law was rich or even affluent. Yet it seems that he provided financially for the childless couple even longer than was required. In any event, this situation was destined to come to an end, compelling Rabbi Moses Sofer to accept a rabbinical post.[66] Initially, like many rabbis,[67] he had tried to avoid the rabbinate, but in his case there was a new twist to the tale.• He supposedly tried instead to become a tailor, but failed because of his age.[68] Yet Sofer was not a man to be forced to enter the rabbinate by somebody else. Once he realized his family's financial distress — his wife once sold her Sabbath garment to buy wine for Kiddush — he decided that he would accept the first offer he received.[69]

Thus, Rabbi Moses Sofer began his career as a rabbi in 1794 at the age of thirty-one, in the small community of Dresnitz. Although he was paid a fair wage, no financial support was given for a yeshivah.[70] In the course of time, however, he persuaded his congregants to maintain several students.[71] Four years later, in 1798, he took a post in Mattersdorf, one of the 'seven communities' under the protection of the Esterhazy family. He served this community until he was selected as Rabbi of Pressburg in 1806. The years 1794—1806 thus marked an intermediate stage in his fame. During this period he received several offers of rabbinical posts. One of these offers was from Prossnitz, where he had once sat in the shadow of other rabbis.[72] All the towns which were interested in Rabbi Moses Sofer were in the area of Moravia and Western Hungary, which in this era had a unified religio-cultural identity.[73] It was from this region, also, that questions on halakhic matters came to him, the first in 1796. It is also reasonable to assume that most of his students during these years came from

---

[66] Plaut, *Likutei*.

[67] Rabbi Akiva Eger relates that his father-in-law forced him to accept his first post (*Igrot Sofrim*, 1.11). The Hatam Sofer reports that Rabbi Yesha 'aia Berlin-Pik, 'fled from the rabbinical office until, finally, the government compelled him to accept a rabbinical postion' (*Derashot*, 2.306a). Plaut reminisces how he escaped and was finally trapped (*Likutei*, introduction to pt 1, 5). This is an almost normative stereotype.

[68] Landsberg, *Eleh Toldot*, p. 16; followed by Sh. Sofer, *Hut ha-Meshulash*, pp. 39—40.

[69] Plaut, *Likutei*, 2.2a; Sh. Sofer, *Hut ha-Meshulash*, pp 40—1.

[70] The rabbinical writ is transcribed in Sh. Sofer, *Hut ha-Meshulash*, p. 41.

[71] *Derashot*, 1.187b.

[72] Sh. Sofer, *Hut ha-Meshulash*, pp. 43—51.

[73] The Hatam Sofer's time in Mattersdorf has recently been summarized in Y. Yosef Cohen, 'He-Hatam Sofer bi-Tekufat Mattersdorf', *She'arim*, 1967; see issues from 20 Adar and following.

nearby communities, though sometimes students did wander to far-away yeshivot. Everything thus points to the fact that among the Jewish communities of Western Hungary and Moravia Rabbi Moses Sofer had begun to be regarded as an outstanding figure. The question is, why?

V

One thing is clear: during this period the Hatam Sofer did not command support as a partisan leader who fuelled civil strife. The dissolution of traditional Jewish society, which was the background for the conflict between the innovators and the conservatives, had actually begun long before. The first public dispute burst forth in Germany at the very moment Moses Sofer left Frankfurt, and it is safe to assume that he heard Rabbi Pinchas Horowitz's sermon against Moses Mendelssohn's Torah translation.[74] News of what was happening in the major cities — Berlin, Breslau and Frankfurt — undoubtedly reached even Prossnitz, Dresnitz and Mattersdorf; events in Prague and especially Vienna were known to the townspeople because of their frequent contact with those cities. An elegy written by Moses Sofer in 1790,[75] when he was still in Prossnitz, expresses 'concern about the neglect of Jewish learning among schoolchildren' because 'these precious children are keen and sharp-witted; still they speak foreign tongues'. The meaning of this phrase, it seems, is that students who were capable of studying Torah in the Holy Tongue were learning it in translation, or were engaged in secular learning. Thus, Sofer continued, 'a threat that Torah will fade away hovers over the classrooms'.[76] It is unclear whether or not there was a special cause which motivated this concern. Perhaps the elegy was occasioned simply by the creation of government-sponsored schools in the Jewish communities of Austria-Hungary, including Prossnitz,[77] Mattersdorf[78]

---

[74] Rabbi Pinchas Horowitz delivered his sermon on the eve of Rosh Hodesh, Tamuz 5542 (1782) (Horowitz, *Frankfurter Rabbinen*, p. 224), whereas Rabbi Nathan Adler's rabbinical writ was only signed on 27 Elul of the same year (Auerbach, *Mishnat Rabbi Natan*, p. vi). As we shall see, the problem of translation occupied the Hatam Sofer a great deal, but he did not mention the author of *Ha-Hafla'ah* (Horowitz) in this context.

[75] A. Sofer, *Shirei Shirim* (New York, 1940) pp. 20–32.

[76] Ibid., p. 21.

[77] D. Kaufman, *Ozar ha-Sifrut*, 3 (1889), pp. 19–20.

[78] B. Mandl, *Das jüdische Schulwesen in Ungarn unter Kaiser Josef II (1780–1790)* (Posen, 1903), pp. 10–11.

and Pressburg,[79] in the late eighteenth century. These schools taught their own brand of civic studies, but otherwise did not encroach upon the traditional, accepted curriculum. Thus most pious Jews made their peace with these institutions, and even the Hatam Sofer did not oppose them publicly.

Problems of the era are reflected in the sermons which the Hatam Sofer delivered in both Dresnitz and Mattersdorf. For example, the drafting of Jewish boys into the army was a problem which the rabbi regarded with great anxiety.[80] He rebuked those members of the community who favoured this development, believing that conscription had the positive benifit of removing 'the thorns from the vine-yard',[81] (the conscripts were taken from the lowest elements in society). As to the opinion of the maskilim, who wanted to encourage the enlistment of Jewish youth for political reasons, he gave no response.[82] Other words of reproof were directed at the failings of the community: negligible financial support for impoverished children and for students of Torah,[83] card-playing by members of the community,[84] attendance at theatres and circuses,[85] carelessness over Sabbath observance,[86] inequitable distribution of the tax burden, to the detriment of the poor,[87] and so on. Sofer bemoaned the heresy which had entered society[88] and the government's tendency to pay

[79] Ibid., pp. 18–23. See also H. Gold (ed.), *Die Juden und Judengemeinde Bratislava in Vergangenheit und Gegenwart* (Brünn, 1932), p. 121.

[80] *Derashot*, 1.120a, 130a.

[81] Ibid., 1.185b–186a. Later, in 1830, he gave his opinion on the issue of conscription to the army, and admitted that the rabbis entrusted the matter to the community leaders, who do 'as they see fit at the time' (*Teshuvot*, 6.29).

[82] This is despite the fact that the view in question was expressed in Hungary, too, as early as 1790. See L. Löw, *Gesammelte Schriften*, 5 vols (Szegedin, 1889–90), vol. 4, pp. 425–7.

[83] *Derashot*, 1.72a, 187b.

[84] Ibid., 1.72a. This was said early on in his service in Dresnitz. In Mattersdorf he realized that card games could not be totally uprooted, and therefore permitted them during Gentile holidays (*Igrot Sofrim*, pt 2, pp. 3–4).

[85] *Derashot*, 1.187a. Theatre-going had been a target of preachers in traditional society long before the Hatam Sofer. See A. Shohat, *Im Hilufei Tekufot, Reshit ha-Haskalah be-Yahadut Germanyah* (Jerusalem, 1961), pp. 37–9.

[86] *Derashot*, 1.187a.

[87] Ibid., 1.72b.

[88] Ibid., 1.17a; and *Teshuvot*, 6.61.

heed to the heretical maskilim.[89] However, these were general criticisms directed at events in the larger world. In his own region he did not encounter such 'deviations'. If he had any struggle at all in these communities, it was against the heads of the community [90] and the burial society,[91] who took advantage of their positions to exploit both their own poor and. defenceless strangers.

It seems that the vigilance of the community and its leaders was still aimed more against old transgressions than new deviations. Counted among these 'old offences' was the Sabbatean heresy, and there are indications that the Hatam Sofer was sensitive to it. It is reported that while he was still in Prossnitz he encountered an individual who cast aspersions upon one of Rabbi Jacob Emden's books, from which he understood that the person was connected to the Sabbatean sect.[92] Another time he recognized a Sabbatean at the recitation of the 'midnight prayer', when the man displayed no signs of grief over the destruction of the Temple.[93] This oral tradition is verified by his own testimony. In a response from the year 1801, when he lived in Mattersdorf, he dealt with the question of whether a community should excommunicate and banish someone who deserved such punishment, even though that person might convert to Christianity. The Hatam Sofer concurred in the opinion of Rabbi Moses Isserles that the punishment should be carried out, unless it was likely that the excommunicant would also remove 'his small children ... who have not sinned' from the Jewish community. In the case of a heretic who inculcated heresy in his children, however, there was no need to display mercy toward the children either. They must be regarded as lost to the religion of Israel. From this the Hatam Sofer arrived at the practical legal conclusion

that the cursed sect which believes in Shabbetai Zvi, may his name be blotted out, should, if, heaven forbid, their hearts do not change for the good, be harassed along with their sons and daughters, for all of them are cursed before God and heresy is part of their very essence. There is no idolatry in the world which is not part of their sham faith, and it is better that they and their children be separated from the Jewish community and

---

[89] *Derashot,* 1.128b.
[90] Ibid., 1.71a—b.
[91] *Teshuvot,* YD 329.
[92] Plaut, *Likutei,* 1a.
[93] *Derashot,* 2.306b; see note.

assimilated among the Gentiles. And to do this will be considered a great achievement.[94]

It is not known from the responsum whether the decree was addressed to an actual event. Perhaps the Hatam Sofer's remarks were occasioned by the animated dispute which had taken place in Prague the previous year and by the publication of Rabbi Elazar Fleckeles' book on the matter.[95] In any event, it is clear that he saw the Sabbateans as constantly establishing families of adherents who transmitted their faith to their children.

Even if we do assume that the Hatam Sofer's judgement refers to an actual event, it was only an isolated occurrence, for there was no civil strife over Sabbateanism in his region. Similarly, no polemic was issued against the fundamental claims of the maskilim. Thus, the time was not ripe for the Hatam Sofer's full personality to emerge.

His students and those who asked him about matters of halakhah certainly were aware of his eminent scholarship. Rabbi Moses Sofer was like an inexhaustible spring: he effortlessly generated problems and solutions, comparisons and distinctions, during the course of his study.[96] He did not refrain from extensive use of the method of *pilpul*, by which concepts and subjects which appeared to be unrelated to one another were combined. However, he generally strove to clarify matters according to their plain meaning — as far as one can speak of plain meaning in relation to the method established by traditional scholarship. For this methodology did not, of course, admit the notion of critical examination — that is, establishing the exact meanings of the words as understood by those who uttered them. (To be precise, this method recognized the need for exactness, but restricted its validity with other presuppositions.[97]) The Hatam

[94] *Teshuvot*, YD 322.

[95] A. Fleckeles, *Ahavat David* (Prague, 1800).

[96] In a letter to Rabbi Daniel Prossnitz from the year 1805 he describes the way he studied and prepared for a sermon: 'My method is to clarify all that is contained in the *sugyah* without omitting anything major or minor. Later I take two or three grains from it and transmit them to the general community.' (*Igrot Sofrim*, pt 2, p. 6).

[97] The dividing-line between plain meaning (*peshat*) and argumentation (*pilpul*) in traditional scholarship is not definable by objective standards. It is decided by the author's own feeling, whether he had meant to find or approach the truth, or allowed himself to depart from it. Such a feeling is sometimes expressed in the author's testimony, when he states that something was said by way of argumentation (*pilpul*) or logomachy (*hidud*). For

Sofer's own method was flexible enough to arrive at conclusions in keeping with his own general views. According to the standards of traditional scholarship, Rabbi Moses Sofer was a plain expounder of the traditional text. He did not construct elaborate casuistic inter-pretations, as was common among writers of the eighteenth century and their successors in his own era.[98] Especially in his responsa, he wanted to arrive at conclusions based solely upon clarification of the doctrines relevant to the matter under discussion. It was also his desire that the decision should be an independent one, and in no way did he shirk responsibility for his judgements. This quality later earned him his position as a great authority in the rabbinic world, and obviously the local inhabitants too, perceived this remarkable quality, however dimly. Nevertheless, great learning and the ability to adjudicate according to Jewish law were not such rare qualities in those days that anyone who possessed them was guaranteed wide-spread fame.

In addition to his outstanding learning, Rabbi Moses Sofer possessed certain character traits which were revealed in simple but meaningful acts. For example, after he had accepted in principle the rabbinical position in Mattersdorf, he received an offer from Prossnitz, a far more important community. In a letter to the people of Prossnitz he explained why he could not change his mind and go there instead:

I have already replied to the holy congregation of Mattersdorf and I have told them that I will come there. I will not, God forbid, deceive them, and I will not search for excuses and pretexts as might normally be done in such a case. For, if I now reversed myself, would they not say in their confusion, 'Every man is deceitful and this man Moses, upon whose shoulders we placed the rabbinical office, is a liar.' Thus, there would be disgrace, anger, and, heaven forbid, a profanation of God's name. And, in a place where there is a profanation of God's name, no honour is accorded the rabbi.[99]

These lines contain allusions to the traditional body of values, accord-

---

an instance of such testimony in the early writings of the Hatam Sofer see *Teshuvot*, 7.18.

[98] This method is justified by Shmuel Landau in his introduction to *Sefer Doresh le-Tziyyon* (Prague, 1827), a collection of the *pilpulim* that his father (the author of *Nodah bi-Yehudah*) made in his youth.

[99] Sh. Sofer, *Hut ha-Meshulash*, pp. 43–44.

ing to which one was expected to be faithful to one's word. The practical possibility of escaping a commitment is recognized, but the Hatam Sofer accepts the more stringent ethical demand.

On another occasion, however, the Hatam Sofer did go back on his word, though not for his own advantage. After four years of service in Mattersdorf the place proved to be stifling for him and his students. Thus, he decided to accept a rabbinical post in Waag Neustadt.[100] He had already preached his farewell sermon [101] when a fire broke out in the town and the Jewish quarter was destroyed. His heart would not permit him to leave his congregation in distress. He asked the people of Waag Neustadt to release him from his promise, and he remained in Mattersdorf. He played an active role in the reconstruction of the community both by enlisting aid from outside sources and by establishing order out of the chaos of disaster.[102] Everything indeed testifies to the fact that in this hour of need he showed a rare ability to fuse spiritual and practical support.

VI

That the Rabbi of Mattersdorf combined great learning, exemplary rectitude and practical talent explains, to some extent, the impression which he made upon the communities of the region. To explain the profound influence that he had upon his students and followers, however, it is necessary to understand his religious personality. Like his master, Rabbi Nathan Adler, he tore himself away from the routine fulfilment of commandments by establishing a personal pattern of religious observance:

As I often say, all the halakhah which is contained in the *Shulhan Arukh* is that which was given equally to all Israel, with no one excluded. Yet he who possesses only Torah does not really even possess Torah, for then his performance becomes merely habit and custom passed on from generation to generation. Therefore, he who would achieve piety before his Creator will be recognized by his deeds — i.e. by those practices which he

---

[100] Vág-Ujhély (Hungarian name), now named Nové Mesto nad Váhom, in Slovakia, and not Neustadt in Austria, as mistakenly identified by A. Katz (*Ha-Hatam Sofer*, p. 17).

[101] *Derashot*, pt 1, 123a–124a. See the editor's note.

[102] Sh. Sofer, *Hut ha-Meshulash*, pp. 40–3.

originates for the sake of heaven, and by all that which his heart desires. In this no two individuals are alike, because no two men love God in the same way. Thus, Israel is called 'children of the Ethiopians', for each one is externally different, but in essence each one is united with all Israel.[103]

The point is that each man must express the depth of his religious consciousness in his own ways, while fulfilling the traditional requirements of religious observance.

The Hatam Sofer fulfilled the general principle which he established in both its aspects. In the many details of religious life which were not fixed and established by Jewish law, he did not follow the example and teachings of others, but rather acted on the basis of his own judgement and reasons. His students collected the entire array of 'the customs of the Hatam Sofer' into a book, in which they detailed his daily regimen, both on weekdays and holidays, from the text of his prayer service to his eating-habits.[104] We cannot always ascertain the reasons for his customs,[105] but it is clear that they were closely connected to the issue of religion and law. Thus, they fell under the category of 'those practices which [a man] originates for the sake of heaven'.

His originality in establishing these customs prevented his actions from becoming merely habitual; it was important to him that the religious consciousness of the individual should not be weakened. Thus, he thought it vital that the proper intention should accompany the religious act.[106] If we take into account his outstanding degree of self-control, it is easy to believe he attained an exceptional degree of religious consciousness. However, his concept of religious consciousness — intention in its plain sense — was not based on the Kabbalah.[107] There is no doubt that the Hatam Sofer possessed a measure of expertise in mystical doctrine.[108] Although he declared not once, but

---

[103] *Teshuvot,* OH 197.

[104] The first to assemble the customs was Plaut (*Likutei,* introduction to pt 3, 1a–5a). See also Sh. Sofer, *Hut ha-Meshulash,* pp. 139–52.

[105] Y. L. Shilal, *Minhagei Ba'al he-Hatam Sofer* (Pressburg, 1930). This author provides source references and specifies the reasons for the customs.

[106] There is a saying attributed to him that from the earliest day he could remember he had never had an impure thought during prayer (Sh. Sofer, *Hut ha-Meshulash,* p. 123).

[107] This is, at any rate, his disciple's account: Plaut, *Likutei,* 3.2b.

[108] A recently published sermon for for the eve of Yom Kippur 5552, in *Nispah le-Sefer ha-Zikaron,* 2nd edn (Jerusalem, 1964), is wholly comprised of Kabbalist concepts.

many times, to those whom he knew were experts in Kabbalah that he did not engage in Kabbalistic practices,[109] he also hinted at his interest in the secret Torah.[110] Thus, while there is no reason to assume that he practised Kabbalah in any regular way, it is clear that as a matter of principle he acknowledged the validity of Kabbalistic doctrine and saw it as a possible or even necessary means for understanding the underlying reasons for the commandments. So, even if he did not *teach* that a special intention (*kavanah*), as defined in Kabbalistic theory, should be present when performing the commandment, he fostered recognition of a connection between the performance and the commandment's hidden dimensions, a connection implicit in Kabbalistic doctrine.[111]

The Hatam Sofer's attachment to the world of mysticism was certainly not purely theoretical. His consciousness was distinguished by its openness to experiences and events whose sources lay beyond the world of normal sense experience and rational calculation. His personal testimony, as well as that of those who were close to him, speaks of occasional dreams and visions.[112] He treated these phenomena seriously and respectfully. Even his waking visions he accepted as allusions to events in the future, and he attempted to interpret his dreams in order to apprehend the meaning or lessons to be gleaned from them. He defined himself as a 'mindful man',[113] an allusion to a statement in the Gemara that 'one who is mindful of

---

[109] *Teshuvot*, OH 145; and also the responsum published in *Kokhavei Yizhak* (1845), pp. 40–1. The meaning is that no law should be decided according to the Kabbalah if it has no halakhic foundation. However, wherever halakhah casts no doubts, he instructs or advises acting according to the Kabbalah. For example, a widow waiting for performance of the levirate rite (*shomeret yavam*) may dispense with the shoe removal (*halitzah*) if she is old and does not wish to be married. But the Zohar claims that the *halitzah* contributes to the peaceful rest of the dead husband's soul, and therefore the Hatam Sofer advises women to perform it (*Teshuvot*, EhE 2.85).

[110] Letter to Rabbi Yuda Asad, *Igrot Sofrim*, 2.13–14.

[111] See below, section VIII.

[112] See Sh. Sofer, *Hut ha-Meshulash*, pp. 46–7 and 52, for such experiences in Mattersdorf. See below, section VII, for dreams and visions in Pressburg during the Napoleonic war. The Hatam Sofer married his third wife after his second wife appeared in a dream, saying that the home must be cared for: Sh. Sofer, *Hut ha-Meshulash*, p. 121. A posthumous appearance by Rabbi Mordecai Benet is mentioned ibid., p. 149.

[113] *Teshuvot*, YD 341.

demons suffers for disregarding them, while one who is not mindful does not'. What he meant was that, although others were free to disregard such things, he was obliged to take careful note of them. There is absolutely no doubt that this openness to signs from beyond the sensory world stemmed from his participation in the group around Rabbi Nathan Adler. Indeed, these people had so cultivated this trait that their opponents assailed them for it. Though Rabbi Moses Sofer left the group during his youth, he retained this trait, as well as other, related ones derived from the tense mystical atmosphere surrounding Adler.

Just as he believed that there was a transmission of signs from the extrasensory world to our own, so he believed that the upper world was susceptible to the influence of man. Yet in practice he adopted a quietistic posture, a viewpoint of submission to the majesty of the higher will: what God decreed in His wisdom man must endure in silence. A letter remains which reveals the Hatam Sofer's position in its every dimension.[114] A father whose young children had died wished to send a representative to pray by the grave of Rabbi Nathan Adler. The Hatam Sofer regarded the man's wish as a type of vow and wanted to help him fulfil it. Due to the connections which 'some righteous men among his students' attained (this in 1818), he sent a financial donation on behalf of the father with instructions on how to act at the time of visiting the grave. At the same time, however, he expressed the opinion that the act was not in keeping with the spirit of Rabbi Nathan Adler and, he added, was at variance with the way in which Adler himself had acted in a similar situation.

Adler had had only one son and one daughter, and the daughter, 'as beloved by him as his wife', died at the age of twelve when Adler was in Boskowitz. The Hatam Sofer was impressed by the conduct of his rabbi, who 'affirmed the righteousness of the divine judgement with a great and wonderful joy that I had not observed in him even during the Festival of the Rejoicing of the Law'. Only when the Haftarah was being recited on the Sabbath during the week of mourning did 'a tear fall from his eye. He caught the tear in his hand and immediately reverted to his former conduct. Again, no hint of sadness could be observed in him, and he did not mention her name at all.' Rabbi Nathan's wife bore him no more children, 'yet he employed no strategem to alter the situation because, I think, she had

[114] The letter was published by Zussman Sofer in *Yalkut Eliezer al Tehilim* (Paks, 1890), immediately following the title page. It was reprinted in Schwartz, *Derekh ha-Nesher, ve-Torat Emet*, pp. 50–2.

stopped menstruating. He thus did not want to protest to Heaven to alter nature, for he feared, God forbid, that he would cause his wife's death.' Up to this point, the Hatam Sofer has described the deeds of his master. The continuation of his testimony, however, provides an instructive autobiographical insight. 'And because of this I, too, never asked him, may the memory of the righteous be for a blessing, to request mercy on behalf of my first wife, may the memory of the righteous be for a blessing, for the reasons mentioned above. For one who does not press time is not pressed by it, and great is his gain and salvation before Him, may His name be blessed.'[115] These words were written six years after his first wife's death, after his second wife had already borne him a son and a daughter (or daughters).

The foundation of the Hatam Sofer's being and religious experience was constructed upon his prolonged contact with the charismatic personality of Rabbi Nathan Adler, and he was fully conscious of the source of this influence. When the news of the rabbi's death (1800) reached him, he gave vent to his feelings, in which a consciousness of gratitude for the past was mixed with a feeling of fatherlessness in the present.[116] He felt that he had unconsciously sensed the departure of his master. Thus he interpreted a dream which he had had about Torah scrolls draped in black, following the custom of the Frankfurt community on public fast days.[117] To an audience the Hatam Sofer described his master not only as a teacher of halakhah who would 'sit and teach just like Moses from the mouth of the Almighty', but also as a miracle-worker who, when the homes on the Jewish street in Frankfurt were being burned − (the Hatam Sofer specifically noted two examples, one in 1774 and the other in 1795, during the French conquest of the city), 'wrapped in a prayer shawl and phylacteries, neither got up nor moved from his study. He prayed undisturbed and neither did God's hand touch his house nor did the fire approach his domain.'[118] In the succeeding section there is something of auto-biographical significance: 'I was not privileged to gaze upon his face while he was on the verge of death, for then his spirit would have been imparted to me in the same way that Elijah said to Elisha, "If you see me when I am taken from you, it shall be so unto you."'[119]

---

[115] Ibid.

[116] Parts of this obituary are cited in Sh. Sofer, *Hut ha-Meshulash*, pp. 55−7. It appears in full in *Derashot*, 2.371a−373b.

[117] *Derashot*, 2.372a.

[118] Ibid., 2.373a.

[119] Ibid., 2.372b.

The reference to the relationship between Elijah and Elisha is instructive. Although the condition for imparting the spirit was not fulfilled in the case of Adler and Sofer, clearly the Hatam Sofer did not perceive the condition as absolute. For, on another occasion, he cited a homily of Rabbi Nathan himself the plain meaning of which was that no student could be elevated to the highest level until his teacher's death.[120] The true feeling of the Hatam Sofer, then, was that a measure of his master's spirit had indeed been passed to him. In our language we would say that the Hatam Sofer, too, attained his master's quality of charisma. In blending charisma with several other qualities, however, he not only concealed it, but also used it to develop a much greater sphere of influence than his master had vouchsafed him.

VII

In 1806 Rabbi Moses Sofer was elected to serve as the rabbi of the Pressburg community. He was then forty-three years old and at the height of both his intellectual and his moral powers. He served the community for thirty-three years and it became the principal arena for his historically significant activities.

The Pressburg community was larger and more important than the communities he had previously served, and, unlike them, it was neither homogeneous nor tranquil. The influence of the Haskalah had been felt, at the very least, among a particular segment of the community, and members of that segment were apprehensive about the arrival of the new rabbi. They turned to him and explained their position:

> Here in Pressburg most of our business-dealings are with non-Jewish merchants, and we are involved with officers and nobles of the state. Consequently, many of us are forced to wear the distinguished dress of the Gentiles, and to cut our hair and shave our beards even during half-holidays and during the counting of the 'omer. Our wives and daughters wear eye make-up and wigs. They go here and there, some to pass the time, some to support the members of their families, and though these customs and matters may not appear to be quite proper in

[120] The autobiographical significance of this paragraph is indicated in Sh. Sofer, *Hut ha-Meshulash*, p. 57.

the eyes of our teacher and rabbi, nevertheless, in a big city like this things cannot be changed.[121]

The authors of the letter added that, according to local custom, the rabbi of the city had no licence to supervise the normal activities of the members of the community. Instead, the rabbi's only task was 'to spread Torah, to instruct people in the way of the Lord by means of ethical instruction, and to issue legal rulings on matters of religious practice'.[122] The topic under discussion here was not one of principled opposition between the demands of the rabbi and the views of the congregants. Rather, these congregants submitted to the needs and spirit of the time, and were simply seeking the right to continue to conduct themselves in accord with their own conception in the future. They asked the rabbi to overlook those flaws, if flaws they were, and, in return, they pledged him both financial and moral support. Their fear was that their consevative opponents would want to rely upon this new rabbi,[123] and thus they advanced this warning to the rabbi before he assumed his post.

In coming to Pressburg, Rabbi Moses Sofer was caught in the struggle between the conservatives and those open to or inclined toward change, a struggle that was taking place in every large Western community at the time. The balance between these two groups generally was dependent upon political, social and personal circumstances. In political and social terms, Pressburg was similar to cities, such as Prague and Nikolsburg, in which the innovators held the upper hand. Developments in Pressburg went in the opposite direction, however, and the community turned into a bastion of conservative Judaism. This turn of events has often been attributed to the strength of the Hatam Sofer's influence. Having traced his development from youth, we are able to appreciate where his great strength lay. Now we shall see, briefly, how he set this strength in motion.

The apprehensions of those community members who feared that the new rabbi would want to supervise their daily activities were unfounded. Indeed, we find no evidence of any such tension between

---

[121] Y. Schwartz, Zikhron le-Moshe (Oradea, 1938), pp. 101–2.

[122] Ibid., p. 102.

[123] 'If you turn your heart and listen to the voice of the charmers, men who lack culture, wicked people who wear fur coats for the sake of deceitfulness, who chastise us with scorpions and make heavy our yoke with unnecessary and impossible demands, then our hearts will be agitated and the fire of argument will always rage among the people of God' (ibid.).

the Hatam Sofer and the members of his community. To a realistic, commonsensical person such as the Hatam Sofer, it was obvious that there would be differences between the small towns he had formerly served and a large city such as Pressburg. He made good use of the opportunities that Pressburg afforded by expanding his yeshivah, so that after only three years he had about 150 students.[124] As for adult education, he personally saw to it that rabbis were placed in houses of study to teach the average person the Pentateuch with Rashi, Mishnah and laws, according to their level of understanding.[125] He himself preached more often than was customary among rabbis in large cities.[126] He used these public sermons not only to impart knowledge and moral teaching, but also to spellbind the congregation and thus to win them over to his opinion on specific issues of the day.

Their hearts and minds were not conquered in just a year or two. During his first year in office one woman boldly brought the rabbi to court because of a dispute between her and the congregation in which the rabbi had ruled against her.[127] The Hatam Sofer's earliest opponents did not disappear, and he did not stand above all criticism even in the eyes of the general public. In his third year in Pressburg a severe crisis beset the community in the wake of Napolean's war against the Austrians, which by the summer of 1809 had reached the city's gates. The French besieged the city and shelled it intermittently. Three months later they conquered it.[128] The damage to the city was considerable, and during the compaign the population, Gentile and Jewish, was thrown into disarray and despair. Some of the residents fled to nearby towns, only to return to Pressburg when the dangers of war paled against the hardships of flight. In the Hatam Sofer's life the event generated a genuine personal crisis. According to his own testimony, he had sensed the approaching danger ever since the

---

[124] *Sefer ha-Zikaron,* ed. J. Schwartz, rev. M. Stern (New York, 1956), p. 50.

[125] Plaut, *Likutei,* 2b,

[126] In *Hut ha-Meshulash*, p. 106, Solomon Sofer lists ten regular yearly sermons and additional ones 'as time and occasion dictate'. The printed sermons bear witness to their frequency. Leopold Zunz, *Die Gottesdienstlichen Vorträge der Juden* (Berlin, 1832), p. 468, reports that the Rabbi in Pressburg delivers moral sermons on the nights before the four fasts, and women attend them too.

[127] This is probably the meaning of *Sefer ha-Zikaron,* p. 42.

[128] The details are given in *Sefer ha-Zikaron.* S. Bettelheim translated into German and annotated most of *Sefer ha-Zikaron.* See Gold, *Die Juden...Bratislava,* pp. 99–108.

autumn, through dreams and visions.[129] When the war finally struck
the city, he too had to decide whether to remain or flee, and within
him rational and ethical considerations — on the rights and wrongs of
leaving his congregation in a time of distress — vied with non-rational
motivations which were impossible to reveal to anyone else. Finally
he left the city, only to return to it in the middle of the campaign. He
did not return to his own home, however, but lived in a house that
was thought to be better protected. He thus failed to escape the
criticism of members of the community in general and of his entrenched critics in particular, who could find no logical reasons for
their rabbi's conduct.[130] He himself felt that his actions had not lived
up to the justified expectations that his fellow men had of him, and
was pulled this way and that, so that he felt that he 'was always
swaying, like the movement of the tress in the forest before the wind.
And the heart knows the bitterness of my soul.'[131] It is clear that at
this stage the irrational elements in his being held the upper hand and
that he had willy-nilly to abide by them.

Yet during the siege we see him engaged in a ceremony called
'redemption of souls', i.e. offering charity to members of the community and comforting them by sending messengers to the graves of
the righteous.[132] This was a semi-magical ceremony of a sort that
most of the community, apparently, expected their rabbi to perform.
They looked to him, to his merit and the merit of his Torah, to shield
them. In the sermons that he delivered during the siege, the rabbi
demurred from taking on himself the role of protector of the community.[133] However, this restraint was nothing more than a gesture
of humility. The truth is that he took it for granted that he had a
special role in determining the fate of the community; 'therefore, I
did all that a humble man like me could do'.[134] Although his actions
were controversial, many undoubtedly interpreted them as praiseworthy. Several of his dreams and visions, and his reactions to them,
were known publicly, and they earned him — justifiably — the title of
'one who engages in mysteries'.[135] Yet even those who concerned
themselves only with what they could see had something to which

---

[129] *Sefer ha-Zikaron*, pp. 2–3.
[130] Ibid., pp. 27–8.
[131] Ibid., p. 28.
[132] Ibid., pp. 4, 16.
[133] Ibid., p. 38.
[134] Ibid., p. 3.
[135] See Bettelheim's German's translation, nn. 5 and 15.

they could point. Also, during this time of tribulation the rabbi maintained his daily schedule of prayer and study. During the entire summer of the siege a day did not pass but he held a class with some of his students.[136] This was the public task which he set for himself and by which, above all, he wished to be judged in this world and the next.[137]

VIII

The following years in the Hatam Sofer's life can be seen as a time when he consolidated his position within his city and extended his fame both within Hungary and beyond.[138] Legal questions now came to him from all corners of Hungary, and in 1810 an appeal reached him from Germany. This urged him to make common cause with some of the noted rabbis there against the rabbinical council of the Westphalian Consistory, which condoned the abrogation of a custom which had been accepted by all Ashkenazic communities: the prohibition on eating legumes at Passover.[139] The Hatam Sofer did not comply with the request to issue either a protest against the council's action or a ban on those involved, for he saw a 'danger' in doing so.[140] It seems that he feared involvement with an institution under the jurisdiction of another state, and one which at that time especially was on friendly terms with the Austrian Empire. He did, however, respond to the query, and, as a matter of fact, he took a principled stance against the tendency which loomed behind this abrogation of custom.

The prohibition on eating legumes at Passover had no basis in the Talmud and it was among the restrictive measures which were extended throughout Ashkenazic communities prior to the thirteenth

---

[136] *Sefer ha-Zikaron*, p. 24.

[137] Ibid. The editor's notes include testimonies concerning his insistence on teaching publicly until his very last day.

[138] Until that year he had received only one query from outside his own region. This came from Trieste, and referred to the authorities' decree that civil marriage should take place prior to the rabbinical wedding-ceremony (*Teshuvot*, EhE 2.108, 109). The responsa date from 5564–5 (1804–5).

[139] *Teshuvot*, OH 122.

[140] 'I am not involved in this matter, and in any case it is a matter where there is a danger.' This sentence was included in the covering letter, which was not meant for publication.

century.[141] Therefore, in times of distress — years of drought, for example — it was customary to lift the restriction.[142] The Westphalian rabbis claimed that such an emergency existed, owing to the years of war and the difficulty, for Jewish soldiers, of finding kosher food during Passover.[143] So far, the decree removing the prohibition was well-founded. However, in the Consistory's formal proclamation halakhic reasons for the decision were mixed with Reform argumentation. Israel Jacobson, head of the Consistory, signed the proclamation, and its Reform orientation was his doing. It was this that created the controversy about a ruling which, at first sight, seemed almost uncontestable.[144]

The traditional rabbis were alert to what had happened, however. Protests reached the Consistory from many different sources, and the extremists among the rabbis, headed by Rabbi Abraham from Glogau, attempted to organize a joint action of famous halakhic authorities to get the decree rescinded.[145] They wanted to include the Hatam Sofer among their number. The Consistory's actual proclamation had not reached him, but he understood the basis for the permission, and acknowledged that those who had issued it were able to base it upon traditional authority.[146] With this 'acknowledgement' he released himself from any obligation to react publicly against those who had issued the permission, though he was far from agreeing with it. On the contrary, he strengthened the ban against legumes by basing it upon a completely new foundation. He turned what had been a custom into a type of *gezerah* (decree) which he claimed had been issued by the sages among the *rishonim* (early medieval rabbis)

---

[141] The prohibition of legumes and its historical sources are described in Rabbi Sh. Y. Zevin, *Ha-Mo' adim ba-Halakhah*, 7th edn (Tel Aviv, 1960), pp. 255–62.
[142] Ibid., pp. 260–1.
[143] The proclamation is printed in B. H. Auerbach, *Geschichte der israelitischen Gemeinde Halberstadt* (Halberstadt, 1866), pp. 215–6.
[144] This is implied in Rabbi Menahem Mendel Steinhardt, *Divrei Igeret* (Rödlheim, 1812), 1.1a. Steinhardt supported the ruling and published his reasoning in this responsum.
[145] Auerbach, *Mishnat Rabbi Natan*, pp. 217–27. A proclamation of the Fürth law court is printed in *Jahrbuch der jüdisch-literarischen Gesellschaft*, 6 (1908) pp. 229–30.
[146] The matter had recently been much discussed in halakhic literature. It is treated by Rabbi Jacob Emden in *Mor u-Kezi'ah*, OH 453 (quoted in Steinhardt, *Divrei Igeret*). The Hatam Sofer repeated Emden's reasoning without mentioning him by name.

in accordance with God's will. ('And the Lord desired this when He said, "Establish a guard around the guard."') He then defined the entire Ashkenazic community as one congregation which had accepted the decree, so that it became a sort of eternal vow which no sage or group of sages would ever be permitted to annul.[147]

A comparison of the Hatam Sofer's responsum with those of the other rabbis shows that he transformed the matter from a halakhic question into a public one of defending the walls of tradition against any breaches.[148] The method of argument in his responsum demonstrates this, but the fashion in which he presented such matters before his congregation reveals it even more clearly. He composed his responsum on the 21 Adar I, and by this time he had already announced his intention to speak on the matter 'on the day of assembly on the Sabbath before the holiday', i.e. on the Great Sabbath which precedes Passover. In this sermon he established the principle 'that the Holy One, blessed be He, granted authority to the sages in each generation to establish customs in Israel, and once they are spread, it is forbidden to uproot them, if those who established them were sages of pure intention wishing to build a hedge around the law. Thus, there is absolutely no right to undo these customs.'[149] The earlier and the later generations are described as a single unified organic body ('For the son is a part of his father and rooted in him'[150]), and this was the ideological justification for his halakhic conclusion that the sons' authority to annul a vow was less than that of their fathers in establishing it. Here we have an outstanding example of the development of a conservative system of thought that can persuasively influence public opinion.

It is clear that at this time the Hatam Sofer had already begun to construct a general theory regarding the sanctification of the tradition, the essence of which was to abolish distinctions between accepted standards — i.e. between the absolute law of the Torah and customs sanctioned by the rabbis. The entire system of traditions had to be observed in its entirety. While the Hatam Sofer was unable to compel the members of his congregation to observe the traditions, he was able to teach them that a violation blemished the essence of Judaism. His promulgation of this principle bound to him those who inclined

---

[147] Ibid., in the responsum.
[148] See for example the responsa of Beit Halevi given by the Hatam Sofer, and the one mentioned in n146.
[149] *Derashot,* 2.243a—b.
[150] Ibid., 2.243b.

toward conservatism — then in the majority in his congregation — and the conservatives were delighted to find that the great rabbi championed their cause, explained it and inflamed passions for it. On account of his principled leadership, the Hatam Sofer acquired a bedrock of supporters among his congregation, and was thus able to take a firm stand against innovations.

To be sure, the innovators did not disappear on account of the Hatam Sofer's presence in Pressburg. On the contrary, in the course of time they became stronger. If, when he came to Pressburg, they seemed no more than a group which deviated slightly from the traditional way of life, they now appeared as advocates of educational reform — long a cause of strife between the conservatives and the innovators. In the winter of 1811 it was announced that the innovators intended to open a school which would combine secular and religious learning in accordance with accepted Enlightenment policy. The Hatam Sofer attempted to prevent this development,[151] and, when he did not succeed, launched a vigorous attack on the innovators, characterizing them as heretics who had licentiously cast off the yoke of the Jewish religion.[152]

The Hatam Sofer's protest against this 'enlightened' education was a continuation of the battle waged by the great rabbis — Ezekiel Landau of Prague, David Tevle of Lissa, and Pinchas Horowitz of Frankfurt — following the publication of Naphtali Herz Wessely's *Divrei Shalom Ve-Emet* ('Words of Peace and Truth') and Moses Mendelssohn's Torah translation.[153] The Hatam Sofer, however, added a personal note to the debate by basing his opposition upon the absolute value of the study of Torah according to the old order and method.

The Hatam Sofer did not negate the value of engagement in 'external wisdom' (i.e. secular studies). On the contrary, he felt that it was both necessary and essential for a wise student to complete his education by receiving such secular instruction, for it served as a

---

[151] According to Plaut, *Likutei*, 2b, the initiators of the plan notified the Hatam Sofer, who responded in his sermon the next day. The sermon implies that he had previously given them his opinion in writing (*Derashot*, 1.113b).

[152] The sermon on this occasion appears in Plaut, *Likutei*, 2.6a—9b; and in *Derashot*, 1.112a—116b.

[153] Both debates are much discussed in the literature. See for example M. Eliav, *Ha-Hinukh ha-Yehudi be-Germanyah bi-Yemei ha-Haskalah ve-ha-'Emanzipazyah* (Jerusalem, 1961), pp. 33—51.

handmaiden to the Torah. He especially emphasized the study of surgery, mathematics and geometry, as they were essential for a proper understanding of several central halakhic problems.[154] He was vigorously opposed, however, to 'philosophical wisdom',[155] by which he meant the study and investigation of the general significance of Judaism, the rational definition of its principles, and the rational justification of its commandments. Moses Mendelssohn, in the generation before the Hatam Sofer, had developed this 'old – new' way of approaching Judaism in his book *Jerusalem,* and his pupils and all those who came under the influence of rationalism in general and the Jewish Enlightenment in particular continued it. There is no reason to assume that the Hatam Sofer investigated Mendelssohn's works; however, he was familiar with the journals of the maskilim, *Ha-Me'assef* and *Bikurei ha-Itim.*[156] In any event, he clearly perceived the character of the 'enlightened' orientation and the danger it posed to the survival of tradition. 'The deviant members of our people attempt to give a reason for every commandment in the Torah. On account of this the Torah will fade away, for they will say that once the reason is invalidated, so, too, is the commandment.'[157] His chief concern was that rational explanation granted the one who offered the explanation a standard of evaluation by which to deny the absolute validity of the tradition. He counterposed to this his own theory, which was a resurrection of one put forward by the thirteenth-century Spanish Kabbalists.[158] ('God forbid that we should maintain that there is not

---

[154] *Derashot,* 1.112b.

[155] Ibid. The issues are made clearer in the obituary for Rabbi David Sinzheim, cited below (*Derashot,* 1.81a). A sermon from the year 5569 deals with 'the impurity of philosophy' (*Derashot,* 2.320).

[156] In a responsum concerning postponment of burial overnight (*halanat meitim*), in *Teshuvot,* YD 338, he rebuked the questioner for being unacquainted with the opinions of Moses Mendelssohn and Rabbi Jacob Emden, published in *Ha-Me'assef* and *Bikurei ha-Itim.* The editors of the *Teshuvot* omit the questioner's name, but he is known to be Rabbi Zevi Hirsch Chajes according to his own responsum in *Darkhei ha-Hora'a,* 4, appendices.

[157] *Derashot,* 1.19a.

[158] Nahmanides' influence on the Hatam Sofer is especially marked, Nahmanides being the chief anti-rationalist spokesman of his times. See Y. Baer, *Toldot ha-Yehudim bi-Sefarad ha-Nozrit,* 2nd edn (Tel Aviv, 1959), pp. 144–8. The Hatam Sofer said of Nahmanides' Torah commentary, 'In my humble opinion, this book is truly a foundation of faith and a source of religion' (*Teshuvot* 6.61). In his will he exhorted his sons, 'Study and teach

a reason for *each* of the commandments; but it may be involved and unknown.'[159])

> For it is known that all the Holy Torah is composed of Holy Names, and that which is secret and hidden in the Torah is eternally more holy than that which is manifest in it ... And we pray that He will open our hearts to His Torah and that we be vouchsafed to live and see ... And may no obstacle blur our sight, heaven forbid, to deceive us so that we might say that the external dress, the plain meaning of the biblical text, is the essence of our faith and not the extra meaning contained in it ... However, the deviants, in their lawlessness, state that there is only one Torah and that there is nothing in Scripture except the plain meaning.[160]

This, then, was the basis of his opposition to translation of the Torah. For translation removed 'the dress of precious stones, the allusions and secrets contained in the Torah, and the rabbinic traditions emanating from it, and garbed it, instead, in the scarlet clothing of philosophical wisdom alone'.[161] Use of a translation thus undermined the traditional foundation of biblical learning.[162] His

---

your sons the whole Bible with Rashi's commentary, as well as the Torah with the commentary of Nahmanides, for they provide fundamental instruction in the faith.' The will has been printed many times, recently from a manuscript appended to *Sefer ha-Zikaron*, p. 119. See Weingarten, *He-Hatam Sofer*, p. 47.

[159] *Derashot*, 1.19a.

[160] Ibid., 1.142b. The expression 'all the Holy Torah is composed of Holy Names' is derived from the introduction to Nahmanides' Torah commentary.

[161] Ibid., 1.81a.

[162] The connection is explicitly stated in the following paragraph: 'Behold ... what would happen if we came to provide reasons for the commandments. It would then be proper to translate the Torah into German or some other non-Jewish language. It would become a minor book that we would study two or three times. After that, it would be fluent in our mouth like flowing water and we would never need to ponder it again. If a doubt about a matter would arise, we would discover the reason for the command-ment and we would know immediately why it was forbidden or permitted. For example, we could ask, 'What is the reason that pork is forbidden?' The rationale might be that it is poisonous and harmful. However, what if a certain ingredient was mixed into it so that it was no longer harmful, or, in a particular place, it caused no ill effects... Thus, if we perform the com-mandments of the Torah without searching for a reason, but accept it instead

opposition to the Haskalah and his disapproval of Mendelssohn's Torah translation were thus united into a single vigorous denunciation.

The translation of the Torah was an issue which had engaged the Hatam Sofer ever since he had first opposed the breach created in the walls of the tradition by the maskilim,[163] for it symbolized to him the danger that was to come. He blamed the breach on the 'lawless among our people', but he could not escape the fact that changes in the civil status of the Jews were a major reason for this development.[164] Secular rulers wanted to learn about the nature of the Torah of Israel — just as in the days of Ptolemy Philadelphus, who had commanded the translation of the Torah into Greek.[165] Of course, the Hatam Sofer knew about the acts of the Paris Sanhedrin, whose members had been compelled by the Emperor Napoleon to answer questions on the issue of the relationship of the religion of Israel to

---

as a decree issued by the King, then we will simply assert, 'Her ways wander.' Reluctantly, we will acknowledge that we do not possess the ability to investigate the letters of the Torah in order to derive new meanings from them daily, nor can we fully employ the thirteen hermeneutical principles of Rabbi Ishmael through which the Torah is properly interpreted. Therefore, even if the law is contrary to reasons such as the ones given above, we would still perform God's statutes and His Torah because it is a divine law, one that needs no reason. The decree of the King, may God's Name be blessed, is simply what it is. Thus, even if every man observes the Torah and commandments correctly, but in his heart provides a cause or reason for his observance, then the deed is not acceptable before God' (ibid., 1.19b).

[163] The earliest sign is the dirge mentioned in note 75, written in 1790. The Hatam Sofer himself made two statements dating the beginning of the breach. In his sermon against the maskilim in 1811 he wrote, 'As is well known, it has been more than sixteen years since the community of observant Jews there has declined and the power of the sages to erect a barrier and to protest against transgressors of the law at all has been completely taken away' (*Derashot*, 1.113b). In a letter to his father-in-law, Rabbi Akiva Eger, in the year 5579 (1819), he said, 'It has been approximately thirty years since the day that the handmaidens, violators of the religion, removed their kerchiefs and weakened the hands of the rabbis. And the Torah was forgotten as a result of these insignificant, undermining foxes' (*Teshuvot*, 6.86). The time lapses indicated in these passages appear to point to the first half of the 1790s.

[164] The first statement in note 163 lays more emphasis on the weakening of the rabbis' authority by the governments, while the second stresses the distancing of the maskilim themselves from traditional discipline.

[165] The example of Ptolemy had already been given in a sermon from the year 5556 (1796): *Derashot*, 1.70a.

the nations among whom the Jews lived. Rabbi David Sinzheim, whom the Hatam Sofer had known from his youth, gave him a report on what had transpired and on the manner in which he, as head of the Sanhedrin, had attempted to satisfy the Emperor's demands.[166] The Hatam Sofer praised Rabbi Sinzheim's manner, for, 'when he was asked about several matters, he responded to his questioners. However, in revealing a little, he hid twice as much.'[167] Thus, there was an obligation to explain Judaism to the nations according to their level of understanding. This task was placed upon 'the righteous, people of accomplishment who are full of wisdom, and who stand between the Gentile rulers and us'.[168] However, these interpreters were aware that only explanations which were couched in the language of partial or evasive truth could be offered the nations. In internal Jewish dealings, though, and especially in education, there was no room for this type of explanation.

'If when children first grow up they learn only the plain meaning of Scripture and secular subjects external to Torah, then before they grow up and begin the needed study of the Oral Law, which is the essence of Judaism, they will have already chosen lawlessness and denied God and His Torah.'[169] It might seem that one should initially introduce 'the learning of man and only later the great kindness', i.e. the singular teaching of Israel — and this was Wessely's position in his time.

> But the truth will guide His path, for it is revealed before Him, may His Name be blessed, that it is impossible to distinguish the people Israel from the Gentiles unless Israel completely separates itself from them and their ways, and refrains from

[166] 'I was his acquaintance in my youth and now, through an exchange of letters with him, I view his righteousness and his blamelessness' (*Derashot,* 1.81a). It is known that Rabbi David Sinzheim saw fit to explain his attitude to the great halakhists of his times. See N. M. Gelber, 'Die böhmisch-mährischen Juden und das Napoleonische Sanhedrin', *Zeitschrift für die Geschichte der Tschechoslowakei,* 1930, pp. 60–1. The Hatam Sofer makes it clear that he too received, and accepted, the explanation.

[167] *Derashot,* 1.81a. This is a most apt definition of Sinzheim's approach, which in fact held on to all traditional details, yet gave them explanations intelligible to those unacquainted with halakhic language. The common view, that Sinzheim's responses were compromised, is unfounded; see J. Katz, *Exclusiveness and Tolerance,* (Oxford, 1961), pp. 184–6.

[168] *Derashot,* 1.81a.

[169] Ibid., 1.112b, in the sermon from the year 5571 mentioned above, in note 152.

studying subjects which they share with us, including Scripture propounded in accord with its plain meaning, for in this they are our equals.[170]

The uniqueness and continuity of the people of Israel depended upon transmitting the tradition according to the accepted procedure. One who broke with this severed the chain of the generations and consigned his descendants to heresy — something more serious, perhaps, than apostasy. Those who were educated according to the theory of the maskilim were fortified, perhaps, to reject Christianity, but not to embrace the religion of Israel. 'They cast off the yoke of religion altogether, believing neither in this one nor that.'[171] These words of the Hatam Sofer were not idle rhetoric. They point, in fact, to the effort to present the maskil as an absolutely undesirable type in the eyes of the Gentiles. If earlier the Hatam Sofer believed that an unbreakable bond had been forged between the governments and the maskilim, he now thought it possible to break that connection.

> Secular rulers help and aid us and defend us in the maintenance of our religion, and they have absolutely no desire to abrogate even a single one of our commandments from the Torah. If in some countries the rulers have listened to the voice of these charmers, they have intended only to do good for us, for they do not know and have not been told that this contradicts the foundation of our faith. However, if they hear and understand that this thing is opposed to our Torah and that these persons possess no religion whatsoever, they will pay no heed to them at all. And God is with us.[172]

The significance of these words is to be found in their extremism: for the Hatam Sofer, it was necessary to maintain Judaism in its traditional form, and anyone who deviated from it would be considered to have abandoned the religion — all religion.

IX

The Hatam Sofer's views and theories regarding the administration of public affairs crystallized during his early years in Pressburg. The

---

[170] Ibid.
[171] Ibid.
[172] Ibid., 1.113b.

thirty years of his life that remained tested the utility of the principles that he had established. The essential events of those years — the struggle against Reform, the strengthening of the traditionalists' position in the communities of Hungary, activities on behalf of the settlement in the land of Israel, and the progress of emancipation (which he viewed with distrust) — require further detailed examination and investigation.[173] Here a summary must suffice.

After his fight with the maskilim in his community in 1811, the Hatam Sofer's position in Pressburg was strengthened, and after the Hamburg controversy of 1819 he became a recognized leader outside his city and country, a figure to whom all turned. His self-assertion resulted from a strengthening-process which had been sustained by a set of mutually reinforcing elements. His aggressiveness earned him a position of leadership on public questions, and his status, as well as his imposing personality, attracted students and admirers. These students and admirers used him as a support and source of strength in their administration of public affairs. His students increasingly gained rabbinical positions throughout Hungary — and not without his active support.[174] As early as 1820 he complained that he was being abused because of his students, saying that they 'diminish the honour due to Torah scholars because they feel that the earth was given to them alone'.[175]

But the success of his students had more far-reaching consequences. For the new type of rabbi that the Hatam Sofer produced stood for a new approach marked by consistency and zealotry. Communities had to choose between a rabbi of this new type and one with Reform tendencies. Those who were prepared to compromise became increasingly rare, and Hungarian Jewry in the end was divided into two extreme camps.

In the 'new traditional' community the rabbi possessed more authority than his predecessors had had in the days when there were no attempts to undermine the tradition. Now the unity of the communities depended upon the strength of rabbinic authority. On account of and in conjunction with this strengthening of rabbinic authority, the rabbi's status was also enhanced. This strengthening of

---

[173] Moshe Samet, 'Halakhah and Reform' (unpublished thesis, Jerusalem, 1967) explores the ways in which the teaching of the Hatam Sofer was influenced by his views on public issues.

[174] Some of his letters, collected in *Igrot Sofrim*, deal with recommendations to support his disciples' rabbinical candidatures.

[175] *Igrot Sofrim*, 2.101.

the rabbinate began in the Hatam Sofer's time and he lent it his full moral support.

In his youth the Hatam Sofer had shared the perennial doubts about the office of rabbi, for it seemed inappropriate to take money for performing a task which had to be considered a *mitzvah* (commandment). Later, these doubts evaporated. He believed that the sustenance of a congregation depended upon the rabbinical office, and he warned congregations not to leave the office vacant[176] and not to be stingy in allotting a salary.[177] He declared that a rabbi had no need to be ashamed of receiving wage and reward for his office.[178] Previously, rabbis had been appointed for a fixed term, usually three years.[179] By the Hatam Sofer's era, they were generally appointed without a time limit.[180] He supported this tendency and ruled that, even if a limitation of three years was stipulated in a rabbinical contract, it was nothing more than a formality and did not empower the community to dispense with the rabbi's services.[181] Also, the rabbinate had come to be regarded as an office that a father could bequeath to his son after him.[182] At first the Hatam Sofer opposed this tendency, and in 1820 he still ruled that a son had no right to demand the office of rabbi for himself 'on the grounds that it was an

---

[176] *Teshuvot*, HM 197. In his will, written in the year 5597 (1837), he instructed his community not to leave the rabbinical seat vacant for more than two years (Sh. Sofer, *Hut ha-Meshulash*, p. 154).

[177] *Teshuvot*, HM 5.

[178] Ibid., HM 21; YD 230.

[179] J. Katz, *Tradition and Crisis* (New York, 1971), p. 87.

[180] In his rabbinical writ from Dresnitz and Pressburg there is no time limit (Sh. Sofer, *Hut ha-Meshulash*, pp. 41, 61–3). However, he says himself that 'It is customary in most of the Diaspora to issue a time-bound rabbinical contract — some for three years, others for five' (*Teshuvot*, OH, 205).

[181] *Teshuvot*, OH 205.

[182] The question was first discussed in *Teshuvot*, OH 12, in the year 5580 (1820), in reaction to an event that took place in the vicinity of Munkács: 'In a certain district, there was a distinguished rabbi who wanted to succeed his father, His Excellency, may the memory of the righteous be for a blessing, who had been the rabbi in that district. Moreover, the son was fit to inherit his mantle. Nevertheless, one leader opposed seating him on the chair of his father and the matter came to court. His Excellency, Rabbi Zevi Avigdor of Munkács, who was rabbi of the adjacent district, fought vigorously to aid the son of the above-mentioned rabbi and attempted to secure his father's inheritance for him.' In the year 5590 (1830) the Hatam Sofer said, 'up to this day several cases akin to this have come before me' (ibid., OH 13).

inheritance from his fathers'.[183] However, over the next decade he changed his mind, on the grounds that, since this service had been transformed into a job, the rabbi was 'like an employee of the community, servicing their needs in return for compensation'.[184] He was thus grateful that he had been permitted to 'transform the office into one of the rights of Jewish scholars and their sons after them'.[185] This ruling paved the way for the transference of his office to his son and to the establishment of a rabbinical dynasty for several generations.

X

The Hatam Sofer's first wife died in 1812. A few months later he married a young widow, the daughter of Rabbi Akiva Eger, who was then Rabbi of Markisch-Friedland, and, two years later, of Posen. Rabbi Akiva Eger's friends and relatives encouraged him to accept this new post in order to raise his family's status, including that of his son-in-law, the 'Gaon'. To this suggestion Eger replied, 'What is such illusory honour to us, and to my son-in-law, may his light shine? Praise be to God, the fact is that I am honoured by him. However, he has no need to be honoured through me.'[186]

In any event, these marital connections served as an additional source of strength and authority, if not to the Hatam Sofer himself then to his sons. His wife bore him four sons (one died in childhood) and seven daughters, and he did not lack the means to support his household 'in a manner fit for deputies and nobles'.[187] If he himself did not emphasize the family's lineage, his wife did not overlook the

---

[183] Ibid., OH 12, and also 13, concerning those 'several cases' brought to him: 'I issued a practical ruling that no preference should be given the son if there was another more fitting than he. And this applies all the more if the community desires another.'

[184] Ibid., OH 12.

[185] Ibid. The shift in the Hatam Sofer's opinion on rabbinical inheritance is noted by L. Löw in *Ben Chananja*, (1858), p. 399; H. Flesch, 'Das Geistige Leben in Pressburg', in Gold (ed.), *Die Juden ... Bratislava*, pp. 25–6. Flesch also points out the context of the statement, the election of Rabbi Mordechai Benet's successor as State Rabbi of Moravia. When the post of state rabbi was concerned, the Hatam Sofer did not approve the son's right to inherit the post.

[186] *Igrot Sofrim*, 1.14.

[187] Y. Hirsch, *Mor Deror* (Vienna, 1892), 1.8. The author studied in the Hatam Sofer's yeshivah.

matter. After her death, the Hatam Sofer said of her that she was meticulous 'about matches and marriages as well as associations ... And she said we should avoid infusing improper elements into our family.'[188] That the talented sons — the eldest, Abraham Samuel Benjamin, and the second, Simon — were destined for the rabbinate, was taken for granted. Precisely when the idea emerged that Abraham was destined to occupy his father's post we do not know. He was fifteen when the Hatam Sofer ruled that sons possessed the right to inherit their father's office. It is difficult to believe that the thought that he was dictating his son's fate did not cross the Hatam Sofer's mind when he issued the ruling. The family tradition does not conceal the fact that he prepared his son for the office.[189] After his marriage, Abraham remained in his father's shadow in Pressburg for six years, during which time he was supported by his rich father-in-law from Gorlitz in Galicia. When his father-in-law's support ended, Abraham expressed his concern to his father and displayed signs of impatience. It is reported that the Hatam Sofer jumped from his chair and rebuked his son, saying, 'Should I arise today from my seat in order to place you upon it?'[190] This scene, which surely was not invented, bears witness to the intention to establish a dynasty and to the problems that this entailed.

In his will, written in Kislev 1836, three years before his death, the Hatam Sofer asked his congregants not to leave the rabbinical position open for more than two years after his death.[191] At the same time he expressed the desire that the yeshivah, 'in any event', should not be idle for 'the year of mourning'. 'And how wonderful it would be if my son, Abraham Samuel Benjamin, would deliver the public lecture [after my death].'[191] Since the offices of head of the yeshivah and community rabbi had previously been occupied by the same individual, this last line was an obvious recommendation to the community to accept Abraham as his successor. And even the day before his death, on the day following Sukkot 1839, he announced an addition to his will which stated that he had ordained his son, 'and he is fit to

[188] *Derashot*, 2.386b.
[189] Rabbi Solomon Sofer, the author of *Hut ha-Meshulash*, says simply, 'From the final outcome it is obvious that my grandfather, may the memory of the righteous be for a blessing, intended, after his death, that our father, may his memory protect us, succeed him and sit on his chair.' (p. 238). His account of the facts (pp. 233—7) supports this statement.
[190] Ibid., pp. 236—7.
[191] Ibid., p. 154.

teach and judge in any community which is great and famous in Israel'.[192] This, too, has been understood as a suggestion that he wanted his son to succeed him as Rabbi of Pressburg.[193] Those near him understood, and appealed to the majority of the community's leaders to sign a written request to the rabbi that he should appoint his son head of the yeshivah and transfer to him several tasks of the rabbinical office while he yet lived, on the understanding that the community would select Abraham as the community rabbi after the Hatam Sofer's death.[194] At this point, the Hatam Sofer called for his son in order to bless him, and to strengthen and fortify him by calling on the merit of his fathers, Rabbi Akiva Eger on his mother's side and Rabbi Samuel Sofer on his father's, to support him. The Hatam Sofer himself promised his son that he would always be with him.[195]

The Hatam Sofer's ruling that a son possessed the right to inherit his father's rabbinical position did not absolutely assure that this would happen. For the condition imposed upon this law of inheritance was that the son could fill his father's position only in the event that he was qualified for the post, and the right to determine this remained, ostensibly, with the community. When Rabbi Moses Sofer's post was transferred to his son, the task of choosing was, in fact, taken out of the community's hands. From the time when the rabbi fell ill, on Hoshanah Rabbah 1839, the congregation was seized by a state of constant excitement which sometimes approached ecstasy. As soon as the danger to the revered teacher's life became known, the whole community stood together in prayer and the sages of the city engaged in appropriate liturgical ceremonies — redemption of the soul, name-changing, and so on. Detailed and reliable descriptions of

---

[192] Ibid.

[193] Ibid., p. 159.

[194] Plaut, *Likutei*, 5.26a–28a. This is a reprint of a letter the author wrote to his friend only three weeks after the event. The letter was also published as a separate pamphlet entitled *Kontres Matzevet Moshe* (Galanta, 1937).

[195] Plaut, *Likutei*, 5.27b. The appeal to the rabbi that he should appoint his son head of the yeshivah is mentioned in the community's formal announcement of the rabbi's death during the seven days of mourning (Sh. Sofer, *Hut ha-Meshulash*, p. 162), but the date is omitted and it might be thought that the initiative came from the community leaders. A third description of the rabbi's death is given by the community clerk and trustee in the community book (printed in *Zikhron Moshe*, pp. 46–8). This source too reports that the appeal came to the rabbi the night before his death, but the last will was written one day earlier.

what transpired in Pressburg during those days remain, and it seems that only the Hatam Sofer, the sick man about to die, managed to retain his composure.[196] The same combination of confident attachment to the world above and exact reckoning of his steps in the world below as had marked him and given him composure throughout his life served him also in his hour of death. While beset by the illness — urinary poisoning, it seems — he heroically continued scrupulously to observe every detail of the commandments. He also continued to decide halakhic questions and to offer homilies. News of his exceptional conduct moved his followers to admiration, until finally his soul departed. His funeral — conducted by the light of torches which lit up the night — turned into a moving and elevating experience for many.

Of course, in such a state of spiritual crisis, the rational considerations which normally determined the choice of a rabbi and leader in the congregation of Israel did not come into play. The appointment of the son — talented and learned, but young and far from possessing the stature of his father, was already a *fait accompli*. Contemporaries did not overlook the irregularity, the like of which 'not even the great scholars of this age have been vouchsafed'.[197] Even at the time when the matter was decided, reservations were expressed about its propriety. One of the Hatam Sofer's outstanding pupils, Rabbi Zalman Bonyhad, a member of the Pressburg Bet Din, found fault with his master for ordaining his son himself, thus disregarding the views of great authorities who opposed such a procedure.[198] Others wanted to postpone the decision over the son's succession to his father's post to a calmer moment. Yet those who clung to the will of the rabbi forced the doubters to sign the son's rabbinical contract prior to the burial, and anyone who refused to sign was not permitted to approach the coffin, as was customary, to seek forgiveness from the deceased.[199] The first of the signatories was

---

[196] In addition to the three sources mentioned in the two previous notes there is also an account by the son Simon, given in Sh. Weiss, *Avnei Beit ha-Yozer*, pp. 52–5. He ignores the appointment of his brother to succeed his father as rabbi. There is also a general report in the *Allgemeine Zeitung des Judenthums*, 1839, pp. 574–6.

[197] Plaut, *Likutei*, 5.27b.

[198] Sh. Sofer, *Hut ha-Meshulash*, p. 159. It is unclear which authorities Rabbi Zalman had in mind. I have found no discussion of the question of rabbinical ordination by the father.

[199] Plaut, *Likutei*, 5.27b.

Rabbi Daniel Prossnitz, head of the Bet Din, a contemporary of the Hatam Sofer and his faithful trustee.[200] He was also the first to deliver a eulogy, and he declared that he personally accepted the authority of the son, for 'his time to rule has arrived'.[201] Others then followed suit, and the opposition was silenced. In the public announcement of the rabbi's death, issued during the first week of mourning, it was stated that the son was already acting as rabbi.[202] The formal selection took place at the end of the week,[203] but this was mere confirmation of what had already been done. The transmission of the post from father to son was thus effected by the charismatic power of the father, who had succeeded in turning the post into a family possession.

[200] Ibid., 5.28a. For Rabbi Daniel's life see Sh. Weiss, *Avnei Beit ha-Yozer*, pp. 56–61.
[201] Ibid.
[202] Sh. Sofer, *Hut ha-Meshulash*, p. 162.
[203] The election took place on Sunday (Plaut, *Likutei*, 5.28a). The seven days of mourning ended on the previous Thursday.

11

Zevi Hirsch Kalischer and the Origins of Religious Zionism

JODY ELIZABETH MYERS

I

Since the destruction of the Second Temple, the Jews have regarded themselves as in exile. They believed that the loss of the Temple, their dispersed existence, and other national privations were a divine punishment for their sins. They imagined that, unlike the Egyptian and Babylonian exiles, this one would culminate in a final Messianic Age. As early as the failed Bar Kokhba rebellion, the rabbis adopted a passive messianic outlook: only God could bring the Redemption, and He would do so at an unexpected moment with a series of supernatural events. They insisted that the Jew should refrain from trying to end their exilic condition by themselves; the most they could do was to engage in repentance. These attitudes of national guilt and messianic passivity became major themes in Jewish literature, from rabbinic commentaries to the liturgy. Although here and there over the centuries alternative viewpoints were voiced, expressing belief in a gradual redemption assisted by human efforts, the dominant messianic tradition remained the passive one.

This conception of passive messianism was increasingly rejected during the nineteenth century by religious and non-religious Jews. Several traditional rabbis began to promote a more active version of messianism that turned the older religious values on their head. They found precedents in Jewish literature for initiating the return to the land of Israel and restoring its pre-exilic character. Among non-religious Jews, passive messianism was a casualty of the secular and scientific thinking that undermined the providential view of Jewish history essential to traditional Judaism.

While much attention has been given to the secularist and Zionist rebellions against traditional religion, the religious rejection of passive messianism has been relatively neglected. Yet it is here that the impact of the modern world is most subtle and far-reaching. It is in this context that an examination of Zevi Hirsch Kalischer (1795—1874), a Central European rabbi who was the most articulate of the revisionists, is valuable. Through the prism of his experience we can begin to understand the nature and formation of modern messianic thinking.[1]

---

[1] Academic scholarship has focused on the latter part of Kalischer's life, beginning with his sixty-fifth year, when he was promoting the agricultural development of the Yishuv. Kalischer's activism is, however, impossible to understand outside the context of his youth and middle age, and this imbalance has resulted in myriad historiographical problems. From the vantage point of his final years alone, Kalischer appears as a forward-looking nationalist. The traditional elements of his life are minimized, with the messianic content of his writings made secondary or merely a passing phenomenon. Thus, most early twentieth-century works on Kalischer identified him with the Hibbat Zion Zionism of the 1870s and 1880s. This literature was reviewed and criticized by Jacob Katz in his seminal articles on Kalischer and the forerunners of Zionism: 'Tzevi Hirsch Kalischer'. in Leo Jung (ed.) *Guardians of our Heritage* (New York, 1958), pp. 209—27; and 'The Forerunners of Zionism', *Jerusalem Quarterly*, 7 (Spring 1978), pp. 10—21. Katz too, however, differentiated too sharply between Kalischer's pre- and post-1860s work and minimized his continued messianism. Contemporary historians likewise have paid too little attention to Kalischer's pre-1860s Prussian environment and his earlier writings. Sensitive to the anti-Reform animus of his 1860s writings, they have incorrectly assumed that Kalischer always operated within the context of the Reform — Orthodox struggle and was motivated by opposition to Reform. As a result, they also give Kalischer's messianic ideology short shrift. See especially Jay Ticker, 'The Centrality of Sacrifice as an Answer to Reform in the Thought of Zvi Hirsch Kalischer', in *Working Papers in Yiddish and East European Jewish Studies*, 15 (Max Weinreich Center, New York, 1975); and the articles by Joseph Salmon, especially 'Tradition and Modernity in Early Religious-Zionist Thought', *Tradition*, 18, 1 (summer 1979), pp. 79—98 and 'The Rise of Jewish Nationalism on the Border of Eastern and Western Europe: Rabbi Z.H. Kalischer, David Gordon, Peretz Smolenskin', in *Danzig, between East and West; Aspects of Modern Jewish History* (Cambridge, 1985), pp. 121—38. The most complete treatment of Kalischer's writings and his messianic ideology is my 'Seeking Zion: The Messianic Ideology of Zevi Hirsch Kalischer, 1795—1874 (PhD dissertation, University of California at Los Angeles, 1985).

II

Zevi Hirsch Kalischer was born in 1795 in Lissa, one of the larger towns in the Posen region and a centre of Talmud study. His family proudly traced their lineage back to renowned scholars and community leaders such as Judah Löw (the Maharal) of Prague and Mordecai Jaffe, the author of the *Shulhan Arukh* commentary *Ha-Levush*. Determined to perpetuate its heritage of religious scholarship, his family gave Zevi Hirsch the best rabbinic education available in Poland. His earliest teacher was his uncle, Rabbi Judah Leib Kalischer, the head of the local rabbinic court. Kalischer then attended the yeshivah of the highly regarded halakhist Rabbi Jacob Lorbeerbaum (known as Havvat Da'at). He finished his formal schooling in Posen, about 50 miles north-east of Lissa, when the great Talmudist Rabbi Akiva Eger opened a yeshivah there in 1815. Both of his teachers were renowned for their exceptional personalities: Lorbeerbaum's humility was legendary (he published his *magnum opus* anonymously), and even Eger's detractors praised his great humanity and beneficence.[2]

Kalischer's married life was quite traditional. His parents arranged his marriage to a woman named Gittel nine years his junior. The date of their marriage is unknown, but Kalischer was living in Thorn, her family's town, by 1818.[3] Thorn was a small town about 50 miles

[2] The most reliable sources of biographical information are A.I. Bromberg, *Ha-Gaon Rabbi Zevi Hirsch Kalischer* (Jerusalem, 1960); and Israel Klausner's introduction to his collection and edition of some of Kalischer's works, *Ha-Ketavim ha-Tziyyonim shel ha-Rav Zevi Kalischer* (Jerusalem, 1947) (cited as *Ha-Ketavim*). For a complete bibliography, see Myers, 'Seeking Zion'.

[3] Kalischer's gloss on the Mishnah, which was published in the 1908 Vilna edition, is dated '1818 Thorn'. Gittel's age was ascertained from Kalischer's death announcement in *Ha-Maggid*, 18/1874, p. 374. This age difference makes it unlikely that Kalischer married her when he was eighteen, as Bromberg surmised, following the Eastern European Jewish pattern of early marriages; see Bromberg, *Ha-Gaon Rabbi Zevi Hirsch Kalischer*, p. 14. A marriage at eighteen would also have been in violation of Prussian law, which forbade non-emancipated Jewish men to marry before the age of twenty-five; see Bernard D. Weinryb, 'East European Jewry (since the partitions of Poland, 1772−1795)', in Louis Finkelstein (ed), *The Jews: Their History* (New York, 1974), p. 351. We do not know whether Kalischer was emancipated, but since he had no trade it is unlikely that he was. His children married quite late. According to a letter he sent to the Alliance Israélite Universelle (*Ha-Ketavim*, p. 455), Kalischer was seventy-eight when his youngest daughter was betrothed.

north-east of Posen at the border of the Posen district; in 1823 it had 248 Jews, belonging to fifty-two families.[4] Its first rabbi began serving in the late eighteenth century. He was still there, serving without pay, when sometime in the 1820s the community asked Kalischer to serve them as well. Kalischer accepted on the condition that he would receive no remuneration of any kind. This refusal to take a salary was based on the rabbinic warning against making the Torah 'a spade for digging'. Accepting a salary was by no means against Jewish law: there were legitimate halakhic opinions approving it, since financial support for Torah scholars had been recognized as necessary for the preservation of Torah study. Remuneration had always been widely practised, and by the late Middle Ages in Europe some rabbinic authorities even regarded refusal of payment as behaviour that 'shamed' the Torah. Nevertheless, it was still regarded as a mark of great piety to refuse a salary, and all of Kalischer's teachers honoured it during part or all of their careers.[5] By the time Kalischer began serving Thorn, however, this behaviour was increasingly rare.

When Thorn's first rabbi died in 1847, the community paid his replacement, but Kalischer continued to refuse a salary. Still, his service to Thorn was minimal: he taught the advanced students, served as the final authority in Jewish law, and occasionally officiated at community events. He was essentially a scholar-in-residence.[6] He consistently rejected payment or gifts from the Thorn community,

---

[4] Jacob Goldberg, 'Torun', in *Encyclopaedia Judaica* (Jerusalem, 1972), gives the following population figures: 248 Jews in 1823; 1371 Jews in 1890 (5 per cent of the total population). S. Neumann, *Zur Statistik der Juden in Preussen: von 1816 bis 1880* (Berlin, 1884), p. 40, cited by Jay Ticker in *Working Papers in Yiddish and East European Jewish Studies* 15, p. 1, gives different figures: 344 Jews in 1840; 1530 Jews in 1880. Unfortunately, more complete figures are unavailable, and I have been unable to find total population figures for this period.

[5] The rabbinic discussion over the use of the Torah is in Mishnah Avot 4:5. For a historical discussion of this principle, see Yeshayahu Leibovitz, *Sihot al Pirkei Avot ve-al ha-Rambam* (Tel Aviv, 1979), p. 33, particularly with reference to the opinions of commentators on the *Shulhan Arukh*. On the Kalischer family's adoption of this principle, see Bromberg, *Ha-Gaon Rabbi Zevi Hirsch Kalischer*, pp. 14–15.

[6] The biographical literature refers to Kalischer as though he were the sole rabbi of Thorn during his lifetime. The names of the rabbis who served Thorn continually from the late eighteenth century to the beginning of the twentieth are listed in I. Rosenberg's article 'Thorn' in the *Jewish Encyclopedia* (New York and London, 1907).

and he donated the profits from his books to charity.[7] Gittel's earnings from her small business were the only means of support for themselves and their four children. Mindful that his piety was dependent on his wife's goodwill and labour, Kalischer acknowledged her sacrifices and credited his scholarship to her in the introductions to his first two books.[8]

The Jewish community of Thorn, though not an old-established one with a history of rabbinic scholarship, nevertheless respected religious traditions. This was typical of Jewish communities in the area until well into the nineteenth century. Prussia, which had annexed the region in 1793, allowed the traditional rabbinate to retain its dominance in Jewish community life. Furthermore, the economic stagnation of the region during the first half of the century led to the emigration of ambitious Jews who were likely to have pressed for religious modernization.[9] According to Kalischer's description in 1846, Reform Judaism had not yet penetrated Thorn. The few requests for religious innovation were easily silenced by his opposition.[10]

---

[7] In a letter written to his friend Elijah Guttmacher in 1870, Kalischer mentioned that he had always given the money received from circumcisions and weddings to charity; see the letter dated 24 Av (1870) in *Ha-Ketavim*, p. 319. On his book profits, see his published letter to S. Goldberg of Vilna in *Ivri Anokhi*, 23/1872.

[8] According to Nahum Sokolow, 'Rabbi Zevi Hirsch Kalischer', *Ha-Olam*, 112 (1924), p. 1031, she was engaged in money-lending. Kalischer's praise of his wife can be found in *Emunah Yesharah*, 2 vols. (Krotoszyn, 1843, and Lyck, 1871), vol. 1, p. 9, and in the introduction to vol. 1 of *Moznayim le-Mishpat*, 2 vols. (Krotszyn and Königsberg, 1855).

[9] Herbert Strauss, 'Pre-Emancipation Prussian Policies towards the Jews, 1815–1847', *Leo Baeck Institute Yearbook*, 11 (1966), pp. 132–5, describes the conservative tone of the bureaucracy. He is cautious about attributing the advance of religious reform to government decisions, because government decisions varied regionally and Jewish communities were simultaneously transforming themselves. Posen's economic decline and its demographic losses are examined in Julian Bartys, 'Grand Duchy of Poznan under Prussian Rule: Changes in the Economic Position of the Jewish Population, 1815–1848', *Leo Baeck Institute Yearbook*, 17 (1972). Steven M. Lowenstein, in 'The Pace of Modernisation of German Jewry in the Nineteenth Century', *Leo Baeck Institute Yearbook*, 21 (1976), documents the connection between religious and economic modernization in Germany.

[10] For example, Kalischer successfully intervened in 1846 when some people expressed the desire to omit the *mehitzah*, the architectural barrier dividing men and women, from the new Thorn synagogue under construction that

Kalischer believed that the failure of Reform to take root in Thorn was due to the division of labour within the community leadership. He had remained true to traditional rabbinic intellectual pursuits and community functions. His subordinate, a preacher (the other rabbi), used extra-traditional sources to inspire community obedience to the rabbi and to the Torah. The problems of contemporary Jewry, wrote Kalischer, stemmed partly from the recent conjunction of the rabbi's and preacher's duties in one person. The result was a free-thinking rabbi who was less capable and desirous of implementing and teaching Torah. This dual leadership structure, Kalischer wrote with smug self-assurance at the height of Reform − Orthodox strife, had been and could still be successful in stemming irreligiousness.[11]

Not until after the middle of the century did Kalischer change his mind. By then the Prussian government had granted civil emancipation to a wider segment of the Jewish population and had become more insistent upon the modernization of Jewish educational institutions. The extension of the Prussian railway in 1857 had stimulated Thorn's economy and facilitated contacts with other cities and regions. Jews eager for religious reform began to make their presence felt. Kalischer's report on the changed environment in 1863 conveys shock and a new feeling of helplessness. Though coloured by an idealized memory of the past, it is nevertheless a powerful testimony to the town's previous obedience to its paternalistic rabbi:

> Until now, this city in which I have lived for some forty years has been faithful. Crooked ways were stopped by choosing the straight path, and the footsteps of the sheep made a path to our God through zealous guarding of our holy ancestors' ways. But now new faces have come here. And, though their hands have not found much room in which to make reforms and to root out everything, God forbid, nevertheless, little by little they begin to make a breach in the wall of the house of Israel. From the depth of my broken heart I see that this is just their beginning.

---

year. His account of this can be found in his commentary on the Torah, *Sefer ha-Brit al ha-Torah*, 5 vols. (Warsaw, 1873−6), vol. 2, p. 77 (on Exodus 10:11).

[11] Z. H. Kalischer 'Das Leben Israels und der Rabbinismus', *Der treue Zionswächter*, 3/1846, p. 58. A similar message can be found in *Sefer ha-Brit*, vol. 5, p. 135 (Deuteronomy 17:18).

Who knows what more they will add, they and their children
after them. . . .[12]

During his first forty years in Thorn, immersed in scholarship in the
cultural backwater of the Posen district, Kalischer had minimized the
seriousness of the liberalizing religious trends that he read about in
the press. His major works, written prior to the advent of religious
Reform in Thorn, should be understood as emerging from this insular, tradition-bound environment.

The course that Kalischer chose upon finishing his rabbinic education testified to his pious studiousness and retiring personality.
With his training and family background, he could have enjoyed a
larger community, greater influence, and the possibility of training a
new generation of rabbis. But he refused all offers of rabbinic office.
Except for occasional trips to other Prussian Jewish centres, Kalischer
spent his entire life in Thorn. Perhaps he was emulating Jacob
Lorbeerbaum, who, after years of communal service and despite
lucrative offers from prestigious communities, retired in 1822 and
devoted the rest of his life to study.[13] Kalischer spent his first few
decades in Thorn studying and writing, only minimally involved in
Jewish affairs elsewhere. By the beginning of the 1840s he had
completed several manuscripts, most of which reflected the narrow
Ashkenazic curriculum that he had studied with his teachers. Soon
after he arrived in Thorn he published, like Eger, a gloss on several
tractates of the Mishnah. His *Moznayim le-Mishpat* was, like
Lorbeerbaum's *Havvat Da'at*, a commentary on a segment of the
Shulhan Arukh. It focused on the civil and criminal laws, an area of
halakhah (Jewish law) burdened by differing interpretations — some
strict, some lenient — that generated voluminous discussion.
Kalischer's interest in this area may have been sparked by Jacob
Lorbeerbaum, who wrote extensively on the subject; in the in-

[12] *Ha-Maggid*, 25/1863. It is significant that, relative to the demands of
Reform Jews elsewhere in Germany, the changes sought by the innovators
were quite minor: improvements in synagogue decorum; a pulpit at the head
of rather than in the middle of the synagogue; and omission of liturgical
passages calling for divine vengeance on recalcitrant Gentiles and slanderous
Jews. The opening of the Thorn connection on the Prussian railway was
announced in *Ha-Maggid*, 17/1857.
[13] On Lorbeerbaum see L. Lewin, *Geschichte der Juden in Lissa* (Pinne,
1904), pp. 204–22.

troduction to his work, however, he mentioned that his model was Rabbi Abraham Danzig's popular summaries of the *Shulhan Arukh*'s daily ritual and dietary laws.[14] Like Danzig, Kalischer restated the older decisions, discussed the conflicting opinions and available options, and presented a conclusion. It was an ambitious project, and the publication of the book established Kalischer's reputation as a first-rate halakhic scholar.

More fundamental as a heritage, though, was the spiritual anxiety that Kalischer's teachers had nurtured in him. Lorbeerbaum's negative view of the Exile is evident in his rebuke of reformers who advocated a more celebratory approach toward prayer. While the Temple stood, he wrote to them, the sacrificial offerings cleansed the Jews of their sins, and they were enjoined to be happy. Now, without the sacrifices, 'we have nothing by which to be forgiven' and must plead tearfully to God through mere prayer.[15] Throughout his life, Kalischer struggled with this problem, concerned less with the inefficacy of prayer than with the fact that the sacrifices were not being offered. Were there the slightest chance that the government of Palestine could be swayed to allow sacrifice, he wrote, 'then every day we are violating a positive commandment to offer sacrifices'.[16] His worry about the neglect of the sacrifices was exceeded only by his enthusiasm for the ritual itself. One typical comment is the following explanation from his Haggadah commentary, published in 1864, on the reason why adult males don a white garment at the Seder meal:

On this night the common Israelite is considered a priest ... Henceforth, your souls will be enthused, for it is not often that your clothes are white like the High Priest's. You will be happy that you were deemed worthy ... to worship just as if the altar were built and the burnt offerings rose as a savoury smell to please God. The love in the Israelite's heart is for his Rock and Creator, and when he offers a savoury-smelling sacrifice to him, his joy will increase like one who finds a great treasure, and he will give thanks to God with all his heart and soul that he was

---

[14] *Hayyei Adam* (Vilna, 1810) and *Hokhmat Adam*, (Vilna, 1812).

[15] Jacob Lorbeerbaum, *Eleh Divrei ha-Brit* (Altona, 1819), pp. 79–80.

[16] This was from one of his 1837 letters to Akiva Eger that was included in the halakhic responsa on the sacrifices included in *Derishat Tziyyon* (Lyck, 1862). All references to this work, cited as *Seeking Zion*, are to the critical edition included in *Ha-Ketavim*. The letter referred to above appears on p. 84.

sustained in life until this night when he donned white clothes like a priest.[17]

Not only did Kalischer believe that sacrifice was the highest form of communication with God, but he could not imagine that a pious Jew might feel otherwise.

The absence of the Temple was not the only privation that Kalischer felt; he also lamented the other conditions of the Exile that diminished the realm of religious observance. He took to heart the fundamental belief that the Jews should live united in the land of Israel under a Davidic king and the elders of Israel, fulfilling all the commandments of the Torah. In most pious individuals, sorrow over the Exile was usually mitigated by the engaging involvements of daily life and by the rabbinic teaching that study, prayer and pious deeds were substitutes for pre-exilic rituals. Kalischer was not so easily comforted. Perhaps it was because he felt that he had attained the rabbinic ideal — guiding his flock and studying Torah freed from everyday concerns — that he was so acutely aware of the distance between the present and the Messianic Age.

III

The earliest record of Kalischer's interest in messianism is a letter he sent in 1836 to the Frankfurt banker Amschel Mayer Rothschild. Kalischer informed Rothschild that it was incorrect to think that the Messianic Age would arrive suddenly and miraculously with no human assistance. Rather, the Messianic Age would slowly evolve with human help once God signalled readiness to begin the Redemption — and Kalischer already discerned this in the elevation of men such as Rothschild to greatness and in the Gentiles' new love for Jews, evident in civil emancipation. Kalischer urged Rothschild to fulfill his role as God's instrument by purchasing Palestine, or at the very least the Temple Mount, from the Egyptian ruler. Then, with the co-operation of the nations of the world, many poor and pious Jews would emigrate to Palestine and make the land agriculturally productive. This would constitute the first, natural stage of the Redemption. By rebuilding the altar and offering sacrifices again, the

---

[17] Z.H. Kalischer, *Seder Haggadah shel Pesah im Biyur Yakar Yetziat Mizrayim* (Warsaw, 1864), p. 18.

Jewish people would re-establish their intimate connection with God and trigger the second, miraculous stage of the Redemption. This included the complete ingathering of Jews, as well as the rebuilding of the Temple, a Davidic kingdom and a rabbinic Sanhedrin. Kalischer insisted throughout the letter that Jewish law supported this venture. He adduced numerous biblical and rabbinic proof texts, and at the end appended his halakhic research on the permissibility of restoring sacrificial worship.[18] Written when Kalischer was forty, this letter contains all of the elements and much of the text of what he later published, in 1862, as *Seeking Zion (Derishat Tziyyon)*, part III of *Emunah Yesharah*.

An analysis of the basic elements of Kalischer's messianic ideology thus far shows that it was harnessed and shaped by his rabbinic training. Guided by normative Jewish literature, he anticipated a Messianic Age that would restore previous institutions rather than establish radically new and unprecedented ones. Furthermore, because he was a committed student of Jewish law, the potential antinomianism of messianic fervour was supplanted by the desire for a greater extension of halakhah over daily life.[19] Indeed, Kalischer's major halakhic work, *Moznayim le-Mishpat*, confirms this sentiment. The book focuses on Jewish civil and criminal law even though it was an area of halakhah that the state — even in Posen — was removing from rabbinic jurisdiction. Kalischer remarked in his introduction that his choice of subject and methodology was dictated by his desire to ease the decision-making process and establish some uniformity of opinion. This optimism and ambition is reminiscent of the legal philosophy of Maimonides, who had argued that the present narrow dominion of Jewish law was an anomaly, and therefore should not be allowed to limit the scope of halakhic study.[20] Messianic anticipation

---

[18] *Ha-Ketavim*, pp. 1–14, transcribes Kalischer's copy of the letter; the original has never been found.

[19] This discussion of the relationship between halakhah and messianism is based on Gershom Scholem's classic article 'Toward an Understanding of the Messianic Idea in Judaism,' *The Messianic Idea in Judaism* (New York, 1971), pp. 17–24.

[20] Kalischer's goals for his book can be found in the introduction to volume 1 of *Moznayim le-Mishpat*. In the introduction to volume 2 he discusses the burdensome complexity of the work and expresses his hope that, with God's help, he would be able to complete volumes 3 and 4. His later writings do not mention this completed manuscript. On Maimonides' legal philosophy, see Isadore Twersky, *Introduction to the Code of Maimonides (Mishneh Torah)* (New Haven, Conn., 1980), p. 206ff.

underlay both Maimonides' and Kalischer's legal philosophies. Kalischer's promotion of sacrifice renewal, which was an expression of dissatisfaction with the truncated religious options of the post-Temple period, brought this latent messianism into the open.

Kalischer's attraction to Jewish philosophy also gave form to his messianic feelings. He had received no formal education in philosophy, but was familiar with the philosophical writings of the Haskalah, particularly of moderates such as Moses Mendelssohn, Naphtali Herz Wessely and Isaac Reggio. By 1840 Kalischer was composing *Emunah Yesharah*, a philosophical defence of Judaism for enlightened religious Jews who wanted to have a rational basis for religious belief and practice without sacrificing piety and observance. As in his legal works, here Kalischer modelled himself on Maimonides, but he also relied heavily on other medieval Jewish philosophers and quoted selectively from non-Jewish philosophical works.[21]

Kalischer's major argument was that a large part of Jewish belief was rational and accessible to all those with a trained intellect. The other part was beyond the realm of philosophy, and this God had revealed in the Torah. Kalischer cautioned against regarding these revealed truths as contrary to reason. Judaism (unlike Christianity, he explained) did not demand belief in any matter *against* reason, such as a logical impossibility, but it did include matters *beyond* reason. By defining these two different types of belief and the appropriate realm of each, Kalischer was attempting to satisfy the desire for a rational faith while limiting reason's potential damage.[22] This commitment to rationalism, though quite limited, was put to service in Kalischer's messianic ideology. There he argued that the enlightened person realizes that God exercises His providence over humanity

[21] His knowledge of non-Jewish philosophy does not appear to have been extensive, and, judging by the references to it in *Emunah Yesharah*, it probably came from Hebrew translations and summaries found in Haskalah publications.

[22] Z. H. Kalischer, *Emunah Yesharah*, vol. 1, pp. 12–19; vol. 2, p. 93. These works have rarely been included in surveys of modern Jewish thought. An exception to this is Eliezer Schweid, *Historiyah shel ha-Mahshavah ha-Yehudit be-Eit ha-Hadashah* (Jerusalem 1977), pp. 379–81. This is a good introduction to the work, although it does not place it in its social and religious context. It is an exaggeration to argue, as Jay Ticker and Joseph Salmon have done (see above, note 1), that Kalischer's arguments were aimed only at the problem of irreligiousness in his own day. He felt that the temptation to follow unrestrained reason was an endemic problem. The examples of temptation that he cited were not drawn from contemporary life.

without abrogating natural law; God's occasional miracles were acts 'beyond reason' and were few and far between. So, too, would God bring the Messianic Era by working 'through' normal, historical events.

This messianic theory was not original. The notion that the Messianic Age evolves gradually and naturally with human assistance is alluded to in midrashic and mystical literature and in the writings of Maimonides and his commentators.[23] The advantage (for rationalists) of this messianic theory is that it does not necessitate miracles, but merely requires positive events suggesting that God is ready, with the Jews' help, to reverse their exilic status. Like Maimonides, Kalischer wanted to cleanse his religious beliefs of irrationality, so far as possible. This desire, previously ignored, was certainly one of the factors contributing to his rejection of passive messianism.

Many of Kalischer's messianic ideas were not in themselves original. Rather, he was one of the first to gather the scattered references to active messianism into a systematic ideology. Furthermore, he did this at a time when traditional rabbis were preoccupied with preventing any modifications of belief and practice. They were particularly concerned with preserving the messianic idea, since liberal and even traditional Jews were denying its national features, and conversion to Christianity was on the increase. Kalischer must have been aware of this, since his revision was partly motivated by the desire to defend Jewish belief. Yet nowhere in these early discussions of active messianism did he respond to the current attacks on the messianic idea. Rather, he was challenging the naive thinking of orthodox practitioners of Judaism. Kalischer regarded himself as a revisionist. He was absolutely convinced that his was the most accurate version of the messianic prophecies and one that the great rabbinic scholars of the past had taught. Yet these teachings had been so misapprehended over time that even his teachers and colleagues were unaware of them. It did not occur to him that his correction of tradition might encourage others to make additional, heretical corrections. He felt secure enough about the survival of traditional Judaism to take on the common understanding of one of its fundamental assumptions. This confidence reflected his insular Posen environment.

Kalischer's proposal to Rothschild may appear fantastic, but in its context is was not that extraordinary. Many Jews certainly shared his perception of Rothschild as God's instrument. It was a venerable

---

[23] See Myers, 'Seeking Zion', pp. 25–7. A good summary of Maimonides' messianic theory is Amos Funkenstein, 'Maimonides: Political Theory and Realistic Messianism', *Miscellanea Mediaevalia*, 11 (1977), pp. 81–103.

Jewish literary motif, beginning with the story of Joseph's elevation to power in Egypt in the book of Genesis, that Jews who were prominent in Diaspora governmental or financial circles and still active in Jewish causes were sent by God to deliver them from trouble. Nor was his call for the purchase of Palestine unique. Suggestions that some European government or rich individuals should procure Palestine from the Muslim regime appeared regularly in European newspapers during the first part of the nineteenth century. This was a period in which increased European intervention in Palestine coincided with widespread ignorance of the Middle East — except for knowledge of the Ottoman and Egyptian regimes' huge debts.[24] Kalischer's high regard for the state was also typical of German rabbis. He shared their belief that the state favoured religious orthodoxy, and like them believed in the beneficence of the state in granting civil emancipation.[25] What was unusual about Kalischer's outlook was his conviction that these events were divine portents of the imminent Messianic Age, and that they demanded specific human responses in order to trigger Redemption.

The only consequence of the Rothschild letter — since Rothschild never responded — was that writing it encouraged Kalischer to get other rabbis to embrace his plan for the renewal of sacrifice.[26] Soon

[24] These suggestions came most frequently from England and France. See Nahum Sokolow, *A History of Zionism, 1600–1918*, 2 vols (repr. New York, 1969), pp. 89–90, 116, 122. Arnold Blumberg, *Zion before Zionism, 1838–1880* (Syracuse, NY, 1985), contains interesting material on the changing European perception of the Middle East.

[25] Robert Liberles, *Religious Conflict in Social Context: The Resurgence of Orthodox Judaism in Frankfurt am Main, 1838–1877* (Westport, Conn., 1985), pp. 80–6, shows that traditionalist rabbis throughout Germany agreed that the state was dependent on religious orthodoxy for its existence. This was the case even for those who had experience of the destructive effects of civil emancipation on Orthodoxy. That Kalischer concluded as much in Posen, where the state allowed the traditional rabbinate to dominate Jewish community life and where the disruptive aspects of civil emancipation were less apparent, let alone enforced, is unsurprising. See his statement in 'Einiges zur Widerlegung der Ansichten des Herrn Dr. Samuel Holdheim', *Literaturblatt des Orients*, 1/1846, p. 2. This was a response to Samuel Holdheim's pamphlet *Über die Beschneidung in religiös-dogmatischer Beziehung* (Schwerin and Berlin, 1844).

[26] Rothschild never responded, even though Kalischer travelled to Frankfurt to pursue the matter. In his introduction to *Ha-Ketavim*, Klausner maintains, without substantial evidence, that Kalischer sent a similar letter to Sir Moses Montefiore and that this inspired Montefiore's 1839 trip to Palestine.

after he wrote to Rothschild, Kalischer sent his research on the sacrifices to Akiva Eger for his approval. His messianic motives must have been apparent, for Eger responded vaguely and ambivalently. Eger asked his son-in-law, the great halakhic authority Moses Sofer (known as the Hatam Sofer), what he thought about the renewal of sacrifices. Sofer wrote to Eger that the entire matter was academic, since the Muslims would never allow it, but he agreed that otherwise it was permissible to offer the Passover sacrifice. Eger did not send Kalischer a copy of Sofer's response. Instead, he informed Kalischer that Sofer considered the matter impossible. Shortly after, both Eger and Sofer died. Kalischer dropped his sacrifice-renewal plan for almost twenty years.[27]

IV

The late 1850s were a watershed in Kalischer's life. He spent the 1840s and early 1850s preoccupied with writing and publishing his philosophic and halakhic books.[28] He wrote several rather abstract

[27] A detailed analysis of the sacrifice-renewal responsa is presented in Myers, 'Seeking Zion', pp. 144−57.

[28] Getting something published was usually a laborious and time-consuming process. An author such as Kalischer who lacked a patron, independent wealth or a supportive printer would generally travel to various towns (or hire someone to do this for him) getting subscribers for the book. At the same time, if not earlier, the author would solicit respected rabbinic leaders for approbations (*haskamot*) which, printed at the beginning of the book, testified to its acceptability and worth. Interested subscribers would sometimes pay in advance, but often would wait until they had received the book. The number of books printed depended on the number of subscribers. The entire process took years: getting approbations and subscribers, printing the books, delivering them, and collecting payments. Kalischer's first volume, *Even Bohan* (Krotoszyn, 1842), a short excerpt from his larger halakhic work *Moznayim le-Mishpat*, indicates on its title page that he was going through this process. He mentions that *Moznayim le-Mishpat* and *Emunah Yesharah*, his philosophical defence of Judaism, are also available for subscription. He managed to establish a reputation for himself fairly quickly, for he had been able to publish in 1840 and 1841 two shorter philosophical essays in Hebrew and German Jewish journals. Volume 1 of *Emunah Yesharah* was published the next year, and other articles followed. The first two volumes of *Moznayim le-Mishpat* were finally printed in 1855, but many of Kalischer's other halakhic writings remained in manscript form and were eventually lost. See Myers, 'Seeking Zion', for full bibliographical information. Years after Kalischer's death, his son Louis expressed to Nahum

and intellectual articles against Reform for the Jewish press. Over the course of the 1850s, however, he made several important discoveries. First, he gradually realized that his kind of pious and orthodox Jew was increasingly a minority and perhaps even an anachronism in Germany. He began to refer to himself as 'one of the remnants of Israel who fear God in their hearts'.[29] Second, he came across material published in the previous decade favouring the renewal of sacrifice. For the first time Kalischer learned that Hatam Sofer had permitted the renewal of the Passover sacrifice.[30] Never suspecting that Eger had intentionally hidden his son-in-law's positive response, Kalischer imagined that Eger had been thrilled with the answer but had been too weak on his deathbed to copy the details.[31] He also discovered that while he had been absorbed in his studies in Thorn, other rabbis had responded favourably to the Hatam Sofer's opinion.

Heartened by the appearance of support, Kalischer tried to gain rabbinic approval for the resumption of other sacrifices as well. He seems to have been unaware of the polemical, anti-Reform context of the pro-sacrifice literature. The authors had neither shared Kalischer's messianic enthusiasm nor had any serious intention of implementing sacrificial worship. Rather, by arguing that sacrificial worship was still desirable and permissible under Jewish law, they were rebutting assertions about the irrelevance of age-old Jewish traditions.[32] Nevertheless, Kalischer found some like-minded colleagues. He re-estab-

---

Sokolow his bitterness that his father's manuscripts were not being published; see Sokolow, 'Rabbi Zevi Hirsch Kalischer', p. 1031. It is presumed that these manuscripts were destroyed during the Second World War.

[29] *Ha-Maggid*, 17/1858.

[30] Unbeknownst to Kalischer, the Hatam Sofer had sent a copy of his response to his young protégé Zevi Hirsch Chajes, who was living at that time in Galicia. Chajes published it, along with an essay showing evidence of the post-Destruction offering of sacrifices, in his book *Darkhei ha-Hora' ah*. Kalischer explained in *Seeking Zion* that he had discovered the original version of the letter when he read Chajes' book, shortly before Chajes's death in 1855. He probably came across the book while in Kalisz seeking Chajes's approbation for *Moznayim le-Mishpat*, which appeared at the beginning of volume 2. For more on the Hatam Sofer and Chajes' correspondence, see Jody Elizabeth Myers, 'Attitudes toward a Resumption of Sacrificial Worship in the Nineteenth Century', *Modern Judaism*, 7, 1 (1987), p. 34.

[31] This is how Kalischer explained the matter to Azriel Hildesheimer in 1862 (*Ha-Ketavim*, p. 189). Though later opponents of sacrifice renewal questioned Eger's approval of the matter, Kalischer always insisted that Eger was enthusiastic.

[32] For a detailed analysis of this debate see Myers, in *Modern Judaism*, 7, 1.

lished ties with a classmate from Eger's yeshivah, Rabbi Elijah
Guttmacher of Grätz. Guttmacher, a respected halakhist and widely
known as a holy man, shared Kalischer's enthusiasm for active messianism and introduced him to Kabbalistic teachings supporting it.[33]
Kalischer's serious study of the Kabbalah probably began under
Guttmacher's influence. Kalischer also met Rabbi Nathan Friedland,
a Lithuanian preacher who had recently completed a treatise promoting active messianism which emphasized the messianic function of
settlement in the land of Israel.[34] Contact with these men probably
showed Kalischer that his messianic theory, which had never been
validated by a living scholar, was quite plausible and would be well
received.

Kalischer's growing mindfulness of the new era before him, and
probably his awareness that his life was drawing to a close, lent a
greater urgency to his mission. His immediate focus became the
agricultural development of Palestine, the mainstay of the sacrificial
system.[35] At first he took steps that, had they been successful, would
have kept him in the private realm: in 1858 he wrote to Sir Moses
Montefiore and Rabbi Nathan Adler of London asking to be appointed overseer of Montefiore's newly purchased plantation in
Palestine. They refused on the grounds that the position was already
filled.[36] Two years later he presented two proposals to Albert Cohn,

[33] People flocked to Guttmacher from all over Central Europe, despite his
public disavowal of possessing any special powers. As late as 1874, Rabbi
Shimon Berman commented that the crowds flocking to Guttmacher were so
great that, were Guttmacher to collect one Reichstaler from each person, he
would accumulate 10,000 in just a few months; see *Ha-Ketavim*, p. 519
(Kalischer's copy of this letter). According to Akiva Eger's great-grandson,
the crowds of people visiting Guttmacher were so distracting that Guttmacher
requested the town leaders to prohibit these vistors from entering the town.
The leaders refused, since they did not want to lose the income that the
visitors brought the town, and they rebuked Guttmacher for his lack of civic
concern. See *Igrot Sofrim*, ed. Shlomo Sofer (Tel Aviv, 1970), part 1,
81–5 nn.

[34] They met when Friedland, travelling through Europe seeking approbations for his manuscript, sought out Kalischer in Thorn. See Klausner,
introduction to *Ha-Ketavim*. The similarities in his thinking to that of the
disciples of the Vilna Gaon is probably more than coincidental. As far as I
know, however, this link has not been established.

[35] This tactical change is discussed in detail below, section V.

[36] Israel Klausner, 'Rabbi Zvi Hirsch Kalischer's *Derishat Zion*', *In the
Dispersion*, 5–6 (Spring 1966), p. 286. Kalischer's letter has not been
preserved, but Montefiore and Adler's reply is in the Schwadron Collection
of the National Library in Jerusalem.

administrator of the extensive charities of the Paris Rothschilds: that
Cohn appoint him to supervise the expenditure of the Rothschild
funds for the agricultural development of the Yishuv (settlement, i.e.
of Jews in Israel), and that Cohn publish the manuscript of *Seeking
Zion*.[37] This effort also failed.

In 1860 Kalischer changed his approach, beginning the public
activism that was to characterize the rest of his life. He called a
conference in Thorn of rabbis and community leaders to discuss ways
of building support for the agricultural development of the Yishuv.[38]
When an organization with the same goal was founded the next year
in Frankfurt, the Society for the Settlement of Palestine (Kolonisations-
Verein für Palästina), Kalischer joined it and soon became one of its
leaders. Eager to carry its message to a wide audience, and especially
to persuade traditional Jews that its goals were legitimate, the organization published *Seeking Zion* in 1862. When the society disbanded
in 1864, Kalischer and Guttmacher took over its name (using the
Hebrew equivalent Hevrat Yishuv Eretz Yisrael) and pursued its
goals independently from their homes in the Posen district. This soon
proved unsuccessful, and in 1866 Kalischer convinced the Alliance
Israélite Universelle to serve as their parent agency. His involvement
in these organizations, and especially the publication of *Seeking Zion*
(which went through two more printings in his lifetime), gave him
the international exposure needed for his cause. From then until his
death in 1874 he wrote extensively for the European Jewish press
(which had recently expanded into monthly and bi-monthly periodicals and was in need of contributors), solicited rabbis and prominent
Jews for support and donations, established local charters of the
organization, and corresponded with anyone who questioned him
about his ideas and projects.

V

While the last fifteen years of Kalischer's life were the most productive in terms of their practical contribution to the Yishuv, his
most intellectually creative years had passed. He had formulated the
theoretical basis of his activism in the 1836 Rothschild letter and the
accompanying responsa on restoring sacrifical worship. His new

---

[37] Kalischer to Albert Cohn, 1860, in *Ha-Ketavim*, p. 180.
[38] Nahum Sokolow, *Hibbath Zion* (Jerusalem, 1934) pp. 20–1. Sokolow
heard a report of this conference from Kalischer's son-in-law, M. Grünberg
of Przesnysz, who had been present.

writing on the subject, including *Seeking Zion*, elaborated and refined his earlier work. His turn to agricultural settlement at the end
of the 1850s must be seen in this light. It did not reflect a change in
theory: the *eretz noshevet*, the settled land of Israel, was the precondition for the renewal of sacrifice, which in turn would bring on
the miraculous phase of the Messianic Age. Kalischer considered his
work to promote agricultural settlement part of his original plan.[39]
More knowledgeable in the late 1850s about the Yishuv, he concluded that neither the Jews nor the Arabs were ready for the renewal
of sacrifice. Since sacrifices could not occur without Jewish farm
produce, the immediate tasks were to purchase, settle and farm the
land. This fusion of the spiritual and pragmatic is consistent with
Kalischer's general commitment to rationality.[40]

Kalischer's turn to agricultural settlement also indicates his awareness of and ability to exploit the current interest in the economic
reform of the Yishuv. European Jews had become increasingly conscious of the poverty of the Jews in Palestine, and their activism was
kindled by humanitarian concern as well as the fact that Diaspora
charity — the *halukah* welfare system for Torah scholars — was the
mainstay of many Jews there. Yishuv Torah scholars, especially the
Ashkenazim, denounced suggestions that jobs should be created to
decrease dependence on the welfare system. They maintained that
the *raison d'être* of the Yishuv was its exclusive devotion to prayer
and Torah study. They particularly denounced proposals to expand
Jewish agriculture, for they regarded these as a threat to the urban
framework of religious life. By the late 1850s, however, the Jerusalem

[39] This is first indicated in Kalischer's 1860 letter to Albert Cohn. While the
letter focuses on building agricultural settlements, Kalischer points out that
he had dwelt on 'this holy task' for some twenty-five years and had corresponded with Eger (and indirectly with the Hatam Sofer) on the matter.
See *Ha-Ketavim*, pp. 178–9. In *Seeking Zion* Kalischer made this point
explicit. He also explained that Nahmanides' understanding of the commandment to conquer and settle in the land of Israel included the obligation to
restore sacrificial worship as well (*Ha-Ketavim*, p. 48).

[40] Katz (in Jung, *Guardians of our Heritage*, p. 219) argues that Kalischer's
1860s activism marked a break with his past. His turn to agricultural settlement was more in line with the spirit of the age, which 'dissociated itself
from mere contemplative expectations'. Katz also erroneously maintains
(ibid., pp. 218–19) that Kalischer altered the order of messianic events in
Seeking Zion, making the settled land the immediate precondition of the
miraculous Redemption. This is incorrect: the sacrifices still held this
position.

Ashkenazim had consented to minimal urban development. When Kalischer heard of this, he and his son immediately began to collect funds for the cause.[41] Yet, because of his messianic beliefs, he consistently expressed greater approval of agricultural development and consequently provoked the wrath of the Yishuv Ashkenazim.

Kalischer's increased sensitivity to public opinion at this stage in his life is evident in the way he toned down the controversial aspects of his work. As early as his 1860 letter to Albert Cohn, and most obviously after the negative reaction to the messianic content of *Seeking Zion*, Kalischer began to minimize explicit references to his messianic theory. He restricted discussions of sacrifice to private correspondence with select individuals, his 1868 pamphlet *Shivat Tziyyon* ('The Return to Zion'), and his exegetical works. These writings manifest his enduring. desire to re-establish sacrificial worship.[42]

A more creative tactic minimizing controversy was Kalischer's development of arguments for the non-messianic benefits of agricultural settlement. If detached from his messianic views (as they readily could be, except in *Seeking Zion* and certain private letters), these gave the impression that Kalischer was merely a religious Jew trying to find a rational solution for the impoverished Jews of Europe and Palestine. He had developed non-messianic arguments before the 1860s, but they had appeared as sketchy afterthoughts. For example, at the end of the Rothschild letter he had pointed out not only that the philanthropist's purchase would help bring the Redemption, but also that in the meantime the country would grow and prosper (since many Jews would flock there, including the victims of anti-semitism) and Rothschild would profit from his investment.[43] In contrast, in

---

[41] See *He-Maggid*, 24/1861, in which the emissary M. Sacks praised Kalischer and his son for their efforts on behalf of the guest houses (*battai mahseh*) as early as 1859.

[42] One of the most poignant examples of this is the letter that Kalischer wrote a few months before his death to the Hatam Sofer's son Simon, pleading with him to support his activities despite the opposition of the Jerusalem rabbis: 'One thing I ask of you: please do not pay heed to the words of the deceivers, but follow the lead of your father who strengthened the holy. For when many study the holy words and observe the commandments, God will then send His spirit and we will inherit the altar place for a savoury offering before Him, and gradually the Redemption light will illuminate us, may it come speedily in our day, amen' (*Ha-Ketavim*, p. 518).

[43] Letter to Rothschild, in *Ha-Ketavim*, pp. 13–14.

Seeking Zion and the later articles, Kalischer promoted the purchase of land and the agricultural communes on social, economic and religious (non-messianic) grounds, accompanying each point with documentation or rabbinic proof texts. He argued, for example, that the agricultural communes would help eliminate food shortages, poverty and unemployment in the Yishuv, would provide Eastern European refugees with a destination preferable to irreligious America, would facilitate the fulfilment of the agricultural commandments, and would give the poor a marketable skill and a sense of accomplishment. Kalischer borrowed most of his economic arguments from articles in the European Jewish press and Haskalah literature. He probably also was inspired by the effort of Rabbi Solomon Eger (Akiva Eger's son) to establish agricultural colonies in the Posen district in 1846.[44]

Kalischer's most original non-messianic argument was that agricultural communes would facilitate a greater appreciation of the religious value of labour. Yet his own high regard for labour was contingent on its role in creating the conditions (the 'settled land') for the Messianic Age. He pegged his praise of labour to the rabbinic dictum that it is good to have 'Torah with a worldly occupation'.[45] While his more Westernized contemporary Rabbi Samson Raphael Hirsch used this passage to defend the study of secular culture, Kalischer thought that it expressed the religious ideal of earning a livelihood alongside Torah study. Yet for him the means of livelihood had to be agricultural labour, and the setting the land of Israel. He heartily disapproved of the notion of a Jewish agricultural colony in Europe and agricultural training for Jews that did not require them to live and farm in Palestine; he regarded these as a rejection of the land of Israel and a frustration of 'our main goal'.[46] He also felt that agricultural labour in the Yishuv without observance of the agricultural and other commandments was pointless and sinful. This is not to suggest that

---

[44] Jacob Toury, 'An Early Movement for Agricultural Settlement in Inowraclaw (Poznan Province) in 1846' (in Hebrew), *Ha-Tziyyonut*, 2 (1970—4).

[45] Pirkei Avot 2:2. This is sometimes translated as 'Torah with worldly knowledge'.

[46] In *Ha-Levanon*, 45/1868, Kalischer speaks highly of Solomon Eger's agricultural-labour program because 'every man will sit under his vine [Micah 4:4] and not wander about studying the sciences, for irreligiousness has increased as a result, due to our many sins'; yet he condemns the notion of a Jewish agricultural 'commonwealth' (*ma' arakhah*). See also Kalischer's letter to the Berlin branch of the Alliance, in *Ha-Ketavim*, p. 489.

Kalischer was insincere in his advocacy of economic reform of the Yishuv. He truly believed that the agricultural development of the Yishuv in the manner in which he suggested could solve all sorts of social, economic and religious problems. On occasion he even admitted that, if his messianic theory were wrong, at least his proposals would improve the Jewish situation.[47] But all of his non-messianic arguments had their ultimate ground in his messianic hopes.[48]

The underlying messianism of Kalischer's non-messianic arguments is also evident in his comparison of Jewish with European nationalism. His praise of European nationalist movements has been cited to show that he was forward-looking and receptive to non-Jewish culture. Kalischer was not, however, a nationalist in the accepted sense of the word. His comments were meant to goad the Jews into action, as in the following frequently quoted passage:

Why do people of Italy and of the other countries sacrifice their lives for the land of their fathers? How much more so should we [sacrifice] for this land, which all peoples of the world call holy. But we stand distant like a man without strength and courage.[49]

Kalischer actually scorned the normative goals of European nationalists as narrow and ephemeral. 'We do not wait for our own [Redemption]', he wrote, 'but for that of all the people of the world ... Everyone will profit and be illuminated by divine light when we are redeemed.'[50] While he complained about the Ottoman regime's onerous taxes, poor security, restrictions on land purchase, and pos-

---

[47] This is generally a comment Kalischer reserved for the Yishuv critics he wanted to assuage, such as Meir Auerbach. See the open letter in *Ha-Levanon*, 8/1863.

[48] Even when Kalischer gave economic reasons for his preference for agricultural settlement, he often added a messianic aside. For example, in a private letter to Azriel Hildesheimer (*Ha-Ketavim*, p. 304) he minimizes the importance of the Jerusalem guest-houses project because they would not fulfil the messianic prophecy of Ezekiel 36:8 (on the future flowering of the land of Israel).

[49] In *Ha-Ketavim*, p. 29. This use of shame is found in the three other references that Kalischer made to European nationalism. See the new afterword to the second edition of *Seeking Zion* (*Ha-Ketavim*, p. 129); *Der Israelit*, 27/1863; and Kalischer's letter to the Berlin chapter of the Alliance, 1873 (*Ha-Ketavim*, p. 457).

[50] *Ha-Levanon*, 34/1868.

session of the Temple Mount, he did not think that Jewish sovereignty in Palestine was necessary for the early stages of the Redemption. Full sovereignty under the Davidic dynasty would come during the miraculous phase of the Messianic Age. He denounced those who felt that the presence of the Muslims impeded reform of the Yishuv and stressed that they must be treated with respect.[51] In fact, Kalischer elevated the rights of (sympathetic) Muslim residents over those of irreligious Jews, whose presence in the Yishuv he would not countenance.[52] He was convinced that the Muslims' high regard for religion and the relative lack of Jewish freedoms in Palestine made the region more amenable to Orthodoxy than Europe, where rabbis who preached heresy were tolerated.[53] Nor was he impressed by the standard tactics of the national movements. When he heard that Rabbi Joseph Natunek of Hungary proposed a military conquest of Palestine, Kalischer argued that this was not only contrary to God's will but also unneccessary. According to his messianic theory, the nations of the world would help (and, in fact, were actually helping) the Jews return to their land, because they knew that this would ultimately lead to their own Redemption.[54] Kalischer's use of nationalist rhetoric was just another attempt to inspire messianic activism.

[51] *Der Israelit*, 3/1869.

[52] Kalischer maintained that an Arab labourer could perform the agricultural commandments for a Jewish landowner if supervised by a Jew (though the ideal was that each Jew should perform the commandments for himself). This comment was based on an actual question asked by a Jewish landowner in 1874. See Kalischer's letter to Meir Auerbach, Mordechai Jaffe and Fischel Lapin, in *Ha-Ketavim*, p. 538.

[53] *Ha-Levanon*, 34/1868. This was a frequent theme in Kalischer's correspondence with Rabbi Azriel Hildesheimer, who opposed agricultural settlement on the grounds that the workers would be tempted to desecrate the Sabbath. See letter from Kislev 1862, in *Ha-Ketavim*, p. 188.

[54] Kalischer expressed his disapproval of Natunek in two letters to Guttmacher in 1866 (*Ha-Ketavim*, pp. 237, 240). His belief in Gentile assistance can be found throughout his writings, but see especially *Seeking Zion* (*Ha Ketavim*, p. 63); *Ha-Maggid*, 3/1871; and his letter to Abraham Ashkenazi, 1874, in *Ha-Ketavim*, p. 539. It is noteworthy that Arthur Hertzberg's translation of a critical paragraph of *Seeking Zion* omits the mid-paragraph phrase stressing the flow of all the Gentiles to Zion. The result is that Kalischer appears more normatively nationalistic than he was. See Arthur Hertzberg, *The Zionist Idea* (New York, 1960), p. 112, and compare the text in *Ha-Ketavim*, p. 42.

VI

Kalischer's increased receptivity to modern sensibilities during the 1860s and 1870s was accompanied by a deepened attachment to tradition. He remained rooted in Thorn, and though he occasionally lamented his distance from cities where he would have had readier access to a large Jewish audience and to those of wealth and influence, he refused to move. He did not travel much, but depended on Nathan Friedland and other friends to serve as emissaries. Nor did organizational work interest Kalischer: he preferred a role behind the scenes writing promotional literature.

With his predilection for armchair activism, it is not surprising that Kalischer continued to write books. He published two exegetical works: *Yetziat Mitzrayim* ('The Exodus from Egypt', 1864), a commentary on the Passover Haggadah, and *Sefer ha-Brit* ('The Book of the Covenant', 1874–6), a five-volume commentary on the Torah and Ecclesiastes. Their mode of discourse is similar to that of *Emunah Yesharah*: Kalischer wrote in a simplified philosophical language and addressed himself to the concerns of deeply religious and educated Jews who wanted their beliefs and observances to conform to reason. His specific aim in *Sefer ha-Brit* was to show that the Torah contained all that was necessary for a just life and human fulfilment. As a result, the commentary, the product of many years of reflection and teaching, is an extremely wordy synthesis of philosophical, mystical, halakhic and homiletical material.

Yetziat Mitzrayim is more focused, addressing the meaning of the central symbols and commandments of Passover, particularly those connected to the sacrificial system. In addition to Kalischer's characteristic philosophizing, it contains lengthy passages from the Zohar and Kabbalistic symbolism. Kalischer may have written this volume in order to strengthen his earlier conclusions about the power of sacrificial worship. Also largely mystical are his additions to the second Hebrew edition of *Seeking Zion* (1866), and his collaborative defence, with Guttmacher, of the sacrifice-renewal plan (1868).[55] In all these works, Kalischer's essential concerns are the same as in his writings from before the 1860s, and reflect his deep commitment to traditional concepts.

---

[55] This collaborative venture was 'Shelom Yerushalayim'. It was appended to *Kontras Shivat Tziyyon*, Kalischer's 1868 rebuttal of Rabbi Jacob Ettlinger's criticism of the sacrifice-renewal responsa.

VII

Kalischer's writings and activities during the last ten years of his life reveal his frustration at the disparity between his goals and his achievements. He had not anticipated the slow pace of progress and the many obstacles to success. He expressed this by denouncing opponents and decrying the timidity and faithlessness of contemporary Jews. Indirectly, he revealed his impatience by discovering encouraging messages in the current events of the 1860s and 1870s. He interpreted all events that promised advancement for the cause of agricultural settlement as Heaven's vindication of his cause and as further divine signals of the approaching Redemption: the increase in agricultural settlement in Palestine, the more vocal Christian interest in the Jews' return to Zion, the opening of the agricultural school Mikveh Yisrael, and the emigration to Palestine of Turkey's chief rabbi and his agreement to help purchase land. All setbacks reinforced the notion that the messianic process was gradual and that God accommodated His will to the natural flow of events. For example, Kalischer did not let the outbreak of Romanian anti-semitism change his conviction that God had put new love for Jews in the hearts of the Gentiles; instead, he suggested that it would lead to increased emigration to Palestine.[56] He even managed to find a bright side in outright opposition. When the Reform rabbi Abraham Geiger denied the concept of a restorative Messianic Age, Kalischer declared that such men would provoke a counter-attack by the pious and thus strengthen the movement for agricultural settlement of the land of Israel.[57] He had a more difficult time dealing with the pious Jews who publicly denounced his plans. God would surely punish them, Kalischer frequently wrote, and, when several prominent opponents in the Yishuv died in a plague, he attributed it to divine wrath.[58] If

[56] This was a repeated theme in 1873. See for example *Ha-Maggid*, 20/1873; Kalischer to Guttmacher, Kislev, 1868, in *Ha-Ketavim*, p. 281; Kalischer to Zevi Hirsch Bernstein, ibid., pp. 411–12.

[57] *Ha-Maggid*, 8/1870.

[58] One example of many is Kalischer to Guttmacher, 1866, in *Ha-Ketavim*, p. 230. These comments are reminiscent of Dr Chaim Lorje's reference to the death of Yehiel Michal Zacks, the influential emissary who would not support the Society for the Settlement of Palestine. Lorje's comments were instrumental in his removal from the leadership of the society. See Getzel Kressel, 'The First Palestine Settlement Society' (in Hebrew), *Zion* 1/1941, p. 205. It would be interesting to analyse the relationship between Lorje's removal, Kalischer's continued defence of him, and the public perception of both men.

this was no consolation, he observed that, the greater the holiness of the plan, the greater the opposition.[59]

Also evident during Kalischer's later years was his awareness of the contradictions between his stated values and his own life. First, he never resolved the problems raised by his advocacy of combining Torah with a worldly occupation. Neither in his writings nor in his own personal life could he consistently defend this ideal. He criticized the rabbinic elitism that denigrated labour, even labour that involved the fulfilment of the agricultural precepts. Yet he always stipulated that a portion of the profits from the communes should be given to the Yishuv Torah scholars. Furthermore, he eventually retreated from his high valuation of agricultural labour by insisting that all workers should spend some time in religious study.[60] Most problematic, though, was that his own refusal to earn a living rendered him a hypocrite.

Second, Kalischer viewed the ideal Torah scholar as one who, like himself, refused to make the Torah 'a spade for digging' by living off community funds.[61] At first glance, it would appear that he wanted his own high standards, already exceptional in the Diaspora, to be institutionalized in the Holy Land. Yet he never did demand that the Yishuv Torah scholars should refuse community funds. He even occasionally defended them from charges of laziness, pointing out that some were not physically capable of labour.[62] This inconsistency was only partly due to his need to gain this group's support. He had genuine respect for Jews who wanted to devote themselves to full-time

[59] Kalischer to Z. L. Berit in *Ha-Levanon*, 3/1872.

[60] See for example Kalischer's letter to Azriel Hildesheimer, 1863, in *Ha-Ketavim*, pp. 188–9, in which he suggests that the farm workers should return to the villages on the Sabbath to pray and listen to teaching, and that anyone who objects should be excommunicated and expelled.

[61] He contended, in opposition to the values of the Torah scholars defending the Yishuv welfare system, that refusing to accept the monetary support of others denoted a higher level of piety than studying full-time and accepting aid. Only a self-sufficient scholar, Kalischer argued, could truly claim that his study is for its own sake and not for any material gain. Elsewhere he asserted that to live by the support of others was sinful. His first clarification of this argument is in *Seeking Zion* (*Ha-Ketavim*, pp. 28,30). See also the extremely derisive comments in the unused part of an article written for *Ha-Maggid*, 34/1863, published by Israel Klausner in *Sinai*, Iyar 1939, pp. 613–14.

[62] *Ha-Levanon*, 3/1872; *Seeking Zion*, in *Ha-Ketavim*, p. 28.

study, since that was the life that he had proudly and stubbornly chosen for himself.

These tensions emerged in Kalischer's plans to settle in Palestine. In 1858 he first expressed his desire to move to Palestine and to work in the communes there, supervising the workers' observance of the commandments. Only this option, it seems, could have resolved the tension between his roles as an activist and a scholar-rabbi, perhaps leading to more impressive gains for his cause. Yet, though he repeatedly made plans to depart, he never did, claiming that family obligations detained him. At the age of seventy-six he was still planning the move. He finally admitted that he was too old and ill for the journey.[63]

Shortly after this, Kalischer decided that it was time for him and Guttmacher to purchase land in Palestine, though the funds they had raised fell short of what they needed. Negotiations were begun in 1873 through their agents in Palestine and Frankfurt, and issued in the purchase of a small plot of land outside Jerusalem in summer 1874. Kalischer, who barely lived to hear of the acquisition, joyfully announced it in the papers, requesting donations from readers to pay the last instalment.[64] He died two months later, leaving it to his sons to complete the transaction.[65]

VIII

Kalischer's primary teaching was that Jews must initiate the messianic proeess through concrete action. He himself, however, largely devoted his efforts to convincing others to act.

His influence rests partly on two features of his writing-style. The first was his presentation of supportive biblical and rabbinic texts. An

---

[63] The following contain a sampling of Kalischer's statements after 1860: *Ha-Ketavim*, pp. 189 (1862), 255 (1867), 266 (1868), 302 (1870), 339 (1872). At the end of summer 1872, he admitted that he could not go (p. 367).

[64] *Ha-Maggid*, 37/1874.

[65] The death announcement appeared in *Ha-Maggid*, 41/1874. The funeral account appeared in the following issue. According to Isaac Arigur, in *Zevi Hirsch Kalischer* (Jerusalem, 1928), p. 160, Kalischer's son Judah Leib made the final purchase arrangement. According to Getzel Kressel, in his *Encyclopaedia Judaica* article 'Kalischer', Kalischer's son Ze'ev Wolf, who was living in Palestine, purchased land with his father's estate. It is unclear to me whether these were two separate pieces of land.

anthology of proof texts is extremely important to the religious community in legitimizing a new course of action, and Kalischer prepared his with a mass audience in mind. He explained the texts with a minimum of exegesis and connected them to several familiar narrative and visual metaphors. Key points were hammered home as slogans. Thus his ideas were easily grasped, yet effectively manipulated public fears and hopes. Many of them became standard fare in the writings of subsquent religious nationalists.[66]

Second, the messianic and non-messianic aspects of Kalischer's reasoning enabled him to serve two constituencies: religious Jews, motivated by active messianism, who sought the continued development of the Jewish community in the land of Israel; and religious Jews who participated in the same activities but who, wary of messianism, were motivated solely by the desire to improve the physical and spiritual lot of their people.

It is critical to differentiate between these two types, because, although in Kalischer's lifetime they were not clearly distinguished, they eventually developed into the two main strands of modern religious Zionism. Shortly after Kalischer's death, religious Jews began increasingly to embrace the idea of a contemporay return to Zion, but they generally rejected messianic thinking. Religious Zionists such as rabbis Samuel Mohilever, Isaac Elhanan Specktor and Jacob Reines regarded Kalischer as a model and an authority for their goal of a rejuvenated Jewish homeland in Palestine where Jews fully participate in all realms of economic life. Against Kalischer, though, they declared their loyalty to the tradition of passive messianism. The Hibbat Zion movement of the late nineteenth century and the Mizrahi party of the early twentieth generally followed suit.[67]

By the second decade of the twentieth century, however, religious Jews had begun to turn to active messianism. Today, most religious

---

[66] One might argue that later active messianists drew their ideas from pre-Kalischer sources without being aware that he had used them. However, *Seeking Zion* was widely read by this circle. See for example *Shivat Tziyyon* ('The Return to Zion'), ed. Abraham Slutzki (Warsaw, 1891), a collection of rabbinic testimonies favouring the Hibbat Zion movement, in which references to Kalischer and borrowing of his material are obvious. The anthology *Religious Zionism*, ed. Yosef Tirosh (Jerusalem, 1975), also contains a wealth of examples.

[67] Rabbinic testimonies of support for Hibbat Zion can be found in *Shivat Tziyyon*. For representative statements of the early Mizrahi Zionists, see Hertzberg, *The Zionist Idea*.

Zionists espouse a messianic ideology reminiscent of Kalischer's. They are convinced that the Zionist successes of the twentieth century constitute the beginning of the fulfilment of the messianic prophecies. They maintain that the messianic process is a gradual and outwardly natural one that requires human assistance. Unlike the early religious Zionists, they talk about acting in accordance with the messianic process and thus eschew political normalcy. Paradoxically, these messianic Zionists, who have little use for objective historical scholarship, have correctly grasped Kalischer's importance as a forerunner. They place him near the beginning of a chain of religious thinkers — including the students of the Vilna Gaon, Judah Alkalai and Rabbi Abraham Isaac Kook—who correctly understood the messianic idea, realized that the Messianic Era had indeed begun, and tried to hasten it.

Kalischer's continuing influence lies in his delineation of and response to certain modern challenges to traditional Jewish thought. Because he accepted the prevailing positive attitude to rationalism, he was bothered by the traditional belief in a miraculous messianic process. He was puzzled by the meaning of the unprecedented positive events of the modern age that reversed the age-old pattern of Jewish existence. Finally, he was beset by the endemic religious desire for the spiritual wholeness promised in the Messianic Age. Searching within the Jewish tradition for a solution to these dilemmas, Kalischer found it in the fragments of activist messianic thought. He revived and systematized these into a messianic ideology that met his needs: it assumed a rationalistic course of history, viewed the unprecedented events as divine intervention, and provided a concrete method for Jews to restore their spiritual wholeness. Paradoxically, the solution he derived from traditional Jewish sources posed a challenge to tradition. Kalischer's radical course of action nevertheless provided a direction for his religious contemporaries, and it continues to do so for their successors today.

12

The Anglicization of Orthodoxy: the Adlers, Father and Son

EUGENE C. BLACK

In February 1988, Rabbi Dr Immanuel Jakobovits was conducted to his place as one of the peers of the realm. Baron Jakobovits of Regents Park had, when signing the book in the House of Lords, achieved one of the ultimate ambitions of the Adlers: shared acknowledged status with the Archbishop of Canterbury. But if the Adlers would have beamed at the scene, many Jakobovits concerns would also have been familiar to them. Secularism, doctrinal reform, and rigid traditionalism still challenged the Orthodoxy they had been at such pains to shape. Assimilation, intermarriage, even apostasy continued to lure some who felt that the community was still too isolated from British life or who chafed under the constraints of Orthodoxy. A few argued that Jewish observance, even Jewish theology, must be better adapted to the contemporary world. Other restive souls saw Anglo-Jewish compromises as sterile, unwarranted tamperings with halakhah and tradition.

Nathan Adler and his son Hermann, the first two chief rabbis of Great Britain and the British Empire, had known these tensions well. Nathan Adler assumed his office at the end of 1844 in a community divided by Reform. Nor was the world of Orthodoxy at peace. English Jews were increasingly restive with the Aldgate-bound world of their own old-established synagogues. Hermann Adler, in his turn, would confront theological challenges from Claude Goldsmid Montefiore and the Jewish Religious Union demanding modernization in the form and content of Jewish belief and practice. Observant Jews, on the other hand, bristled at any signs of compromise. By the end of the century, moreover, secularization was making broad inroads among Jews in all walks of life.

Nathan Marcus Adler, the third son of Marcus Baer Adler, Chief Rabbi of Hanover, was born on 15 January 1803. The family, so tradition had it, had come to Germany from Crete. Its lineage reached back in Frankfurt history to the fourteenth century. Originally *Kohanim* with the surname Kahn or Kayn, the family assumed the name Adler in the sixteenth century and achieved lasting prominence in the Jewish community. Not only did Nathan Adler stand in a long rabbinic tradition, but he had what proved to be the good fortune of being born a subject of King George III. The union of the Hanoverian kingdom with Great Britain was not dissolved until the accession of Victoria in 1837, so Nathan's academic and professional career in Germany and Hanover was well known in British royal circles.[1] Adler received his rabbinical diploma at Würzburg and his doctorate from Erlangen in 1828. Nathan was a precocious child, singled out by his father as the most promising of his sons, destined to be a scholar and community leader. It was a custom in the Adler family for sons to be selected for the rabbinate according to prospective talent, not seniority. Nathan would, in his turn, choose his second son, Hermann (1839–1911), to be his aide, his intimate and his successor. Hermann spoke movingly of his father as his mentor from childhood and his teacher as an adult. He studied Talmud intensively from the age of ten. Nathan firmly but lovingly taught and trained his son, moulding Hermann into his successor, repeating what his father had done for him.

Nathan also trained his other sons for a public role. Marcus Adler (1837–1911), Hermann's older brother, was active in Jewish communal affairs, being, among other things, a founder and manager of Stepney Jewish Schools. Marcus Adler, however, applied family discipline and regularity as a mathematician. An actuary and fellow of the Royal Statistical Society, Marcus founded the London Mathematical Society. He designed the London County Council system of train and tram fares, which proved of great benefit to the working classes. His work also served the Jewish community, for it eased the dispersion of inhabitants of the Jewish East End, lessening the burden of slum congestion.[2] Elkan Nathan Adler (1861–1946), half-brother

[1] See Nathan Adler's patriotic sermon *Des israeliten Liebe zum Vaterlande: eine Predigt zur Feier des Geburtstags seiner Majestät des Königs Wilhelm IV,* 27 Aug. 1836 (Hanover, 1836). For Nathan Adler's certificate of naturalization, see H. Waddington to N. Adler, 24 Nov. 1856, in the Mocatta Library Quartos, B 20 ADL Nathan Adler, University College, London.

[2] *Jewish Chronicle,* 17 Jan. 1879, 5 June 1896, 9 June 1905. Marcus Adler's son Herbert (1876–1940) followed in the family tradition, serving as director of Jewish education in London.

of Marcus and Hermann, was a lawyer who is best remembered as one of the great Jewish bibliophiles. His collection of books and manuscripts was sold to the Jewish Theological Seminary in New York, making that institution a significant research library. Elkan, like Marcus, committed himself to Anglo-Jewish education and played an important role on the Jewish Religious Education Board.

All Adlers seem to have been devoted to learning. Nathan Marcus Adler early displayed a particular propensity for classical and modern languages. Encouraged and pushed ahead at home, he went on to study at Göttingen, Erlangen, Würzburg and Heidelberg. Not only did he make a mark for himself in secular studies, but he was destined by temperament, ability and background to be a voice for tradition in a modernizing world. In 1830, at the age of twenty-seven, he was appointed Chief Rabbi of Oldenburg. Within a year, he succeeded his father as Chief Rabbi of Hanover. Benign and authoritative in appearance, Nathan commanded respect both for who he was and what he stood for. He was an esteemed Talmudic scholar, a quality which even his critics were quick to concede. He was a man of unflinching Orthodoxy in an age of intellectual and religious ferment. He was sincere, zealous and benevolent.

Warm and devoted as rabbi and as a parent, he demanded unflagging commitment and effort from his flock and family, holding himself and them as models for the world to see and emulate. He married well. Henrietta Worms was the sister of Baron Solomon Benedict de Worms and daughter of Jeanette von Rothschild (a sister of Nathan Mayer Rothschild), so the match connected Nathan with the Jewish elite and buttressed his ambitions. At the same time, it appears to have been very harmonious. Marcus and Hermann, the sons of Nathan and Henrietta, sought, successfully it would seem, to replicate in their own marriages the family and home life they remembered. Nathan and Hermann depended upon the family to sustain them in their public and private lives. For father and son a Jewish home nourished by love, supportive of all, was the cornerstone of life. The home was their refuge from the intensity of public life. Henrietta seems to have devoted herself to her domestic role, venturing little into more public Anglo-Jewish life. After her death, Nathan, then in his fifties, remarried. He and Celestine Lehfeld had one son, Elkan, for whom Marcus and Hermann appear to have had great fraternal and filial affection. Family bonds remained close throughout their lives. Love of family, concern for children and dedication to education — for their own offspring and for the community — was to be a dominant theme for the Alders from generation to generation. That bond tied father to son, and, in Hermann Adler's case, even was to bring husband and wife together.

When Nathan Marcus Adler arrived in Britain, British Jewry was enjoying increasing prosperity and anxious to play a fuller role in British public life, but also confronting serious internal divisions and tension. Disunity seemed a real threat. The Reform secession of 1840, however small a challenge it ultimately posed, held some appeal for those who sought to be more 'British' while retaining a Jewish identity.[3] (A similar appeal proved to be one of the abiding attractions of Reform for Jews in the United States). The battle lines had already been drawn. Solomon Hirschel, as Ashkenazic Chief Rabbi of London, and David Mendola, the Av Bet Din (head of the Sephardic court of law) of the Spanish and Portuguese congregation, met. Their findings, published on 22 January 1842, and distributed to all Spanish and Portuguese and Ashkenazic congregations in Great Britain and the Empire pronounced a *herem*, an excommunication, against those using the West London Synagogue *Forms of Prayer*. The reaction proved more mixed than upholders of Orthodoxy would have wished. In London the Western Synagogue rejected the *herem* and returned it. Congregations in Manchester and Liverpool did the same. Outraged Plymouth Jews burned it.

Sir Moses Montefiore, England's foremost Jew, earnestly sought to bring Orthodox Askhenzic and Sephardic Jews together, but he resisted every attempt to accommodate or come to terms with Reform Jews. The leading layman in the community was anxious to find a new Chief Rabbi of sufficient authority and capacity to save British Jewry for Orthodoxy. A relationship by marriage to the Worms family and the Adler family connection with the Rothschilds may or may not also have helped, but the Chief Rabbi of Hanover, Nathan Marcus Adler, could not have been other than the most highly favoured candidate. He was much praised by the Duke of Cambridge, former Viceroy of Hanover and uncle of Queen Victoria. Adler's

---

[3] See, in general, M. Leigh, 'Reform Judaism in Britain (1840–1970)', in D. Marmur, (ed.), *Reform Judaism: Essays on Reform Judaism in Britain* (London, 1973), pp. 3-52. Accounts of the Burton Street Synagogue controversy tend to be wise after the event and play down its significance. Both *The Voice of Jacob* and the *Jewish Chronicle* took it seriously' at the time. The Reform service curtailed the Siddur, abolished the Aliyot and Mi Sheberah, and eliminated 'sacred days which are evidently not ordained in Scripture'. The Orthodox regarded abolishing the second day of festivals as the rejection of Oral Law and an impossible breach with tradition.

reputation as both a scholar and an administrator preceded him, and he even enjoyed a family tie to an eighteenth-century Chief Rabbi of London. His father had served as Chief Rabbi of Hanover for the previous fifty-two years, so the Adler connection with the British royal family's domains was well established, a point not lost to a British Jewish community seeking full political recognition.[4]

Adler's election was more severely contested than the decisive vote would imply. Thirteen candidates, none of them from Britain, were originally considered. The list shrank to four finalists, of whom only three actually had votes cast in their favour. Since the office was no longer merely that of Chief Rabbi of London but that of Chief Rabbi of Great Britain and the British Empire, every recognized Ashkenazic congregation was polled. Three provincial synagogues declined to vote, and the West London synagogue voted for Adler's leading opponent.[5] Adler moved circumspectly but firmly. Although elected in 1844, he did not come to Britain until June 1845. Citing his need to give a year's notice of relinquishing his post in Hanover, Adler carefully considered the most pressing problems he would confront. Not everyone waited patiently. The Reform controversy had so unsettled the community that one leading layman wrote to Adler asking him 'to settle a difficult religious affair'.[6] Adler did not need to be told about that, and the Reform dispute in various forms outlasted father and son in office.

Adler took the opportunity to circulate all Ashkenazic synagogues in the British Empire with a questionnaire that allowed him simultaneously to sample opinion on various issues and symbolically to

[4] N. M. Adler, *The Adler Family* (London, 1909). Nathan Adler's doctoral testimonials are in Mocatta Library Quartos, B 20 ADL Nathan Adler. The same files include a manuscript description of his installation 'in great splendour'. Adler was formally placed in the contest for election (the short list) on 21 August 1844, (S. Oppenheim to Adler, 21 Aug. 1844). J. H. Ellis informed him of his election and announced Adler's starting salary as £800 plus marriage fees. He was granted a further £120 for travelling and 'fitting your establishment' (Ellis to Adler, 6 and 20 Dec. 1844).
[5] The communal hunger for the sort of leadership the Adlers were to provide can be found in the contemporary literature. See particularly *A Few Words Addressed to the Committee for the Election of a Chief Rabbi of England and to the Electors at Large. By a Friend of Truth* (London, 1844). Adler received 121 votes, Hirsch Hirschfeld 13, and Samson Raphael Hirsch two.
[6] Lyon Barnett, who denounced the defectors to Burton Street in a letter to Adler, 1 Apr. 1845, Mocatta Library Quartos, B 20 ADL Nathan Adler.

assert himself as head of all British Ashkenazic Orthodox Jews. The inquiry allowed Adler to lay out his programme. Education came first. Organizing the religious life of the community would begin with schools for infants and reach 'up to such as are to extend their salutary influence to the future, by training proper and efficient teachers'. The formalities of religious ceremony stood next. Order and decorum must be brought to the synagogue, Adler wrote, for 'it is necessary that quiet and decorum, dignity and solemnity should prevail there during divine worship, so that it may awaken the fear of the Lord, foster feelings of devotion, and promote brotherly union'.

Third came religious and charitable institutions, all of which could inculcate 'the cherishing of industrious habits and useful activity among our co-religionists'.[7] Nathan Marcus Adler pursued that agenda for the rest of his life. The public and private person merged, and the Adler family became an idealized microcosm of the world that the Chief Rabbi hoped to shape.

I

British Jewry needed an able, determined religious leader. Jews were, by the 1840s, moving towards comfortable acculturation within British society. It was their good fortune to find rabbinical leaders well suited to the task at hand, building accommodations to British life while preserving Jewish culture, spirit and indentity. British Jews had small, active provincial communities, particularly in Manchester, Leeds, Bradford, Liverpool and Hull.[8] Small groups could be found in the port towns, Scotland and Ireland. But the Jewish world centred on London, and the death of Solomon Hirschel, Chief Rabbi of London, was the occasion for an important change. Provincial Ashkenazic congregations were invited to send representatives to vote for a new Chief Rabbi, this man to be Chief Rabbi of Great Britain and the Empire.

The title and role were new, the demands unprecedented. The

---

[7] Quoted from, R. Apple, 'United Synagogue; Religious Founders and Leaders', in S. S. Levin (ed.), *Century of Anglo-Jewish Life 1870–1970* (London, 1970), p. 14. For Nathan Adler's religious position simply defined, see in particular N. Adler, *The Jewish Faith. A Sermon Delivered in the Great Synagogue...(29 January 1848)* (London, 1848).

[8] See particularly Bill Williams, *The Making of Manchester Jewry, 1740–1875* (Manchester, 1976).

three old London Ashkenazic synagogues – the Great, the Hambro' and the New – no longer answered metropolitan communal needs. All three lay close together in the old centre of Jewish settlement, while more and more of their members, particularly the most affluent and successful, had moved away. The three could ill afford to lose their wealthiest and most dynamic members and resisted any movement to establish new, more conveniently located synagogues. Walking across the West End and the City of London to services taxed the devotion of such men of affairs. Few considered following the example of Sir Moses Montefiore, who constructed a private synagogue in his house on Park Lane. Some mechanism that would protect the interests of existing synagogues while taking account of the changed population distribution had to be found.

Informal non-poaching agreements were deemed insufficient. By a treaty of 1834, the three synagogues not only reaffirmed those understandings but also set in motion the co-operative movement that would ultimately lead to the organization of the United Synagogue in 1870. The treaty also defined proportionate responsibilities in maintaining communal social institutions, making it the first step in the creation of the Jewish Board of Guardians in 1859. What the treaty could not do was to provide an acceptable mechanism for responding to the shifts of population. The wealthier and more successful had already begun their westward migration, but the institutional response to their wishes for convenient places of worship was grudging at best.

Such concerns had already contributed in part to the Reform secession of 1840. Drawing more followers from Sephardic Jews annoyed with their synagogue in Bevis Marks than from Ashkenazic supporters, Reform sounded more divisive than it actually was. Borrowing principally Sephardic forms, the Reform Jews had no desire to cut themselves off from their co-religionists. They wished to contribute to Sephardic communal charities, but were not permitted to do so. By the time Bevis Marks lifted its ban on Reform Jews in 1849, that point was moot. Both Ashkenazic and Sephardic authorities preferred to stamp the movement out. But the *herem* against those using the West London Synagogue *Forms of Prayer* failed to bring the dissidents to heel.

Into this world strode Nathan Marcus Adler, his programme proclaimed and his ambitions clear. Judaism depended upon sound education and training. Jews' Free School had already been started from the rudiments of a Talmud–Torah and would grow into the largest primary school in the United Kingdom. A comprehensive educational programme and institutions to serve the needs of a growing community remained to be developed. Order and discipline in synagogue worship remained lax. The rudiments of the constitutional structure of what the Adlers would forge into the Chief Rabbinate of the British Empire were in place, if somewhat ill-defined. The Bet Din (chief rabbinical court) existed, for instance, but as part of the Bet ha-Midrash.[9] Haphazard charitable institutions supplemented synagogue relief.

Adler believed that sustaining traditional Orthodoxy in religious practice was best accomplished through judicious adaptations to British culture and a high degree of centralization of religious authority. This demanded, among other things, an Anglo-Jewish rabbinate, but as a way of enhancing his own authority, he carefully appropriated the title to his own gift. Ministers with the title of 'Reverend' presided over synagogues. Adler took the lead in promoting Jews' College to train them.[10] Those seeking rabbinical certification, however, could only secure it on the continent or by Adlerian fiat. One critic denounced the system as 'un-Jewish, un-orthodox, undignified and unfair', running counter to the spirit of Judaism and displacing great continental rabbis with 'nondescript ministers'. A defender replied that Adler's organization had worked well for gen-

[9] Nor did Nathan Adler do much to clarify the situation in the case of the Bet Din. Judges sat at his discretion and pleasure. During Adler's incumbency only one permanent *dayyan*, Aaron Levy, held office. He retired in 1872, and Adler appointed no permanent successor until Bernard Spiers took office in 1876, retaining the post until his death in 1901. Adler made sure that the rulings of his Bet Din would be politically credible. For what Raymond Apple (in Levin, *A Century of Anglo-Jewish life*, pp. 17-18) somewhat unkindly calls a gesture to keep the East End happy, Nathan Adler used Jacob Reinowitz as an 'unofficial *dayyan*', a revealingly vague term.

[10] C. Roth, 'The Chief Rabbinate of England', in I. Epstein and E. Levine (eds) *Essays Presented to J.H. Hertz, Chief Rabbi* (London, 1942); V. D. Lipman, *A Social History of the Jews in England, 1850–1950* (London, 1954), pp. 34–40. Nathan Adler, however, sought to recruit middle-class Jewish boys to an appropriate Jewish preparatory school and move them on to the rabbinate. As Jews became middle-class, they preferred to send their sons to elite British schools and colleges, and Jew's College perpetually teetered on the brink of disaster on just such issues of social recruitment. The Adlers also had some difficulty in controlling the use of the term 'Reverend.' The spiritual leaders of congregations appropriated it, regardless of qualifications. By the end of the century, Hermann Adler was willing to concede it to qualified cantors, but he drew the line at *shohetim* (ritual slaughterers) using it.

erations. 'At the head of this system to-day stands, Saul-like, a Chief Rabbi, honoured and beloved by the "whole" community of Jews in Great and Greater Britain, renowned for scholarship and unostentatious piety, gifted with those rare qualities of tact essential in the exalted and difficult position he holds.'[11] Not until the beginning of the twentieth century were statutory arrangements agreed upon that defined the British training-prerequisites for the rabbinate. British ministers otherwise had to go abroad to receive a *hattarat hora'ah*, their rabbinical certification. Simeon Singer, later the author of *The Authorised Daily Prayer Book* of 1890, did so, as did Hermann Gollancz. Even Hermann Adler, who first obtained a degree from University College, London, was sent abroad, to earn his doctorate at Leipzig and his rabbinical diploma at Prague in 1862.

For more than half a century the Adlers moved away from the traditional view of a congregational system of autonomous congregations, to an episcopacy with a clerical caste of 'reverends' ordained by themselves. The London Bet Din was not permitted to rule upon provincial matters save in a consultative capacity. The Chief Rabbi preferred to supervise each Bet Din himself. The Adlers personally organized the supervision of provincial synagogues and schools. No body of clergy or laymen was allowed constitutionally to intrude upon the Chief Rabbi's authority. Centralizing authority and imposing discipline upon a scattered and diffuse community was a point upon which the lay elite and the Adlers could work in common purpose. Each, as the nineteenth century went on, found the enhanced power of the other useful for its own purposes. They flourished together. Critics worried that this stratified, anglicized community was, in the most profound sense, anti-Jewish. Jews were becoming Anglo-Saxon, finding their historical roots at Runnymede, not Jerusalem. A chief rabbi who adopted episcopal style clothing and wore bishop's gaiters had, such critics argued, gone too far.[12]

Adler hoped that the establishment of Jews' College would bring sons of the elite to religious careers. He even established a Jews' College school to train young men, but was forced to give up that

[11] *Jewish Chronicle*, 29 Dec. 1900, 4 Jan. 1901.

[12] See, in general, E.C. Black, *Social Politics of Anglo-Jewry, 1880–1920* (Oxford, 1988); and, in particular, 'Anglicisation on Jewish Lines', *Jewish Chronicle*, 4 Apr. 1902, and 'Diploma of a Rabbi', *Jewish Chronicle*, 20 Feb. 1903. Aubrey Newman has some pointed remarks on substantive and symbolic anglicization in *The United Synagogue* (London, 1980), pp. 93–4. For provincial concerns, see Nathan Adler's circular letter of May 1882 in Mocatta Library Quartos, B 20 ADL.

enterprise in 1879. Adler simply could not recruit the students he needed. Even Jews' College itself barely stayed afloat. Anglo-Jewry had an ambiguous relationship with its principal ministerial training-institution. Created in 1856, Jews' College had a history of ups and downs, with far too many of the latter. Professor Israel Gollancz was determined to understand why British Jews, with their commitment to learning and veneration for their religious institutions, could not create a major and respected centre. Jews' College was brought to Tavistock Square and associated with University College, London. Neither a central location nor attachment to a major centre of learning produced an institution such as American Jews had created with their Seminary in New York half a century before.

Abler English Jews, for what seemed to them good reasons, avoided the ministry. The children of the elite rarely even considered it. Most British-trained ministers lacked status. Ministers, even on those rare occasions when granted the title of rabbi, were all too often regarded as cultural decorations, a kind of synagogue status symbol. When seeking a minister for a major synagogue, therefore, elite laymen cast their eyes on distinguished veterans or on well-regarded Europeans. Demand, moreover, conditioned supply. The graduate of Jews' College could look forward to life as the minister of a provincial synagogue for a paltry annual salary of £100 with little prospect of promotion to the great world of the United Synagogue. The minister of a small provincial congregation, Nathan L. Cohen, reminded Jews' College students that a minister

> must needs be almost an expurgated edition of human nature. He must cultivate patience, tact, invariably a fair judgement, and, above all, that very difficult attribute, a true sense of proportion, and always imperturbable courtesy in the face even of unwelcome opposition ... He must abstain, as a rule, from acute, at least, secular controversies, under the danger of losing his influence for good with those from whom he may differ. [His lay superiors instructed him] to conduct the service, and to attend to religious requirements, to teach and train the young, to visit and comfort the suffering and those in trouble, to evoke high conduct and to do religious observance, and he is to do all this mainly by periodical sermons warranted not to exceed twenty minutes![13]

[13] Prize-giving, Jews' College, 3 May 1903, reported in the *Jewish Chronicle*, 8 May 1903.

In spite of all its limitations, Jews' College nevertheless attracted a handful of industrious and dedicated students. A few, such as the Revd J. F. Stern, made distinguished careers for themselves.[14]

Institutional centralization and the establishment of an anglicized heirarchy led Nathan Adler's agenda. The Bet Din was his Bet Din, a point about which there would be no confusion. Critics of what came to be called 'Adlerism' mumbled about chief rabbis who presided over no rabbis. Each congregation had its lecturer or reader, who by mid-century was called a minister and addressed as 'Reverend'. The control of each congregation, however, was firmly in the hands of laymen, for whom the minister provided a service. At the beginning of the nineteenth century, many synagogues had a lay head who presided over services and monthly meetings of a committee of management in alternation with two wardens.

An oligarchic system was well entrenched. The wardens, officers and seven elders (supplemented in some congregations by five governors) determined who would or would not attend the quarterly meetings of the vestry and even who would or would not be invited to general meetings. The Ashkenazim had a system of privileged membership as distinct from mere seat-renters.[15] Lay concerns dominated communal and even synagogal life. Disorder was commonplace, a point to which repeated, ineffective legislation on decorum bears sad testimony. People wandered in and out of services as they pleased. Stock-exchange quotations were known to be fetched and passed from hand to hand during Yom Kippur services. The synagogue 'turned into a veritable bear garden' for Simhat Torah. The wives of those chosen to read from the Torah would toss almonds and raisins down for the boys in the congregation. When the beadle was called

---

[14] I. Finestein, 'Joseph Frederick Stern 1865—1934: Aspects of a Gifted Anomaly', in A. Newman (ed.), *The Jewish East End 1840—1939* (London, 1981), pp. 75—96.

[15] This distinction originated in the higher status accorded heads of families and householders as opposed to the itinerant or those who lived elsewhere and returned for festivals. The cost of membership was high. For the Great Synagogue in 1800, a man paid 8 guineas for his own and his wife's seat. He was then eligible to be elected a privileged member. Privileged membership gave him the right to vote for officers (as could his widow), to stand at marriage or Bar Mitzvah, and to be buried in a plot in the high ground of the cemetery. He also received priority in being called up and in recitation or reading. For a succinct account upon which this section draws see, 'A Hundred Years Ago. Anglo-Jewry at the Commencement of the 19th Century', *Jewish Chronicle*, 11 Jan. 1901.

up with all of the boys, the congregation was much amused by the firecrackers the rowdier among them would set off behind his back.

Such was the world the Adlers came to set in order. And order — both in congregational decorum and in institutional arrangements — was much needed. Nathan Adler promulgated a set of regulations in 1847 defining his supremacy as Chief Rabbi in all matters of ritual and practice. He understood what had to be done to find some middle way between full assimilation and Jewish particularity. He enhanced the position of his clergy while shaping them into a hierarchy over which he presided. He insisted they have neatly trimmed beards or be clean-shaven. He clad them in the mufti of Anglican clergymen. Well into the twentieth century, a Jewish minister staring benignly out of the photograph of a Bar Mitzvah class would be indistinguishable from an Anglican priest with his confirmation class. Adler extended the use of the Established Church vocabulary into British Orthodox Judaism, even endorsing an ecclesiastical architecture that blended Anglican substance with Jewish symbols.[16]

The Adlers also pursued institutional centralization. In this they shared the aspirations of the emerging Ashenazic elite. Lionel Louis Cohen and Nathan Adler, the lay and religious generals of the campaign for order, decorum and anglicization, moved in common purpose and with shared assumptions. They jointly pressed for the systematization of Jewish charity through what would ultimately become the Jewish Board of Guardians in 1859.[17] The Board of Guardians improved upon the arrangements in the treaty of 1834 and opened the way to a decade of negotiations and manoeuvre. Since meeting communal social needs and synagogal life were inextricably linked, the rationalizing of one must, of neccessity, hasten the integration of the other. Joshua Van Oven had proposed a Poor Board with a central managing-committee from each synagogue 'for the management of all the Jewish poor in the metropolis' as early as 1802. Henry Faudel repeated that plea in 1844 to an audience more prepared to listen when he proposed a general council of British Jews to manage all Jewish charities 'to secure an efficient centralisation with wholesome and necessary control'. The existing system, he argued, produced more problems than benefits. It merely encouraged mendicants and idlers instead of training productive artisans and assisting

[16] J. Glasman, 'Architecture and Anglicization: London Synagogue Building, 1870–1900', *Jewish Quarterly*, 34, 2 (1987), pp. 16–21.

[17] For the Jewish Board of Guardians see V.D. Lipman, *A Century of Social Service* (London, 1959); and Black, *Social Politics*, ch. 3.

those anxious to help themselves.[18] That pioneering-exercise in communal joint action was, in turn, an inspiration for creating the United Synagogue. Adler and Cohen supported the systematic development of communal education, taking judicious advantage, as time went on, of state funding and support. Each idea — the rationalization of social policy and administration, the organization and control of education, and the establishment of a religious order — reinforced the others.

The United Synagogue Act of 1870 statutorily defined the function and relationship of the principal London Orthodox synagogues. In doing so, Parliament did more than ratify what had been past practice. It untied the Gordian knot that had constrained orderly communal growth. So long as new synagogues were concessions from existing institutions, the entrenched could block or severely inhibit growth. Existing synagogues feared, correctly, that they stood to lose essential revenue unless some protective umbrella organization existed. The United Synagogue became the institution through which Ashkenazic lay leadership could respond in financially viable and responsible ways to the growth of the community in outer London and the provinces.[19] The United Synagogue simultaneously provided

---

[18] [H. Faudel], *Suggestions to the Jews for Improvement in Reference to their Charities, Education and Central Government: By a Jew* (London, 1844); 'A Sketch of the Early History of the Jewish Board of Guardians', *Jewish Chronicle*, 20 Mar. 1896.

[19] The standard history is Aubrey Newman's *The United Synagogue*. See also C. Roth, *The Great Synagogue, 1690–1940* (London, 1950). For the Adler family, see also M.N. Adler, *The Adler Family*. The original five synagogues of the United were the Great, Hambro', New, Brayswater and Central. The Borough was added in 1873. The United, responding to the pressures that had brought it into being, then founded in relatively rapid order the synagogues of St John's Wood (1876), East London (1877, established in Stepney in response to what were then middle-class needs), North London (1878) and New West End (1879). The pressure of immigration to the East End stimulated more middle-class outward movement. This led to the establishment of Dalston (1885), Hammersmith (1890), West Kensington (1890) and Hampstead (1892) synagogues. The Hambro', steadily in decline, moved out to Mile End Road in 1899. It would not formally merge with the Great until 1936. Stoke Newington Synagogue (1903) accommodated more middle-class Jews moving northwards, and Brondesbury (1905) those moving north-west. The congregations of Poplar, East Ham and Manor Park, and South East London joined the United as associate rather than constituent synagogues in 1902, and were followed by West Ham in 1907. Brixton, established as a constituent synagogue in 1913, was founded after Hermann Adler's death.

the Chief Rabbinate a forum from which, in fact, to preside over the individual congregations. Through the creation of the United Synagogue and by enhancing the office of Chief Rabbi, the Adlers, father and son, shaped Orthodox Jewry institutionally to resemble Anglicanism, with the Chief Rabbi a Jewish equivalent of the Archbishop of Canterbury.

The United Synagogue, like the Jewish Board of Guardians, would owe much of its success to the skill and dedication of a handful of communal civil servants. They were carefully recruited, well-recompensed by the standards of the time, and even covered by a pioneering superannuation scheme. The United Synagogue ran as well as it did thanks in great measure to the labours of its able secretary, Dr Asher Asher. Asher was the first Scottish Jew to be licensed as a physician. He came from Glasgow in 1862, where Lionel Leonard Cohen recruited him to be secretary of the Great Synagogue in 1866.[20] That was the year of the famous Sukkot breakfast (24 September) when Nathan Adler asked the community leaders to rise above their differences for the sake of the community. The event, which looms large in the history of the United Synagogue, was important in symbolic terms rather than for anything it actually achieved. Communal growth and mobility demanded order, and lay leaders had long been building its foundations.

Both Nathan and Hermann Adler proved worthy parents in this enterprise. Nathan brought international standing and social elitism. Anglo-Jewry sought and needed both as it aspired to become an accepted and established sub-culture within British society. Decorum and deference appealed to upwardly mobile lay leaders quite as much as it did to the Adlers. Nathan Adler, for his part, moved cautiously, even tactfully, to establish his authority. When commenting on a work that Dr Asher Asher, the effective hon. secretary of the United, had just prepared, Adler observed that it was 'an admirable translation in a thoroughly religious Godfearing spirit with scientific accuracy'. He then pointed out, however, that Asher had used the word 'Hierarchs', and suggested that 'the term involves too much idea of dominion and authority in sacred things'. 'Priests' might be more appropriate.[21].

---

[20] *Report of the Committee in Reference to the 'Duties and Emoluments Annexed to the Office of Secretary'* ... (London, 1866). The secretary was to receive £275 and certain fees. When the post of secretary of the United Synagogue was established, Asher was paid £500, the salary for a senior government civil servant.
[21] N. Adler to Asher Asher, 14 Mar. 1871, in the Asher Asher Papers,

The common treasure of the community, Nathan Adler observed when speaking to the Sephardic congregation, was the Torah. What bound them together as Jews was the same religion, the same holy language and the same history.[22] But Adler never publicly championed Sephardic Ashkenazic union. He sought only close co-operation. Against Reform Jews he took a firm stand, although he and his successors were to see Orthodox Jews, too, make increased use of English and to witness United Synagogue Orthodoxy stress decorum in the same way as the Reform leaders did. The Rev Dr David Woolf Marks, Reform's first minister, ironically gave Nathan Adler's authority a considerable boost. A Dutchman, Moses Schott, held a *Shohet's* (ritual slaughterer's) licence from the Chief Rabbi of Emden. Adler refused to endorse it in 1868, and Schott sued. A future Lord Chancellor pleaded his case, arguing that Jewish ecclesiastic authorities had assumed a jurisdiction over which they had no right. 'They have thought themselves entitled to issue certificates permitting Jews to exercise the trade of a butcher, and in the absence of such certificates they cannot follow the trade.' 'Such an exercise of ecclesiastic authority', Giffard concluded, 'is inconsistent with the freedom of trade enjoyed in this country.' Professor Marks was called for the plaintiff, explained that he did not recognized Adler's jurisdiction and attached little importance to matters of *kashrut* (dietary law). Marks, however, then upheld Adler's authority for Orthodox Jews, explained the principles of *kashrut*, and observed that the slaughterer must be a man of high moral character, must be examined, and is not qualified for all places simply by having a certificate for one.[23] Although Marks had struck an important blow for Adlerian authority, his testimony also underscored the rift between Reform and Orthodoxy.

Anglo-Jewish Archives AJ 166, Mocatta Library, University College, London.

[22] N.M. Adler, *The Bonds of Brotherhood: A Sermon Delivered in the Synagogue ... of the Spanish and Portugese Congregation ...* (London, 1849), pp. 5ff., 14.

[23] Baron Martin immediately ruled that there was no case to go to a jury, and the plaintiff was non-suited. Schott *vs* Adler, *The Times*, 15 Dec. 1868. The judgement was confirmed and extendend beyond London in Fineberg *vs* Adler et al. at the Liverpool Assizes on 25 Feb. 1904 before Mr Justice Bigham. See *Jewish Chronicle* 4 Mar. 1904. Hermann Adler found himself under considerable pressure to compromise on details. To resist these, he sought the co-operation of the leader of the London Sephardim, Dr Moses Gaster. See for example Adler to Gaster, 19 Oct. 1897, Gaster Papers 89/93 in the Mocatta Library, University College, London. For Nathan Adler's

Within the rapidly growing Ashkenazic Orthodox community, Adler had a well-defined agenda. The minister, as he insisted upon calling the spiritual head of each congregation, must set a public example through his own life. He was the guardian of the Holy Law and must preserve the sacred inheritance 'undimmed and uninjured'. Education, in the broadest sense, must come under rabbinical direction. The Jewish home was 'the first and most important school', 'our little Temple the school for adults'.[24] Demanding such standards of others, Nathan Adler brooked no compromises within his own home. He lived as he preached, imposing discipline and believing in love. There the public and private man became synonymous: 'I feel bound to lay the following religious duties to the hearts of my children, grand-children, and great-grandchildren with my earnest wish that they may always observe them, and thereby keep my memory fresh and green.' The main principle of Judaism (Deuteronomy 6:3) was to love the Lord thy God with all thy heart, and with all thy soul, and with all thy might, and that principle could only be sustained by living Jewish lives in Jewish families and homes. This meant rigorous devotion to *kashrut*, daily prayers and Bible study, careful ob-servance of the Sabbath and celebration of the festivals. Jews must understand and pass to their children the full sweep of Jewish tradi-tion and perserve the Oral Law. Adler's was just such a home, a model for his flock.

> Home, however, a Jewish home, forms the centre of the divine Laws. It is in their house that husband and wife must live in peace and domestic happiness, under all the vicissitudes, the sunshine and cloud of their life. It is here where father and mother must train their children with parental love and solicitude, receiving filial love and affection in return.[25]

The family was the centre from which grew the understanding and love of God's work. The family was also where Jews first learned to

---

rigorous views on Shechita see the discussion in *Jewish Chronicle*, 24 Jan. 1890. On the issue in general see A. M. Hyamson, *The London Board for Shechita, 1801–1954* (London, 1954).

[24] N. M. Adler, *Predigt beim Antritte seines Amtes als Ober-Rabbiner in Grossbritannien gehalten in der Great Synagogue of London am 4ten Tamus 5605 (8ten Juli 1845),* (London, 1845), pp. 5–15. Adler preached his inaugural sermon in German. All his sermons published thereafter were in English.

[25] Ethical Will of Chief Rabbi Nathan Marcus Adler (confidential), 31 Dec. 1883, in the Laski Papers, AJ33/234, Mocatta Library.

appreciate their moral obligations and social responsibilities. The community as a whole, Adler preached, must create and cherish those institutions that provided all Jews with the capacity and opportunity to worship. Since we must deal with others as we would have them deal with us, Adler reminded his flock, we must instruct all of our community. No group, however small, and no individual should be forgotten. To Jews busily financing and contructing an elaborate and expensive network of educational and social-welfare institutions that would be a model for Victorian Britain, he asked that something be done even for the handful of Jewish deaf and dumb.[26]

Nathan Adler and the lay leaders of the community had their vision of social commitment, but it did not include socialism. When Aron Lieberman reached London in August 1875, he bore the battle scars of struggles with Vilna rabbis and Russian authorities. He and nine fellow Lithuanians organized the Hebrew Socialist Union (Agudah ha-sozialistim Haverim) in May 1876. Like most such organizations, it devoted most of its time and energy to heated debates about membership rules and minor points of ideology. It may or may not have been an inspiration for the Bund and Socialist Zionism (Poale Zion), but Lieberman's 'Call to Jewish Youth' (18 July 1876) drew a wrathful response from the Chief Rabbi and the Jewish lay leadership. Even the Jewish trade-union movement wanted no part of Lieberman and the disorder that seemed to accompany him. Lieberman returned to Germany to crusade for Russian liberation and social democracy, but his heirs, such as Morris Winchevsky in *Arbeter Fraint* ('The Worker's Friend'), picked up Lieberman's ideological torch in the next decade for a much larger and potentially more responsive audience.[27]

Nathan Adler remained in titular command as the great wave of immigration from Eastern Europe began, but he was ill, exhausted and aging. Hermann Adler had assumed more and more of his father's duties since 1876. When Nathan severely curtailed his activity in 1880, the Chief Rabbinate effectively passed as the office of Delegate Chief Rabbi to his younger son Hermann. The choice was well made, for the next generation of British Jews demanded a gifted Chief

---

[26] N. M. Adler, *The Morning and the Evening Sacrifice: How to Be Represented in These Days: with Specific Reference to the Claims of Deaf Mutes in the Jewish Community...January 18th 5625* (London, [1864]) pp. 9, 12–14.

[27] Black, *Social Politics*, ch. 7; W. Fishman, *Jewish Radicals* (New York, 1974), ch. 4.

Rabbi who would not question the values and assumptions on which
Anglo-Jewry rested. Hermann was an administrator and a preacher.[28]
He was suited to his age. The fifth child and second son, he was
trained from youth to his place.[29] He attended University College
School in London, then University College, where he won prizes for
philosophy, English and classical literature. Among his friends from
those early years were Lord Herschell, Stanley Jevons, John Morley
and Louis Kossuth. His father had trained him from childhood in
Talmud and continued to be his son's mentor until his death in 1890.
After going abroad to take his doctorate and rabbinical diploma,
Hermann returned to England as his father's secretary in 1862. He
was offered but declined the position of Chief Rabbi of Hanover. He
could not be persuaded to leave England. He tutored privately and
taught at Jews' College. When the lectureship of Bayswater Synagogue
fell vacant, Hermann stood for the post, defeating A.P. Mendes of
Birmingham in what was considered by many as a referendum on
Nathan Adler's Chief Rabbinate. Bayswater Synagogue was both
large and influential. Hermann's gift for preaching and homiletics
suited his congregation. The new generation was prepared to step
into the place of the old.

Nathan Adler had brought his German sense of order, discipline
and the fitness of things to Britain. He never questioned his beliefs,
his value, or his role. He also never overstepped the lines of lay
control or compromised his German sense of *Obrigkeit*, of social and
political deference to constituted authority. Thus he constructed a
clearly defined religious hierarchy, brought discipline to religious
services, and showed Jews to the British world as respectful and
respectable. His politics and sensitivities proved well suited to the
British scene. He could deny that he had made any concessions of
halakhah, while constantly adapting Jewish observance to British
sensibilities. His son Hermann would improve upon his work, while
he, Nathan, lent his authority, prestige, wisdom and experience. For
fourteen years, from 1876 to 1890, two generations of Adlers con-

[28] Though he helped make the sermon central in Orthodox services, Adler
himself spoke a trifle slightingly of it. See H. Adler, 'The Functions of the
Jewish Pulpit', *The North London Pulpit* (London, 1892). For Hermann
Adler's appointment as Delegate see Nathan Adler to the President and
Members of the Council of the United Synagogue, 10 Nov. 1880 in reponse
to theirs of 5 Nov. to him (Mocatta Library Quartos, B 20 ADL).

[29] Marcus N. Adler commemorated the jubilee of his family as chief rabbis
with *The Adler Family. Address Delivered at the Jewish Institute ... on
June 6th 1909* (London, 1909).

tinued a formal process of anglicization in Jewish public life and became themselves thoroughly British Jews.

II

The Adler regimes overlapped. Nathan survived, officially holding the office of Chief Rabbi until his death in 1890. Hermann took over more and more of the work. Some communal clucking could be heard, but Hermann's election in 1891 was a foregone conclusion. The Delegate Chief Rabbi had spent a decade consolidating the work of his father and confronting the great challenge to British Jewry, the sudden wave of immigration from Eastern Europe that washed across the British Isles after 1881. Unlike his father, he made no mark as a scholar. As a preacher, speaker and polemicist, he had no peer. He continued the process his father had begun of anglicizing British Jewry, a task made easier by foundations firmly laid and more difficult by the influx of immigrants.

Nathan Adler made the Chief Rabbinate dignified and imposing. His authority was felt, even if not fully accepted, in all quarters. Hermann continued the process, appreciating the role of symbols as well as substance. The United Synagogue approved designs for buildings that looked dignified, appropriate to the now highly decorous services, with just enough of Gothic and Romanesque to be 'establishment' without being blatantly Christian. Altar and pulpit were segregated in the Anglican manner, both as a reflection of the increased importance placed upon the sermon and subtly to enhance the significance and role of the preacher.[30] Hermann Adler sat on a variety of public bodies and moved easily in the world of churchmen. He adopted full clerical garb and even assumed the title 'Very Reverend'. In a culture in which such things mean much, Adler placed himself on a level with Anglican bishops, while refraining from appropriating a bishop's precise title, 'Right Reverend'. He received the ultimate accolade accorded important British men of affairs, a caricature by 'Spy' in *Vanity Fair*.

He beams out from the caricature officious and confident, busy as ever. Hermann Adler was always doing something. Whether in the home, in some public forum or in the Bet Din, preaching, or dashing off a brief, well-crafted essay on the patriotism of the Jews, their culture and importance in civic life, or the evils of Zionism, he was

[30] Glasman, *Jewish Quarterly*, 34, 2, pp. 16–18.

the picture of activity. The Adler home was as busy as the Adler office. Herzl records a visit to Adler one evening. He stumbled upon a veritable beehive of activity.[31] Rachel Joseph, Adler's wife, a daughter of the Anglo-Jewish elite trained from young ladyhood for philanthropic work, was busily engaged with a social welfare group. Nettie, as Hermann and Rachel's daughter Henrietta was always called, was conducting a girl's club Bible study and prayer meeting (the club did not yet have facilities of its own). She would shortly carve out a distinguished place for herself in education and professional social work.

Adler daughters like Adler sons learned in partnership with their parents. Ruth Adler married Dr Alfred Eichholz, a scholar and pedagogue of much importance, repeating in yet another generation the Adlerian commitment to education. Nettie, who appears to have been offered as a bride for the young Herbert Samuel, but to have been refused made children in schools, clubs and the workforce her family. Alfred Adler, Rachel and Hermann's son, trained for the ministry and was launched on a career that might well have made him the third Chief Rabbi Adler but for his tragic death in 1910, a year before Hermann. Every Adler could claim some unique contribution to education. Rachel Adler, for instance, organized the Jewish Penny Dinners Society, which long bridged the gap for poor children by providing kosher meals at school. She, like Lady Magnus, perhaps even from a spirit of competition with the wife of one of Reform Jewry's citizens, pioneered the club movement among adolescent East End girls.

Rachel Joseph was the perfect wife for Hermann Adler. Her mother had pushed her early into philanthropic work. While still unmarried, she organized the Ladies' Loan Society well before the Jewish Board of Guardians organized its own highly successful and much praised loan department. She and her fellow ladies sat each week in a room at the old Jews' Infant School personally interviewing applicants and taking their shillings and half-crowns as they repaid their obligations. She made her work part of the life of every Jewish woman aspiring to upper-class status. The Baroness de Rothschild took her turn on the Loan Society rota every two months. Rachel Adler's forte, the one which her daughter Nettie would make so much her own, was education. Jewish Children's Penny Dinners

[31] *The Complete Diaries of Theodor Herzl*, trans. H. Zohn, ed. R. Patai (New York and London, 1960), vol. 1, p. 1 278. Patai misidentifies Hermann Adler as Nathan Adler throughout the diary. The date of the visit was 23 Nov. 1895.

helped make life tolerable and education possible for the poor. She then organized the Jewish Boot Fund, the Jewish Children's Holiday Fund and the Jewish Children's Happy Evenings. She championed the Domestic Training Home, which combined social rehabilitation with training Jewish girls for domestic service (an occupation they avoided whenever possible). Rachel Adler also helped to sponsor the Jewish Crèche, a pioneering day-care centre, was active in the management of the Evelina de Rothschild School in Jerusalem, and even sat on the governing council of the Anglo-Jewish Association.

For all of this, Rachel Adler still found time to manage her home, cherish her husband, sustain and support him, and shield him from many of the cares and burdens of day-to-day existence. Thanks to her, Hermann could devote himself to the role of courtly and genial host and be the witty conversationalist and good listener that he was. In a home so well and graciously managed, he could display his great tact and *savoir faire*, to set any guest at ease. In the privacy of that home, moreover, he could retreat to the pleasure of his own library or spoil his visiting grandchildren and other young guests.

The family which Nathan Adler had charged with high moral responsibility was carrying its domestic mission into the wider Jewish and British worlds. Nettie Adler took her mother's social activism even further. She urged the professionalization of social work and aggressively expanded the scope of Jewish and state concerns. She revolutionized the Committee of Wage-Earning Children, personally leading a deputation to the Home Secretary, Sir John Gorst. The committee documented almost 7,000 cases of children working for wages out of school hours. With a precision and forcefulness of which Beatrice Webb strongly approved, Nettie Adler stirred Salisbury's government into action and helped determine the direction of future social legislation and policy. A school-manager under the London School Board for the East End, she enriched and extended the opportunities that school offered East End girls, both in curricular and in extra-curricular terms. She developed scholars' guilds, half-way houses between school and girls' clubs that capitalized upon school camaraderie by providing recreation and instruction for former pupils who had entered the workforce.

Through the guilds Nettie Adler hoped to improve the status and opportunities of Jewish women, whose parents, she felt, set their daughters to work for the best short-term return on the assumption that they would soon marry and so have no need to achieve economic independence. As a visitor for the Jewish Board of Guardians, she saw far too many cases of widows lacking skills with no prospects of making their way in the world. Dependence on charity, she argued, sapped their character. Just such words had come from her father and grandfather as they struggled to create a philanthropic system that elevated self-help and penalized the *schnorrer*.[32] Nathan Adler's sons helped to sustain his struggle. Hermann Adler's entire family joined the fray.

Hermann's prodigious memory enabled him to recall the details even of the coach journey he took from Hanover to Cologne at the age of six when the family came to Britain. That agile mind also allowed him to straddle a thoroughly British world, to which he was committed, and the cosmopolitan world of the continent. Save for his father and his family, the greatest single influence in 'building up his store of scholarship' and shaping his character was Dr Michael Sachs, whom he met at the university in Prague in 1860. A distinguished poet, preacher, and philologist, Sachs gave Hermann advice that he would never forget.

Above all the preacher should speak out plainly to his hearers, or in other words, must have something to say. To address them with effect, he should bring to his task a well-stored mind and a thorough knowledge, combined with a ready command of the matter to be handled. The action will always be suitable and correct if the words proceed from the heart. The preacher should strike every chord, and hold every subject coming within his sphere — now addressing and rousing the congregation as a body, now the members individually. Everyone should be brought to a consciousness of his duty, as part and parcel of the Jewish body and as a representative thereof, and be taught to consider himself bound to act as a champion in the cause of Judaism, to defend it from the attacks of the enemy without and within, and to hand down the religion of his fathers to his children. Far from attempting to accommodate the law to his life, each individual should be enjoined to render his life conformable to the law, and to take it for his rule and guidance. Fully to possess oneself of a blessing, it is necessary to fit oneself for it. In short, one must be fully resolved to practise one's religion in order to be able to do it.[33]

[32] Black, *Social Politics*, ch. 8.
[33] The quotation is actually from Sachs to Dr Asher Asher, who asked for guidance when preparing for a ministerial career, and is quoted from the special memoir of Adler in the *Jewish Chronicle*, 21 July 1911

Hermann Adler completed his father's work of integrating Jewish Orthodoxy into the British world. He felt comfortable among his colleagues in the Anglican Church, sitting on committees with them, joining the Bishop of London's social-morality crusade as vice president. By character and temperament he was well suited to the role he was called upon to play. He moved diplomatically and effectively among the Anglo-Jewish elite. He prodded their philanthropic efforts, laboured for the constant improvement of Jewish education, helped to design the Jewish Religious Education Boards as a way of providing religious training to the increasing thousands of Jewish children in secular board schools. He sought social justice for the Jewish poor, denouncing Jewish landlords who exploited their tenants as 'transgressing Jewish law'.[34]

Autocratic in style and conservative in politics, Hermann Adler presided over the greatest expansion of Britain's Jewish community. He, as much as any single person, moulded the spiritual response of British Jewry to the dramatic problems of adaptation and modernization. He, like other nineteenth-century clergymen, Jewish or Christian, bemoaned the growth of secularism and irreligion. He laboured tirelessly to make West End and East End Jews alike 'loyal subjects and steadfast Jews'.[35] He fought all forms of irreligion, stood as firmly as he could against Reform or Liberal Judaism while steadily anglicizing Orthodoxy, and believed, above all, that the highest form of Jewish culture was to be found in the enlightened Diaspora of the West.

Adler disliked the ways in which immigrant Jews disrupted the tidy fabric of the community that he, his father and the lay leadership had laboured so industriously to weave. East European Jews also annoyed him with their propensity to trigger doctrinal controversy. He had no use for political radicalism and detested Zionism which he considered 'absolutely mischievous'.[36] While he, like other community leaders, denounced that 'jargon' Yiddish, he could talk to the

---

[34] Tenants Protection Association meeting, 14 Jan. 1899, reported in the *Jewish Chronicle*, 20 Jan. 1899. See also H. Adler, *The Duty of the Hour: A Sermon Preached at the Bayswater Synagogue on the Eighth Day of Solemn Assembly, 5659–1898* (London, 1898).

[35] Booth staff interview notes, 1897, in the (Charles) Booth Papers, B 197/11, Library of the London School of Economics and Political Science.

[36] Anglo-Jewish Association council meeting, 11 July 1897, AJA Minute Books, III, pp. 56–7, in the Anglo-Jewish Archives in the Mocatta Library; *Jewish Chronicle*, 16 July 1897.

immigrants in their tongue. He regularly presided at sittings of his Bet Din, always seeking to settle disputes by mediation, to avoid public trials in the courts. Those, he felt, could only be expensive for the parties concerned and were often embarrassing for the community as a whole. If his own authority were not convincing, he would invoke East European rabbis of high standing to endorse his more politically sensitive rulings. One observer found him a man 'of great energy and fervour. He treats nothing lightly and becomes impressive in his intensity.'[37]

While he worked assiduously in the East End, he had, at best, an ambiguous relation to, and view of, foreign Jews. He feared that they endangered the work of generations of British Jews. They were given to ecclesiastical indiscipline. Well they might be, for Adler's Orthodoxy seemed almost incomprehensible to their traditionalist sensibilities. These newcomers threatened British Jewry's harmonious world view. To promote his ideas and policies, Hermann Adler made annual pastoral tours through the provinces. He brought to bear his charm, his pulpit skills and the force of his personality throughout the nation. His schedule was laid out with mathematical precision, neatly camouflaged by his genial goodwill and enthusiam. When the occasion demanded, moreover, he could shift from the English cleric to the Polish *maggid* complete with 'the regulation tone and gestures, and ... flood of rhetorical Yiddish'.[38]

Where the Adlers and the United Synagogue proved ineffective, Sir Samuel Montagu, later first Baron Swaythling, retrieved the situation. Arguing that the Rothschild–Adler conception of West End missionary enterprise to the East End was conceptually wrong and misdirected, he created what he called the Federation of Minor Synagogues, which became the Federation of Synagogues. Although not part of the United Synagogue, the Federation acknowledged the authority of the Chief Rabbi while attempting to remain culturally closer to the traditionalist immigrants. Through a judicious use of carrots and sticks, Montagu drew newcomers into the acculturating network of Anglo-Jewish social and religious institutions. Being himself highly observant, politically sensitive and immensely wealthy, he did much to cover Hermann Adler's vulnerable flank. Montagu presided for years over the Shechita Board, which also proved a valuable weapon in the Adlerian acculturation armory. The administration of Bet Din rules concerning *kashrut*, so crucial a part of

[37] Booth Papers, B 197/29.
[38] *Jewish Chronicle*, 15 July 1898.

Jewish observance, was in the hands of one who shared Adler's view of moral purpose in modern society.

Nathan Adler had fought the Reform movement. Hermann Adler confronted both Reform and twentieth-century Liberal Judaism. Adler appreciated the motives — a desire 'to deepen the religious spirit among those who hold aloof from services — but felt that absenteeism from Sabbath morning service represented on 'unwillingness or inability to hallow the Day of Rest'. To the charge that many Jews had difficulty taking part in a ritual conducted in an unknown tongue, he pointed out that the translations in Singer's *Authorised Prayer Book*, along with English translations of the Bible, made Judaism fully accessible.[39] He rejected the notion that traditional prayers and aspirations jarred with the feelings of modern men and women, and ridiculed the idea that the segregation of the sexes limited attendance. Declining to sanction the Revd Morris Joseph's appointment to the Hampstead Synagogue in 1892, he objected that Joseph had sanctioned the use of instrumental music at Sabbath afternoon services and had dared to express disbelief in the future revival of sacrifices. Yet he simultaneously endorsed a system of 'optional' modifications of ritual which four synagogues had asked of him in the furtherance of anglicization. He contended that they did not violate the statutory liturgy and that by making limited concessions he was attempting to preserve as much Hebrew as possible in the service. Adler roused considerable ire in the community for his testimony before the Royal Commission on Marriage and Divorce at the end of 1910. Conceding that issues of illegal marriage and divorce still plagued the Jewish community in spite of the determined efforts of communal authorities to control it, he asked for state legislation on the matter.[40]

---

[39] Even Nathan Adler acceded to pressure to bring more English into the Orthodox service. See N. Adler to S. Singer, 9 Nov. 1889, Mocatta Library Quartos, B 20 ADL. A discussion about revising Orthodox ritual ran for several years in the columns of the *Jewish Chronicle*, featuring 'Nemo' (Revd A. L. Green) and 'Aliquis' (Dr Asher Asher), and in 1880 a conference of synagogue delegates prevailed upon Nathan Adler to permit the shortening of Sabbath and festival services. Hermann Adler, after his formal election as Chief Rabbi in 1891, resisted pressure to have modifications to services decided by a convocation of Orthodox clergy. The issue then at stake, however, was circumscription of his authority and 'democratization'. See Ellis A. Franklin to the editor, *Jewish Chronicle*, 22 Nov. 1901, on the occasion of yet another proposal 'to bring Jewish Ritual up to modern times'.

[40] Community leaders disliked anything implying the slightest loss of

Hermann Adler asked how the Jewish spirit could be deepened by a Judaism which held out no inducement for Jewish children to learn Hebrew.

> But the principal feature of the service should be the discourse in which the preacher should plead with all the earnestness, all the enthusiasm at his command, for the keeping of the Sabbath; should seek to combat the evils we deplore — religious decadence, with its accompanying materialism and abstention from Divine worship. He should strive to rouse his hearers to a more loyal Jewish life, with the spirituality, the aspiration of the human soul Godward, which it enforces. And these efforts should be seconded by direct personal influence.[41]

Adler fell back on his strengths and values to reject latitudinarianism and the new criticism. He accused Claude Montefiore, Liberal Judaism's sponsor, of omitting the 'essentials of faith and practice', of rendering Judaism indistinguishable from Ethical Culture or Unitarianism.[42]

Just as he stood squarely for an Orthodoxy which he and his father anglicized against the fashions of intellectual change, London preoccupied him at a time when provincial British Jewry was growing in size and self-consciousness. In an increasingly democratic age, he continued to argue for enlightened elite governance in both lay and religious matters. His responses to questions and challenges were tactful, even diplomatic, but they remained authoritarian, however enlightened. Centralization enhanced his authority but may also have deprived synagogues of a flexibility that would have enabled them to

---

autonomy. Letters to the editor took issue with Adler in every subsequent issue of the *Jewish Chronicle* until Adler's death in July 1911. Communal resistance to statutory immigration restriction sprang, to a considerable degree, from the same source. Anglo-Jewry had been practising various forms of immigration restriction for years. It did not want some other authority, particularly the state, making decisions that it felt should be its own.

[41] H. Adler, 'The Old Paths', sermon preached at the St John's Wood Synagogue, 6 Dec. 1902, on Jeremiah 6: 16, published in the *Jewish Chronicle*, 12 Dec. 1902.

[42] Letter to the editor, *Daily Telegraph*, 28 Oct. 1909. Adler, however, wrote a preface to Bishop Colenso's *Pentateuch* in 1865 for the Jewish Society for the Diffusion of Religious Knowledge and was quite untroubled by such exponents of the new criticism as Claude Montefiore and Israel Abrahams sitting on the Jewish Religious Education Board.

adapt more deftly to evolving communal needs. While he gave his clergy status, he imposed hierarchy. Jealous of any challenges to his authority, real or imaginary, Adler unwittingly created opportunities for those of different views.

Hermann Adler's incumbency also witnessed the British campaign for restriction of alien immigration. However disguised, this turn-of-the-century campaign to impose statutory limitations on immigration was directed at East European Jews. They were conspicuous since they crowded into Stepney and a handful of provinicial industrial centres. They were also convenient targets in the growing campaign against the Victorian gospel of free trade in money, people and goods. The Jewish community felt besieged. The Board of Deputies of British Jews began grudging concessions to a broader representation. Anti-alienism helped to bring the United Synagogue to terms with Montagu's Federation of Synagogues. By 1902, the Federation minister was invited to sittings of the Bet Din. The Russo-Jewish Committee intensified its adult-education programme in the East End and funded provincial Jewish boards of guardians to aid the process of resettlement and dispersion from the East End. Jewish women were more readily given scope and authority in communal institutions.

Adler and other leaders looked to flaws in the British Jewish image and asked the community to understand what was at stake:

> Every Jewish scamp, every Jewish money-lender, every Jewish cheat, does more harm to Judaism than a Christian scamp, a Christian money-lender, a Christian cheat does to Christianity. Contrariwise every Jewish hero does us more good. This is the necessary condition of minorities. So may you recognise and understand your importance and your responsibilities.[43]

The moral exhortation also underlined a fact, blurred but never eliminated. The Adlers made Jewish Orthodoxy another acceptable religion in their host culture. But were British Jews simply British people of the Jewish persuasion?

III

Critics of Adlerism were unhappy with anglicization. As Orthodox Jews they should have regarded the repulse of Reform and limitations

---

[43] Jewish Religious Education Board prize-giving, 8 June 1901, reported in the *Jewish Chronicle*, 13 June 1901.

of the Liberal challenge as triumphs. Instead they looked upon
services subtly shortened, the intrusion of English, the symbols of
Christian ecclesiology, the discipline and decorum of services, the
introduction of organ and choir as undesirable compromises. Realism
and acculturation bent if they did not actually violate halakhah,
whatever the rulings of the Adler Bet Din. But this protest reached
beyond the details of observance. The entire process of anglicization
meant, among other things, teaching all immigrant children the
'enormity of un-English habits and customs'. Since, as one critic put
it, children have difficulty 'distinguishing between qualities and de-
fects of manner and character, the first lesson is to despise their
parents'.[44] When taken to extremes, the reaction led to the lawcourts
in Liverpool or the revolt of the Mahzikei Hadass (the True Upholders of the Religion) in London. The two, as it happened,
overlapped.

The case of Fineberg *versus* Adler et al at the Liverpool Assizes on
25 February 1904 grew out of the cumulative mishandling of the
licensing of a provincial *shohet*. Hermann Adler issued an *issur* (a
condemnation of butchers violating the rules of Shechita) upon which
a Liverpool enthusiast improved in Yiddish translation. When Adler
saw what had actually been published, he called the translator and
the Liverpool Board of Shechita to account, but not before an action
for libel had been instituted. Adler was found innocent; his authority,
in so far as the court could define it, for ruling on matters of kashrut
upheld; and, at the cost of some adverse publicity, the authority of
the Chief Rabbi was more clearly defined and extended.[45]

One of those testifying on behalf of the plaintiff was Amram
Werner, the rabbi of the Mahzikei Hadass, a congregation that had
rejected Adler's authority over issues of kashrut. His testimony — the
judge had to question him in German — did Fineberg no good and
proved unsettling to Anglo-Jewish leaders concerned about the public
image of Jews. It also underscored an abiding problem for the Adlers.
The Mahzikei Hadass believed that Jewish tradition had been compromised, and it required all of the diplomatic skill and political
muscle that Sir Samuel Montagu could muster finally to bring the
congregation into the network of his Federation of Synagogues and
under the authority of the Chief Rabbi. A breach that began in 1891
was carefully healed in 1905.

[44] 'Anglicisation on Jewish Lines', *Jewish Chronicle*, 4 Apr. 1902.
[45] The case is described in detail and thoroughly discussed in the *Jewish
Chronicle*, 4 Mar. 1904.

Much had been involved. Solomon Herz, the founder, had established his own Bet Din. He had also appointed Rabbi Werner, 'a rav of the old type', a learned man, who preached no Anglo-Jewish sermons but devoted his services to dealing at length with Talmudic questions and answers(*shaalotu-teshuvot*). Shechita rules were more rigid. The Adlerian compromises were gone. Services were in Hebrew and Yiddish. There were no mixed choirs, no concessions to anglicization in symbols, form or content. Such independence, of course, was intolerable. Montagu made that clear: 'The great and urgent necessity of to-day is that our foreign coreligionists should be brought more and more within the influence of English Jews rather than be estranged from them by needless dissensions, and we hope that this necessity is now well understood in those quarters in which the Machziké Hadass secession originated.'[46]

Reverberations of discontent still sounded, although sheer indifference mattered much more. A large proportion of East London Jews were not observant. More than half of London Jews, observed one of the most able Jewish social workers at the beginning of the twentieth century, worked on the Sabbath. Secularization inexorably burrowed its way into the community. Yet, save for a handful of political activists, the community had few who rejected Judaism. The East European who kept his shop open on the Sabbath still sent his son to a heder, a religious school, through his Bar Mitzvah. He attended services for the High Holy Days. He had no interest in Christian conversionists but retained a sentimental attachment to the synagogue. Alterations in services or enthusiastic preachers were unlikely to change him. Judaism was more and more a secular bond, less and less a living faith. Zionism, with its imaginative appeal to Jewish ethnicity, was an attractive idea distant enough not to be disruptive while capturing a growing sense of pride in self and people.[47]

---

[46] Kashrut remained a touchy point. The Mahzikei Hadass were permitted to select their own special *shohetim*, but their appointments required the sanction of the Chief Rabbi. *Jewish Chronicle*, 17 and 24 Feb. 1905. See also B. Homa, *A Fortress in Anglo-Jewry: The Story of the Machziké Hadath* (London, 1953); *Orthodoxy in Anglo-Jewry 1880–1940* (London, 1969); Hyamson, *The London Board for Schechita, 1801–1954*; ch. 9; and Black, *Social Politics*, ch. 7.

[47] Harry S. Lewis, 'East End Judaism — Need and Possibilities of Reform', paper presented to West London Synagogue Association, 15 Feb. 1903, published in the *Jewish Chronicle*, 20 Feb. 1903. Adler had issued a pastoral

Hermann Adler was resolutely anti-Zionist in an age and a community in which that was receiving more of a hearing. He was a man of the West End acting as a missionary to the East End, whether he inhabited his Finsbury Park residence or not. Adler understood that he was out of tune with the sympathies and culture of those Jews of East European origin who now represented by far the greatest number of British Jews and felt that his successor must be a man to bridge that gap. J. H. Hertz, trained in the United States, experienced in South Africa, was ultimately selected. But from Hertz to Lord Jakobovits, in spite of the turmoil and trauma and change of almost eighty years, the world of British Jewish Orthodoxy remained to a great degree the unique world that Nathan and Hermann Adler forged.

Nathan Marcus Adler came to England prepared for the task ahead of him. He brought his sense of order and discipline, his Orthodoxy and his pride. As an Adler and the descendant of chief rabbis, Great Britian and the Empire offered scope for his ambitions. He stood against Reform Judaism in Germany and circumscribed it in Britain through a judicious mixture of resistance and subtle accommodation within British Orthodoxy. He helped bring organization and order to Jewish education and Jewish social welfare institutions, and created a quasi-episcopacy for British Jewry. He preached and practised the virtues of family life as the cornerstone of Judaism. He was parent, teacher and friend to his children, preparing each for a life of dedicated service to the community. Through his life he became as anglicized as the community he led, although he retained through his scholarship close and deep ties to the world of traditional Judaism.

Hermann, his son, was trained from childhood first to aid, then to succeed, Nathan as Chief Rabbi. From a Decalogue learned at four to Talmud studied from the age of ten, father guided son. Almost to the day he died in 1890, Nathan and Hermann discussed Talmud and issues of Jewish practice. Nathan had placed education first on his agenda for Great Britain. Education brought Hermann and his wife-to-be together and kept them close through their long and happy marriage. It bonded them to the son who died in 1910 and to their daughter Nettie.

---

letter in June 1898 enjoining employers, employees and professionals to end the desecration of the Sabbath, sponsoring a society to that end with Sir Samuel Montagu. To 500 letters dispatched, they received only five replies. See *Jewish Chronicle*, 8 and 15 July 1898.

With Nathan Adler, the public and the private person blended, the one all but indistinguishable from the other. Hermann Adler continued to refine the public persona. But behind the Very Reverend the Chief Rabbi Doctor Hermann Adler, PhD, LLD, DCL, CVO, and away from the fund-raising banquets and public forums, somewhere behind his library door lurked a warm man tumbling young grandchildren without thought to the dignity of his position. Nathan and Hermann Adler created a religious hierarchy, borrowing freely if judiciously from Anglicanism. They shared in the building of Anglo-Jewry's communal organization with its wide-ranging charities and schools, clubs and cultural institutions. Both in spiritual and secular life they did much to shape modern British Jewry.

Contributors

Israel Bartal is Professor of Modern Jewish History at the Hebrew University and chair of the Department of History of the Jewish People. He is the director of the Center for Research on History and Culture of Polish Jews. He is the editor of the second, revised edition of the minute book of the *Council of Four Lands in Poland* (Jerusalem, 1990) and co-author (with Magdalena Opalska) of *Poles and Jews: A Failed Brotherhood* (Hanover, NH and London, 1993). He is the author of several monographs and articles on the history of Eastern European Jewry and the pre-Zionist Jewish community in Palestine (*Exile in the Land,* Jerusalem, 1994).

Eugene C. Black is Ottilie Springer Professor of Modern European History at Brandeis University. His most recent book is *The Social Politics of Anglo-Jewry, 1880–1920* (1988). He is currently completing two projects, a biography of Edwin Montagu and a monographic study, *Lucien Wolf and the Diplomacy of Minority Rights in Eastern Europe, 1918–1930.*

Michael Burns, Professor of Modern European History at Mount Holyoke College, is the author of *Rural Society and French Politics: Boulangism and the Dreyfus Affair, 1886–1900* (1984) and *Dreyfus: A Family Affair, from the French Revolution to the Holocaust* (1992). His essays on French Jewish history have appeared in Jehuda Reinharz, ed., *Living with Antisemitism: Modern Jewish Responses* (1987), and Norman Kleeblatt, ed., *The Dreyfus Affair: Art, Truth and Justice* (1987).

Todd M. Endelman is William Haber Professor of Modern Jewish History at the University of Michigan. He is the author of *The Jews of Georgian England, 1714–1830: Tradition and Change in a Liberal Society* (1979) and *Radical Assimilation in English Jewish History, 1656–1945* (1990). He has also edited *Jewish Apostasy in the Modern World* (1987) and *Comparing Jewish Societies* (1997). He is currently completing a history of the Jews in Britain from the Resettlement to the present.

Deborah Hertz is Professor of History at Sarah Lawrence College in Bronxville, New York. She is the author of *Jewish High Society in Old Regime Berlin* (1988), which has appeared in translation in German. She also edited *Briefe an eine Freundin: Rahel Varnhagen an Rebecca Friedlaender* (1988).

Jacob Katz, born in Magyargencs, Hungary in 1904, received his Ph.D. from the University of Frankfurt in 1934. A member of the Senate of the Lessing Academy (Wolfenbüttel), an Honorary Fellow of the University of Frankfurt, and Honorary Foreign Member of the American Academy of Arts and Sciences, he is the recipient of the Israel Prize for Jewish History, the Kaplun Prize of the Hebrew University and the B'nai Brith International Award. Now Professor Emeritus at the Hebrew University, he served as Rector in 1968–71. He has been a visiting Professor at Harvard, UCLA, and Columbia. He is the author of *Exclusiveness and Tolerance: Studies in Jewish-Gentile Relations in Medieval and Modern Times* (1961); *Tradition and Crisis: Jewish Society at the End of the Middle Ages* (1961); *Jews and Freemasons in Europe, 1723–1939* (1970); *Emancipation and Assimilation: Studies in Modern Jewish History* (1972); *Out of the Ghetto: The Social Background of Jewish Emancipation, 1770–1870* (1973); *From Prejudice to Destruction: Anti-Semitism, 1700–1933* (1980); and *With My Own Eyes: The Autobiography of An Historian* (1995).

Steven Mark Lowenstein is the Isadore Levine Professor of Jewish History at the University of Judaism, Los Angeles. He is the author of *Frankfurt on the Hudson: The German Jewish Community of Washington Heights* (1989), *The Mechanics of Change: Essays on the Social History of German Jewry* (1992), and *The Berlin Jewish Community 1770–1830: Enlightenment, Family and Crisis* (1994).

Frances G. Malino is Sophia Moses Robison Professor of Jewish Studies and History at Wellesley College. She is the author of *The Sephardic Jews of Bordeaux* (1978) and *A Jew in the French Revolution: The Life of Zalkind Hourwitz* (1996). She is co-editor of *Essays in Modern Jewish History* (1982) and *The Jews of Modern France* (1985). She is currently working on a study of the women teachers of the Alliance Israélite Universelle (1868–1939).

Richard Menkis is an Associate Professor in the Department of Classical, Near Eastern and Religious Studies at the University of British Columbia. He is founding editor of *Canadian Jewish Studies/Etudes juives canadiennes,* and is currently conducting research on the cultural history of Canadian Jews.

Jody Myers is Professor of Religious Studies and Coordinator of the Jewish Studies Program at California State University, Northridge. She has published articles on modern messianism and is currently working on an intellectual biography of Zevi Hirsch Kalischer.

Aron Rodrigue is Eva Chernov Lokey Professor in Jewish Studies and Professor of History at Stanford University. His last two books are *The Jews of the Balkans: The Judeo-Spanish Community, 15th and 20th Centuries* (with Esther Benbassa) (1995), and *Images of Sephardi and Eastern Jewries in Transition: The Teachers of the Alliance Israélite Universelle, 1860–1939* (1993).

David Sorkin, Frances and Laurence Weinstein Professor of Jewish Studies at the University of Wisconsin-Madison, is the author of *The Transformation of German Jewry* (1987) and *Moses Mendelssohn and the Religious Enlightenment* (1996).

Index